PRIORITIES

~~[illegible]~~ WALKER

-PAINTER

-BLACK PERSON

-FLANEUR

-ALL AROUND WILD AND CRAZY GUY

-NICE GUY

NOAH DAVIS

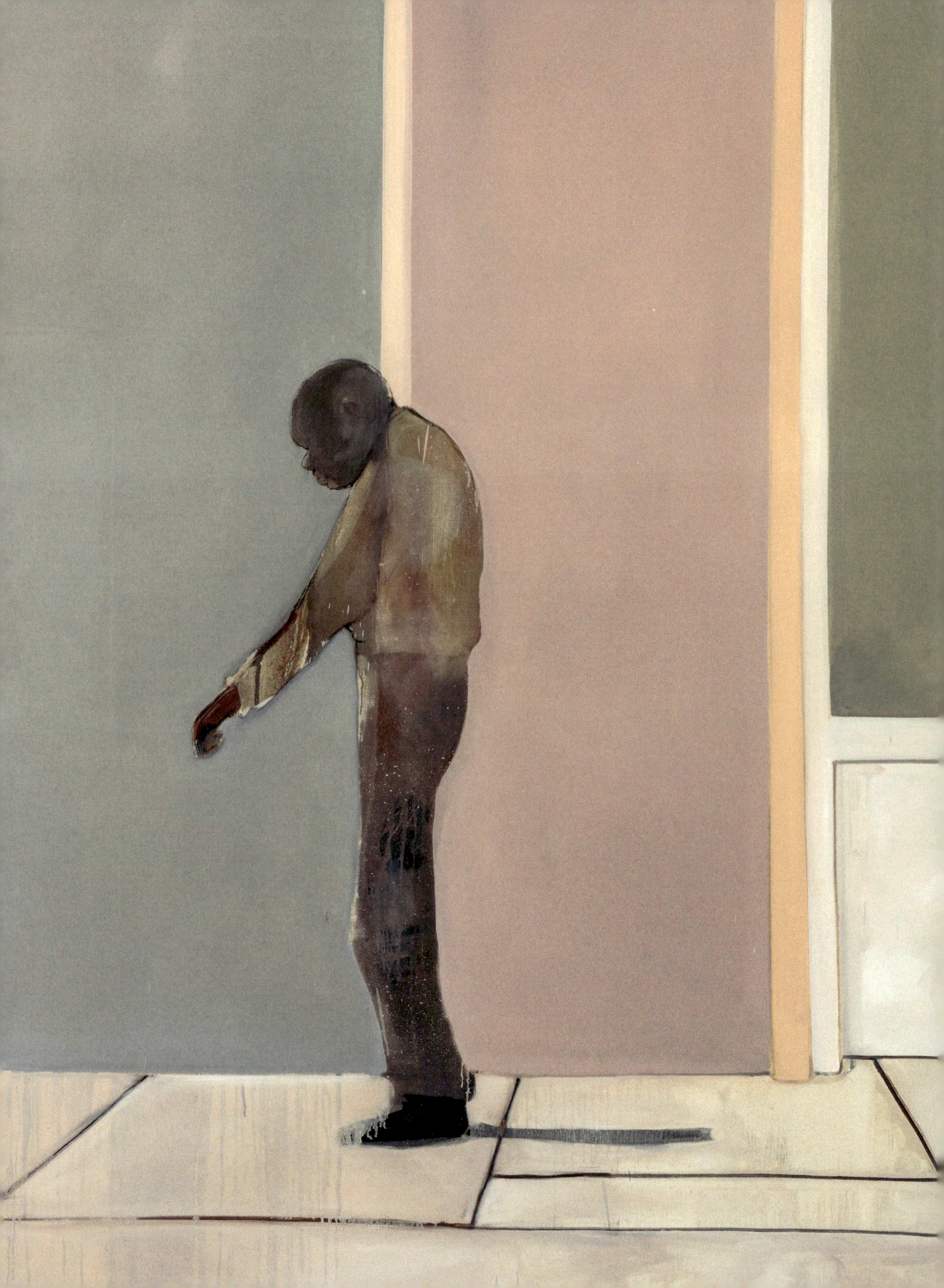

NOAH DAVIS

Edited by Wells Fray-Smith, Paola Malavassi and Eleanor Nairne

PRESTEL
Munich · London · New York

INTRODUCTION by Shanay Jhaveri, Paola Malavassi, Ann Philbin

When painting casts its spell, time marbles. An artist emerges, blinking into the light; a visitor looks up to find people closing in around them. Noah Davis had a keen sense of how a work might strike in an instant and live on for a lifetime. As Roberta Smith noted in the *New York Times*, Davis made paintings that have a remarkable capacity to 'dwell in silence, slow us down and hypnotize'.[1]

Noah Davis was born in 1983 into a Seattle family who encouraged artmaking (even renting him a painting studio as a teenager so he might kindly stop ruining the carpets at home). After moving to New York to study at Cooper Union School of Art, he left before graduating and relocated to Los Angeles in 2004. There, he compiled his own art education from exhibitions, fellow artists and the endless catalogues he'd peruse while working at Dagny Corcoran's Art Catalogues, the former bookstore at the Museum of Contemporary Art (MOCA). He became so well versed in art histories that he could effortlessly move a conversation from Balthus to Francis Bacon and from Odilon Redon to Rothko or switch between their styles in his own work. In 2007, he was included in his first group show. By 2008, he had a solo exhibition in Los Angeles, soon followed by others in New York and Seattle. Beyond his life as a painter, in 2008, he also met and fell in love with the artist Karon Vereen (now Davis) and became a father in 2010 to their son Moses.

Noah and Karon co-founded the Underground Museum (UM) in 2012. Based in Arlington Heights in Los Angeles, the UM aimed to bring 'museum-quality art' to the historically Black and Latinx neighbourhood, offering a space of 'refuge, education, sharing, relaxation and peace'.[2] Complete with a lending library, a Donald Judd-inspired bar and a Purple Garden (in part, an homage to Prince), in the ten years it was open, it hosted exhibitions, talks, concerts, film screenings and wellness sessions for the people of Arlington Heights and beyond.

When Davis died of a rare cancer in 2015, aged just 32, he had achieved a remarkable amount in his tragically shortened life. Beyond devising an institution and contributing to the creative pulse of Los Angeles, he built a prolific career as a painter, had over ten solo shows, curated exhibitions (with such unforgettable titles as *LOOK MOM, NO TALENT* and *Imitation of Wealth*), took part in multiple group projects and supported emerging artists. He provided settings for artists and audiences who otherwise may have felt excluded from cultural spaces. At the UM, visitors could feel witnessed, represented and welcome.

Davis's body of work includes drawings, collages, sculptures, films and performances, alongside the paintings for which he has become celebrated.

Often drawing on art history, his personal archives of photographs, magazines and books, and anonymous snapshots found at Los Angeles flea markets, Davis's figurative paintings include a vibrant cast of characters who are almost entirely Black. Figures sleep, dance, play musical instruments and swim in public pools. Almost always, they seem at ease in the world. It is hard to say exactly when each moment is taking place, lending each scene a kind of nostalgic tranquillity. Davis described how he wanted 'to show Black people in normal scenarios' – an act of refusal against the imagery of Black trauma that has historically circulated and continues to saturate the media.[3]

A fierce critic of his own work, Davis often painted over a single canvas multiple times, turning each painting into a kind of time capsule. As Camila McHugh described in *Artforum*: 'Davis's paintings combine immediacy... with a timelessness – more precisely, a sense of being unstuck in time – that derives in part from his transtemporal source material.'[4] A single work might reference ancient Egyptian mythology, a scene from a Hitchcock movie, a Manet painting, *Game of Thrones*, or a conflation of all of these and more. His curiosity was relentless and capacious enough to hold seemingly disparate influences. As Davis simply put it: 'Things will really come to me.'[5]

The curators Wells Fray-Smith, Paola Malavassi and Eleanor Nairne have only been able to make this exhibition and catalogue – the first international institutional overview of Davis's achievements since his untimely death – because of the immense generosity of his wife Karon, who has been our dearest collaborator throughout the process. It is thanks to Karon that we were able to wade through the reaches of what Davis produced across his far-too-short career. We would like to thank her deeply for sharing her home, her memories and her insight with our institutions. It has truly been a pleasure to work together.

Davis had a remarkable working relationship with the curator Helen Molesworth. In 2014, Davis asked Molesworth, who was then Chief Curator at MOCA, if the museum would lend works to the UM. She agreed and arranged to share a copy of MOCA's 'bible' with Davis: an enormous binder that contained all the works in MOCA's permanent collection. Davis studied the bible and began to curate exhibitions from his hospital bed at Cedars-Sinai, beginning with a presentation of William Kentridge's film *Journey to the Moon* (2003). After Davis's death, Molesworth curated exhibitions of his work at David Zwirner in New York and London (in January 2020 and October 2021), which allowed a wider audience to appreciate the vivacity of his painting. Molesworth also co-curated the first institutional display of Davis's work at the UM in 2022 with Justen LeRoy. We thank Helen for entrusting us to pick up the mantle.

We would also like to thank the David Zwirner team – in particular, Bellatrix Hubert, Katie Priest and Marlene Zwirner – who have been intimate and steadfast collaborators from the very beginnings of this project. Because of the length of the exhibition, lenders have been especially generous in allowing for the works to be shown in Potsdam, London and Los Angeles, and we would like to sincerely thank them for supporting the project across all three iterations: The Estate of Noah Davis; The Andrew W. Mellon Foundation; the Ankner family; Arora Collection, UK; ASOM Collection; the collection of Lindsay Charlwood and Ryan McKenna; the private collection of Aileen Getty; Glenstone Museum, Potomac; the Hammer Museum, Los Angeles; James Harris and Carlos Garcia; the collection of Heidi Hertel and Greg Hodes; William Kentridge and Goodman Gallery; Los Angeles County Museum of Art; the collection of Ryan Murphy and David Miller; the Museum of Modern Art, New York; Miguel; the Rubell Museum; the Studio Museum in Harlem; the Scantland Collection; and all those who wish to remain anonymous.

Preparing for this exhibition required reaching out to gallerists, artists, friends and other members of Davis's creative family, who graciously shared their perspectives on Davis's profound impact on their work and lives. This was an especially painful ask, as memories of Davis's spirit and achievements remain bound up with regret that he is no longer around to share in their recollection. Our special thanks go to Mark Ankner, Laci Blackford, Lindsay Charlwood, Daniel DeSure, Aileen Getty, Tyler Gibney, Eric Gleason, James Harris, Aleen Jaghalian, Justen LeRoy, Melodie McDaniel, Ryan McKenna, Meg Onli, Josh Rabineau, Julie and Bennett Roberts, Connie Rogers Tilton and Megan Steinman.

This exhibition was initiated by Paola Malavassi, Director of DAS MINSK Kunsthaus in Potsdam, and Eleanor Nairne, then Senior Curator at the Barbican and now the Keith L. and Katherine Sachs Curator and Head of Modern and Contemporary Art at the Philadelphia Museum of Art. It has been curated at DAS MINSK by Malavassi with support from Marie Gerbaulet and at the Barbican by Wells Fray-Smith and Nairne with support from Colm Guo-Lin Peare and Ada Egg Koskiluoma. We thank Barbican's former CEO Claire Spencer for championing this project. The exhibition's presentation at the Hammer Museum in Los Angeles is thoughtfully stewarded by Aram Moshayedi,

Interim Chief Curator, with Ikechúkwú Onyewuenyi, Curatorial Associate. We would also like to thank our fantastic colleagues in exhibitions management, production, development, education, events, communications, press, marketing, front of house, security, building services and retail at all three institutions, who are too numerous to name here but whose contributions are deeply felt.

The exhibition at DAS MINSK was beautifully designed by the Kooperative für Darstellungspolitik in cooperation with Fasson Freddy Fuss, who developed the graphic design for the show. At the Barbican, Jonathan Hagos and Tim Coles of Freehaus transformed the galleries, working closely with A Practice for Everyday Life on the graphic design, who are also responsible for the elegance of this publication.

We are so grateful to the artists, writers and curators whose texts in this book capture the complex ways in which Davis's paintings work their power over us. Tina M. Campt contributes new research on Davis's *1975* series, paying particular attention to the Black spaces that unfold within the paintings. Claudia Rankine opens the door to Davis's commitment to community, positioning his paintings and the UM as radical invitations. Dawoud Bey, T.J. Clark, Francesco Clemente, Karon Davis, Marlene Dumas, Helen Molesworth and Jason Moran respond to individual paintings by Davis, setting them alight through words. We thank all the authors for the sensitivity with which they joined our fold and brought their written artistry to bear.

For the curatorial team, it has been crucial to spend as much time as possible with Davis's work while allowing for his philosophy and approach towards artmaking to be their guides. Because Davis knew better than anyone that painting can do 'something to your soul that nothing else can. It is visceral and immediate.'[6]

Shanay Jhaveri, Head of Visual Arts, Barbican Art Gallery, London
Paola Malavassi, Director, DAS MINSK Kunsthaus in Potsdam
Ann Philbin, Director, Hammer Museum, Los Angeles

1 Roberta Smith, 'Noah Davis is Gone; His Paintings Continue to Hypnotize', *New York Times*, 6 February 2020, www.nytimes.com/2020/02/06/arts/design/noah-davis-david-zwirner-review.html.
2 Karon Davis, 'Imitation Suite: Helen Molesworth and Karon Davis reckon with Noah Davis' *Imitation of Wealth*', *Art Los Angeles Reader*, no. 2, January 2016, p. 18.
3 Ben Ferguson, 'Noah Davis', *Dazed Digital*, 9 February 2010, dazeddigital.com/artsandculture/article/6483/1/noah-davis.
4 Camila McHugh, 'Noah Davis: David Zwirner, London', *Artforum*, February 2022, artforum.com/events/noah-davis-249423.
5 'Noah Davis: Interview by Ed Templeton', *ANP Quarterly*, vol. 2, no. 3, p. 15.
6 Ibid.

NOAH DAVIS AND THE MAGIC QUOTIDIAN by Eleanor Nairne

That time
we all heard it,
cool and clear,
cutting across the hot grit of the day.
The major Voice.
The adult Voice
forgoing Rolling River,
forgoing tearful tale of bale and barge
and other symptoms of an old despond.
Warning, in music-words
devout and large,
that we are each other's
harvest:
we are each other's
business:
we are each other's
magnitude and bond.

Gwendolyn Brooks, 'Paul Robeson', 1970

How does an artist render the textures of our everyday, intertwined lives? There is something saline-fresh about the thin, thin paint that Noah Davis used so distinctively, as if his paintings have just been plucked from a bath of developing fluid.

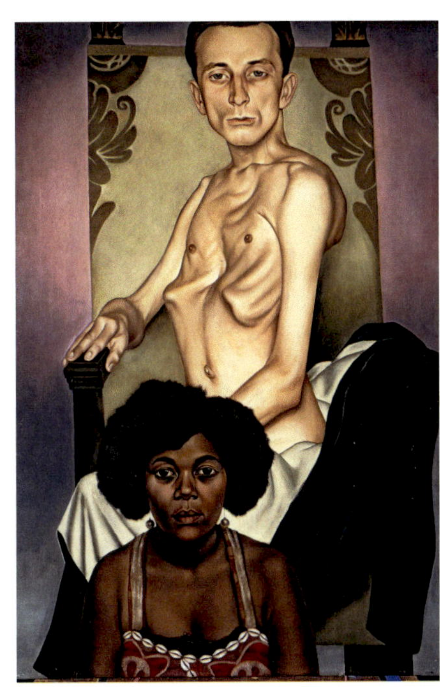

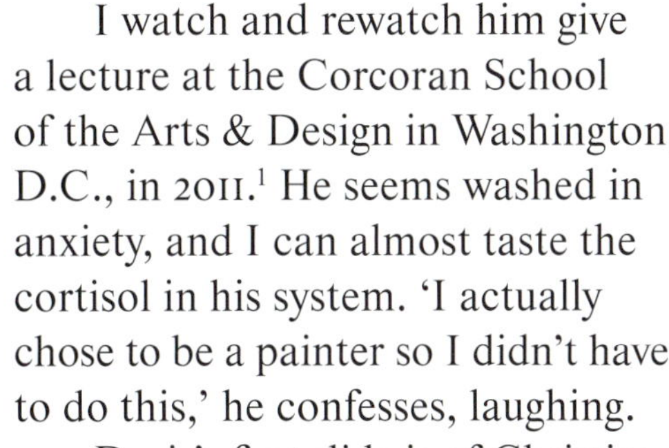

I watch and rewatch him give a lecture at the Corcoran School of the Arts & Design in Washington, D.C., in 2011.[1] He seems washed in anxiety, and I can almost taste the cortisol in his system. 'I actually chose to be a painter so I didn't have to do this,' he confesses, laughing.

Davis's first slide is of Christian Schad's 1929 work *Agosta, the Pigeon-Chested Man, and Rasha, the Black Dove*, which he had encountered at the 2006 exhibition *Glitter and Doom: German Portraits from the 1920s* at the Metropolitan Museum of Art in New York – a precise, exoticised painting typical

Christian Schad, *Agosta, der Flügelmensch und Rasha, die schwarze Taube* (Agosta, the Pigeon-Chested Man, and Rasha, the Black Dove), 1929

of *Neue Sachlichkeit* (New Objectivity) depicting two Berlin fairground performers: Agosta, who had a sunken ribcage, and Rasha, a snake charmer from Madagascar.

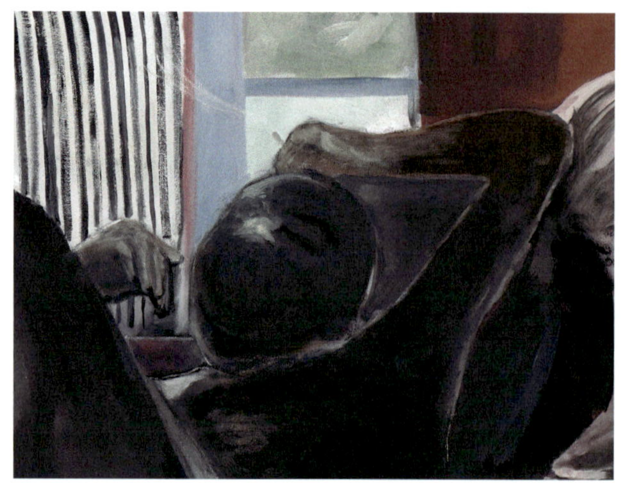

His second slide is of his own painting *Single Mother with Father out of the Picture* (p. 37) from 2007–8. Davis explains how he came to make this quietly arresting image, in which a young woman leans back into a plush, patterned armchair, wearing little more than an oversized t-shirt, her distracted eyes and the glare in her glasses suggesting the light emitting from a nearby television; a little girl between her knees wears little more than white underwear and ankle socks, the colour mirroring the plaster cast cladding her left arm. 'For a time period, I was going to [flea markets] every Saturday, I was collecting as many photographs as I possibly can... trying to pick the ones that felt the most like snap photography... slice of life, it's not necessarily high photography, but it tells a story.' Beset with nerves as he may have been, Davis has total clarity when articulating his artistic purpose: 'I wanted to take these anonymous moments and make them permanent'; or, as he goes on to elucidate: 'I wanted Black people to be normal. That was my whole thing.'

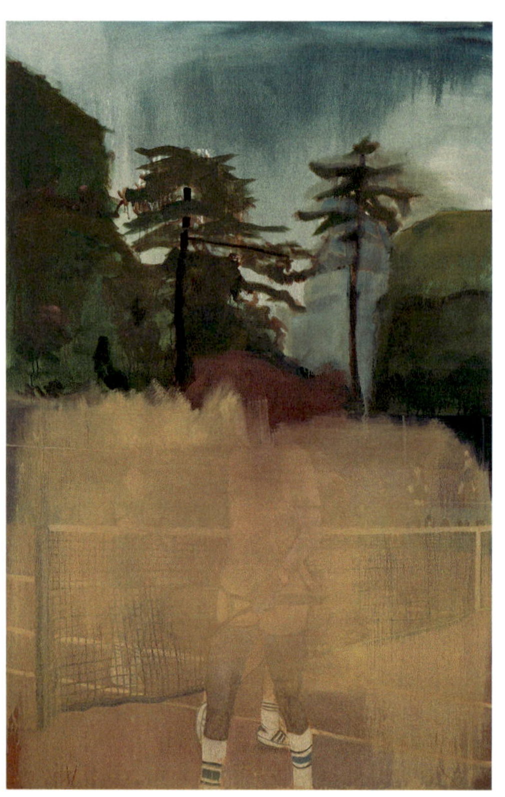

What does it mean to be 'normal' (a word that stems from a right-angled carpenter's square)? To no longer feel the angular assault of othering? His father Keven was a lawyer who had grown up in one of the few Black families in Sacramento,

Top *Sugartown* (detail), 2011
Bottom *Arthur Ashe*, 2013

California, while Davis pointed out that 'I'm from Seattle, so it's not like I'm surrounded by Black people'.[2] Feeling anomalous can bring expectations of exceptionality. As he put it: 'I've seen all [Dad's] clients come in... it always has to be so extra, and it always has to be so over the top'.[3] By contrast, Davis often paints faces that are tender, slack; some are entirely erased, suggesting a rag has been gently rubbed over their features, allowing them to release into the weave of the canvas; no need to perform here.

In his 2013 portrait of the tennis player Arthur Ashe, the first Black man to win a Grand Slam title, Davis casts a Rothko-esque veil over the lower half of Ashe's body while maroon brushstrokes swarm around his head. He must have been especially sensitive to the demands placed on sports stars given his father represented the Williams sisters from when they were teenagers negotiating the junior tennis circuit. Ashe's portrait chimes with an idea expressed by Claudia Rankine in *Citizen: An American Lyric* (2014), in which she describes the masking required when a subject is made to feel like 'graphite against a sharp white background'. 'Watching [a] newly contained Serena, you begin to wonder if she finally has given up wanting better from her peers...This type of [behavioural] ambiguity could also be diagnosed as dissociation and would support Serena's claim that she has had to split herself off from herself.'[4]

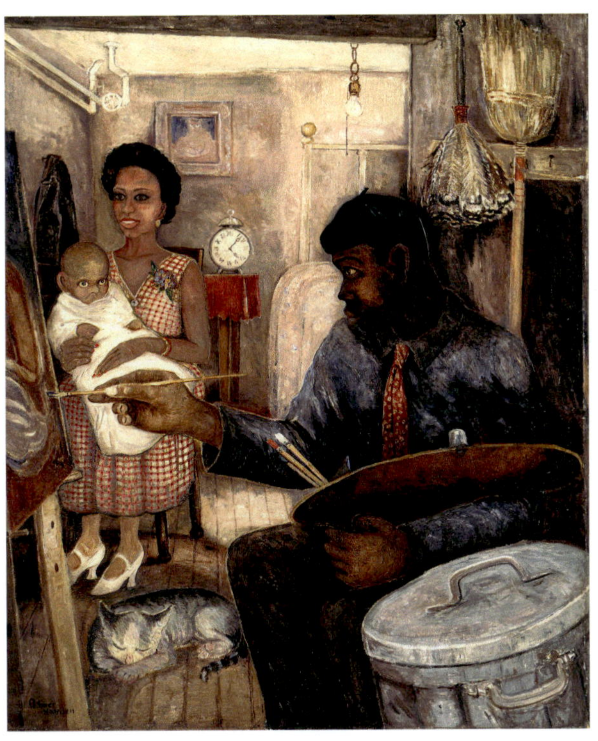

In D.C., a member of the audience mentions their favourite painting – Palmer Hayden's *The Janitor Who Paints* (c. 1937) – and Davis responds: 'I love that!' In the scene, Hayden, who supported himself as a janitor in Greenwich Village, depicts himself crammed into a corner of his apartment, working on a canvas as a woman in a red gingham dress, with her baby swaddled on her lap, sits for him in the opposite corner. The room is lit by a bare light bulb, and the clock has just gone four. With a palette tucked into the crook of his arm, Hayden asserts his status as a painter in defiance of the clutter of his day job, suggested by a trash can, broom and feather duster.

Palmer Hayden, *The Janitor Who Paints*, c. 1937, repainted after 1940

Davis also knew what it was to juggle a multitude of side hustles, including working at the bookstore at MOCA. I find myself wondering about how cramped he must have felt when he stood up to give this talk: the youngest artist to be included in *30 Americans*, a travelling group exhibition of work by contemporary Black artists from the Rubell Family Collection, he had been persuaded to be the special guest speaker for the 'Educators' Night Out', even though he hated talking publicly about his work. Many artists do, but for Davis, it was especially fraught given how he set out to capture moments of quotidian Black life – in all its banality and brilliance – that are essentially ineffable.

That year, he had barely been painting at all. He had rented an apartment in Harlem so that he could be close to his father, who had been diagnosed with late-stage cancer.[5] Not long before his father's death, Davis made *Painting for My Dad* (2011) (p. 99), in which a figure dressed in a faded red t-shirt and a pair of quintessential 'Dad jeans' holds a lantern in one hand as he stares down and beyond into a starry abyss. It is not unusual to contemplate your own mortality or that of a beloved, but to portray the vertiginous experience of imminent grief is an incredible feat.

As his lecture draws to a close, Davis keeps offering his audience reassurances: 'This is the last slide, so you can get out of here!' But as is inevitable on these kinds of occasions, there is still one final question, and it is, of course, ridiculously vast: 'I'm curious – what themes did you want to explore?' Davis draws breath: 'I wanted to create narratives that are based in – almost like a Fellini. You know Federico Fellini, the filmmaker? So, if you take – in terms of casting, finding the right figures, finding these just really basic stories to tell that are about love, that are about death or so forth, that's where I'm kind of going ... But I want it to be more magical. I don't want it to be so stuck in reality.' An enchanted cinéma vérité.

Palmer Hayden described his work as 'a sort of protest painting', and Davis's project is equally political, although not vociferously so.[6] To present Black bodies in repose, at play, going about their daily lives, is to liberate them from the tyranny of white scrutiny. To conjure scenes that are both ordinary and extraordinary is to refute the fiction of difference. This is the humble truth that Gwendolyn Brooks recognised: *that we are each other's harvest / we are each other's business / we are each other's magnitude and bond.*

1 'Educators' Night Out' at the Corcoran School of the Arts & Design, 4 October 2011, online recording, vimeo.com/31541073.
2 Ibid.
3 Ibid.
4 Claudia Rankine, *Citizen: An American Lyric* (London: Penguin Random House, 2015), p. 36.
5 For more information, see Lindsay Charlwood's beautifully authored chronology in *Noah Davis: In Detail* (New York: David Zwirner Books, 2023), p. 187.
6 Artwork description from the Smithsonian American Art Museum, americanart.si.edu/artwork/janitor-who-paints-10126.

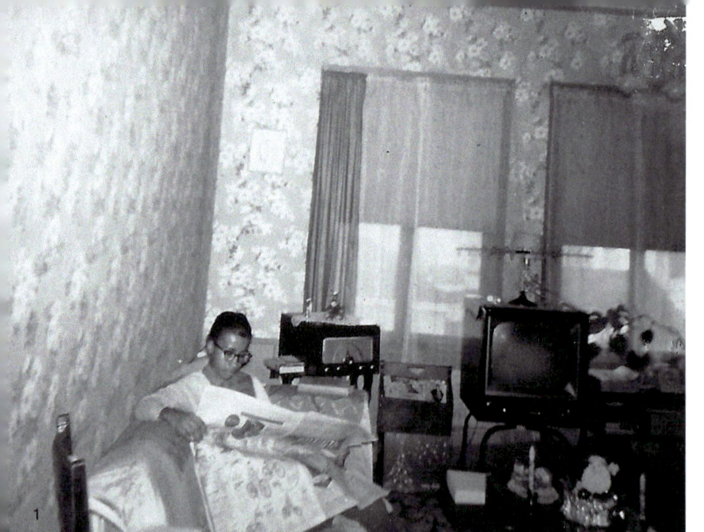

1

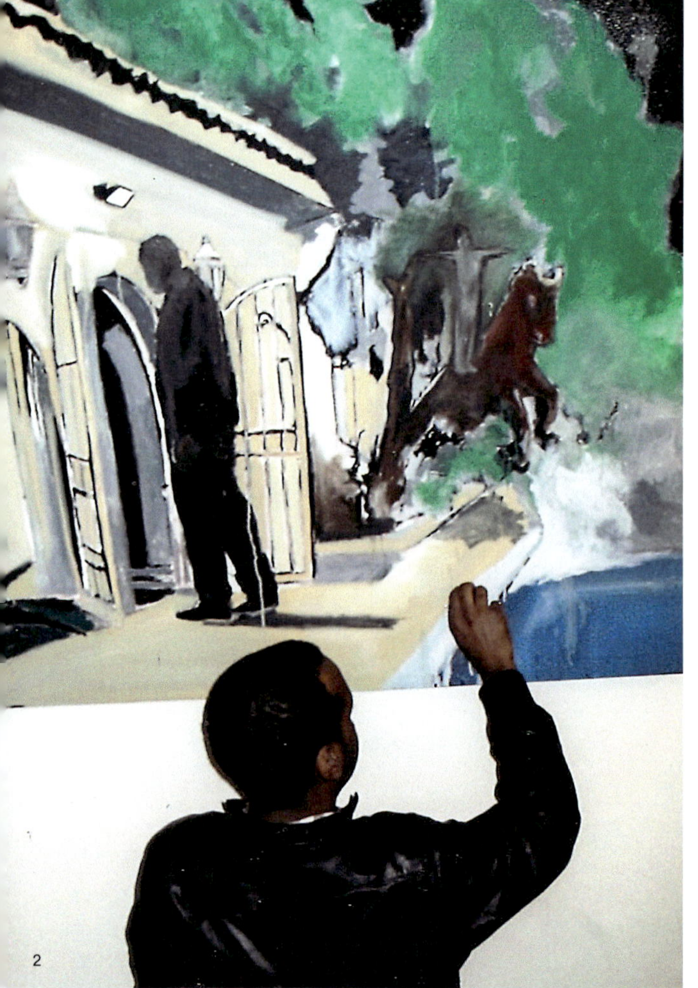

2

"Yet free of violent city noise."

3

Best Fucking Painter Alive

4

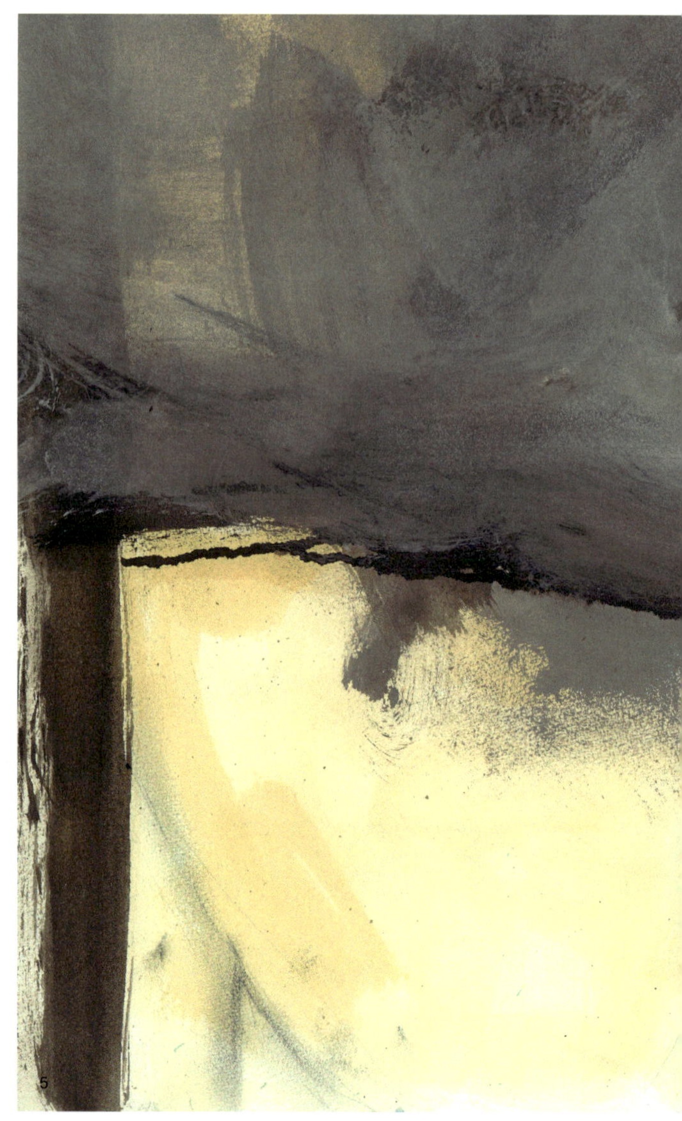

5

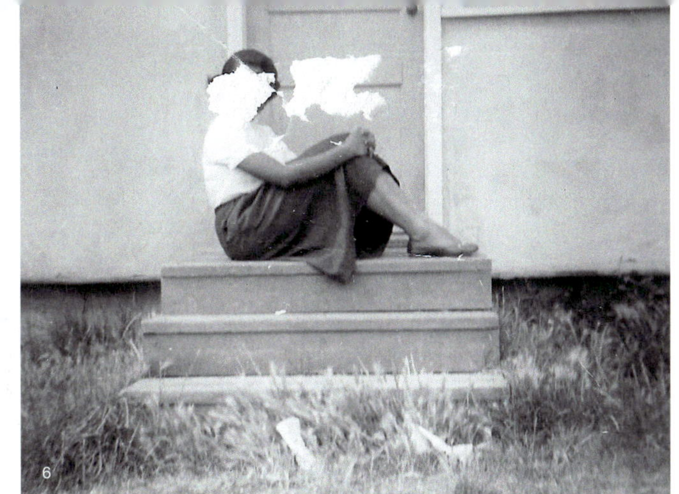

6

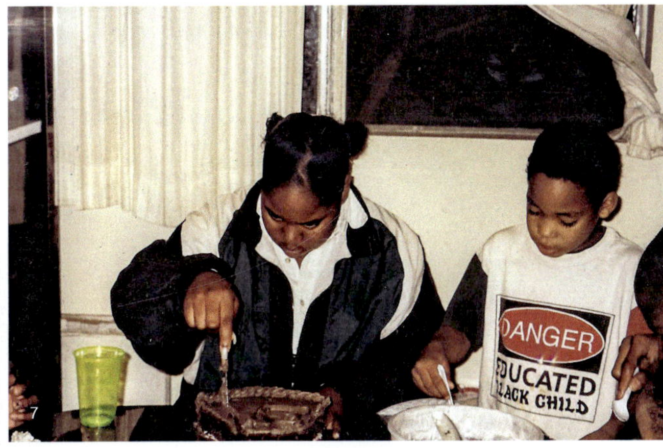

7

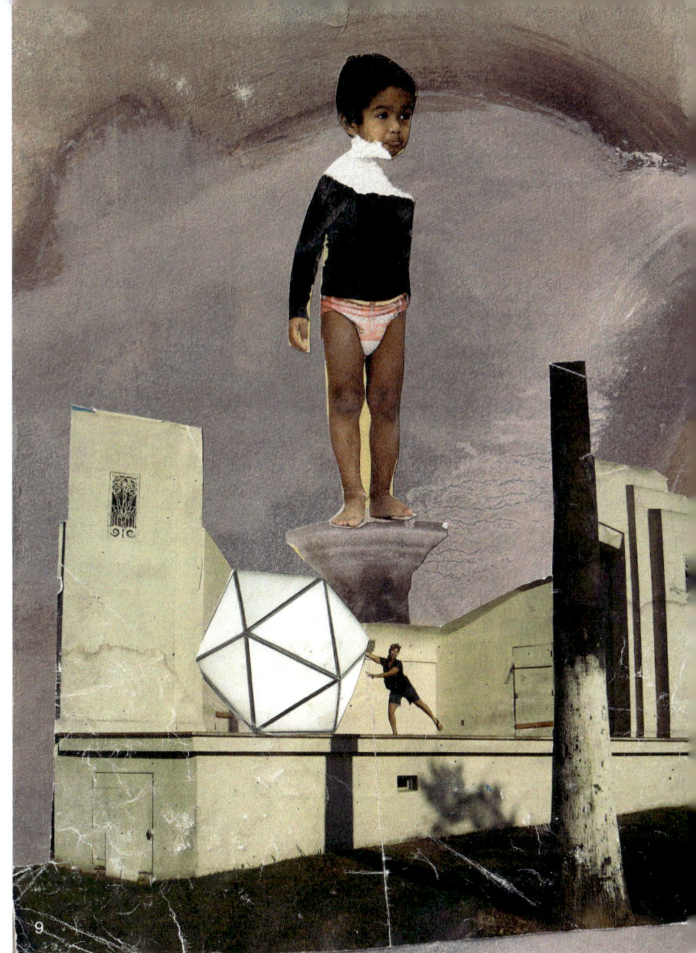

9

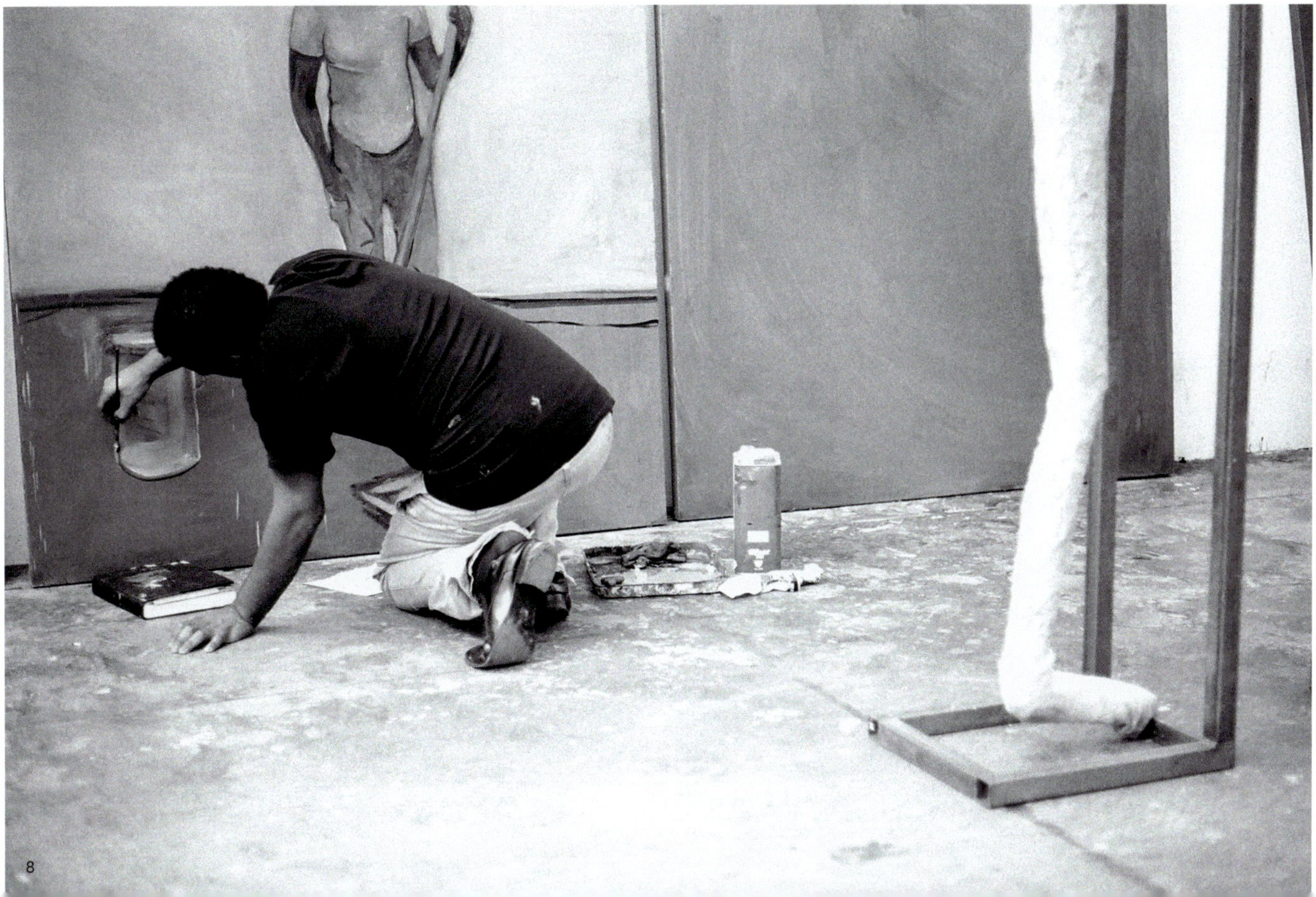

8

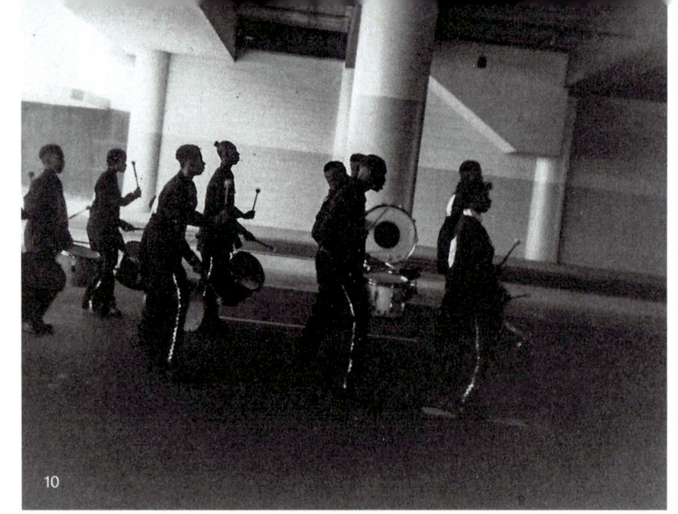

10

PRIORITIES

WALKER

- PAINTER
- BLACK PERSON
- FLANEUR
- ALL AROUND WILD AND CRAZY GUY
- NICE GUY

11

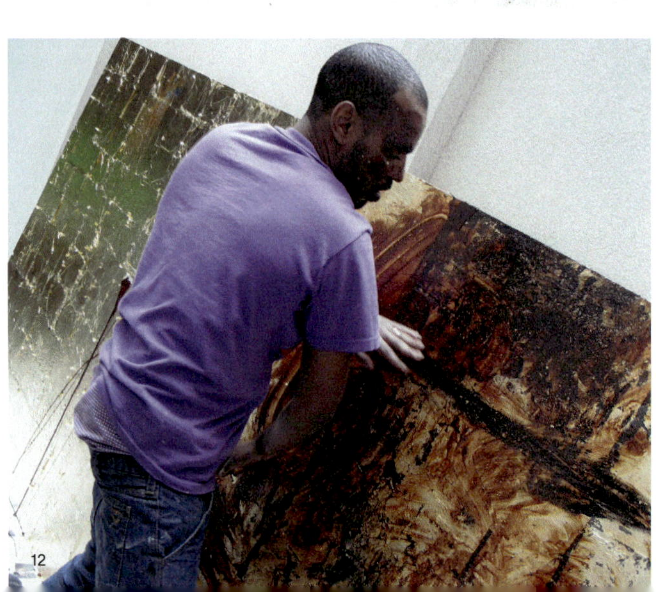

12

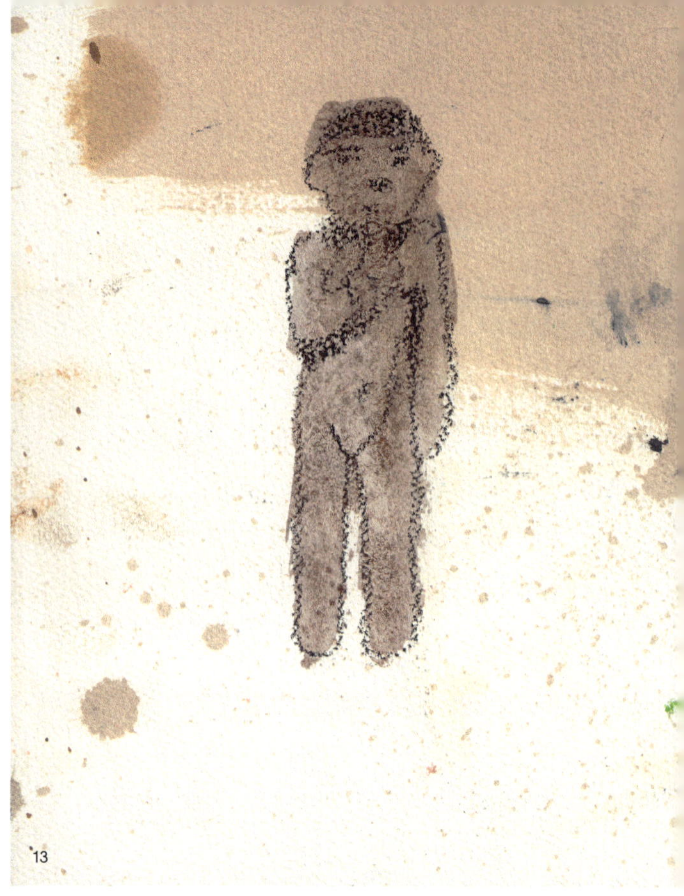

13

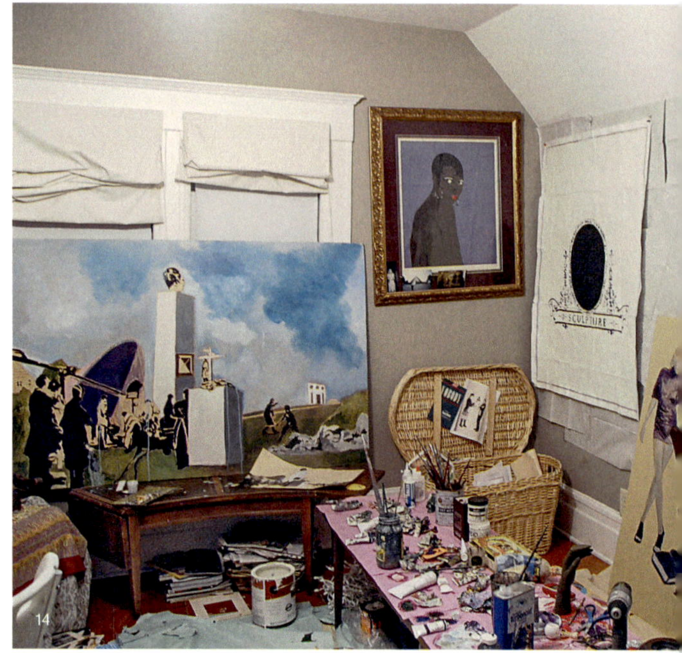

14

- WHAT ARE YOU DOING?

why do you want to become an artist /
- why do you make what you make.

15

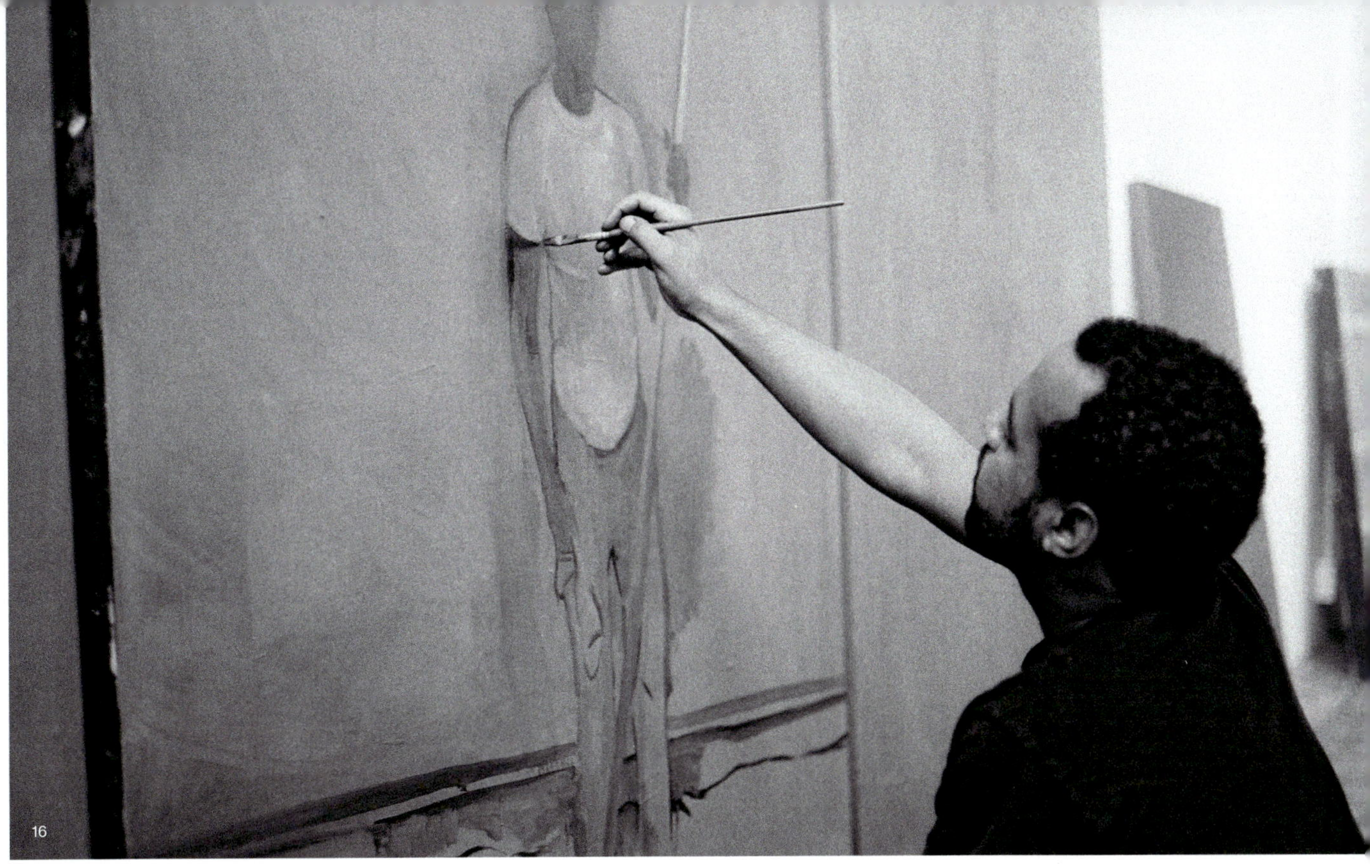

16

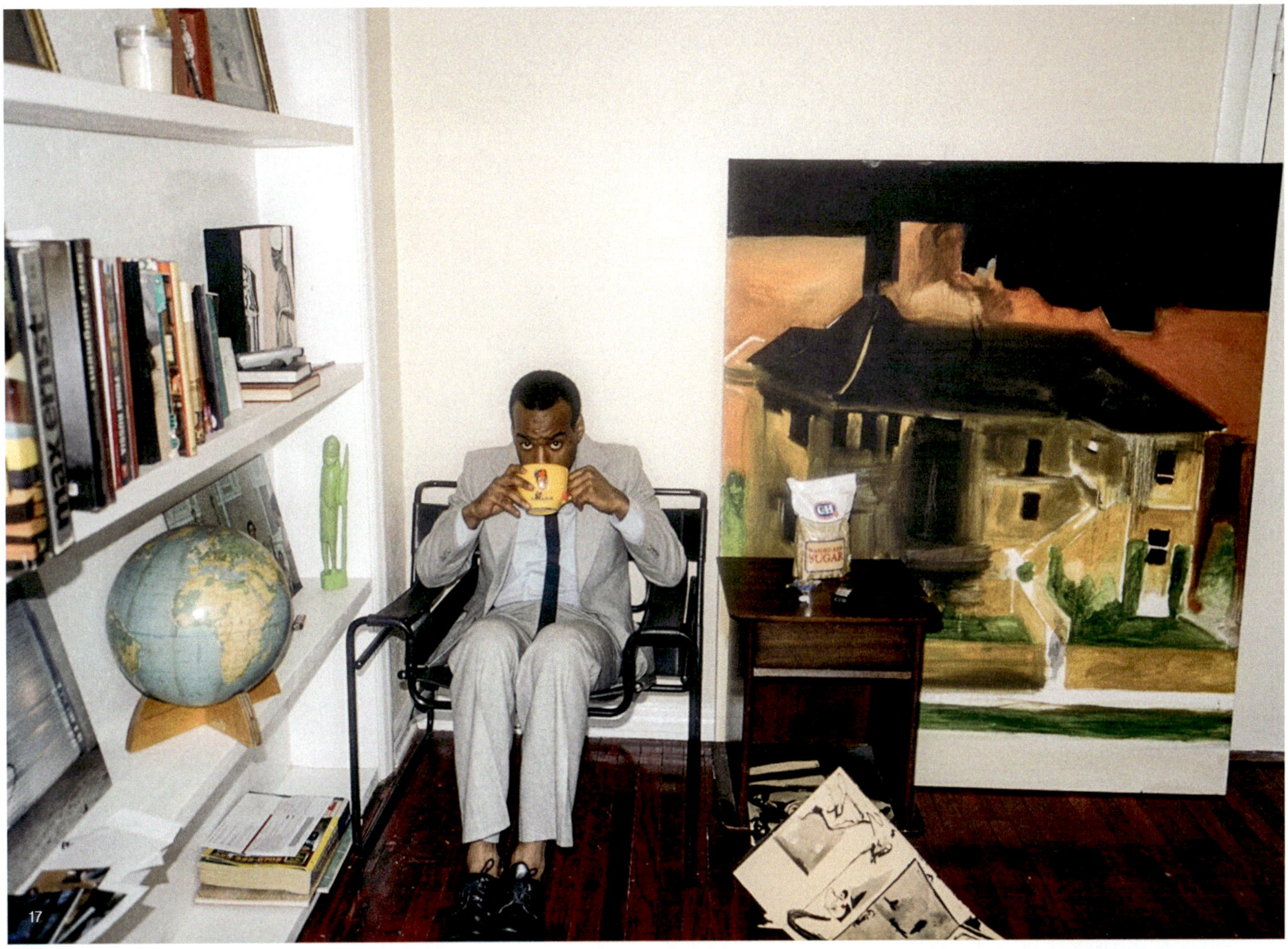

17

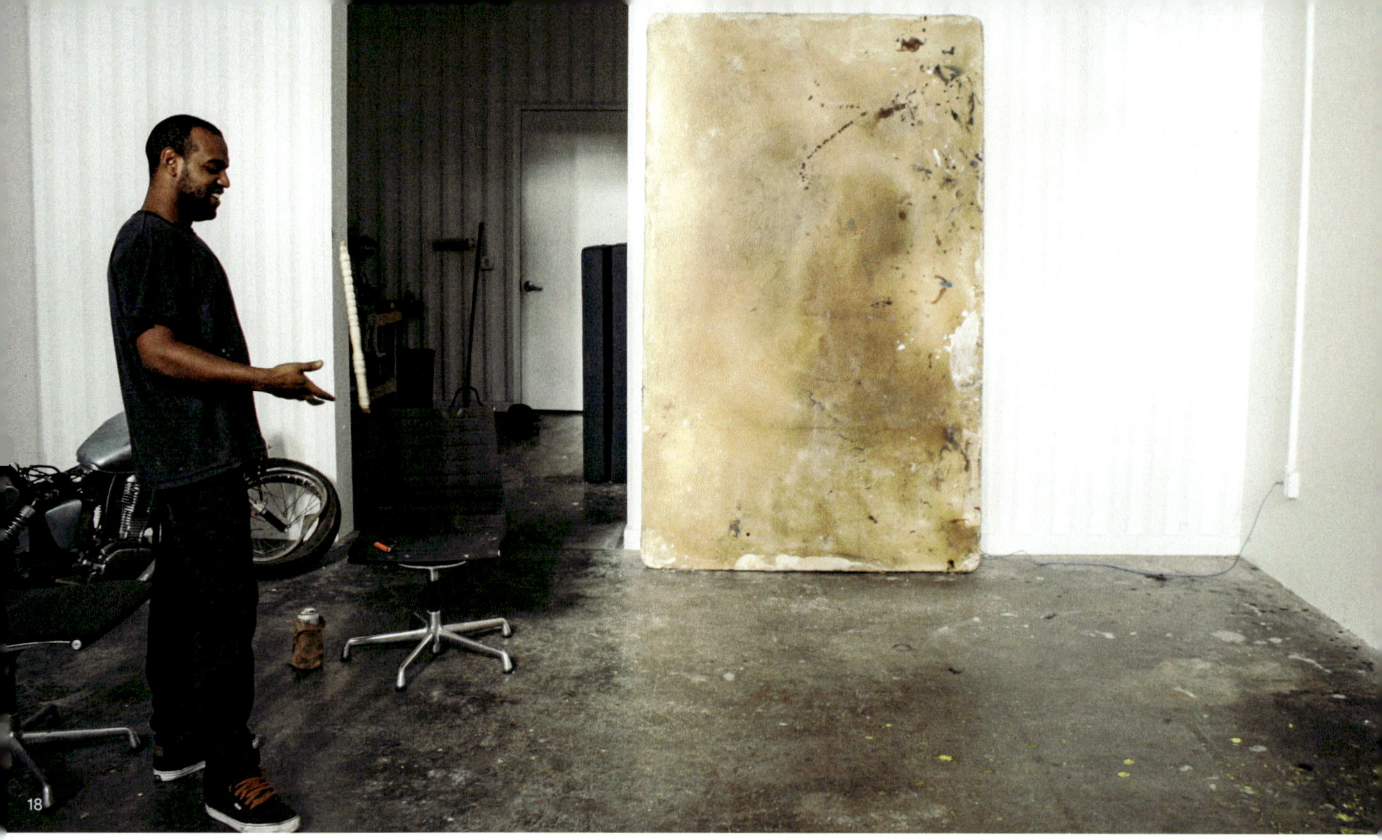

18

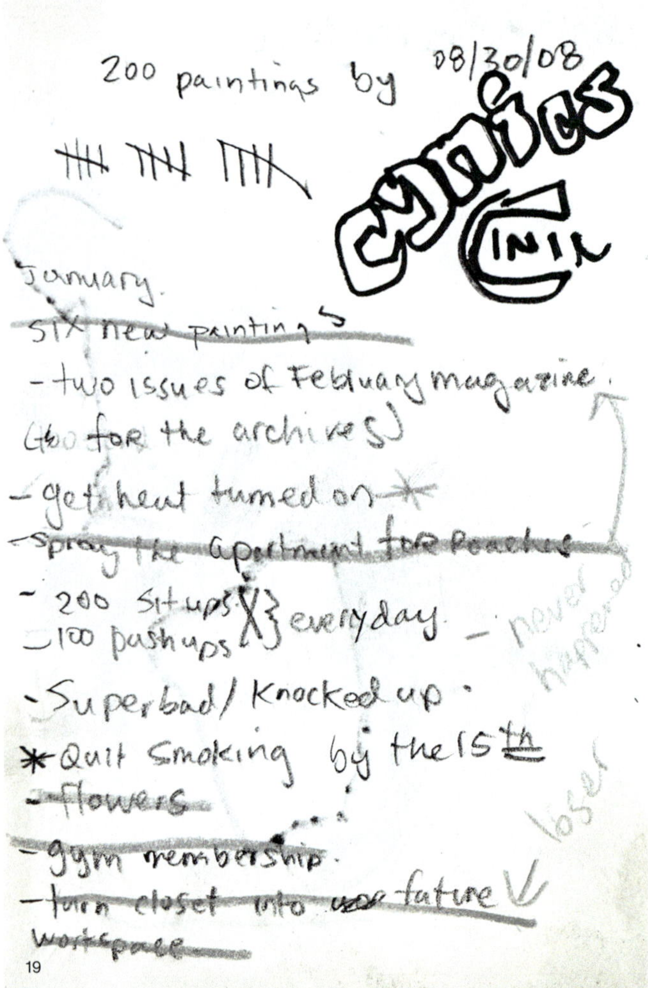

200 paintings by 08/30/08

Cynics

INI

January.

~~six new paintings~~

- two issues of February magazine. (two for the archives)

- get heat turned on *

~~- spray the apartment for roaches~~

- 200 sit ups
- 100 pushups everyday. – never happened

- Superbad / Knocked up.

* Quit smoking by the 15th

~~- flowers~~

~~- gym membership.~~

~~- turn closet into future workspace~~ loser

19

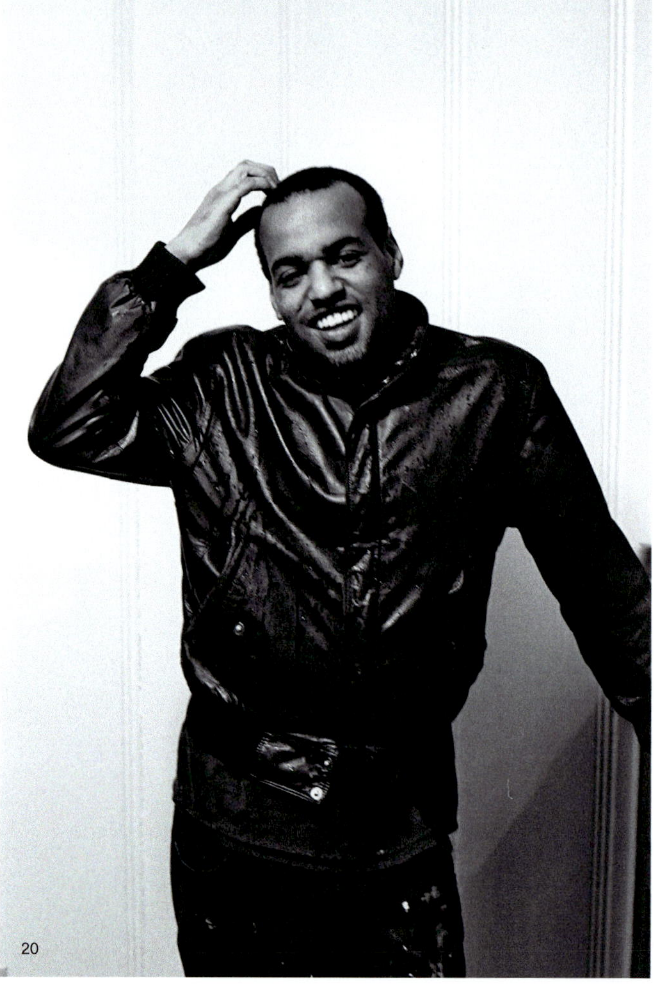

20

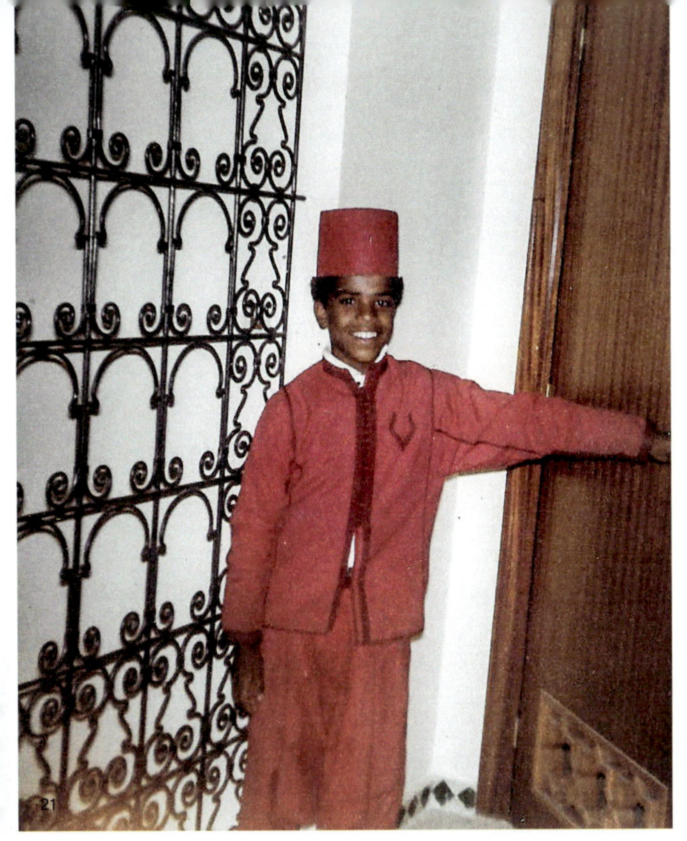

21

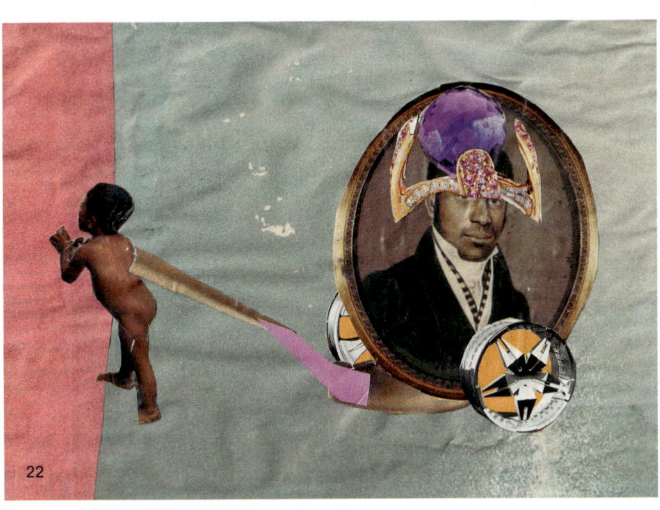

22

Stay Vegan.
Smile.
Don't Worry.

23

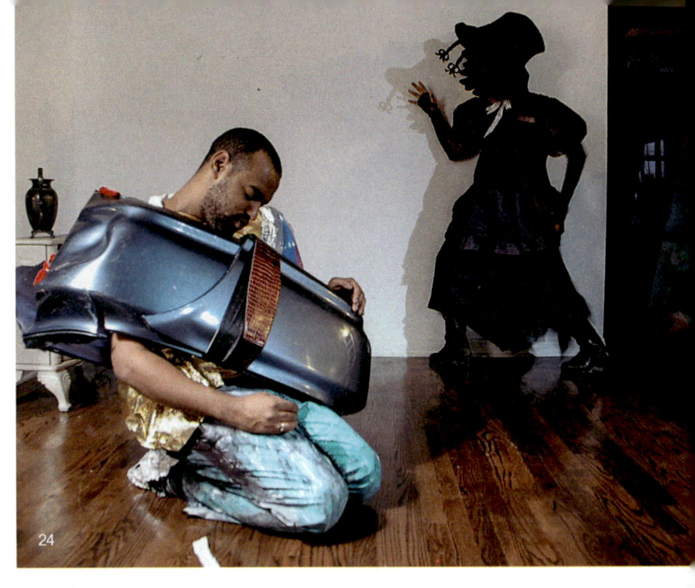

24

25

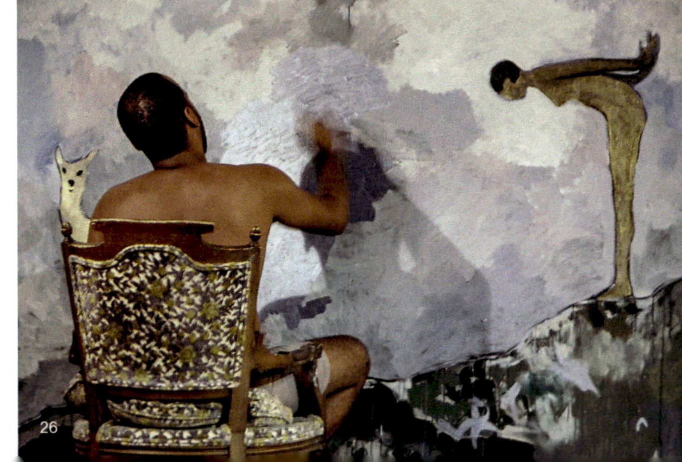

26

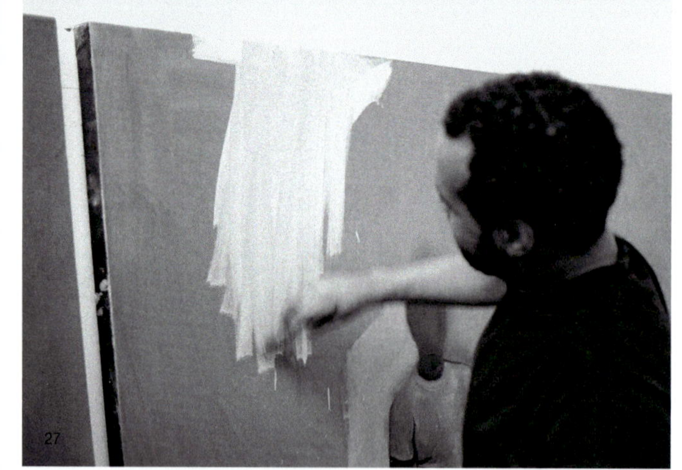

27

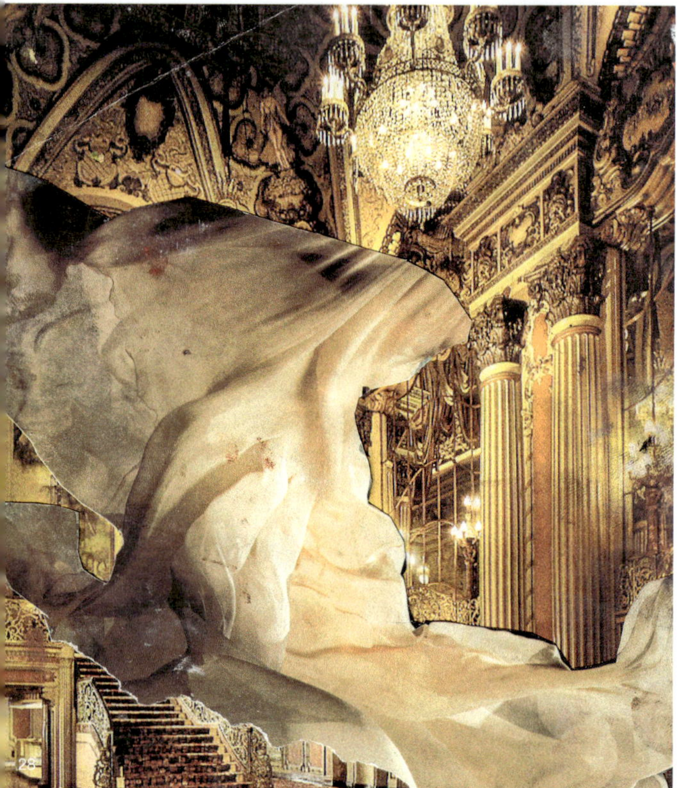

28

Buy Books.
– spend less money on
cigarettes more money on
books groceries, flowers, books
books, books. books.

29

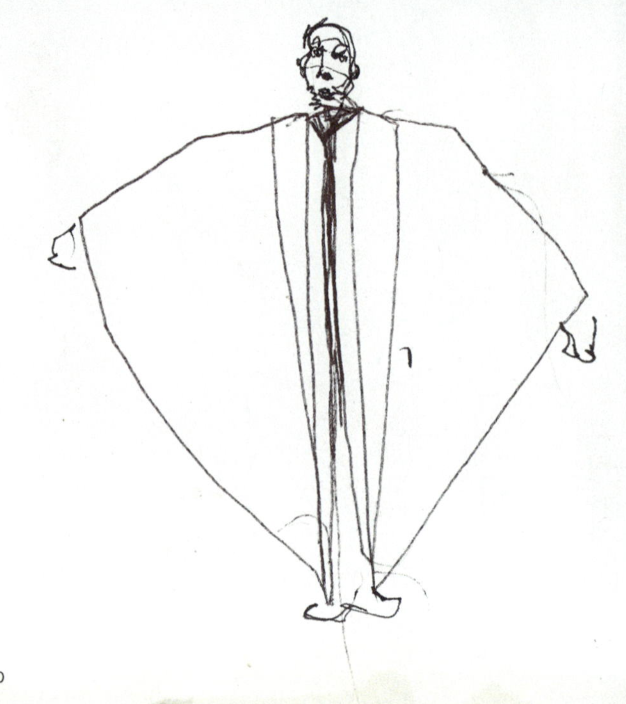

30

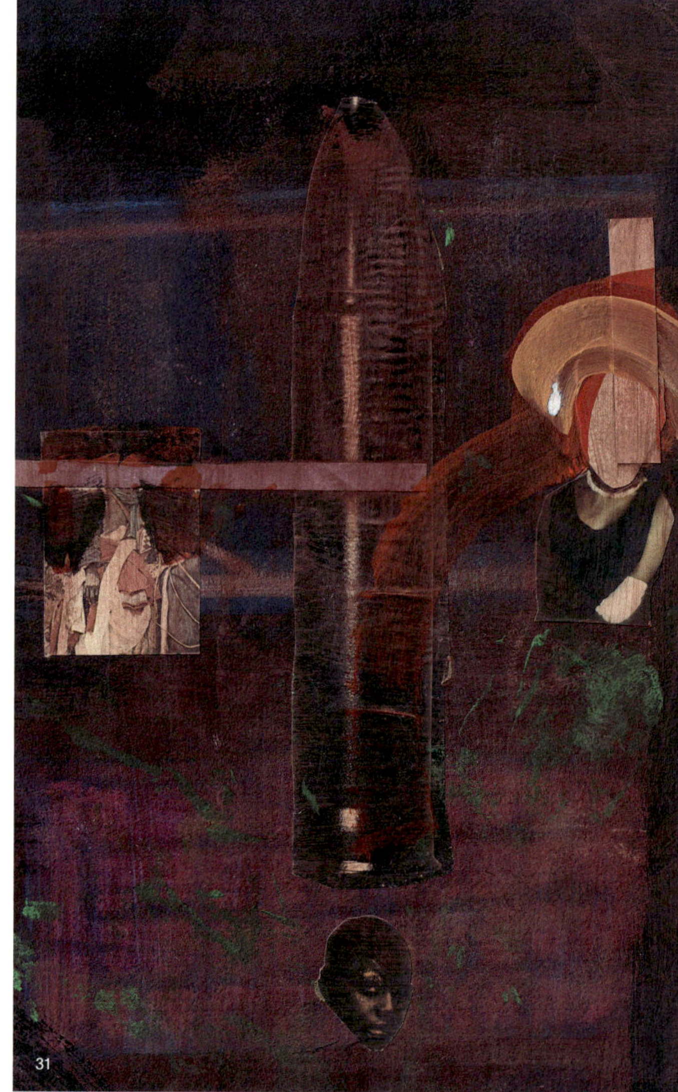

31

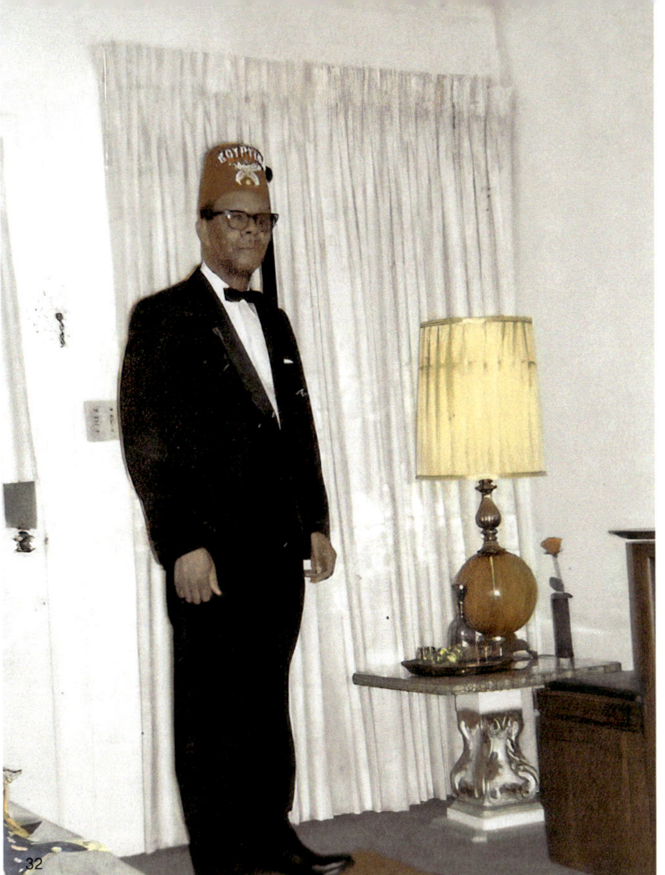

ROBERTS & TILTON
5801 Washington Boulevard
Culver City, CA 90232
T 323-549-0223
F 323-549-0224
www.robertsandtilton.com
info@robertsandtilton.com

October 7, 2010

PRESS RELEASE

Gray Day

Curated by Noah Davis
October 30 - December 18, 2010
Opening reception for the artists: Saturday, October 30th, 6 to 8pm

Joshua Aster, Larry Bell, Michelle Blade, James Brittingham, Bruce High Quality, Juan Capistran, Kristen Calabrese, Alika Cooper, Sylvia Cooper, ~~Aaron Curry~~, Daniel Desure, Mark Dutcher, Andrew Foster, Michael Hayden, Inner City Avante Garde, Charles Karubian, Anthony Lepore, Sydney Littenberg, Mark McKnight, Samia Mizra, Emmeline De Mooij, Ariana Papademetropoulos, Marlon Rabenreither, Pj Risse, ~~Allen Ruppersburg~~, Malik Sayeed, Allison Schulnick, Natasha Snellman, Eric Yahnker.

The exhibition, *Gray Day*, ~~should exist like the aftermath of a failed suicide attempt; it should represent the line that has been blurred between art, commerce and celebrity. Where simultaneously the artist Jeff Koons and the NBA all-star Shaquille O' Neal can assume the same position as curator, I'm unable to differentiate the two exhibitions. *Gray Day* is the idea that one can no longer define the art world, yet, the thirty plus artists in the exhibition more or less situate themselves within it.~~

~~To demonstrate the~~ apathy of the present moment, I felt it would be significant to gather a large group of artists to work individually on a single objective to create a show that is entirely gray. ~~An ode to group shows such as Gavin Brown's "Who's Afraid of Jaser Johns" and the Metropolitan Museum of Art's exhibition of "Jasper Johns: Gray," this exhibition asks thirty artists to create works that best define their interpretation of the color gray.~~ For now let's call all the work in this exhibition "gray matter," and the space that it occupies a "gray area."

Works on view range from Larry Bell's geometric drawings executed in the 1970s to Marlon Rabenreither's film stills that formally echo Bell's current collage paintings. ~~A slide from 2001 by Kevin Galleazi displays a lottery ticket and a photograph of American women on a trip to a third world country, surrounded by natives whom the artist has adorned with stars on their faces to illustrate the exploitation of the voyeur on the indigenous people. The slide itself was taken while the curator and the artist were roommates in college ten years prior. Printed without the artist's permission, the slide has transformed from personal ephemera to an undiscovered moment in recent art history.~~

A survey of contemporary ~~local talent~~ in painting includes ~~standout pieces~~ by Allison Shulnik, Charles Karubian, Joshua Aster, Mark Dutcher and Kristen Calabrese. ~~Each painter maintains their own technique while creating new territory in one of the most illusive mediums. James Brittingham's acrylic and mylar wall pieces are instantly iconic. Bay Area artists~~ Michelle Blade and Mark McKnight ~~both contribute consistent work habits, one in drawing and the other in photography.~~

Works from various private collections consist of shadow boxes by Bruce High Quality, ~~and a portion of Eric Wesley's early sculpture. The new art collective, Inner City Avant-Garde, riffs on the reality of a day job.~~ ~~A smashed disco ball by Daniel Desure lays on the floor as if it has fallen ten feet to the ground declaring the end of the party.~~ ~~A sizeable~~ sculpture by Michaels Hayden ~~is like a severed building that has been rearranged to comment on~~ contemporary architecture. A new sculpture by Natasha Snellman ~~called~~

34

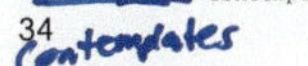

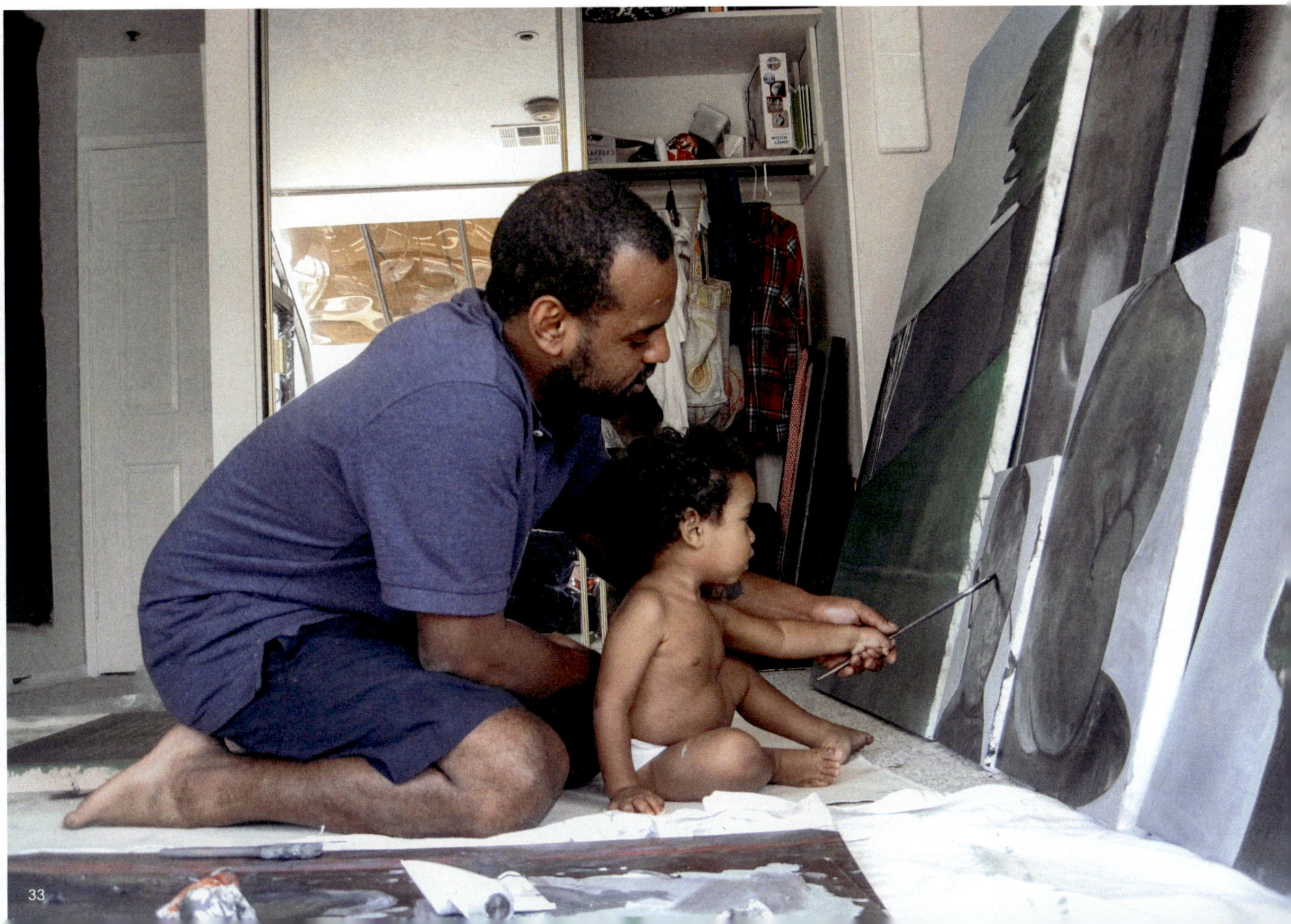

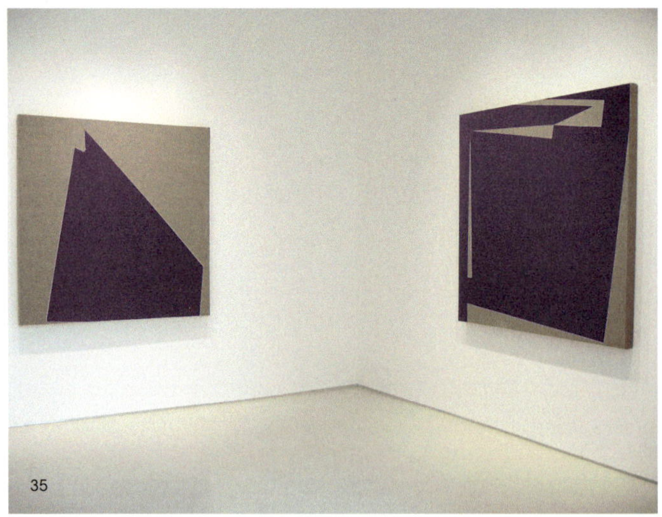

35

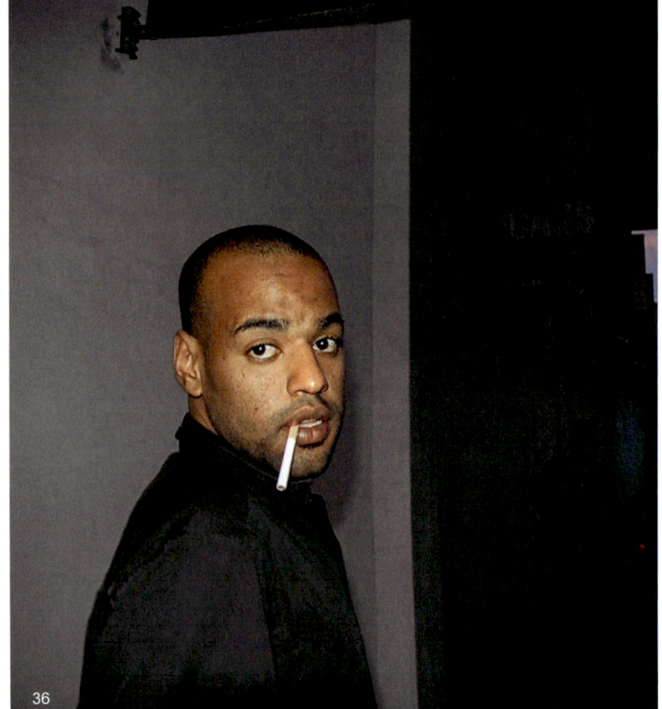

36

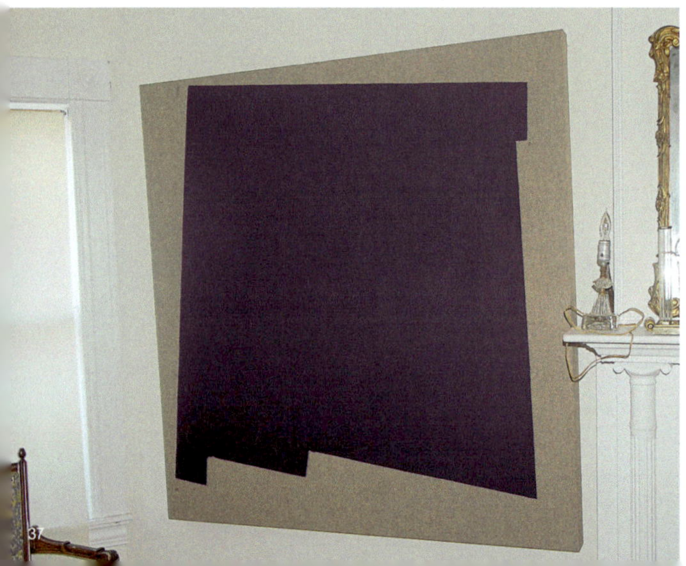

37

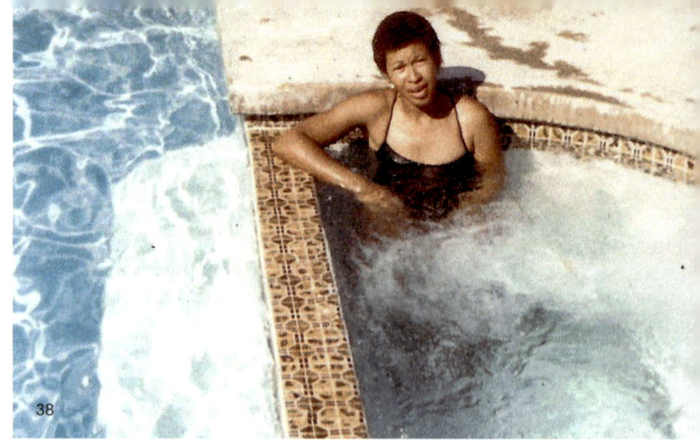

38

In business, you learn at a faster rate than academia.

39

NOBODY

New Paintings by

NOAH DAVIS

October 11 - November 8, 2008
Opening Reception Saturday, October 11th, 6 - 8pm

ROBERTS & TILTON

40

1 Found photograph from Davis's collection
2 Noah Davis painting. Painting no longer exists
3 A line from street poet Bob Kaufman's poem 'Cocoa Morning' (1967) in Davis's notebook, c. 2010–14
4 Notebook page, c. 2010–14
5 *Untitled*, 2014, mixed media on paper, 38.7 × 27 cm (15¼ × 10⅝ in)
6 Found photograph from Davis's collection
7 Found photograph from Davis's collection
8 Davis at Pico Studio, Los Angeles, 2009. Painting no longer exists (painted over by the artist)
9 *Untitled* (detail), 2014, mixed media on paper, 39.4 × 26.7 cm (15½ × 10½ in)
10 Found photograph from Davis's collection
11 Notebook page, c. 2010–14
12 Davis's painting performance with chocolate on gold leaf at Tilton Gallery, New York, 2009
13 *Untitled* (detail), 2015, mixed media on paper, 30.5 × 22.9 cm (12 × 9 in)
14 Davis's home studio in West Adams, Los Angeles, 2009
15 Notebook page, c. 2010–14
16 Davis at Pico Studio, Los Angeles, 2009. Painting no longer exists (painted over by the artist)
17 Noah Davis in his apartment in Koreatown, Los Angeles, c. 2008
18 Davis at Pico Studio, Los Angeles, 2010
19 Notebook page, c. 2010–14
20 Davis at his home in Los Angeles, 2009
21 Found photograph from Davis's collection
22 *Untitled* (detail), 2014, mixed media on paper
23 Notebook page, c. 2010–14
24 Davis in costume as a John Chamberlain sculpture and Karon Davis as a Kara Walker silhouette, Halloween, 2009
25 *Untitled* (detail), 2015, mixed media on paper, 30.5 × 22.9 cm (12 × 9 in)
26 Davis working on *Prey*, Los Angeles, 2010
27 Davis at Pico Studio, Los Angeles, 2009. Painting no longer exists (painted over by the artist)
28 *Phantom Painting, Collage* (detail), 2012, mixed media on paper, 15.6 × 12.7 cm (6⅛ × 5 in)
29 Notebook page, c. 2010–14
30 Notebook page, c. 2010–14
31 *Untitled* (detail), 2015, mixed media on paper, 39 × 27.3 cm (15⅜ × 10¾ in)
32 Found photograph from Davis's collection
33 Noah and Moses, Los Angeles, c. 2010–11
34 Davis's annotated press release for *Gray Day*, Roberts & Tilton, Los Angeles, 2010
35 Installation view, *Noah Davis: Nobody*, Roberts & Tilton, Culver City, 2008
36 Davis at the opening of *30 Americans*, Rubell Family Collection, Miami, 2008
37 *Nobody*, 2008, installed in Davis's home in West Adams, Los Angeles
38 Found photograph from Davis's collection
39 Notebook page, c. 2010–14
40 Invitation for *Noah Davis: Nobody*, Roberts & Tilton, Culver City, 2008

HELEN MOLESWORTH on *40 Acres and a Unicorn*, 2007

The deep grammar of pictures begins with figure and ground. There is a surface (ground) and there is a mark (figure). All pictures have these two things. Meaning emerges from their difference. In Noah Davis's *40 Acres and a Unicorn*, the ground is black. Coal black, midnight black, ebony black, ink black. The black of tar, of velvet, of a raven's feather, of obsidian. The black that absorbs all other colours, the black that is the total sum of all colour. The black of the ocean at night, the black of the galaxy, the black of the universe, the black of the multiverse. Manet's black, John McCracken's black, Kerry James Marshall's black. Vantablack. The black that forms the ground of *40 Acres and a Unicorn* appears bottomless, an endless projection backwards in space and time, a cosmic field, the Big Bang. Out of this non-space emerges a phantom on a mule, a man on a horse, a child on a unicorn. The black ground behind him is resolutely flat. There is no modelling, no illusion of receding space. There is only a subtle shift in tonality from black-black to blue-black in the mere hint of a horizon line, a whisper of surface for the unicorn's hooves to find their footing.

Forty acres of fertile black earth, that was the promise of Special Field Orders, No. 15 – a military decree issued in the final months of the American Civil War, an attempt to reinscribe order as it became clear that America had a problem: what to do with/about/for the formerly enslaved? One suggestion was that the government allot land to these newly freed Black Americans. Who, it must be reiterated, had already been tilling the soil and planting and harvesting the crops for generations without any compensation and who had not been allowed to own the fields they laboured upon through any of the mechanisms open to white people, such as purchase, inheritance, squatting, theft. Thousands of formerly enslaved people were sent to Hilton Head and the Sea Islands off the coast of the Carolinas. The plan was to divide up the land and offer what mules were available. Surely the people who had been working the land without pay were entitled to some small patch of it? Pledges made by a victorious army and Lincoln's government would be rolled back by the very next administration, as American a tale if ever there was one. The house always wins.

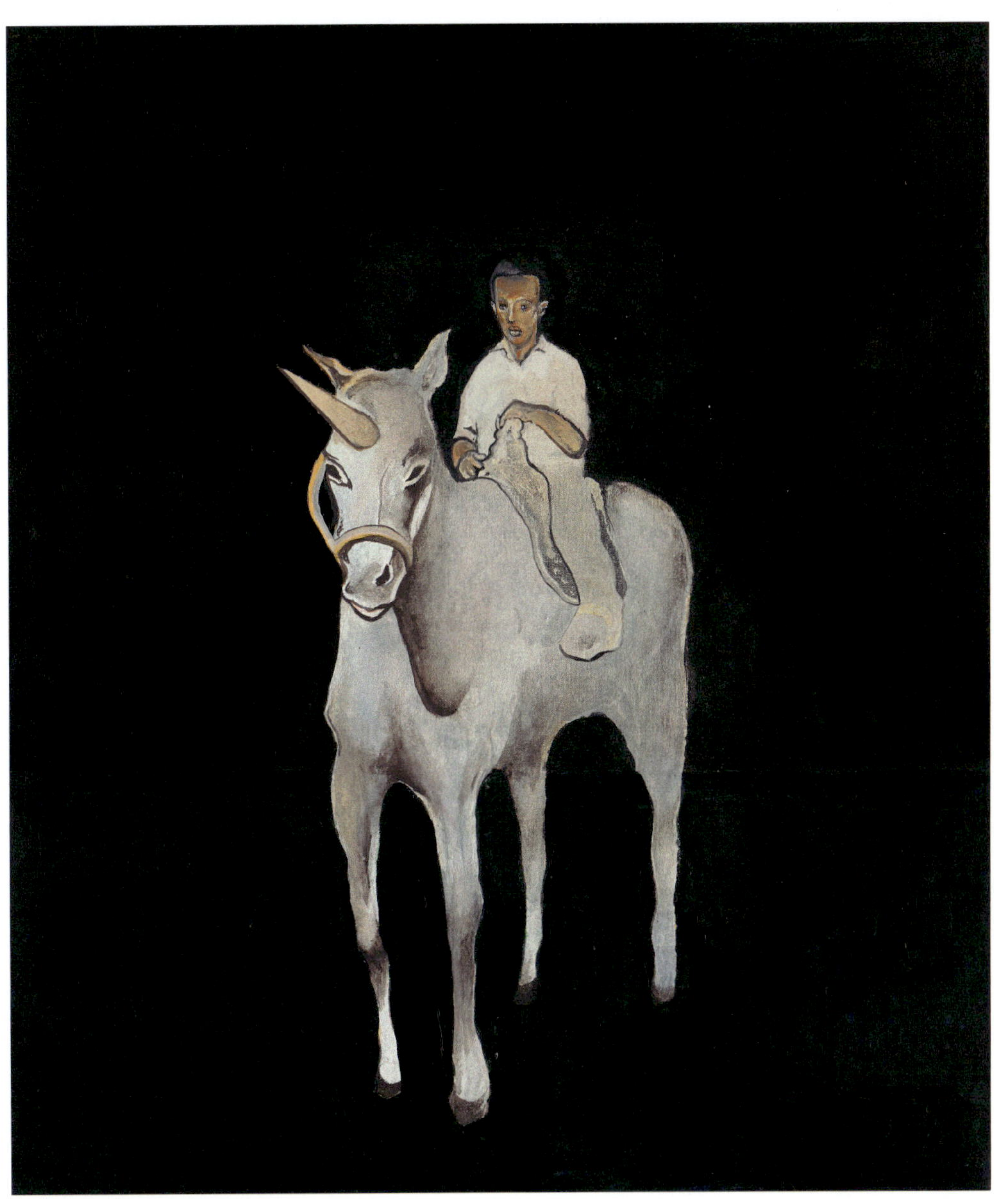

29 *40 Acres and a Unicorn*, 2007

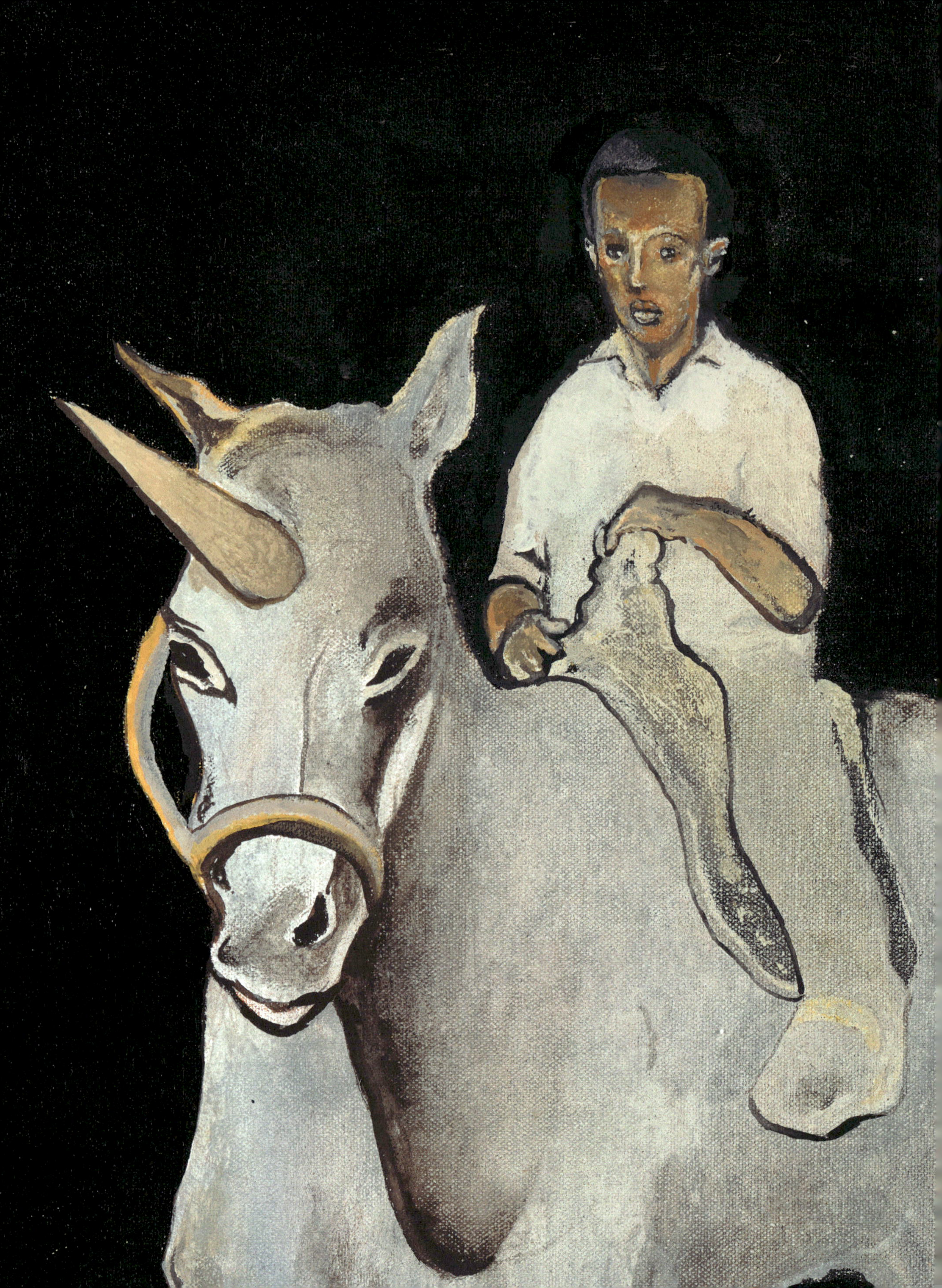

The phrase '40 acres and a mule' would become shorthand for the failure of the postwar Reconstruction era. It would come to signify America's inability to make either restitution or reparations for centuries of enslavement and oppression. Davis offers *40 Acres and a Unicorn* as a sly rejoinder to this broken promise. Out of the blackness of creation appears a mythological animal. If the fantasy of a unicorn replaces a beast of burden, then the endless space-time continuum of the universe replaces the 40 acres. A phantom, a man, a child lightly holds the reins of a future perpetually deferred, a future not contained in the space of the picture. Delicately rendered in this diminutive canvas, the figure and his unicorn are headed straight towards us. In the first line of his poem 'Harlem', Langston Hughes asks, 'What happens to a dream deferred?' In the poem's last line, he answers the question with another, one he felt the need to set in italics: '*Or does it explode?*' Will the myth of the unicorn ever meet the reality of the cosmos? If Americans finally metabolise the figure-ground relations of our country's origin (wealth and power, both accumulated and extracted, each utterly contingent on centuries of enslaved labour), will there be a Big Bang in the socio-political order? And if so, what wild potentiality, what new beginnings would such an explosion bring? What fecund, ever-expanding version of blackness might arise from the painting's modest elegance of phantom, man, child on a unicorn as he emerges from the deep dark past and arrives at our spell-bound present while looking ahead to the glimmer of a barely perceptible future?

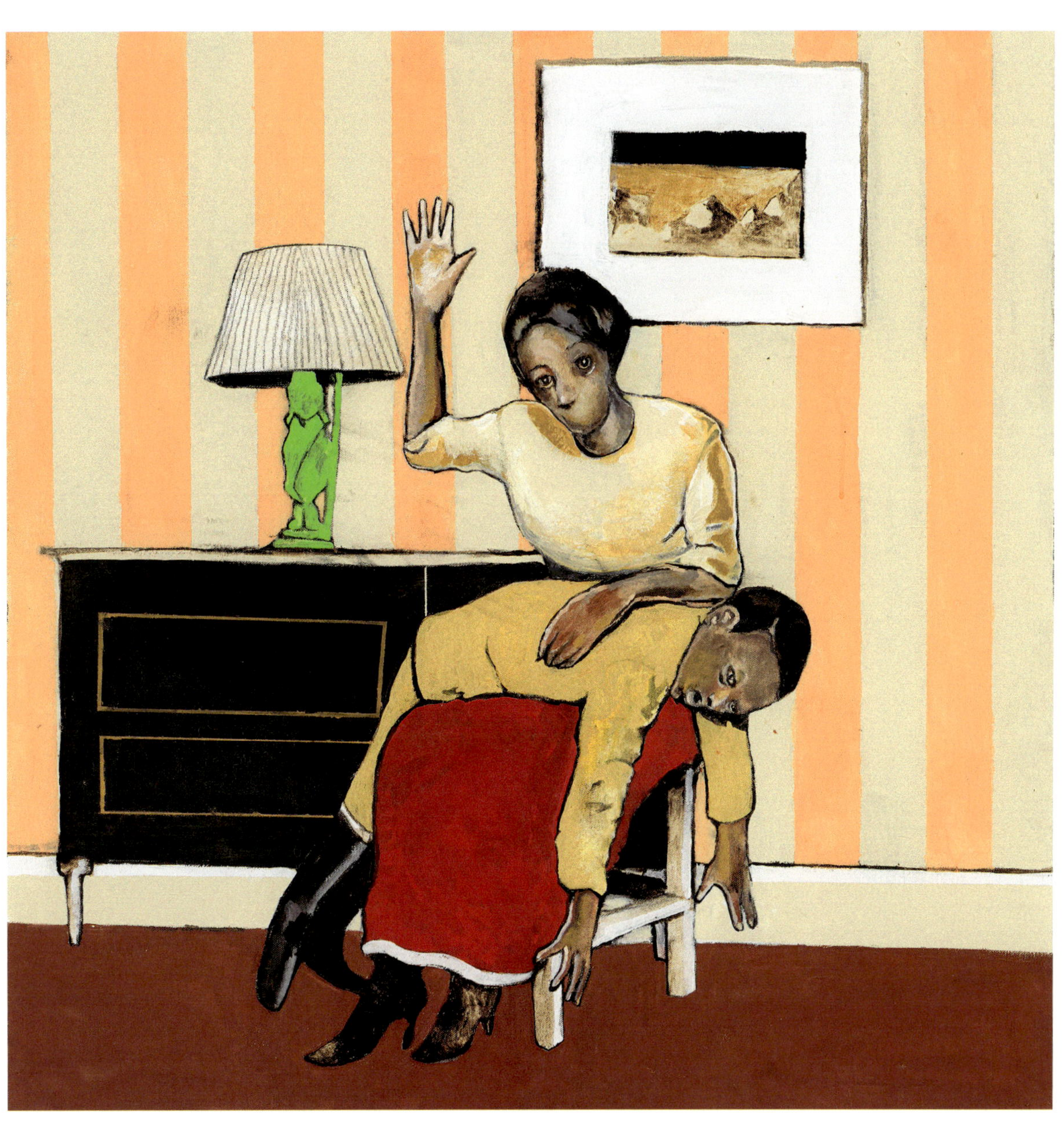

 Bad Boy For Life, 2007

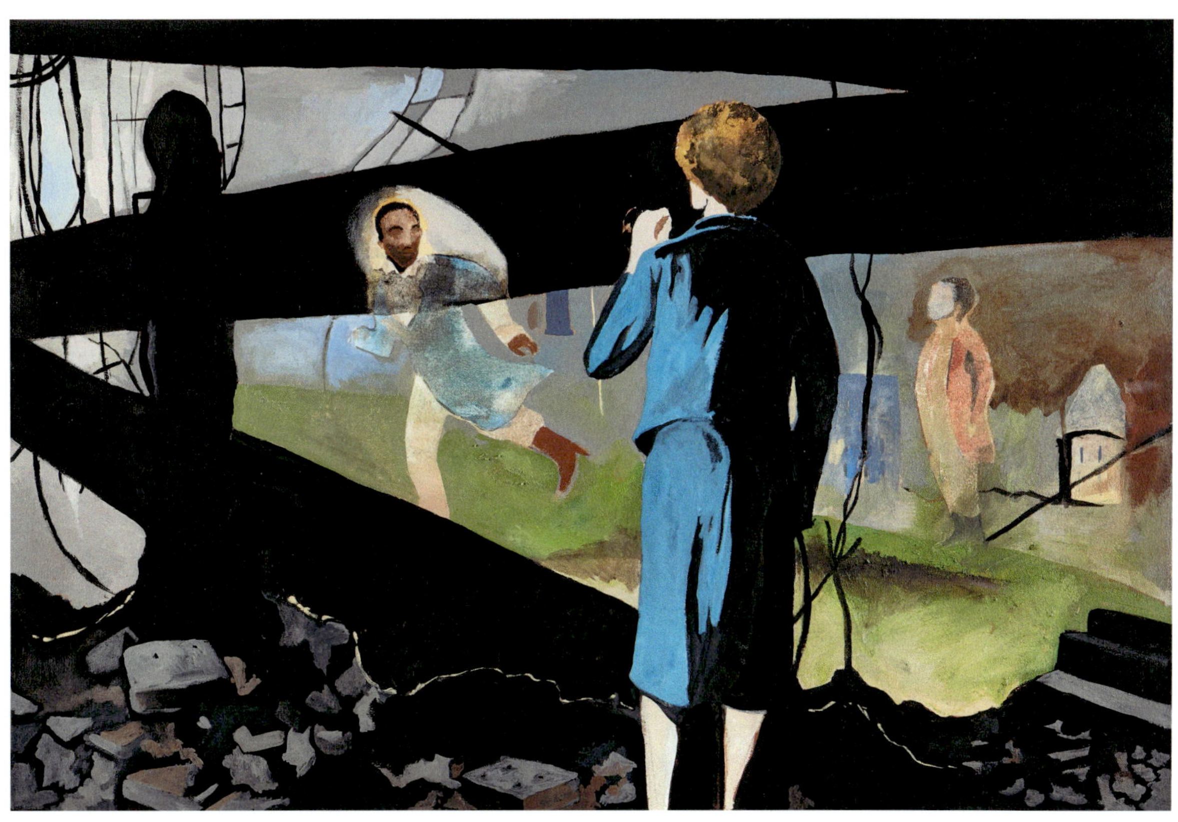

35 *Candyman*, 2007

MARLENE DUMAS on *Single Mother with Father out of the Picture*, 2007–8

Noah Davis's paintings are outta sight! Not the 'out of sight', where 'out of mind' follows from.

Davis saw that sometimes, something is so far away it can't be seen, and, therefore, it can be ignored. He knew how to bring that far-away thing towards us, to touch a nerve with a well-placed hit and a smile. How to pull away and then come back again. An expert in suggestiveness, he understood the concealed, the hidden, the invisible. His work seems to show the everyday in a rather recognisable way, but everything is not always okay. Davis's paintings thrive on ambiguity. Are we sure we know where we are? Hollywood is not LA. He takes us to a place of his own to show the spiritual magic of his art. Listen to his own words on painting: 'The practice has a history so vast and forgotten that it can only exist in the land of the spirits.'

I never met Noah Davis. In person, that is. I did not know the man nor the artist in the real. Did not have the pleasurable privilege to meet him, nor the possibility to confuse the man with the artist, wherever the twain would not be the same. Whatever else, he sure loved painting. And not just his own. He understood the bigger picture. That made his work ambitious but also modest. Proud, not pompous. Purposeful yet playful. And aware of the power of words.

Look at *Single Mother with Father out of the Picture*. It is a good example of how a work can linger longer through the tension created by its title. It is painted with a hand connected to a mind that's critical and wonders. The title makes us think of all the absent fathers who left as soon as there was a child to be taken care of, about double meanings and paintings in paintings. Sometimes children, when asked to draw their families, leave out a member they dislike, saying there was no more space left on the paper to include them.

The child in this painting is looking at someone or something not visible inside the frame but present, just out of sight. The child's arm is in plaster. Did she fall by accident? Or is it just a lump of thick white paint next to thin areas of almost no paint? Her gaze leads you beyond the space of the painting. Even more so with Davis's use of the idiom 'out of the picture'.

Davis's paintings are moving in many different ways. He remains actively present in his work, even if he takes you to places without him.

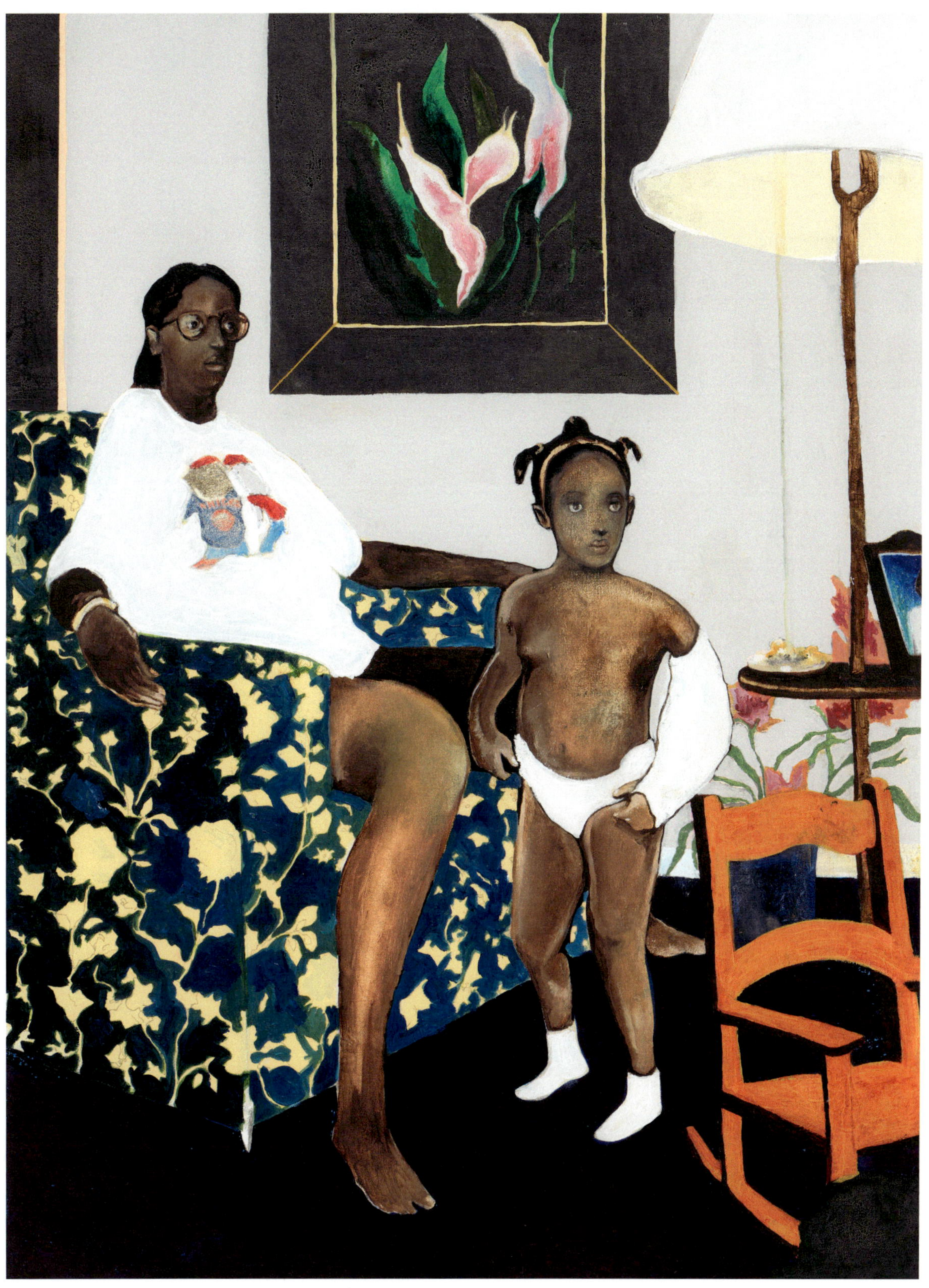

 Single Mother with Father out of the Picture, 2007–8

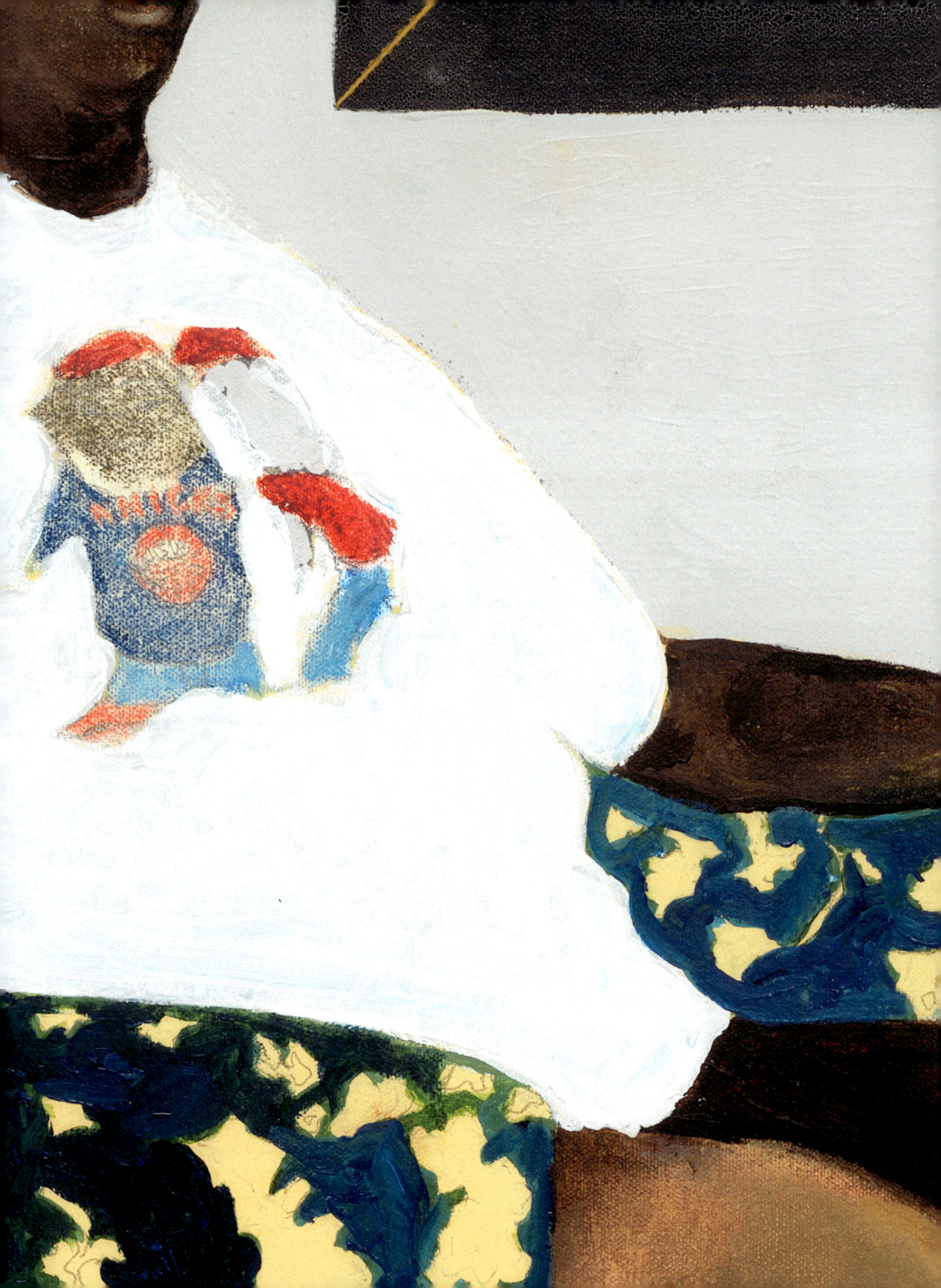
KNICKS

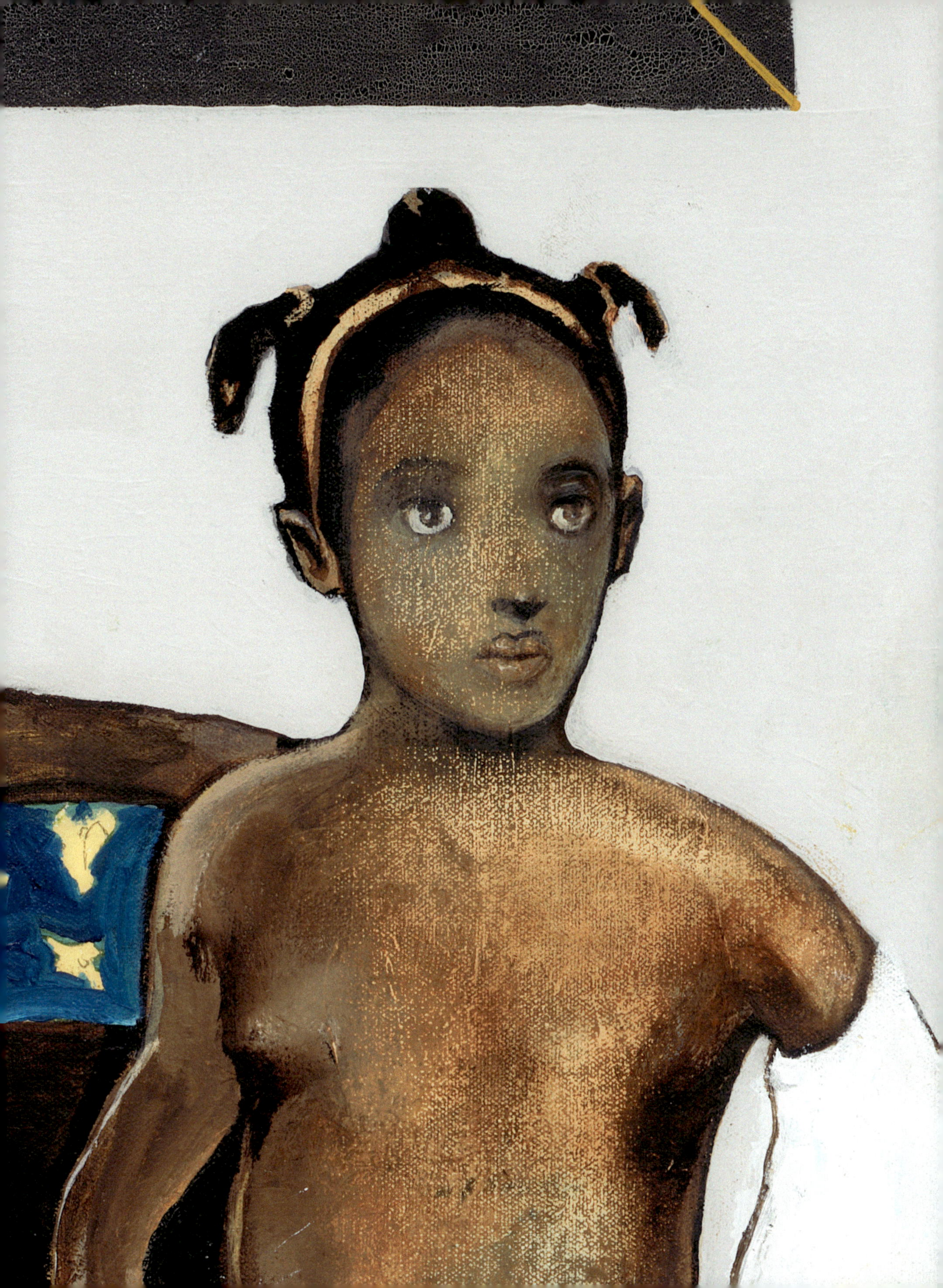

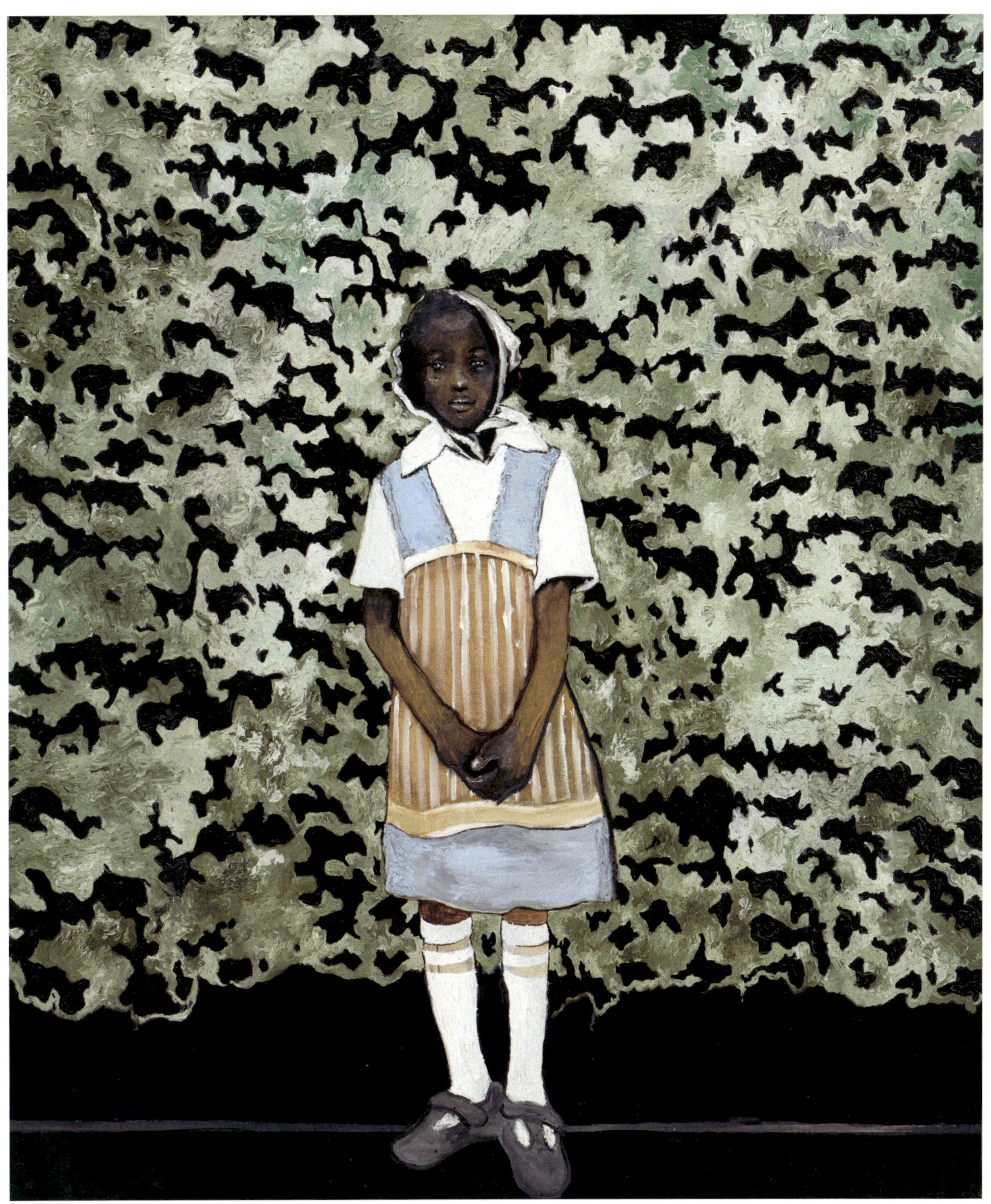

 Mary Jane, 2008

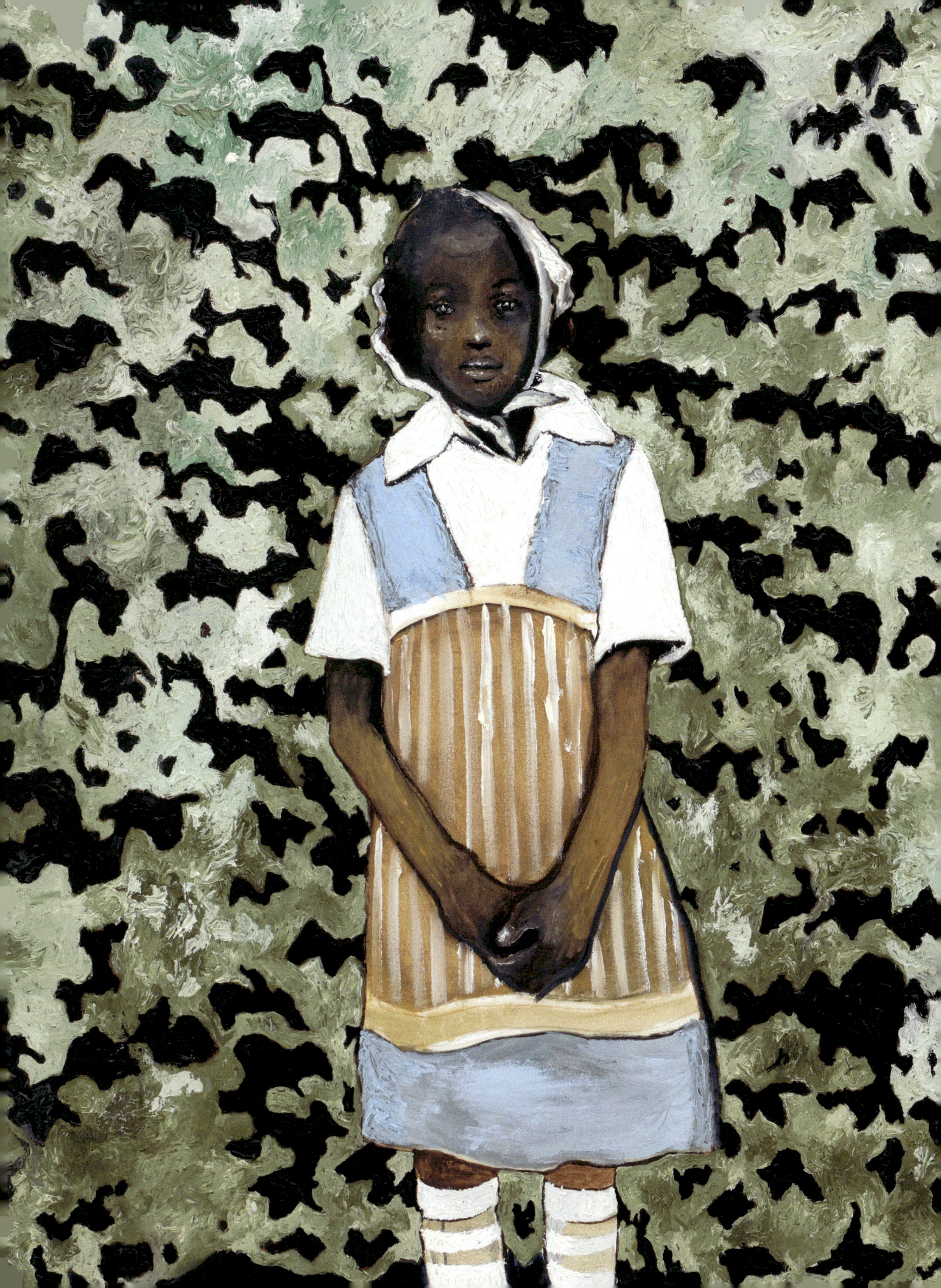

 LA Nights, 2008

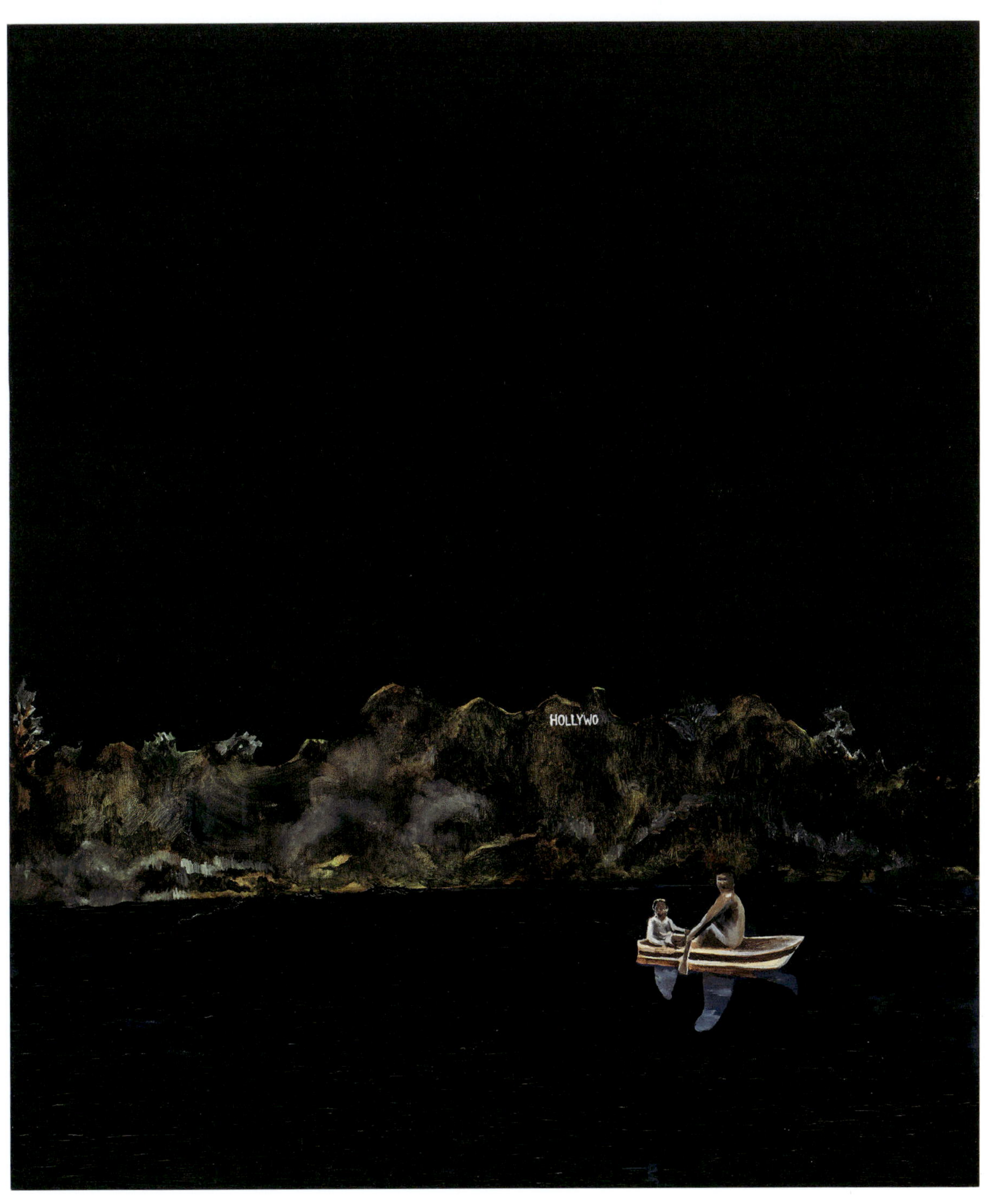

 NO-OD for Me, 2008

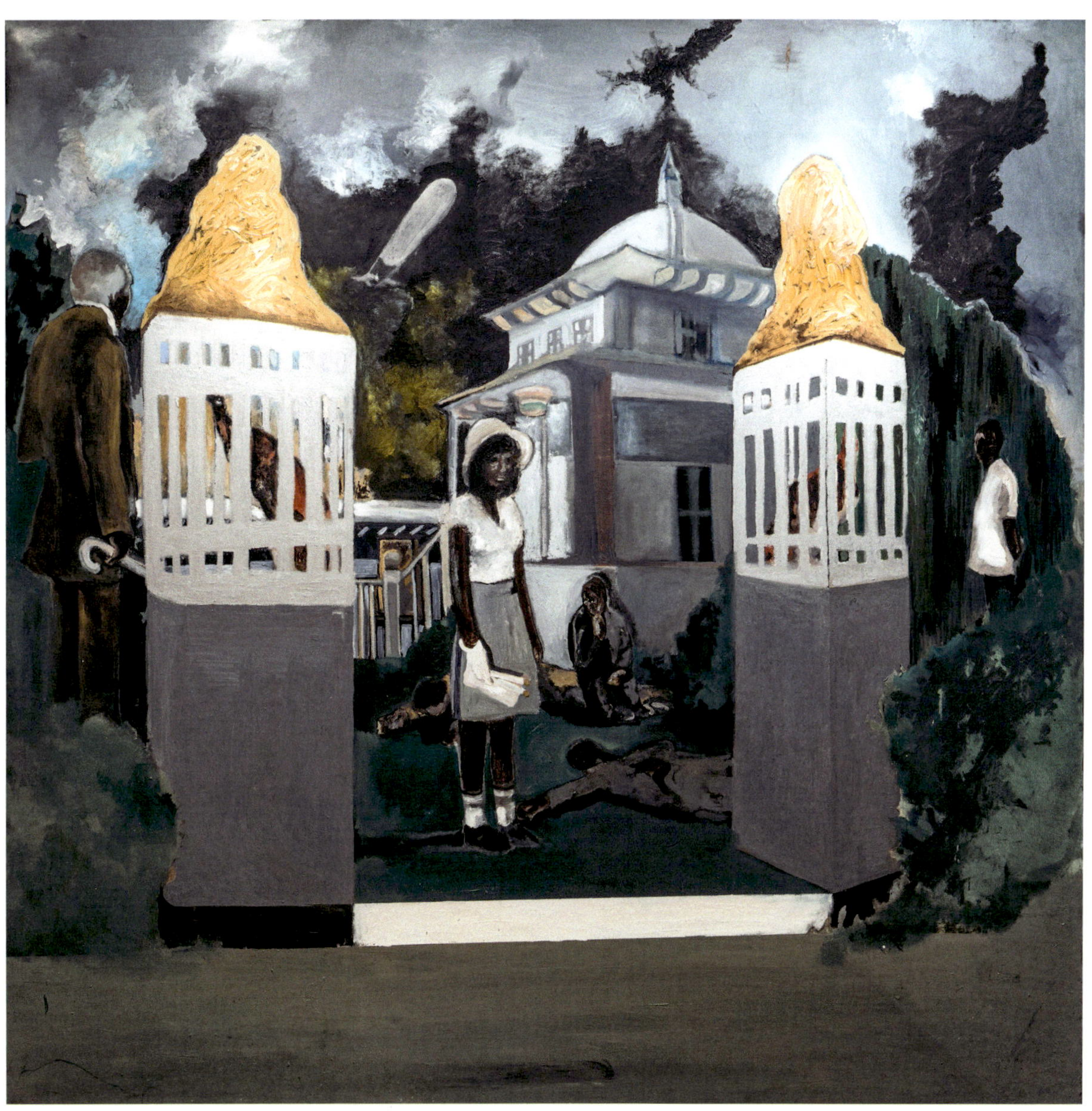

49 *Black Wall Street*, 2008

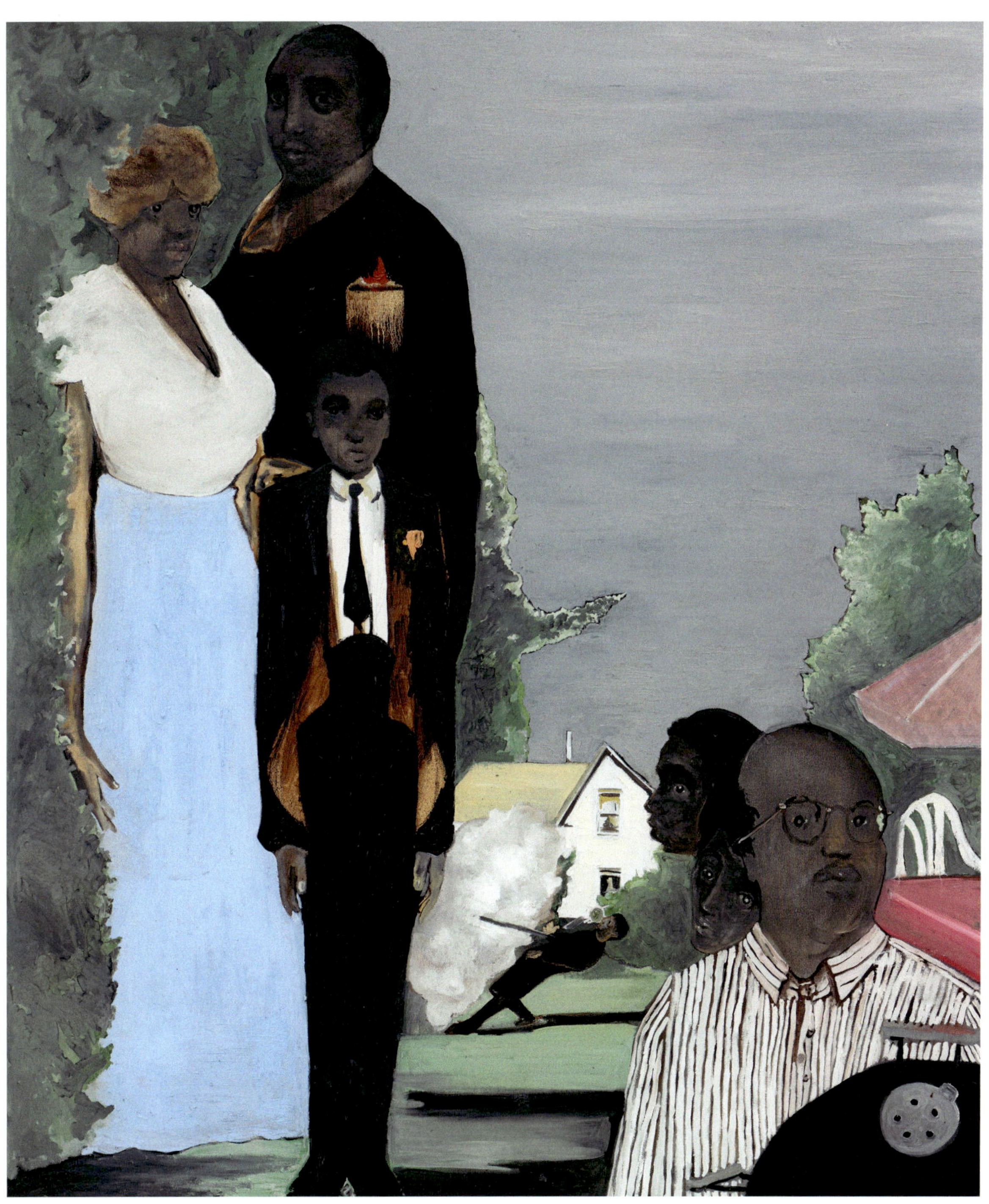

 The Last Barbeque, 2008

53 *Nobody*, 2008

NOAH DAVIS: SO MAGIC, SO REAL
by Paola Malavassi

I feel there is immense freedom in painting to create your own universe – if you don't let 'Art History' or pretense get in the way. I'm actually not a big science fiction guy at all. I'm more of a sappy romantic. These elements of fantasy may arise from my need to 'break the spell,' or the constraints of art theory, and move more into the realm of mysticism.[1] Noah Davis

Did Noah Davis's idea of not letting '"Art History" or pretense get in the way' apply equally to the production of his art and its reception? The curator Helen Molesworth has described how, when speaking, Davis would put categorisations like 'museum-quality art' in quotes with a wiggle of his fingers.[2] Rather than dismissing these terms entirely, this informal distancing reminds us to always look at them with a critical eye. Perhaps, for Davis, not letting 'Art History' get in the way meant not letting it become your sole guide but instead using it to tell different kinds of stories; wielding it to 'create your own universe'. Just as the danger of a single story has long been recognised,[3] Davis's air quotes can be understood as a silent call to break up the 'canon' and the *one* history of art to make way for other (hi-)stories. Indeed, as Molesworth recounts, Davis 'was obsessed with art history, he loved art, and he really loved GREAT art. He thought Black culture was a culture of excellence and that the art historical canon was a place of excellence as well. He knew it was human stupidity that kept us all apart.'[4]

Davis must have had an extensive knowledge of art history thanks to his passion for art books and his work in the bookstore at MOCA in Los Angeles. He would name countless artists who constituted his frames of reference: Francis Bacon, Balthus, Georg Baselitz, Francesco Clemente, Giorgio de Chirico, Peter Doig, Marlene Dumas, Lucian Freud, Paul Klee, R. B. Kitaj, Édouard Manet, Kerry James Marshall, Noah Purifoy, Neo Rauch, Odilon Redon, Daniel Richter, Christian Schad, Eugen Schönebeck, Henry Taylor, Luc Tuymans.

With Davis's constellation of influences in mind, I wanted to use the space of this essay to align his paintings with works by other artists, guided by an approach to exhibition-making I developed at DAS MINSK, which I call *Interplay*. Following this method, I juxtapose works of art – often from very different contexts – to create interactions outside the 'canon'. Think of the artworks as musicians at a jazz club who sit in on an improvisation session with others they may not have known before. They play together, not necessarily in search of harmony, but in search of a challenge. Inspired by Tina M. Campt's concept of 'listening to images',[5] I like to connect works of art to discover what might develop between them if one listens carefully. Art history frequently bases its frames of reference on encounters, friendships, influences and quotations. Creating an *Interplay* between works allows the freedom to intuitively – perhaps even speculatively – go beyond these 'facts' and encounter unpredictable new perspectives. Below, I've sketched out a series of *Interplays* between works by Davis and Max Ernst, Wolfgang Mattheuer, Max Beckmann and Nicole Eisenman.

Bad Boy for Life
Noah Davis and Max Ernst

Max Ernst painted *The Virgin Spanking the Christ Child before Three Witnesses: André Breton, Paul Éluard, and the Painter* nearly a century ago, in 1926. The work pictures just what its title implies: the Madonna with her hand raised to smack the naked bottom of the infant Christ lying across her lap (presumably not for the first time, as the child's buttocks already have a reddish blush). Noah Davis's *Bad Boy for Life* (2007) pictures an almost identical scene: a mother about to spank her son's backside. She stares at us intently with wide-open eyes, the place where her mouth should be a blur of flesh-toned paint. Unlike Ernst's work, where we join a small group of onlookers, here, we are the scene's only witnesses. Davis's title suggests what the mother is wordlessly expressing: that this punishment will leave its mark for a lifetime. In fact, the mothers in both paintings would probably agree in judging their young sons as 'bad boys for life'.

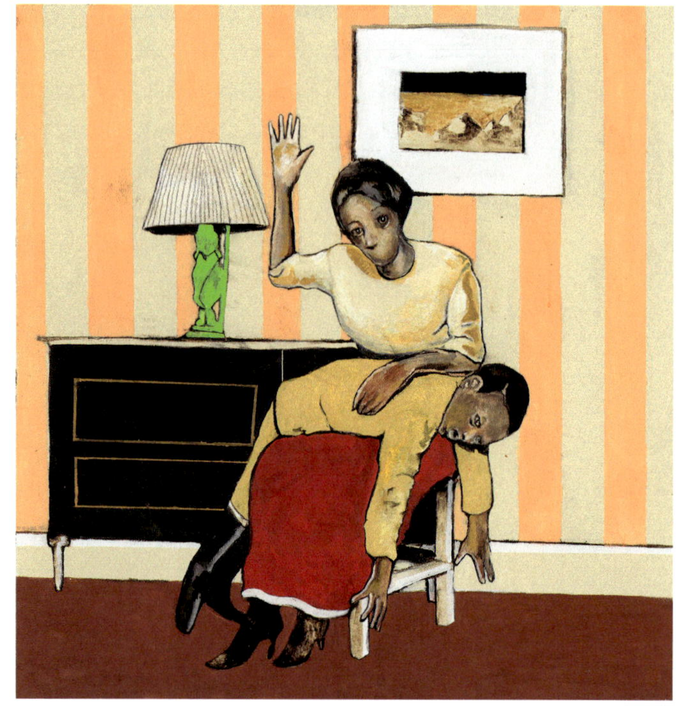

When first exhibited in Paris in 1926, Ernst's painting caused a scandal, not so much because the Blessed Virgin is about to

Bad Boy for Life, 2007

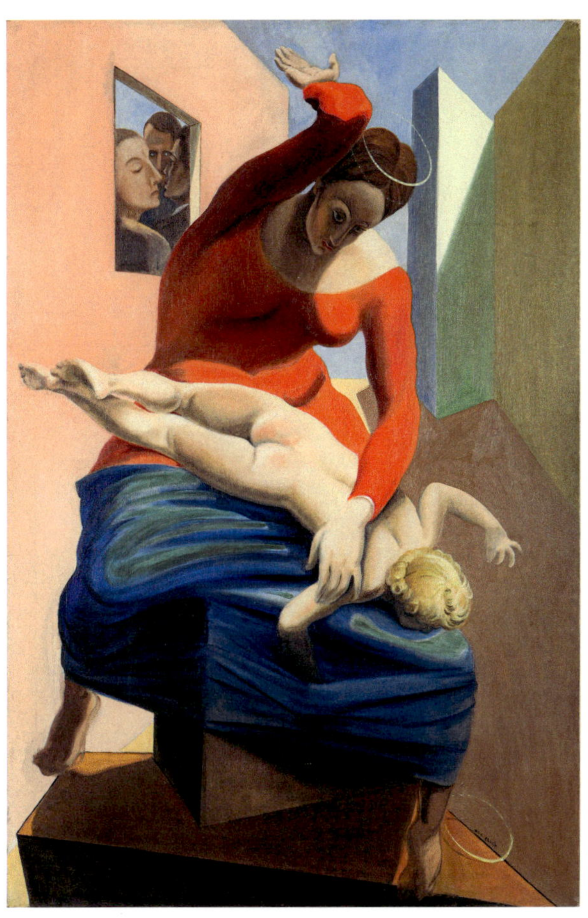

strike her son, but because the child's halo has fallen to the floor, stripping the Son of God of his holy status. Ernst impiously places his signature inside the fallen circle of light. As his halo falls, has Jesus, too, become a bad boy for life?

What happens in the *Interplay* between these irreverent paintings when we place them side by side? What was expected of a mother in Paris in 1926? What about in Los Angeles in 2007? And what is expected today? Who defines the image of *the mother* that is imposed upon us?

In Ernst's and Davis's paintings, both the Mother of God and the mother next door are caught in compromising situations. They have lost their composure, revealing themselves to be all too human. Both artists' sense of humour is evident in the dramaturgy of their painted scenes as well as their choice of titles. Both also break with the 'canon' in that they go against what is expected of depictions of mother-son dynamics, presenting a wholly antithetical vision to the idealised scenes of mothers turned lovingly towards their children that populate historical works of art. These paintings reveal another side of motherhood. Here are two mothers who, perhaps from exhaustion, frustration or psychic strain, are about to resort to violence.

Questions about representation in art arise in the space between these two paintings: how many depictions of Black mothers and Black Madonnas exist in so-called Western art history?

The Neighbour Who Wants to Fly
Noah Davis, Wolfgang Mattheuer and Max Beckmann

Flying, a symbol of yearning for freedom and distant horizons, is the common element shared by Davis's *The Missing Link 1* (2013), *The Neighbour*

Max Ernst, *La Vierge corrigeant l'enfant Jésus devant trois témoins: André Breton, Paul Éluard et le peintre* (The Virgin Spanking the Christ Child before Three Witnesses: André Breton, Paul Éluard, and the Painter), 1926

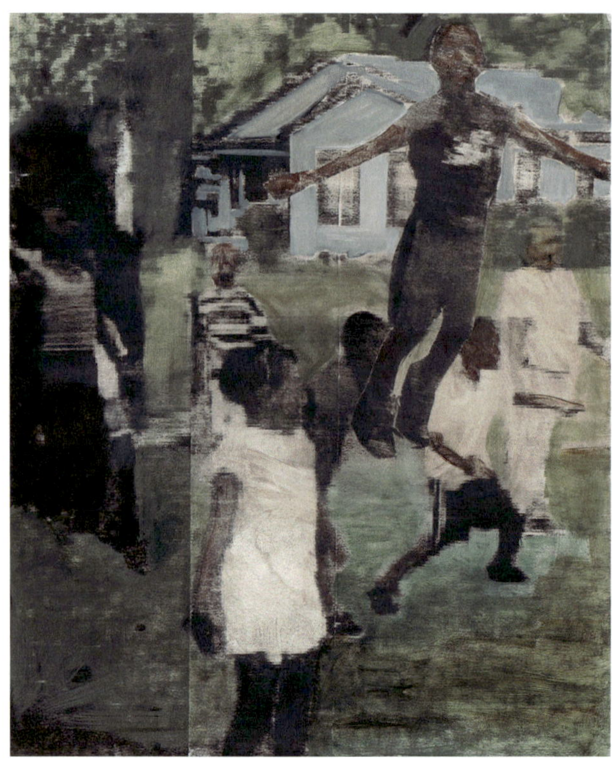

Who Wants to Fly (1984) by Wolfgang Mattheuer and *Falling Man* (1950) by Max Beckmann.

Mattheuer, who lived in Leipzig, worked in the tradition of the Leipzig School in the former German Democratic Republic (GDR). He was deeply influenced by the painter Max Beckmann, who was also from Leipzig. The mythological figure of Icarus appears again and again in Mattheuer's work; at times, he is depicted as half-man, half-bird, at others, all bird. Occasionally, he is seen taking off, as in *The Neighbour Who Wants to Fly*; in other works, he is falling to earth. With outstretched, bird-like wings, the figure in this painting rises up towards the sky, over allotment gardens (*Schrebergärten*) and astonished neighbours (including a child whose arms are outstretched in excited imitation).

In Davis's *The Missing Link 1*, a group of children are playing on a front lawn. It is a perfectly everyday scene, except for the presence of one child, who looks towards the viewer as he levitates with outspread arms several feet off the ground.[6] His playmates appear oblivious to the boy's seemingly effortless flight. As Molesworth has rightly pointed out, weightlessness is a frequent theme in Davis's paintings: 'His figures often seem to float, as if in a nimbus; they are in the picture but not tethered to it by gravity. Look carefully, and you'll see there is rarely a pool of shadow to indicate weight around the feet of his figures.'[7] In *The Missing*

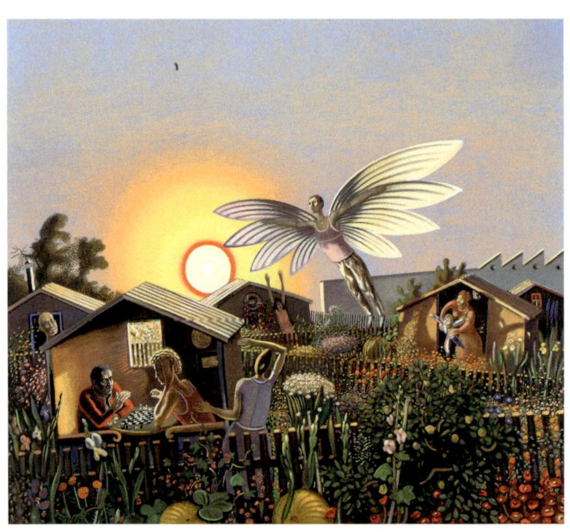

Top *The Missing Link 1*, 2013
Bottom Wolfgang Mattheuer, *Der Nachbar, der will fliegen* (The Neighbour Who Wants to Fly), 1984

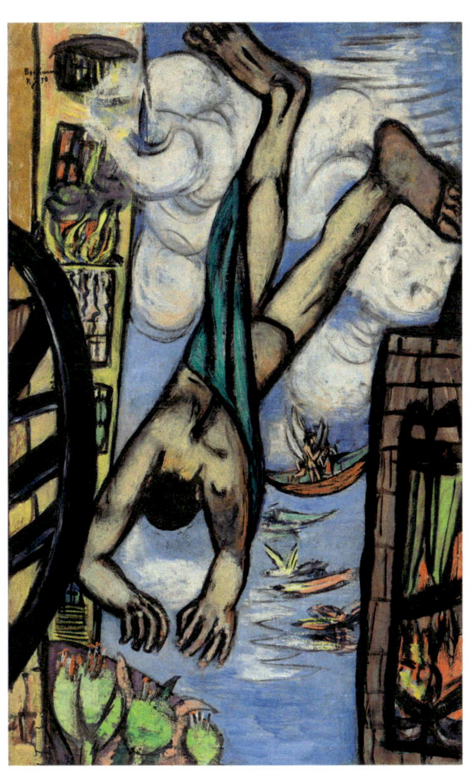

Link 1, the figure's ethereality isn't just gently suggested by a lack of shadow – he is clearly in flight, hovering far above the grass. Is this another neighbourhood Icarus?

The scene is reminiscent of photos of the singer H.R. of the hardcore band Bad Brains, in which he is leaping several feet above the stage; or the image of Boston Celtics player Bill Russell in Paul Pfeiffer's ongoing *Four Horsemen of the Apocalypse* series, in which he appears to hover in mid-air; or Henry Taylor's painting *See Alice Jump* (2011), based on a press image of the legendary Olympian Alice Coachman caught in mid-leap over a high jump bar.

Mattheuer's Icarus and Davis's child both conquer gravity. Hovering presupposes an eventual landing, either planned or accidental. In Max Beckmann's *Falling Man*, a seemingly mythological figure draped in emerald-green cloth plunges headfirst through the air between burning towers. Is this a suicide or an attempted escape from the fire? Behind him, winged creatures wait in boats on the water far below.

Flying is the visualisation of possibilities. In the *Interplay* between these paintings, a kind of existential sound emerges. It is the sound of dreams and self-determination, of adventure, of departure, of leaving – either willingly or under duress – and of escape.

Heading Down River
Noah Davis and Nicole Eisenman

In landscape and history painting traditions, boats often symbolise transition, catastrophe and rescue.[8] Noah Davis's *NO-OD for Me* (2008) and Nicole Eisenman's *Heading Down River on the USS J-Bone of an Ass* (2017) both depict floating vessels, visually referencing Romanticism to convey powerful, uncanny scenes.

In Davis's *NO-OD for Me*, two figures are seated in a boat in a nocturnal landscape. They could be a father and son. It is a mysterious scene of arrival or departure, in which the nakedness of the adult figure 'clothes' the romantic landscape in the 'garment' of an old history painting.

Max Beckmann, *Abstürzender* (Falling Man), 1950

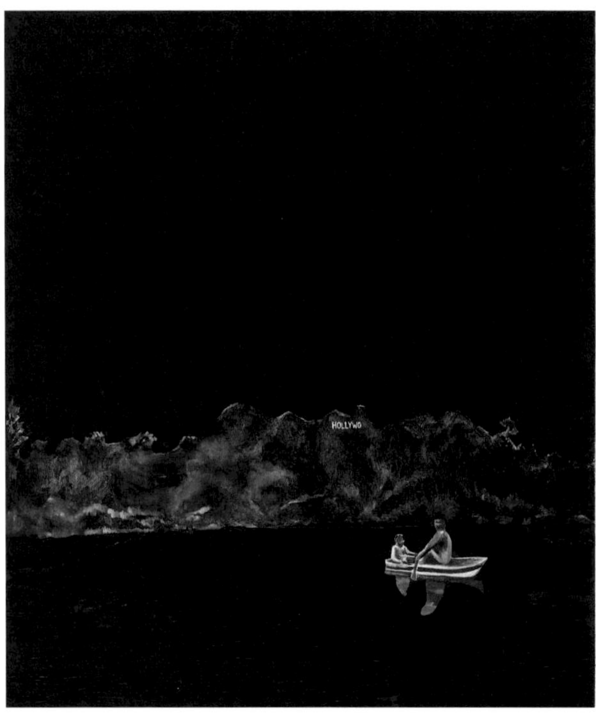

Behind the figures, LA's famous Hollywood sign is brightly illuminated in the distant hills, although it is missing its last two letters (the O and D from the work's title). The truncated sign is the only source of light in the painting – not the moon, the stars or streetlights. Otherwise, the colour black predominates. The sky is black, the water is black. Davis had mastered the colour in all its nuances, fully aware that black is not simply *black* – just as Toni Morrison claimed that 'night black' could be like 'a rainbow'.[9] In its negation, *NO-OD for Me* raises questions about participation and accessibility in the film industry and, tangentially, the art world. Aside from the two protagonists, it is a deserted (and, notably for LA, car-free) scene that suggests the din of the metropolis has been hushed. If we try to 'listen' to this painting, we might perceive that the scene appears to have been plunged into an eerie quietness.

The 'soundtrack' in Eisenman's *Heading Down River on the USS J-Bone of an Ass* is entirely different, underscored by the roar of a waterfall, at the edge of which sit two sailboats on a stretch of bilious green, polluted water. Added to the gushing of the water are the sounds of a drum and a flute, played by sailors who should be steering instead of making music. Indeed, their music appears to be a ploy to distract the viewer and themselves from imminent catastrophe. Seated in the stern of one of the boats (which, as the title describes, is in the form of an ass's jawbone) is a suited man who bears a strong likeness to the former US President (Eisenman made many works that dealt with the Trump administration while he was in power). This man and his companions are visibly ignoring what is about to befall them; it is pointless, too late, to think of rescue. Is this grotesque naval parade a fantasy of the right's final demise or the premonition of our hopeless common destiny?

NO-OD for Me, 2008

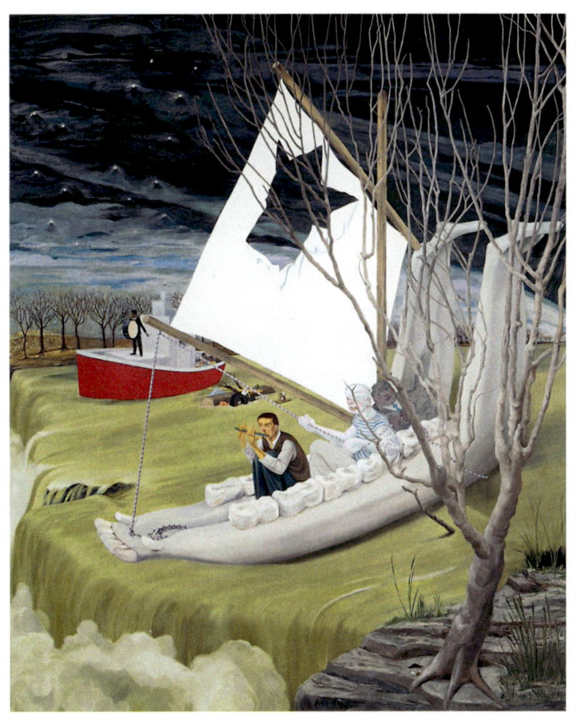

Together, these unsettling works disclose how glamour, power and slogans can dazzle and blind us. In a way, they both seem to present a pitiless antithesis of a Hollywood film with a happy ending. The infinite stillness in Davis's painting allows us, on second glance, to make out the figures' uncanny reflections in the water, which seem to be cloaked in white-hooded robes, evoking, perhaps, the uniform of the KKK. Is this a trick of the water's reflection or a ghostly apparition? Suddenly, this scene seems as ominous as the presence of an evil president in Eisenman's sailboat. The two scenes are very different, yet in the tense *Interplay* between them – in the space between a boisterous parade and absolute silence – we may perceive that the same overtly racist, bigoted spirits occupy both works: in the ass's jawbone, as well as lurking, almost undetected, in the dark water's reflection.

Magical Realism from Los Angeles

Noah Davis said he wanted to paint 'normal scenarios', which is precisely where he found the human, existential and universal.[10] He frequently superimposed both traditional subject matter and magical elements onto images of his Los Angeles neighbourhoods, creating timeless scenes full of references that are both local and universal. For Davis, elevating the everyday lives of Black people by making them subjects of art was a form of self-determination and empowerment. Davis created a 'missing link' between art, himself and his community – an 'alternative canon', as he called it – one full of power, dignity, beauty and poetry.

With the founding of the Underground Museum, Davis brought both his art and that of others into Arlington Heights, a neighbourhood with predominantly Black and Latinx residents. At the same time, he integrated his LA neighbourhoods into his art as subject matter. As Jason Moran

Nicole Eisenman, *Heading Down River on the USS J-Bone of an Ass*, 2017

notes in his response to Davis's painting *Pueblo del Rio: Concerto* (2014) (p. 183), what eventually conquers the world's stages as art, music, sport and dance often originates in 'the hood'.[11]

Through creating an *Interplay* between Davis's work and other figurative paintings from different epochs, the universality and timelessness of his corpus become apparent. His work offers an essential contribution to the development of twenty-first-century art, occupying a space in a progressive, figurative tradition that is neither purely expressionistic nor surrealistic, neither entirely romantic nor *neusachlich*. It lies somewhere between all of these categories – between the real and the magical. Maybe Davis was the magical realist of Los Angeles. Or, as he might have put it, with a wiggle of his fingers, the 'magical realist'. Although perhaps he would have accepted the assertion that his paintings are as magical as they are real.

1 Noah Davis in an interview with Lauren Haynes, '3Qs: Noah Davis', The Studio Museum in Harlem, undated.

2 Helen Molesworth, 'Some Years Count as Double', Helen Molesworth (ed.), *Noah Davis*, exh. cat. (New York: David Zwirner Books/ The Underground Museum, 2020), p. 165.

3 See Chimamanda Ngozi Adichie, 'The Danger of a Single Story', lecture, TED Global 2009, ted.com/talks/chimamanda_ngozi_adichie_the_danger_of_a_single_story.

4 Helen Molesworth (personal communication, 13 June 2024).

5 See Tina M. Campt, *Listening to Images* (Durham: Duke University Press, 2017) and Campt's essay on pp. 163–67.

6 This motif is to be found in a photocollage used by Davis for a never-realised record cover design for the singer-songwriter Cody ChesnuTT's album *Landing on a Hundred* (2012). The collage is now held digitally in Daniel DeSure's Commonwealth Projects in Los Angeles. The painting's earlier iteration explains the vertical line that runs through the scene.

7 Helen Molesworth, 'Noah Davis, an Introduction', *Noah Davis*, p. 7.

8 Théodore Géricault's *The Raft of the Medusa* (1818–19) is one of the most famous examples. While Davis was at Cooper Union, he reproduced this scene with the artists' collective the Bruce High Quality Foundation (see p. 246).

9 Toni Morrison, *Song of Solomon* (New York: Vintage Books, 2004), pp. 40–41: 'And talking about dark! You think dark is just one color, but it ain't. There're five or six kinds of black. Some silky, some woolly. Some just empty. Some like fingers. And it don't stay still. It moves and changes from one kind of black to another. Saying something is pitch black is like saying something is green. What kind of green? Green like my bottles? Green like a grasshopper? Green like a cucumber, lettuce, or green like the sky is just before it breaks loose to storm? Well, night black is the same way. May as well be a rainbow.'

10 Ben Ferguson, 'Noah Davis', *Dazed*, 9 February, 2024, dazeddigital.com/artsandculture/article/6483/1/noah-davis: 'Race plays a role in as far as my figures are Black. The paintings aren't political at all though. If I'm making any statement, it's to just show Black people in normal scenarios, where drugs and guns are nothing to do with it. You rarely see Black people represented independent of the civil rights issues or social problems that go on in the States.'

11 See p. 182.

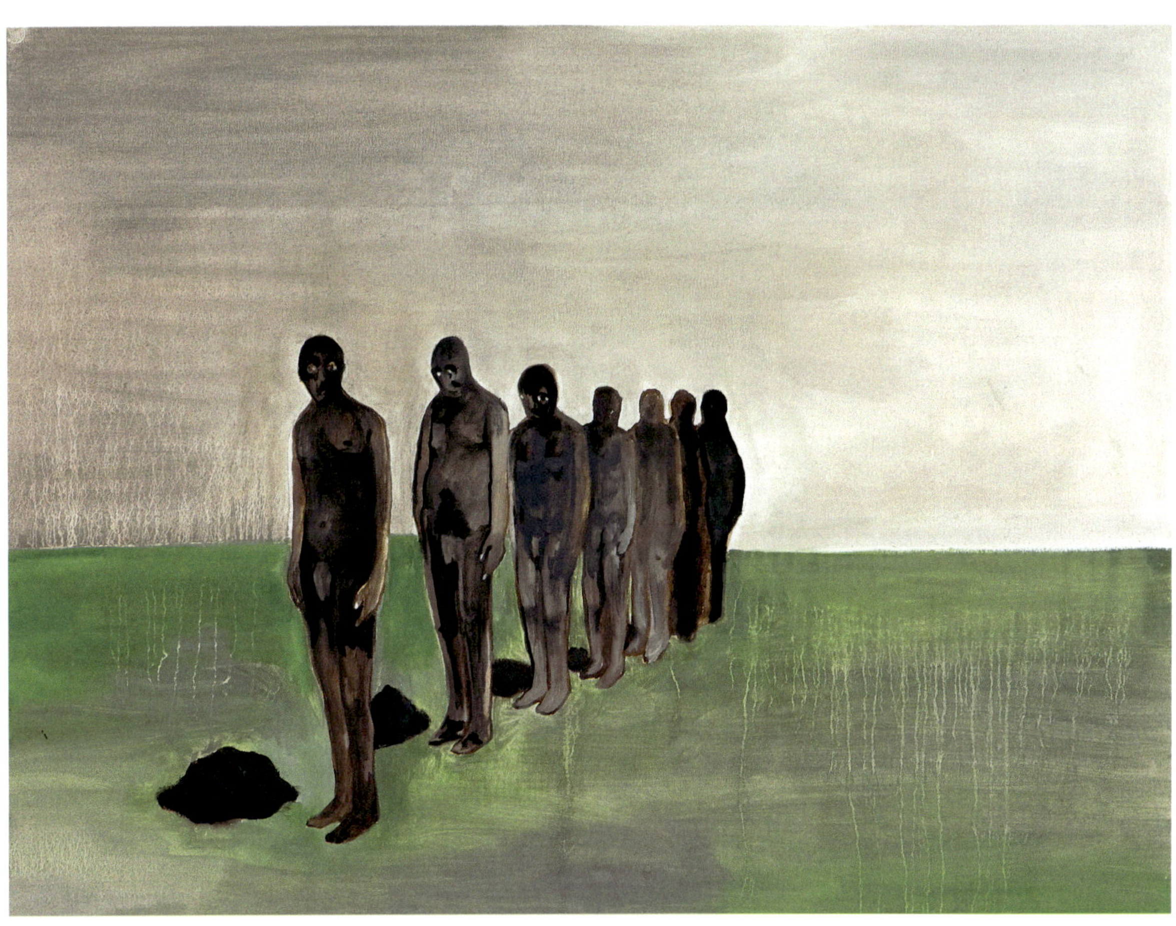

 The Seven Prisoners of the Abyss, 2008

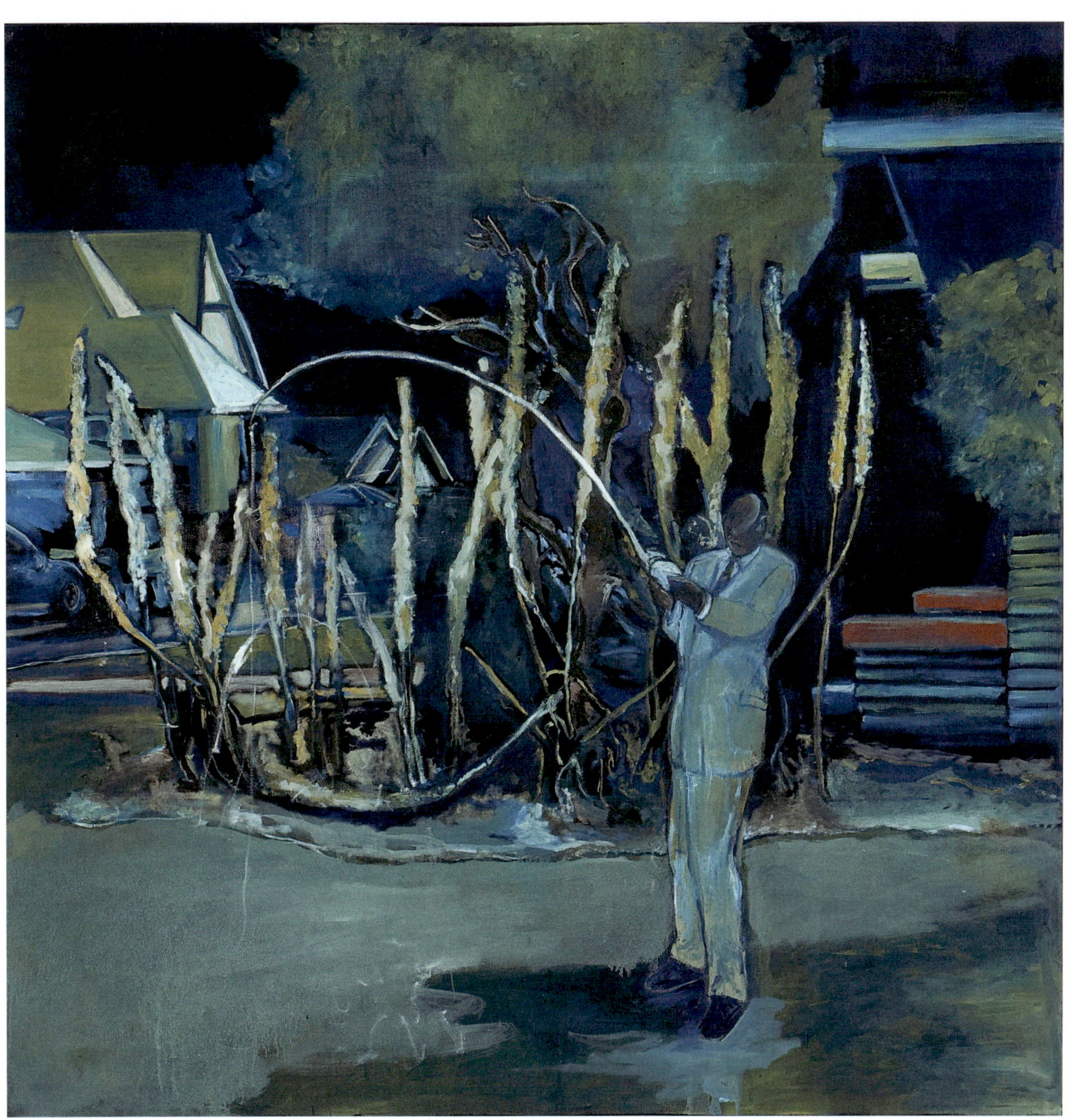

 Museum Guard Fishing, 2009

T.J. CLARK on *The Architect*, 2009

Noah Davis was 25 when he painted *The Architect*. It is an early work by an artist whose work would all be early, though by the time Davis died, aged 32, his art was on the way to a kind of simplicity that most painters don't achieve in a lifetime. *The Conductor* (2014) (p. 193) would be a good example of Davis's 'late' style: ironic, flamboyant simplification, touches of painterly bravura, a slightly corny colour harmony, and yet, a residual stubborn optimism in the thing shown, like a dream you've mostly forgotten but can't shake off. *The Conductor* strikes me as a better painting than *The Architect*. Certainly, it points forward more clearly to paintings to come, problems to solve – ways in which geometry and painterliness (which seem to stand, in Davis's art, for order and disorder, or discipline and spontaneity, or the world rebuilt and the world transfigured) might be put to work together, not displayed as beautifully at odds. It is tragic that the future paintings never got done.

The Architect is an early work, but not like any other work I know by a 25-year-old. I admire its gentleness and recklessness. I like the way geometry – the hard-edge rectangles that come to Davis from Mondrian and Judd, those two strange idols – moves from two to three dimensions as we get closer to the picture plane, ending as a model of a city on a hill. It looks flimsy, the model. The surfaces leading up to the city square don't make sense. Are we supposed to take the Maya-pyramid-cum-Miesian-town-hall seriously? Above all, what kind of white rain is falling on it? The architect – that must be him underneath the splash and dribbles of paint – becomes a god behind the veil. His face multiplies. His expression flickers between gravity, amiability, 'understanding', maybe irrevocable sadness. (We know that the painting began from a photo of the Black architect Paul Revere Williams, who perfected the art of drawing upside down … because he realised that most of his white clients couldn't cope with sitting next to him as he sketched out their dream houses.)

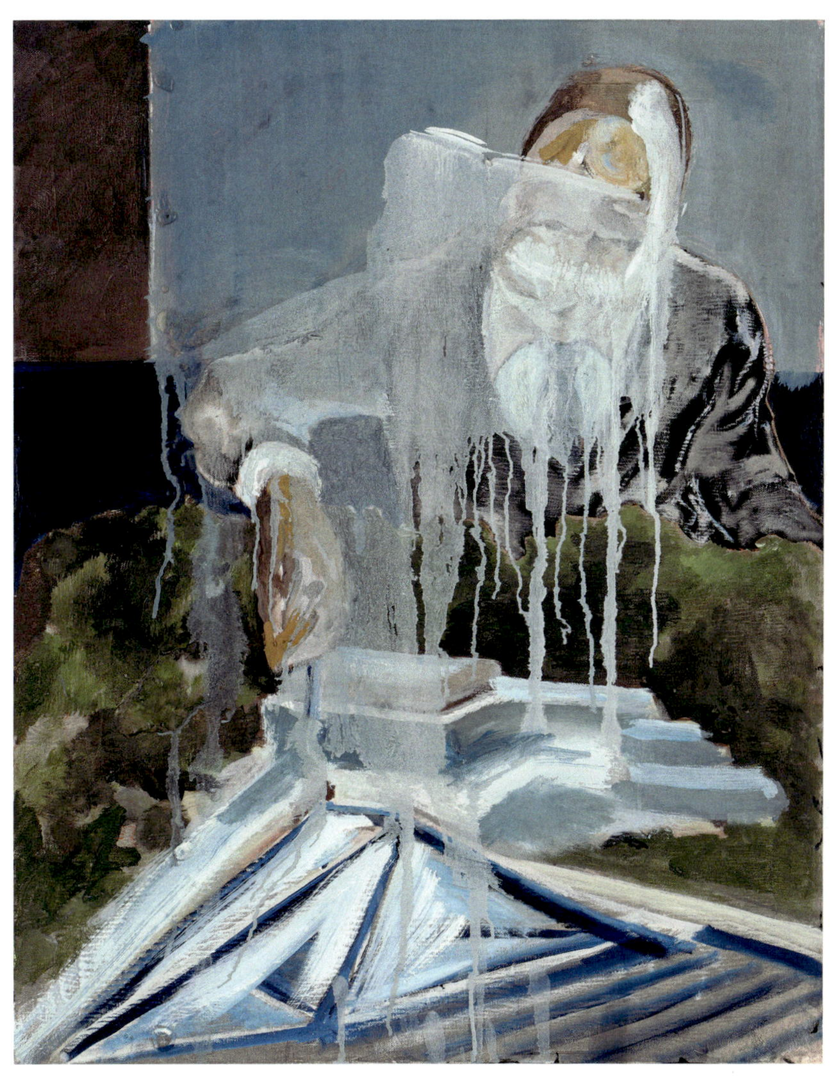

 The Architect, 2009

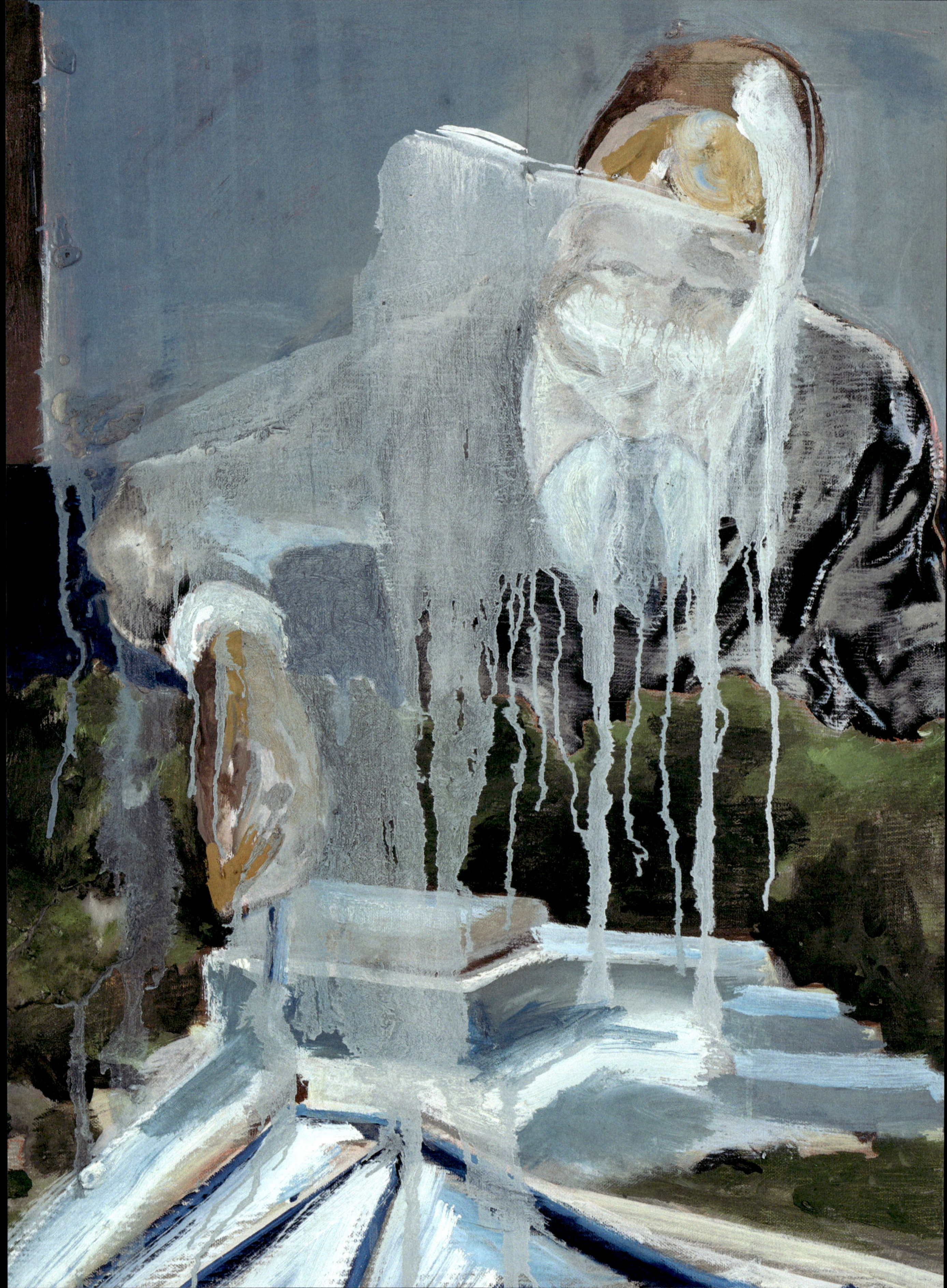

The splash of white that concludes *The Architect* is showy, yes. But I think the showmanship – the risk-taking, the impatience, the 'devil-may-care' in dialogue with the care (the guardedness) that seems to me the painting's subject – is a way of thinking about the subject by obscuring it. Any painter of high seriousness, whatever their age, goes on worrying about how and why painting (painting as messing about with materials, painting as getting good at not being in control) interferes with image-making. The better you are, the bigger the worry. Accidents are attractive – viewers fixate on them. It could be an empty gesture, that splash. It could be a cover-up. Or it could make Paul Revere Williams – 'Black bourgeois', Black success story, Black architect to the stars – come free of the categories and sit on the other side of the table.

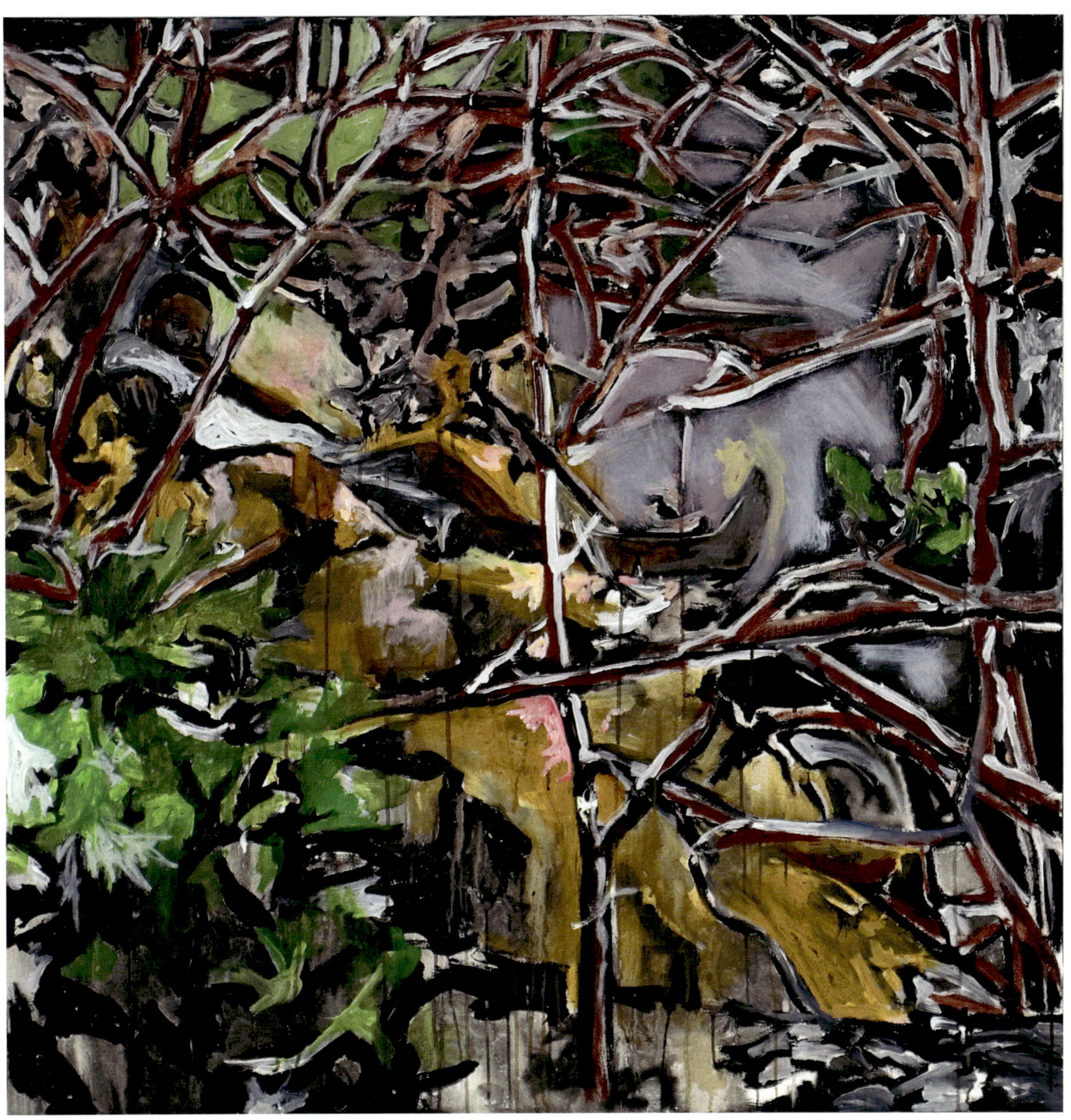

73 *The Gardener*, 2009

KARON DAVIS on *Isis*, 2009

When I look at this painting it takes me back to a time of deep love and nesting. Noah and I had just moved into an old Craftsman house in West Adams. It was the first time I had ever lived with a man, and I was quite nervous about it, but we were so in love, the butterflies soon subsided. We locked ourselves away from the world and dove into each other. We made love. We made art. The house became a love den, a studio and a gallery. Every wall, every room was territory to be conquered. Even the cobblestoned backyard was up for the taking and soon tables, chairs and everyday mundane objects became an outdoor installation – our imitation of Kippenberger's *The Happy End of Franz Kafka's 'Amerika'.*

Isis is based on a photo Noah took the day I unfurled two large fans – each with cheesy images of an Egyptian king and queen printed on their surface – and painted them yellow with house paint. I threw on my sister Naja's old gold dance leotard from the '80s, with sequins lining the hems and tassels that hung off my butt and sparkled like tinsel. Noah said, 'Stand there! You are Isis.' Using the fans as wings, I raised my arms and opened them. He snapped the pic and quickly retreated to paint it.

Egypt has always held a special place in my heart. When Noah and I met, I was studying ancient myths and history. I had just left my production job in Hollywood and was exploring film projects: Black Wall Street, Black cowboys, Stepin Fetchit, The Frogs, Egyptian mythology and so on. Noah joined me on these journeys through history, and our home became a portal where our imaginations could run wild. We exchanged stories, dreams and techniques for making art. He painted, and we lost ourselves in this magical time. You can see both of us in this painting: Noah's reflection is behind me in the window of our home.

This painting holds so much for me. It is our past, and it is my present and future in both painting and in life. I am Isis and Noah is Osiris. In ancient

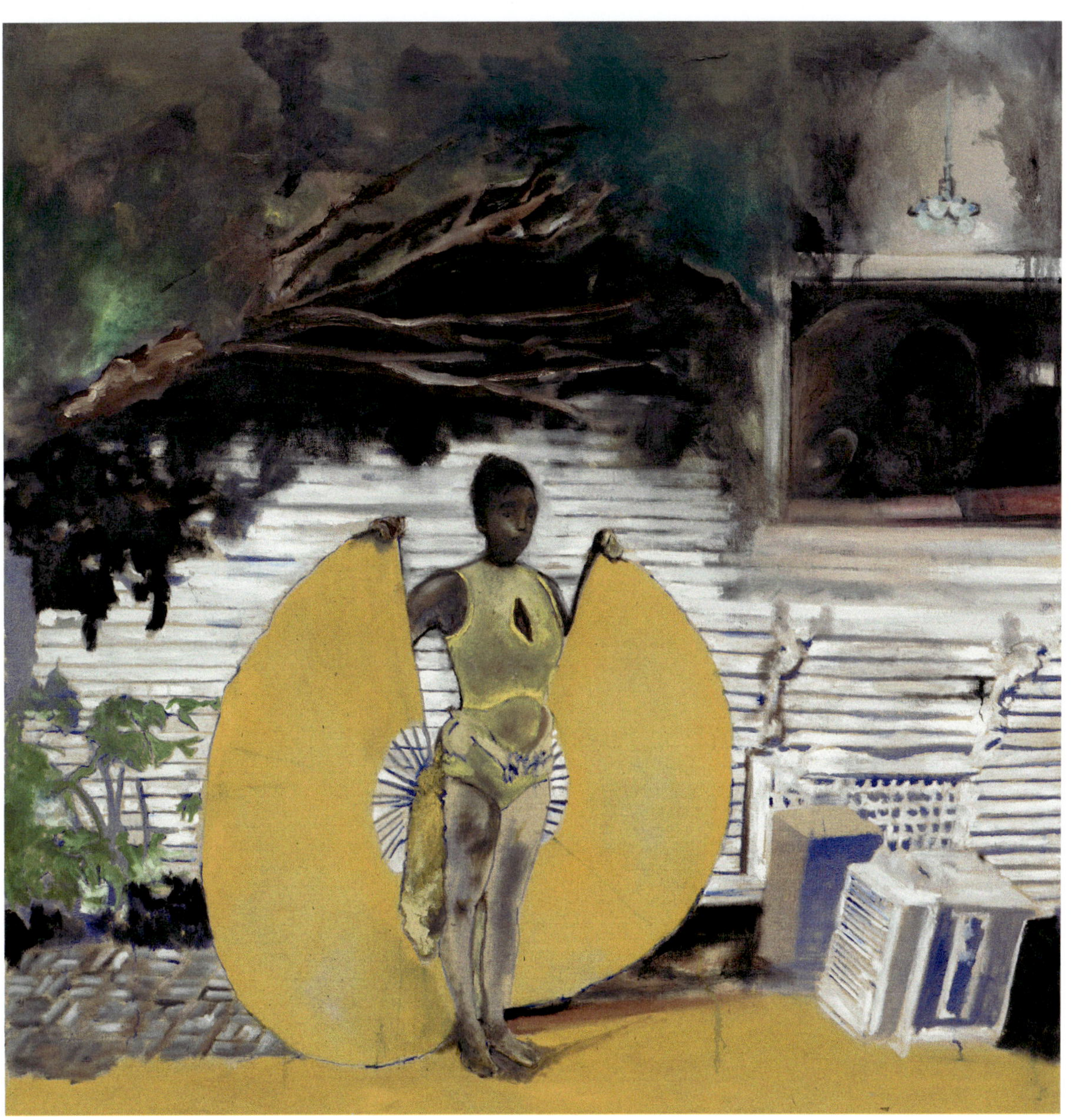

 Isis, 2009

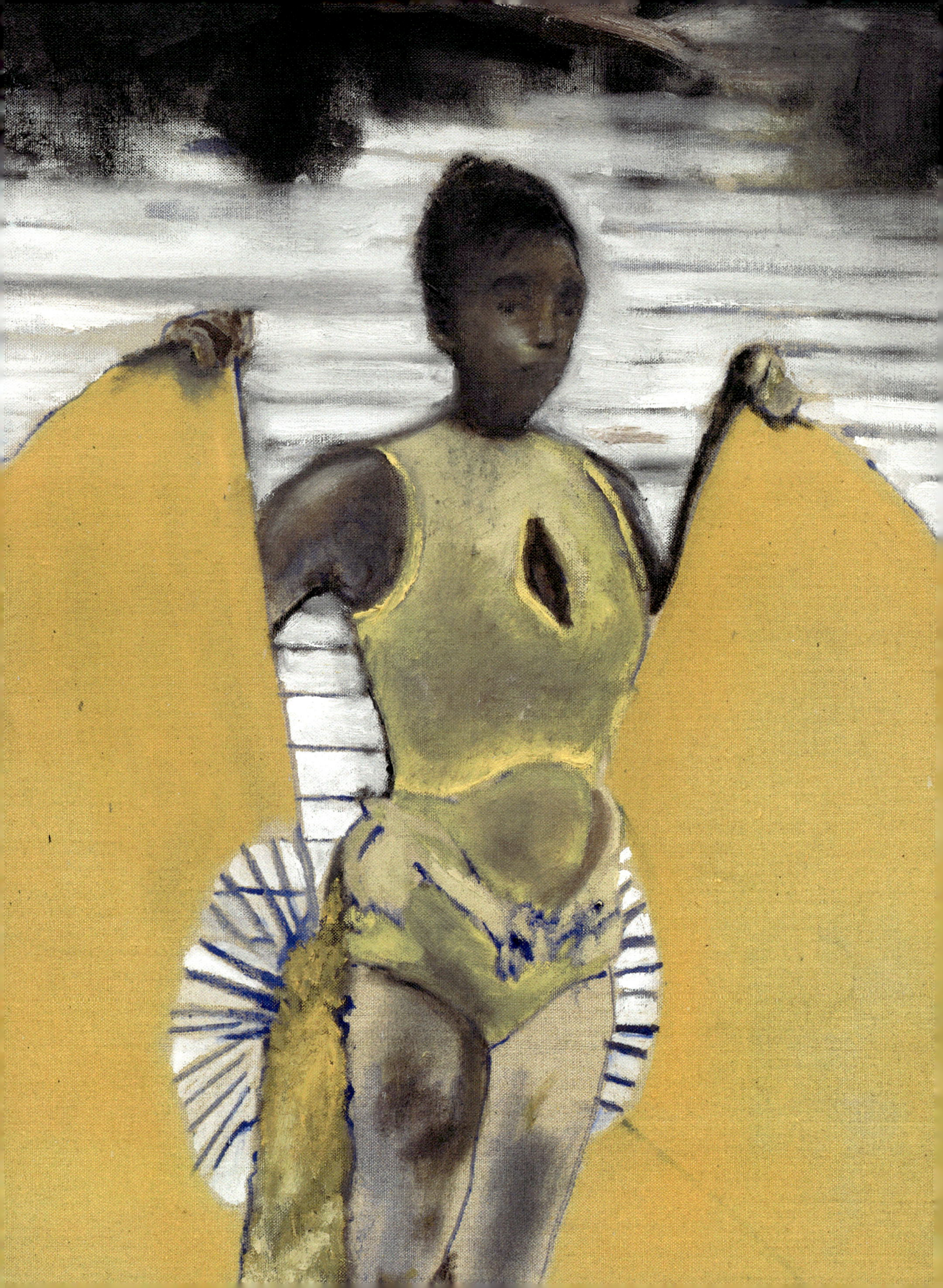

Egyptian mythology, Isis assembles all the scattered parts of Osiris in order to cast a spell to make him whole again so he can live forever as a god. Noah is my Osiris. He will live forever through his work. My assignment is gathering these parts of my love and protecting them.

'Find the babies,' he said to me while fighting cancer at Cedars-Sinai. That is what I promised him, and that is my daily mission – to make the archive whole, to gather his work, to ensure that 'the babies' are there for the world to see. I spend my time and money, my sleepless nights, tracking down these pieces of him to fulfil my promise: to make all he put into this world complete. This journey isn't easy – paintings change hands or disappear into auction houses; some might not be seen again in public for decades, maybe even centuries.

When I stand in a room surrounded by 'the babies', Noah is there with me. The memories of watching him paint, the scent of Terpenoid, oil paint and cannabis, the sound of Vivaldi or Jay-Z in the air. Noah may be gone, but in that moment, surrounded by the parts of him, he is there, whole, in my heart.

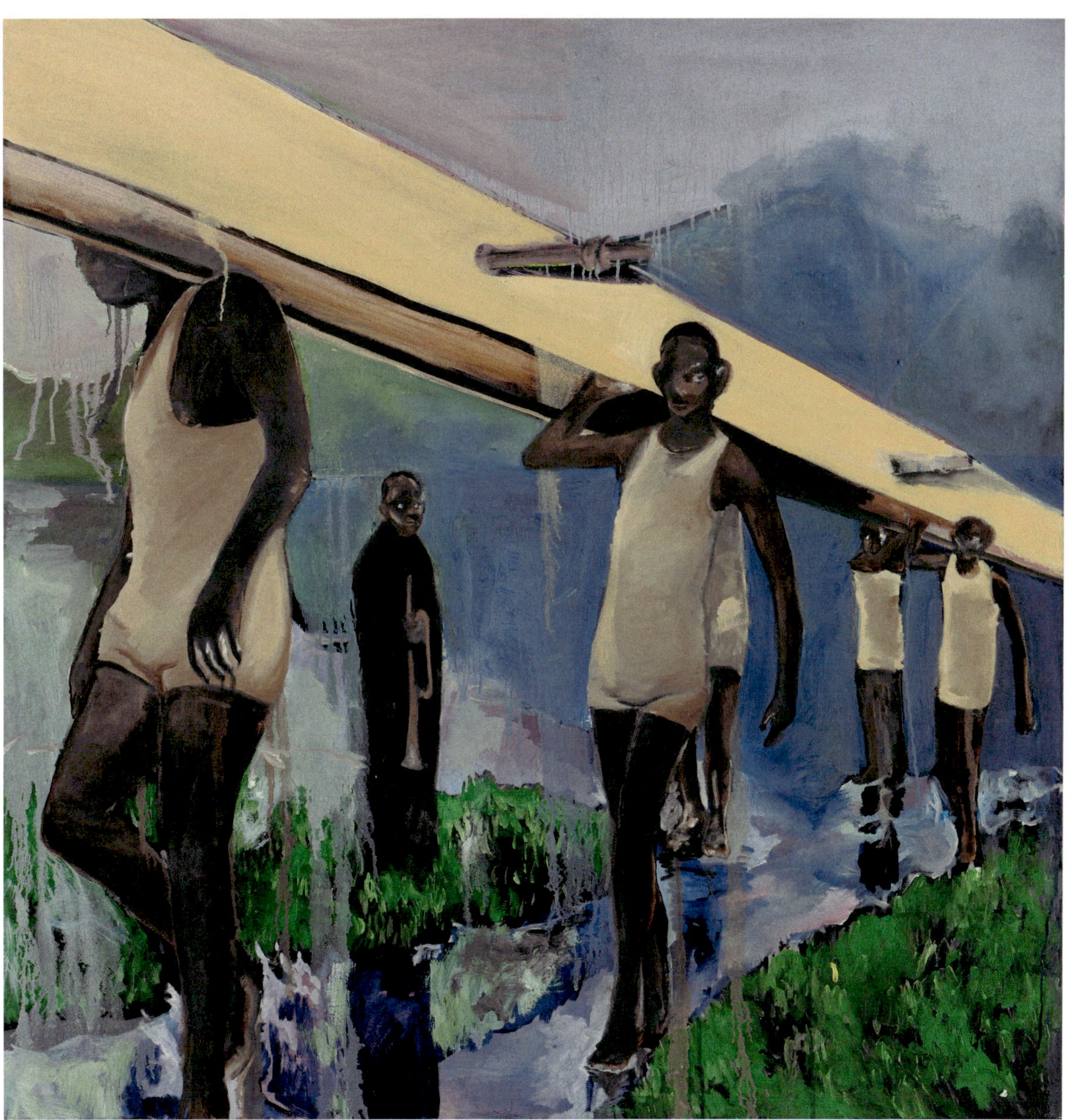

 The Year of the Coxswain, 2009

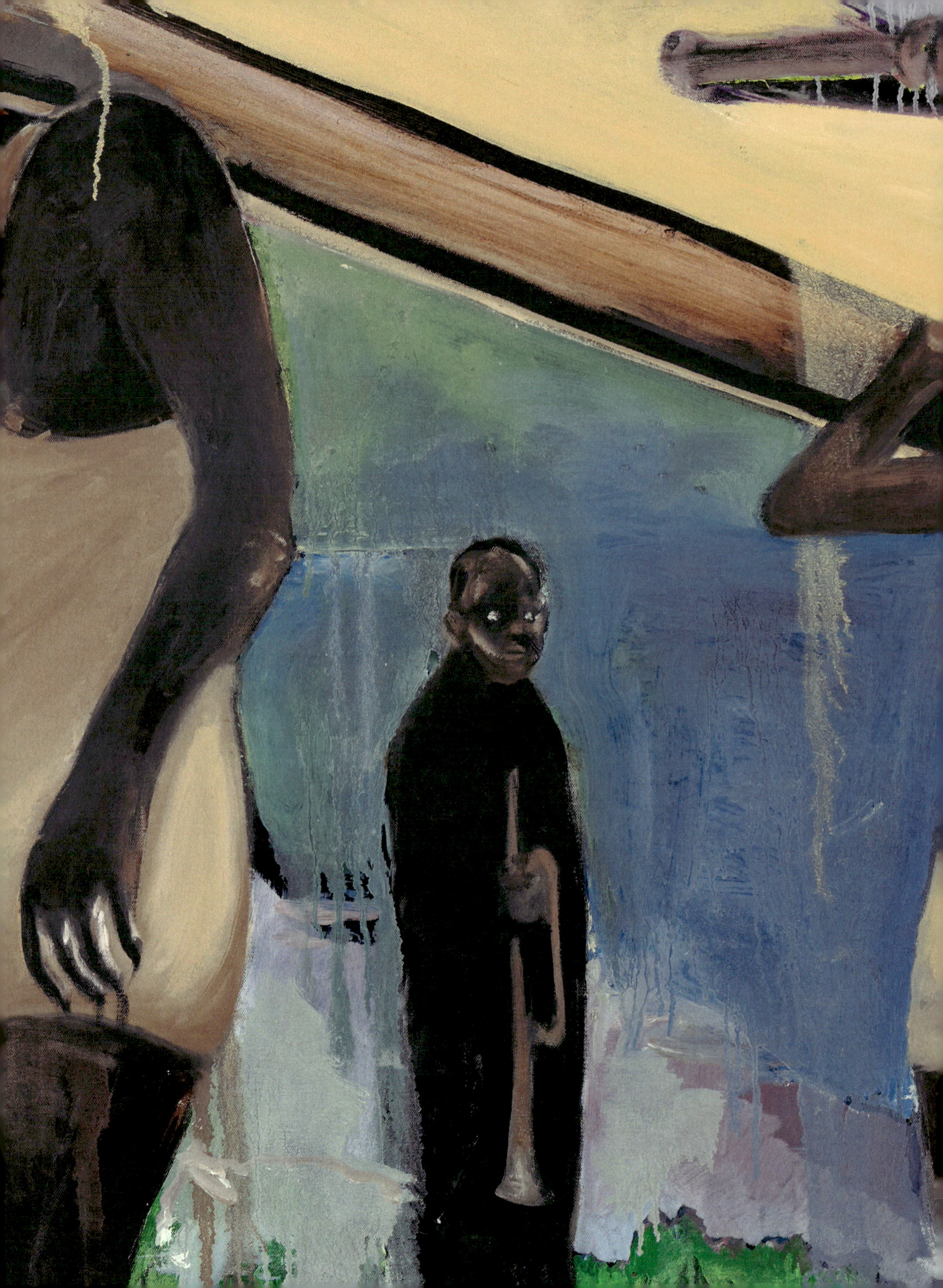

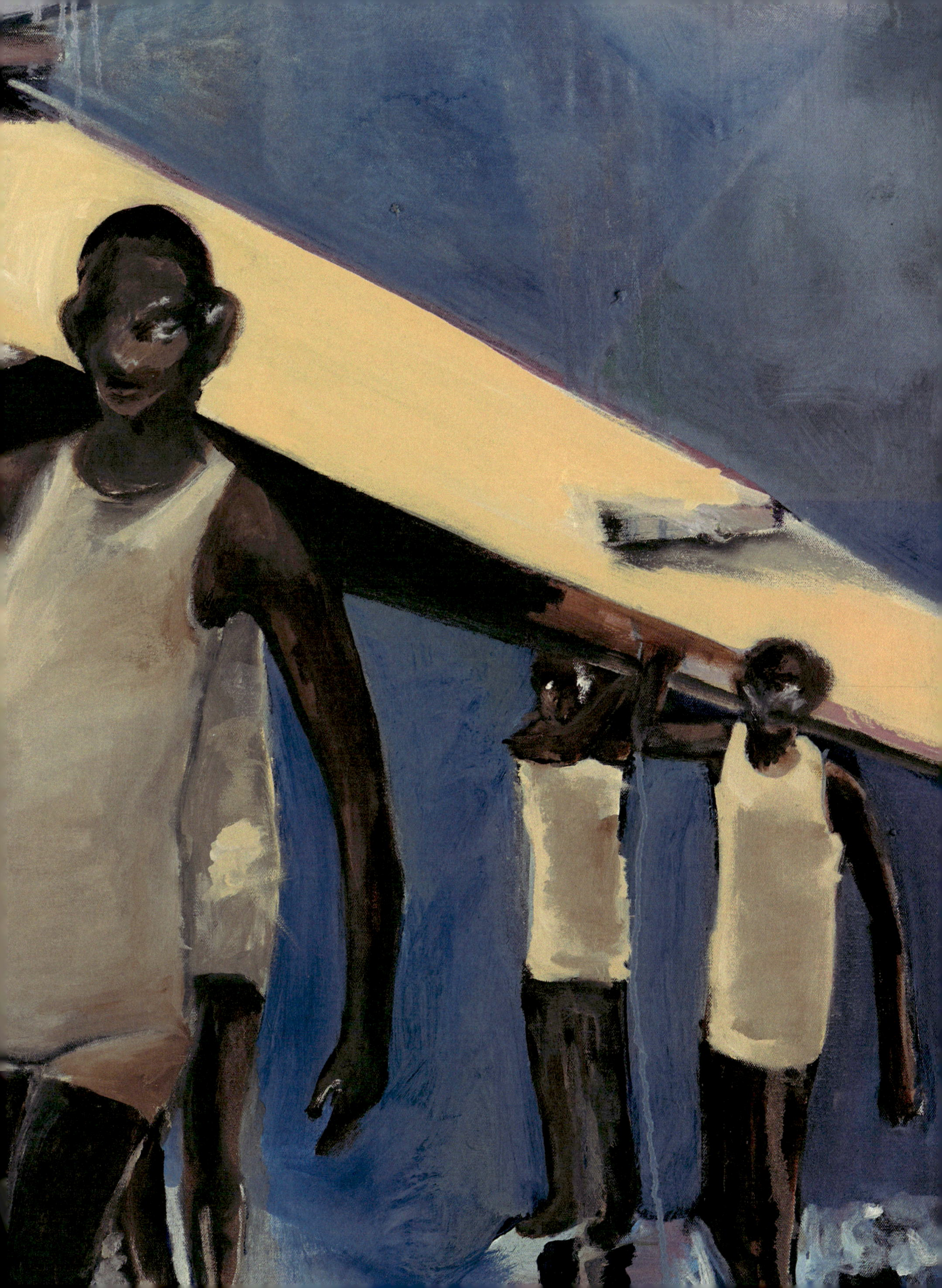

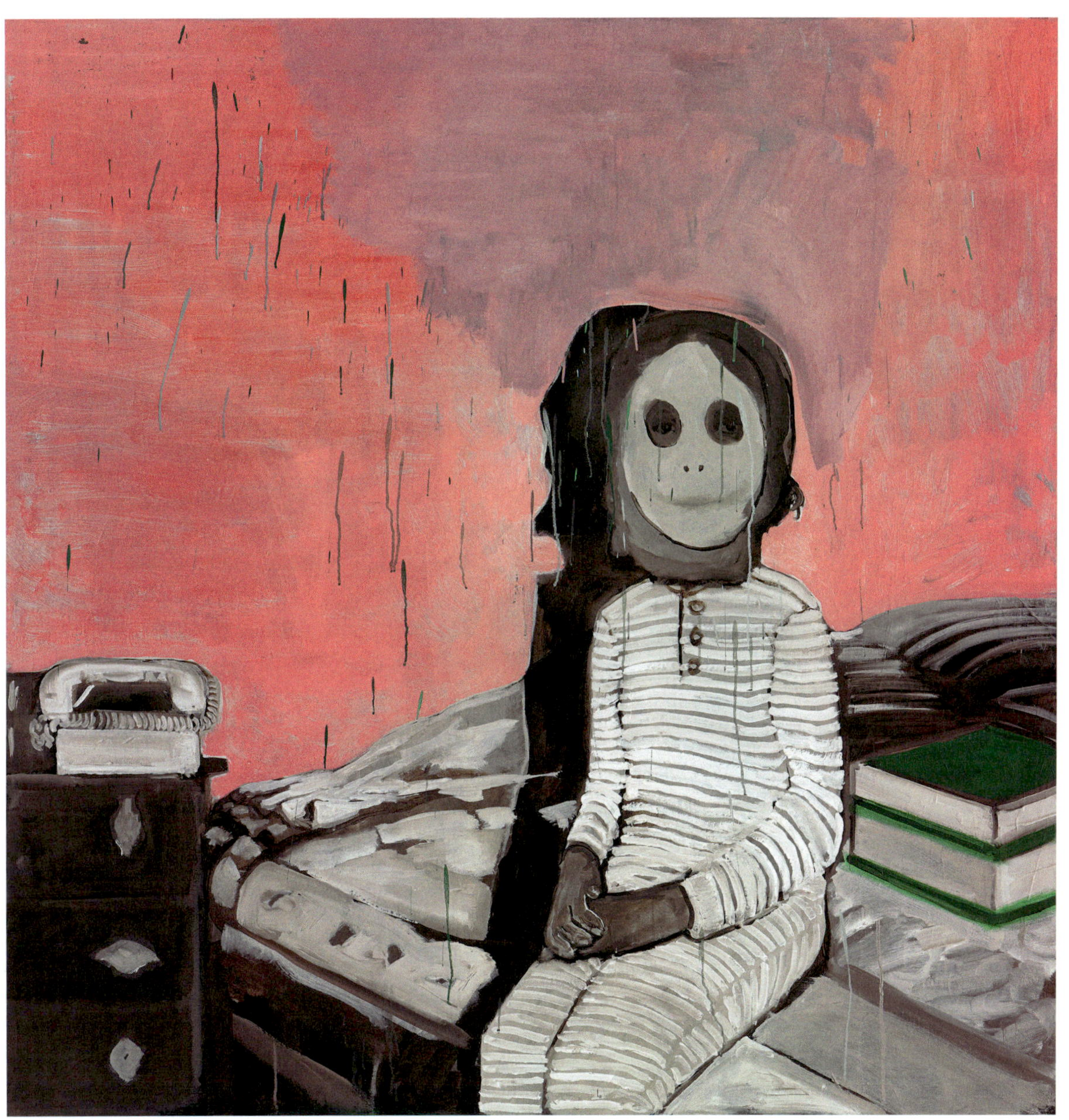

 1984, 2009

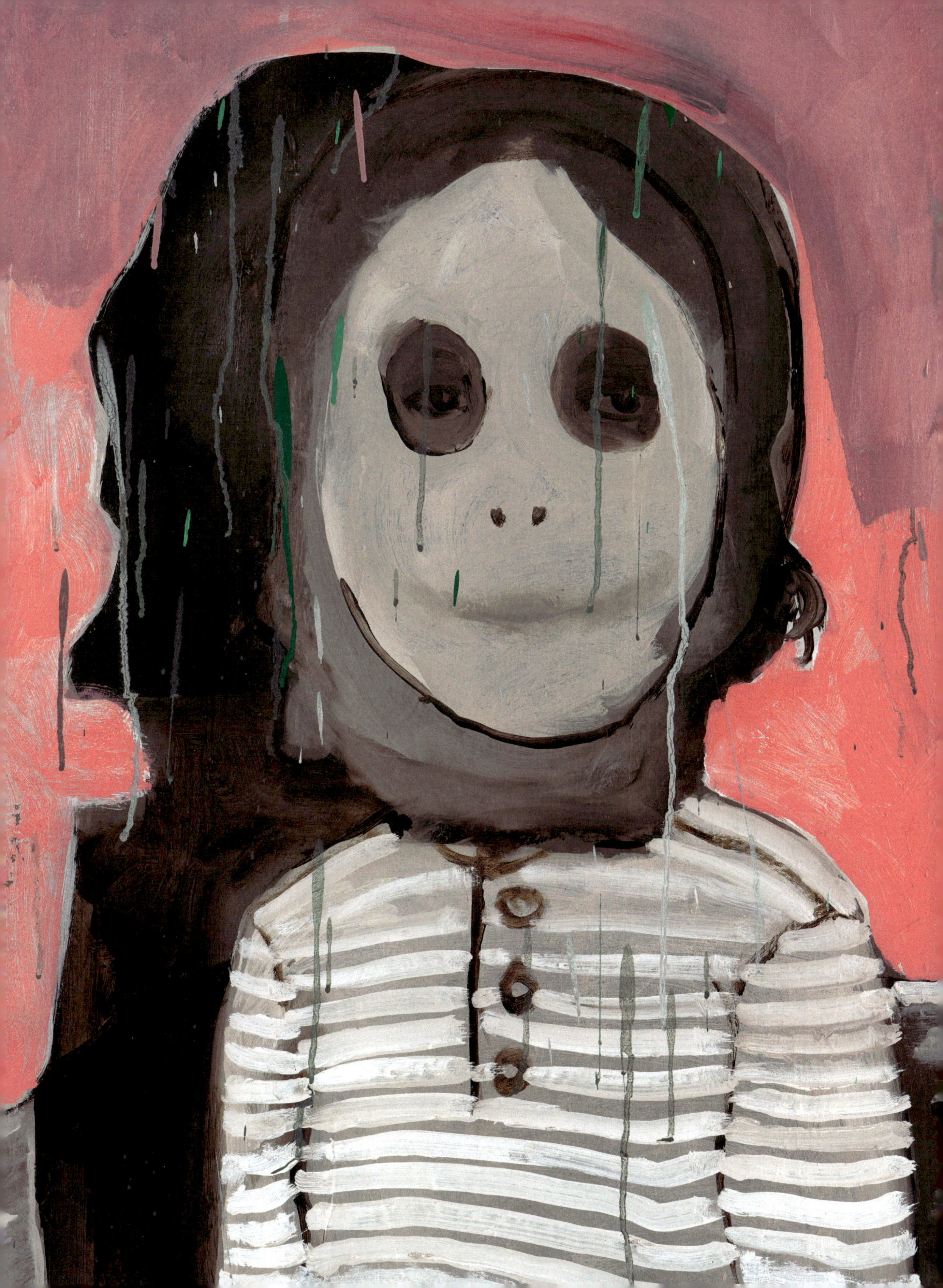

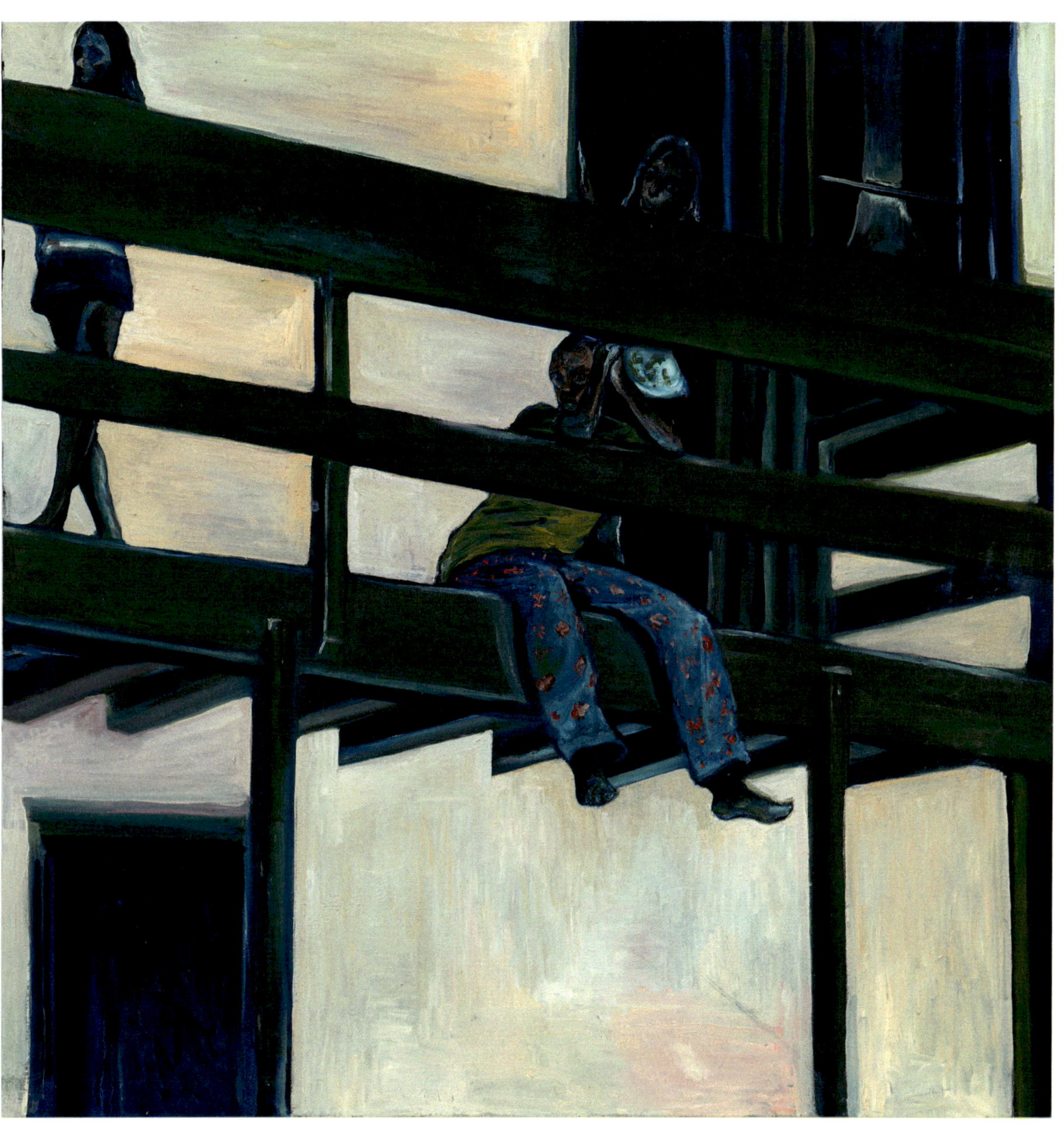

 Another Balcony, 2009

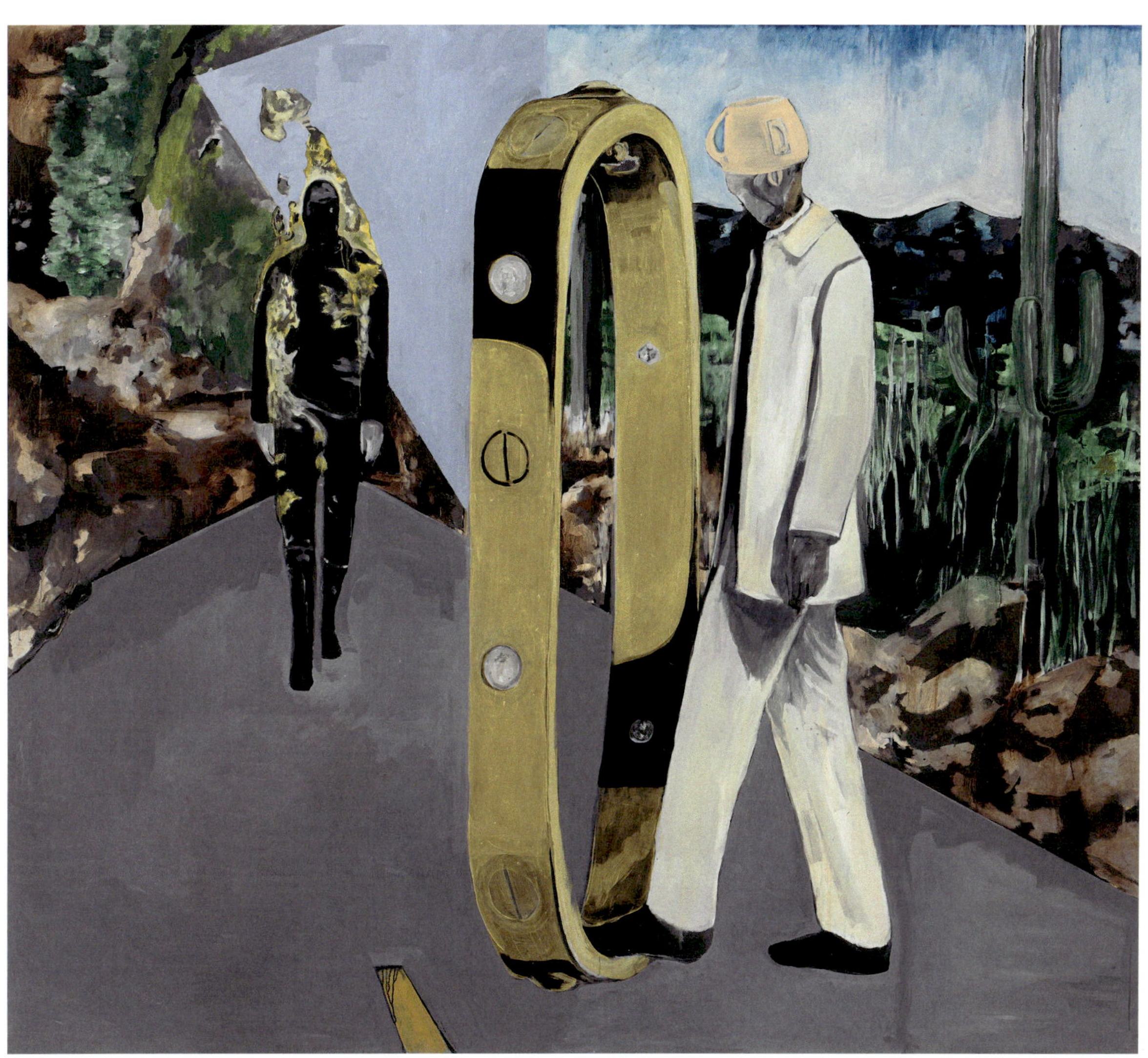

89 *Imaginary Enemy*, 2009

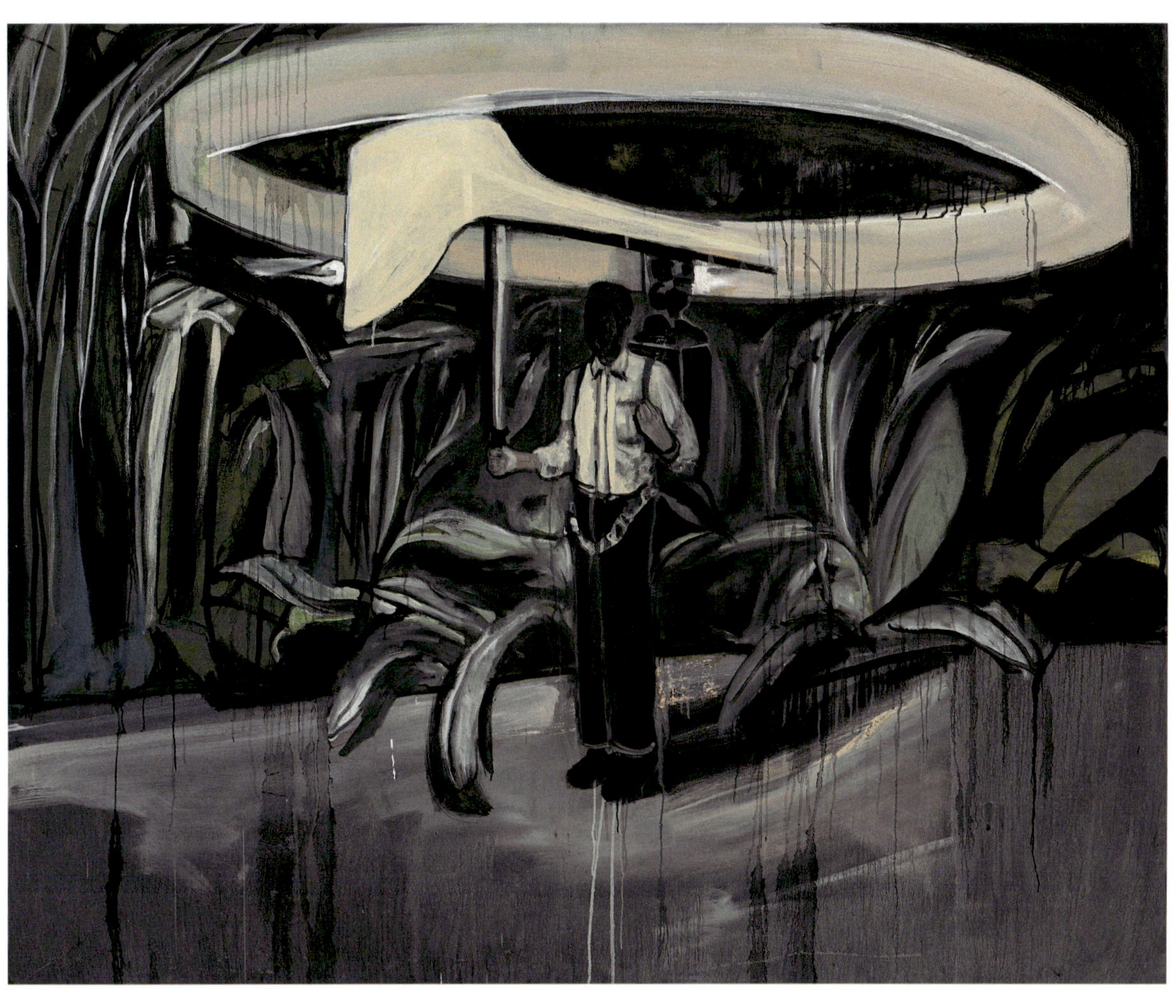

91 *The Future's Future*, 2010

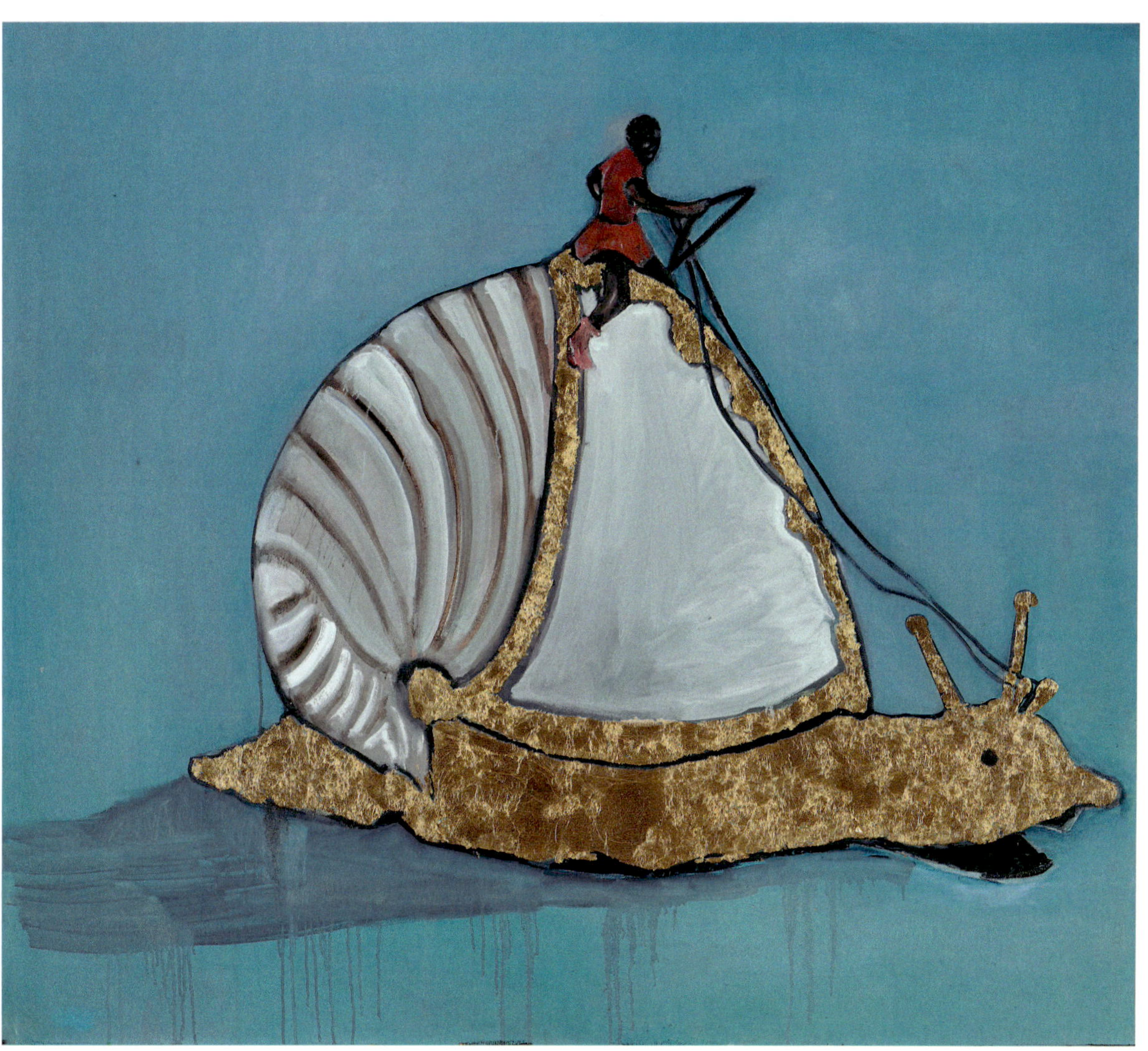

 A Snail's Pace, 2010

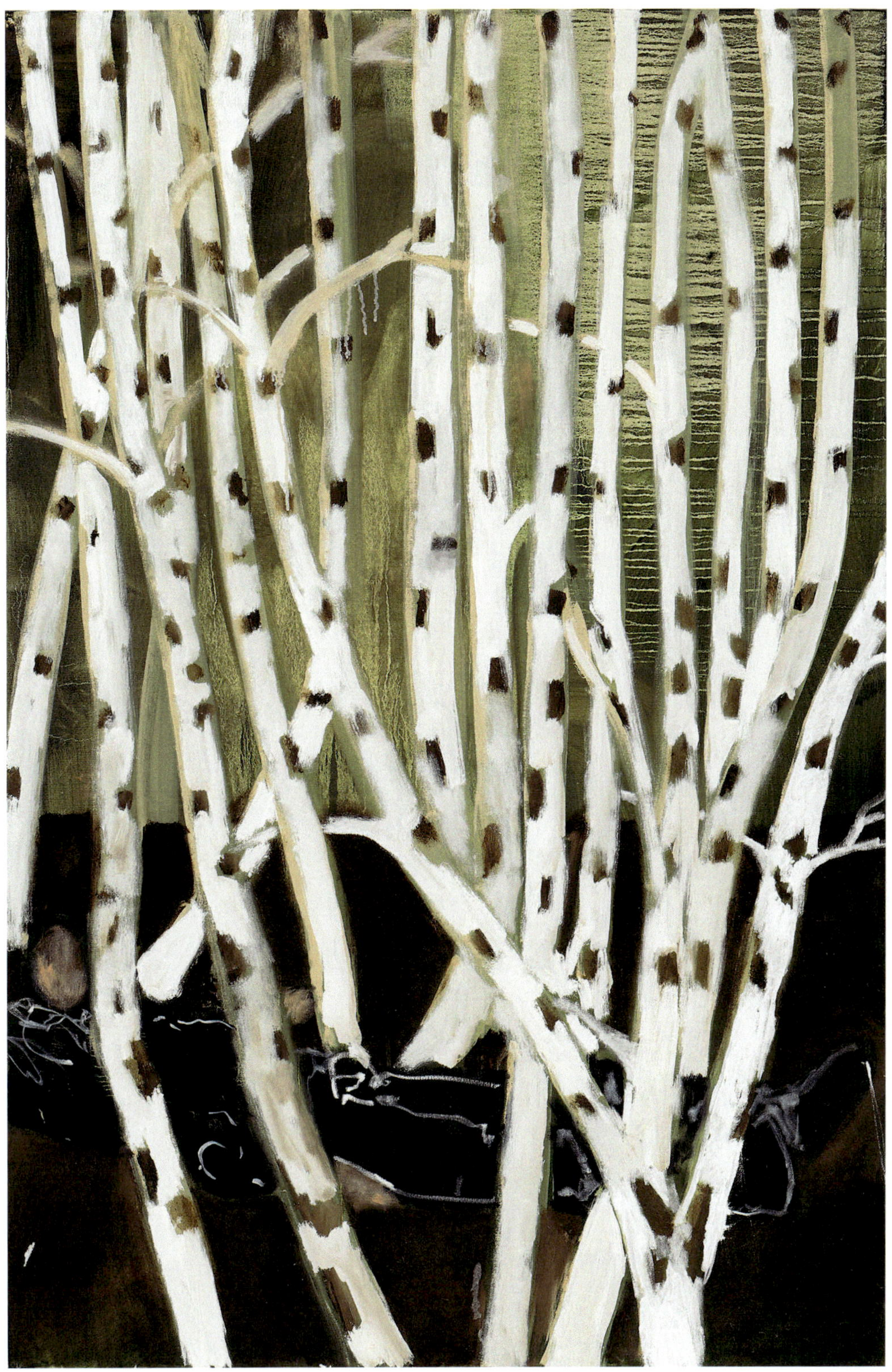

 Untitled (Birch Trees), 2010

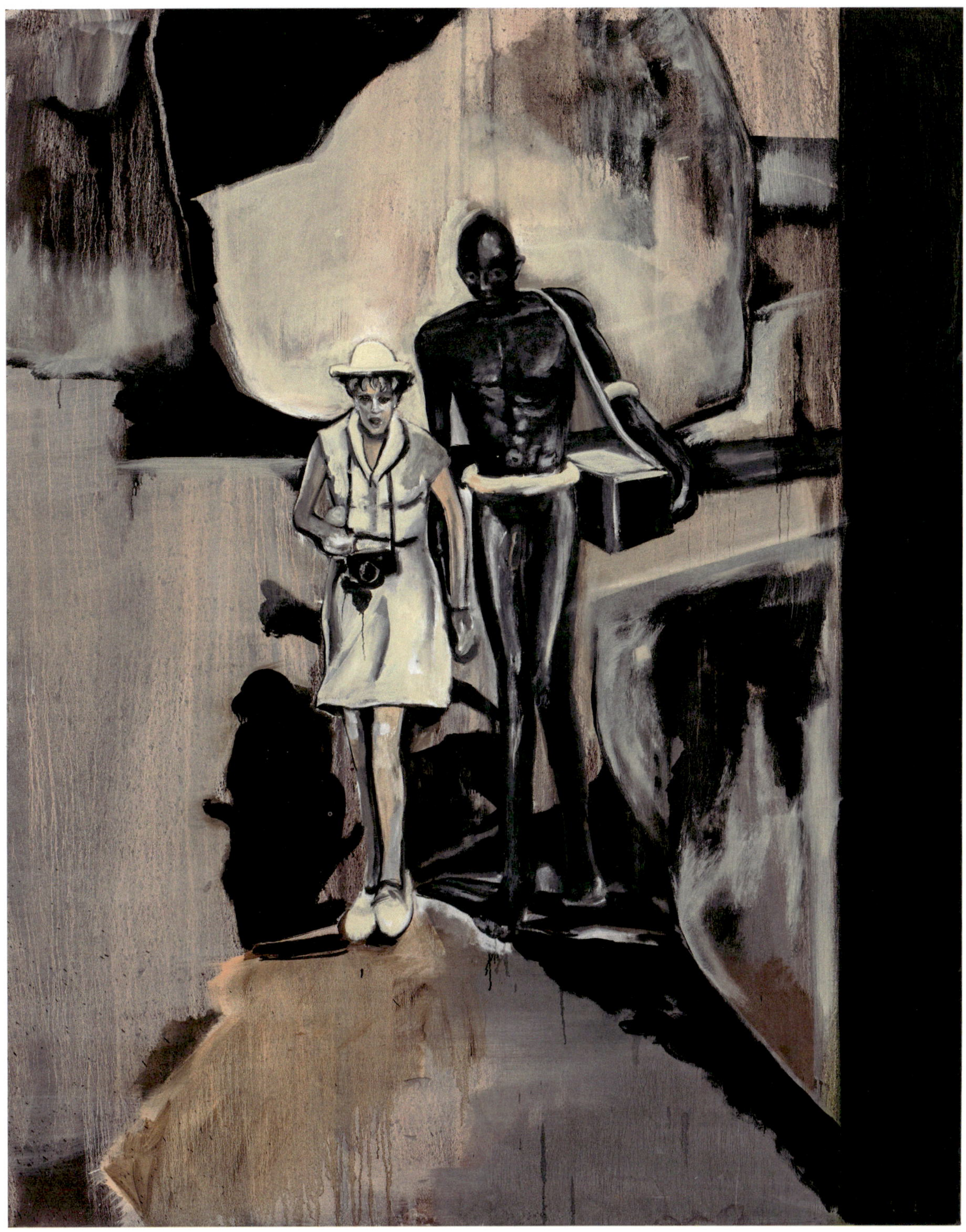

 Leni Riefenstahl, 2010

FRANCESCO CLEMENTE
on *Painting for My Dad*, 2011

Dear Noah, I am not writing of you. I am writing to you.

To write of you would be to bury you again, as you cannot argue with me, and I know you would argue (just as I argue, just as painters must always argue). To write to you, on the other hand, is soothing. It is comforting to talk to you, to think of you, to think of the gentleness implied in your being a painter, to think of the fury implied in your being a painter: the fury necessary to sharpen, with an effort of the intellect, the treacherous vagueness of beauty. You were not afraid of beauty. You knew that beauty, like Rilke said, is the beginning of terror.

I notice you pay attention to the surface and the edges. The measure of legitimacy in a painting is found only there. The edges must be like the marks of the lover's nails, the surface must be like the surface of the lover's skin.

Dear Noah, we never met, but the curators of an exhibition about your work say that you are fond of my paintings. They asked me to choose one of your paintings and write about it.

I intend to talk only to you, and I do not intend to talk of myself. Still, I can't help but feel a sense of affinity with your meandering – both timid and bold – when I notice that your paintings do not emerge from a reactive impulse but stand, self-sufficient, in reference to one another. Your paintings are a family, and they relate to one another not only through palette and treatment but, above all, through the images you chose. The images, which, no matter how much you resist them, come at you and demand to be seen.

I have decided to go through almost all the paintings in your exhibition to find out how they tell the story of what is not shown, of what cannot be shown. I will let your paintings lead me to the one that makes my mind, my pen, fall silent.

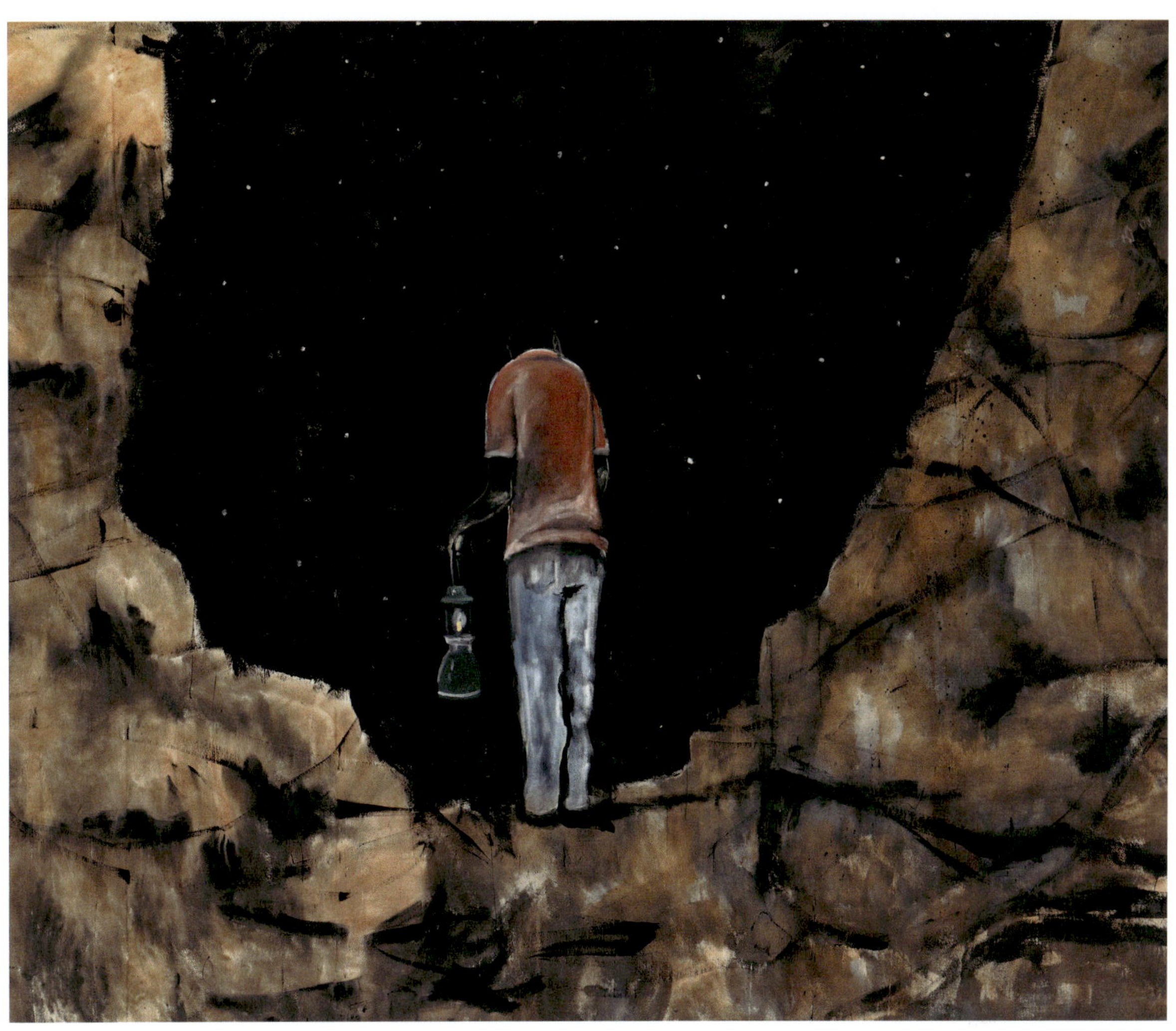

 Painting for My Dad, 2011

Here are the paintings, one by one:

Men by a lake waiting for the sun to peek through the clouds again. It is not a leisurely gathering; it is not a secluded lake. These are foreigners in a landscape that is calmer than they are.

Abstraction in brown and maroon, as if the Puritanism of 1970s minimalism had rusted, militarised, camouflaged, found a new form of calmness in imperfection.

It's not enough to decorate a house with wallpaper in soft colours, lacquered drawers and a bland landscape picture on the wall. A boy-man gets spanked. The high heels of the mother and the boots of the son are incongruent with the situation because, elsewhere, things are also incongruent.

A child and her shadow, a child and her book, a child and her unmade bed, her pyjamas, her bedside telephone. The child is wearing a mask. The child is death.

Where to go from here? Solitude is a step away while he is slouching, holding his arm, making sure not to make eye contact with the pastel-painted panels, whose pleasing proportions are indifferent to a man's toil.

To observe others is to observe them from behind while they cross the street, while they stop to pick up something they dropped, while they are lost in thought. Their colourful clothes do not protect them from the expanse of asphalt, signs and parking lots that are too wide, too grim.

What good is a lawn? What good is the perspective of buildings (neither poor nor rich) if there are no ballerinas dancing on the grass, turning the sky purple? Their costumes are the colour of dawn, their skin is the colour of dusk.

Where there are fences, there is something to lean one's back against, read the paper and wait.

Why is it that all the figures in these paintings do not seem to have made it past a young or a very young age?

Here is a child disguised as a child standing in front of a wall painted in camouflage.

Again, someone turns away from the viewer. Is this the solitude of the observer or the observed? Or is it the solitude of observation?

Hollywood was then. Now, brackish waters cover the city with a metallic mantle, the black water reflecting a starless sky. A father and son in a rowboat finally look at the painter, but they are too far away, and it is too dark, too quiet, too late. There is no contact, only the scar of history, the writing on the hill.

Sometimes, things melt away. A Santa Claus (or a biblical prophet or a Renaissance architect) looks downwards at his own creation, a model of an ice pyramid rising as it disappears.

Houses also melt away, sinking into the quicksands of LA. The opera conductor has had to climb onto a chair to be seen or heard. Are the tenor and soprano standing on the roof? We see their feet.

There is so much outdoors in the indoors. So much indoors in the outdoors. Are we in a billiard parlour? Again, two figures caught in mid-sentence. Movement interrupted.

Children and adolescents, blurred as if seen through the lens of a Super 8 camera from another time.

We know where we are because we are drowning in a field of sensations. When a wall-like building shuts our horizon, we can search for the sky only in a faint reflection in the water. The bathers, too, cannot decide if they are there or not there.

The image of a hunter suggests references one should research, but the foliage and the tree trunk surrounding the hunter say otherwise. The themes of waiting, solitude, observation and death are all there, and so are a distinctive pink and green.

Water is important, and land is not that solid, either. After the boat race, the youth carry the boat on their shoulder. A trumpeter in black looks at them in vain. They look away. Is it a boat they carry or a coffin? Is this a race or a funeral?

Men at a funeral. The sky is so big, the house so small. The dead is already out of the picture. The image is cropped too soon and almost leaves him out. The world of adults is a world of funerals.

Dear Noah, as you will have noticed, I had to write about almost every painting in the show to make my way to this one: the one I wish I had painted, the one I painted, the one I will maybe paint.

In *Painting for My Dad*, as usual, you are observing someone from behind. But this time, the person you are observing is you. You stand at the bottom of the deepest hole. But the hole is at the top of the highest peak. You cannot remember if you climbed up or down. What is certain is that even if you are deep down below, you are also looking at the stars from above. You did not bring the lamp you hold to make your way here. You brought your own light to give light to the stars. Now, along with the stars – for the first time, not alone – you observe life continuing below; life small, but not without meaning.

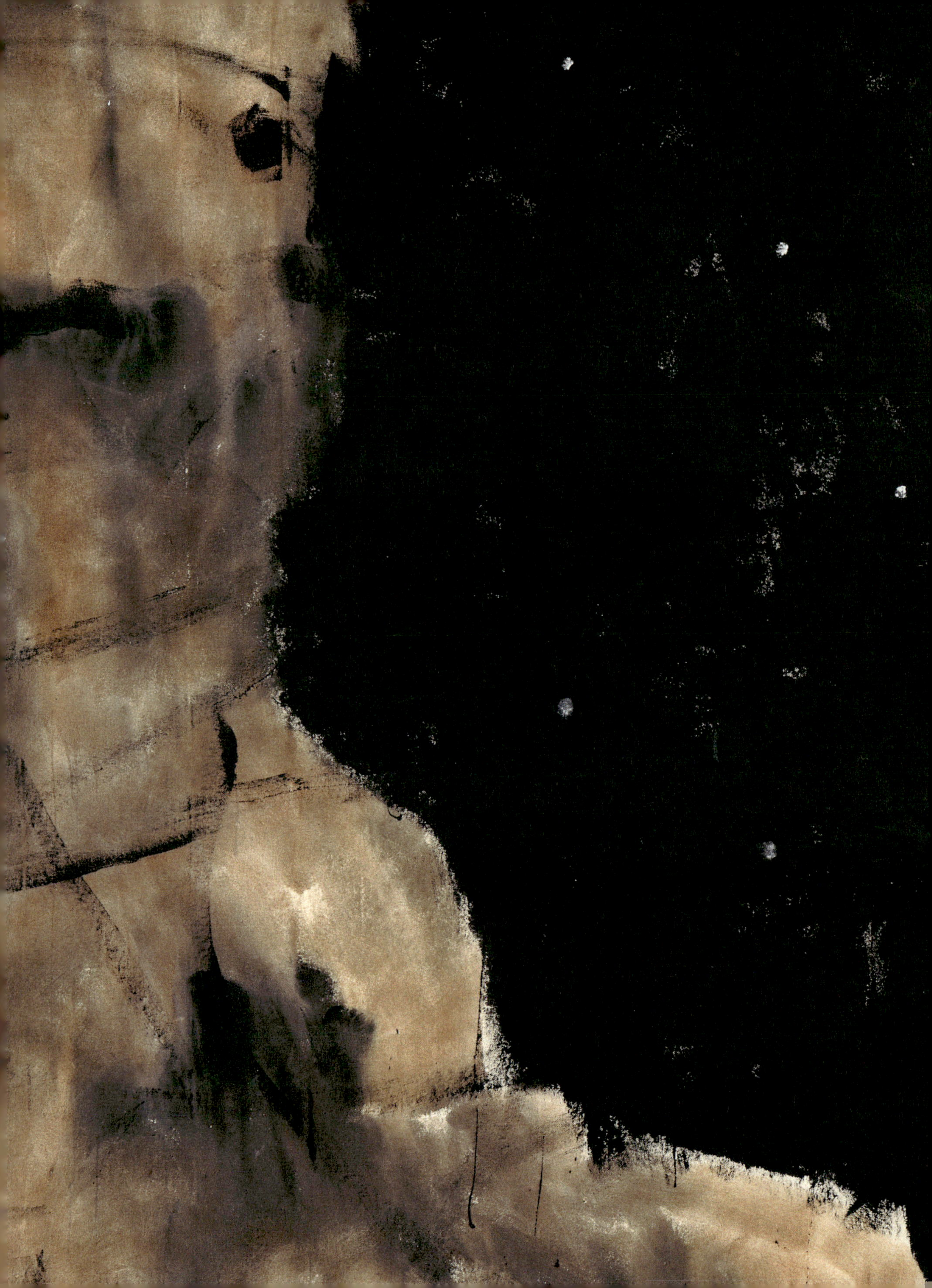

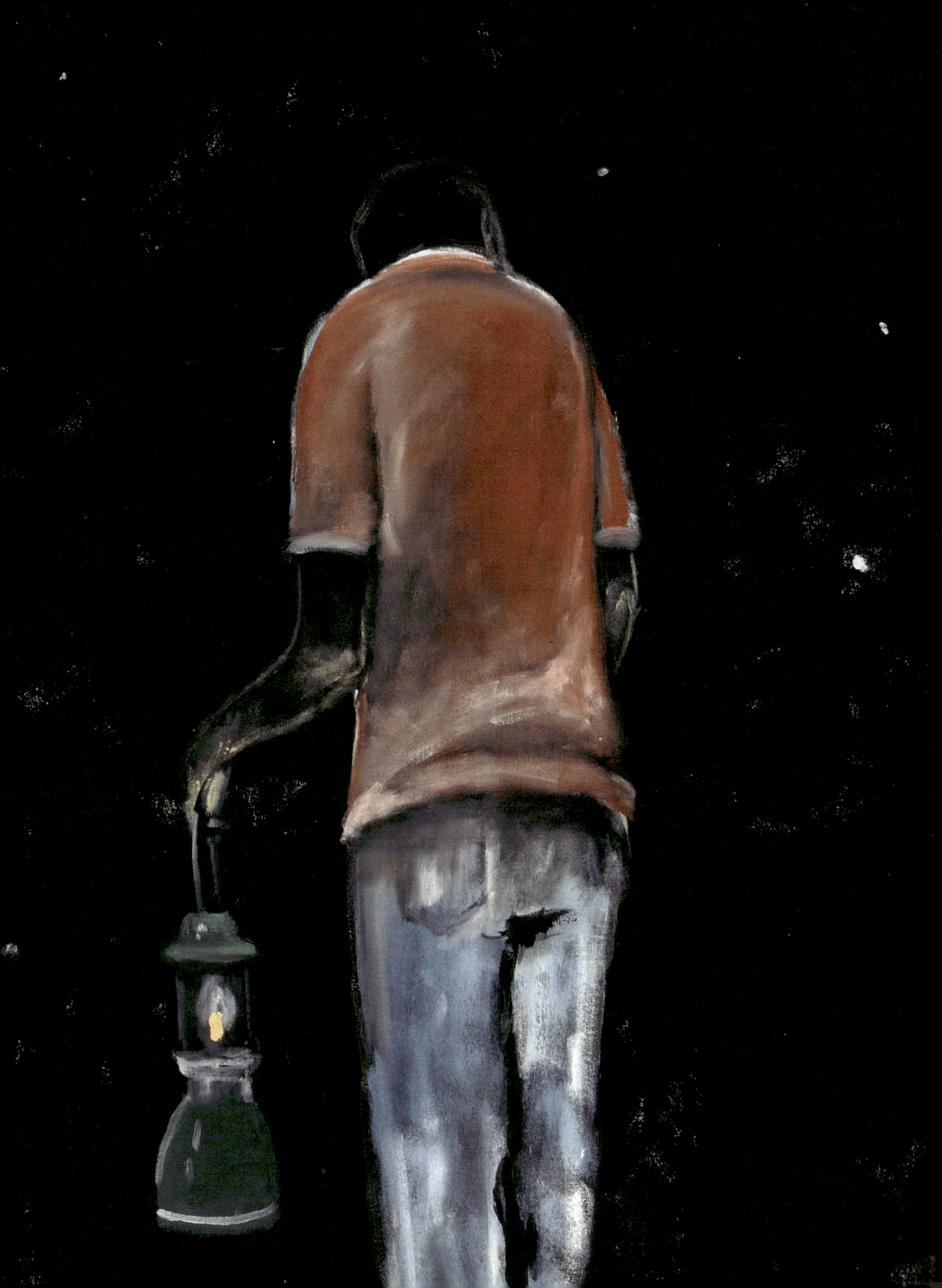

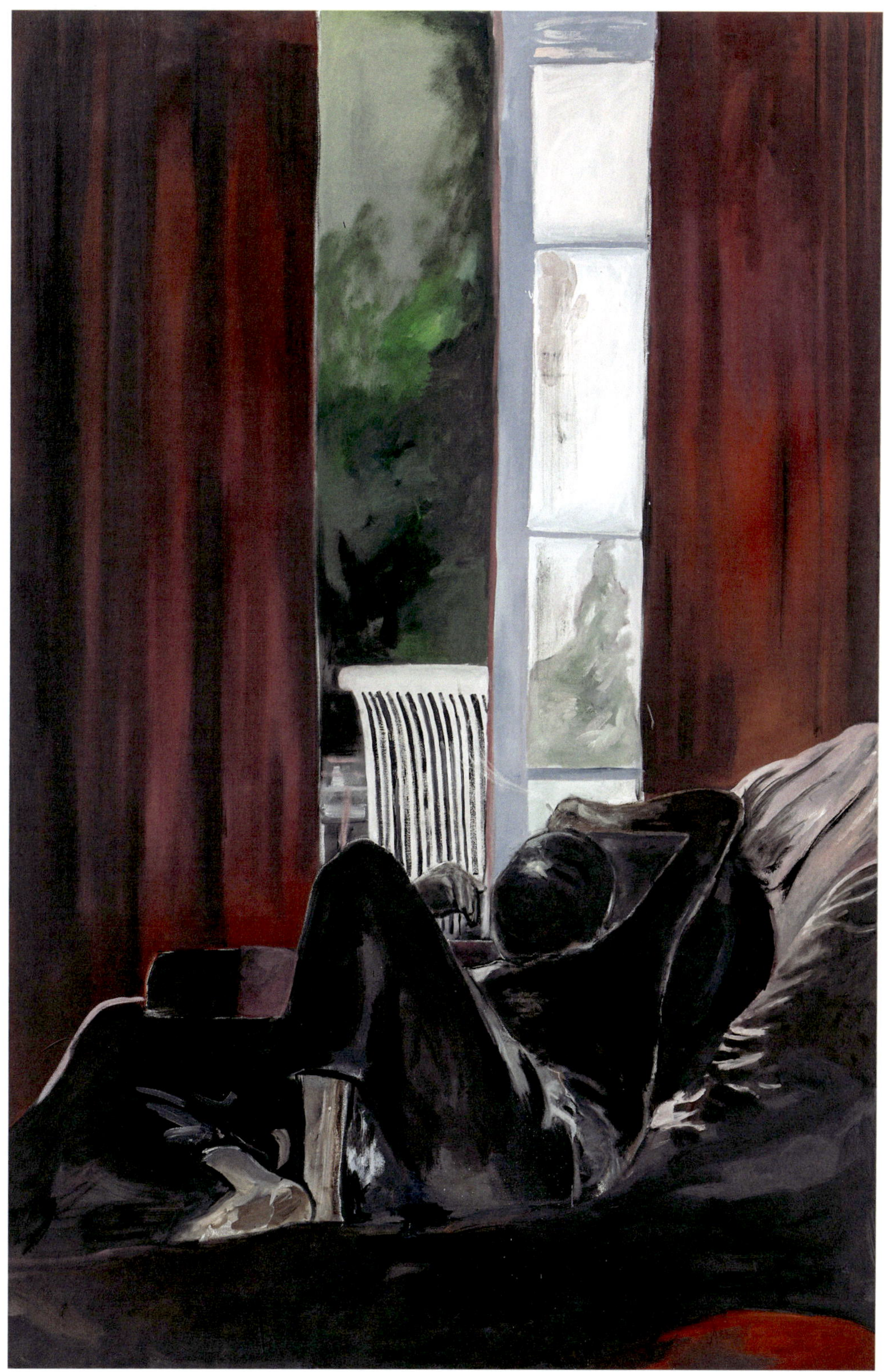

 Sugartown, 2011

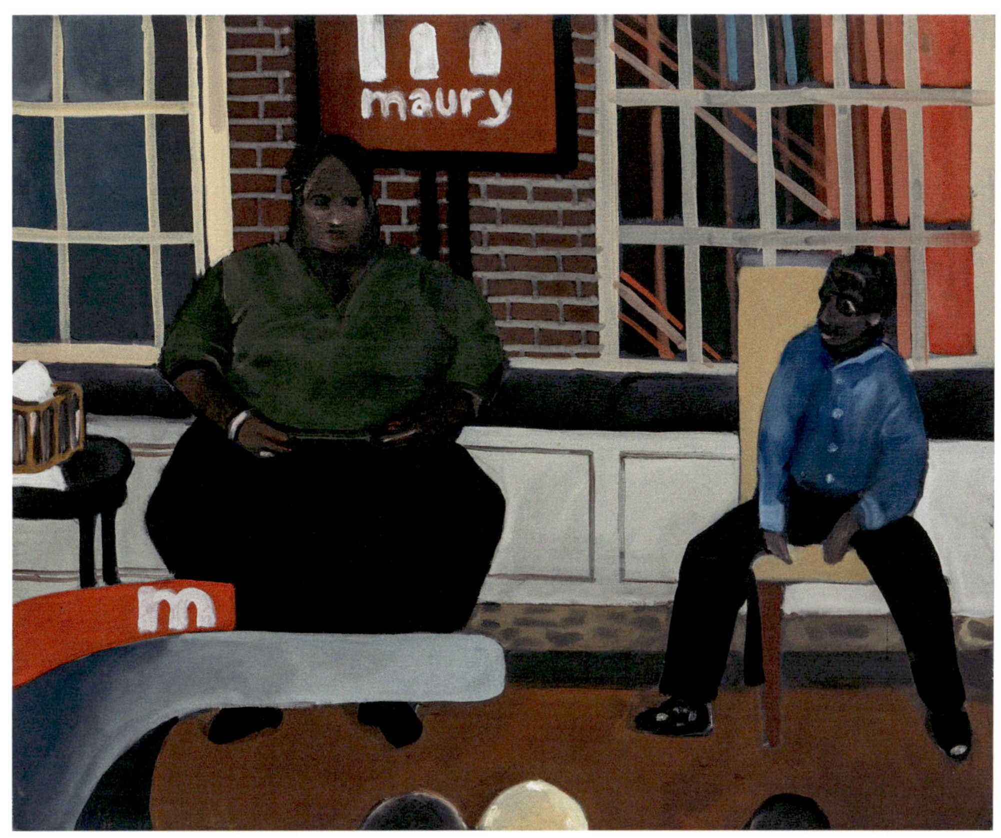

 The Maury, 2012

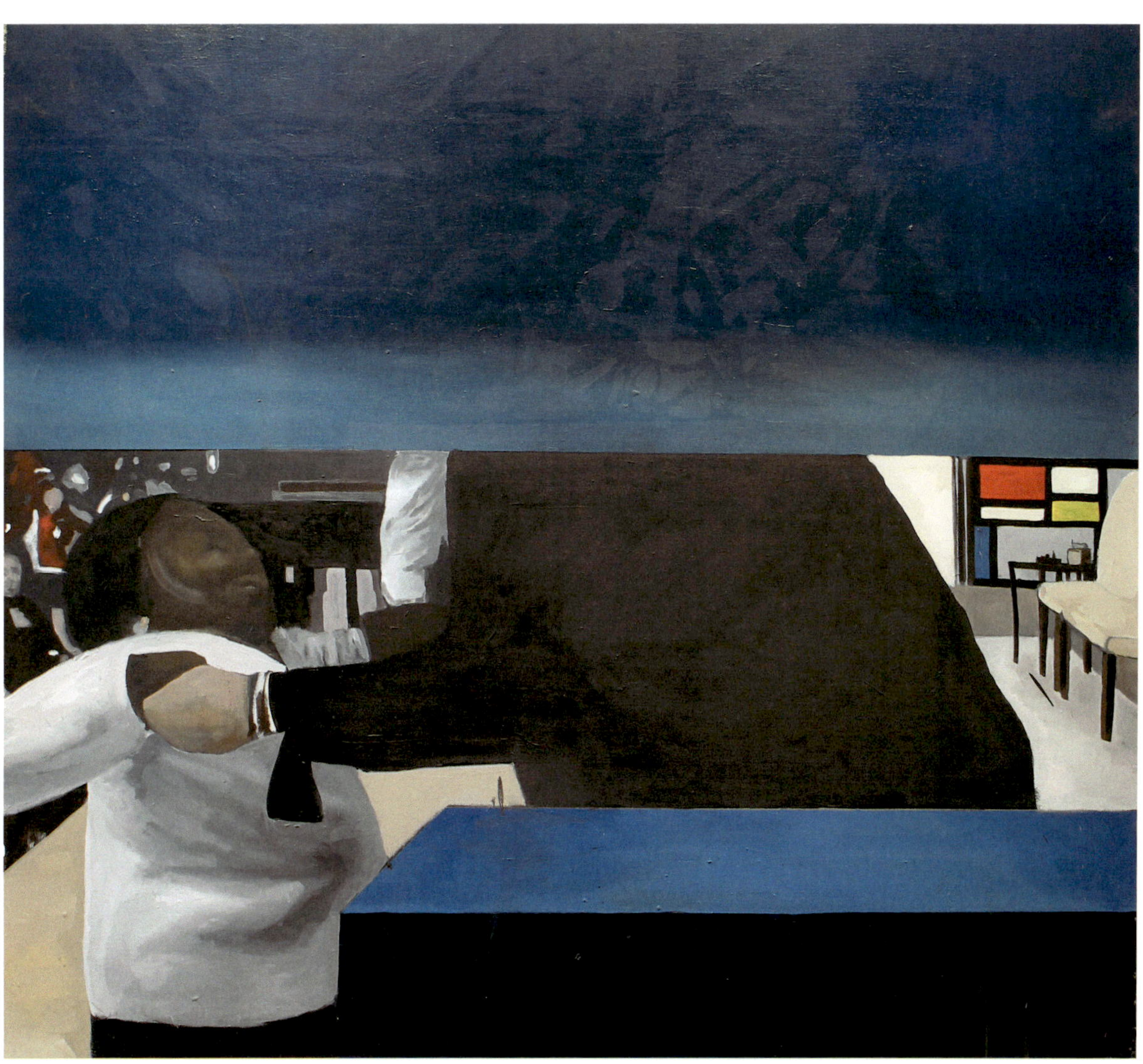

 Maury Mondrian, 2012

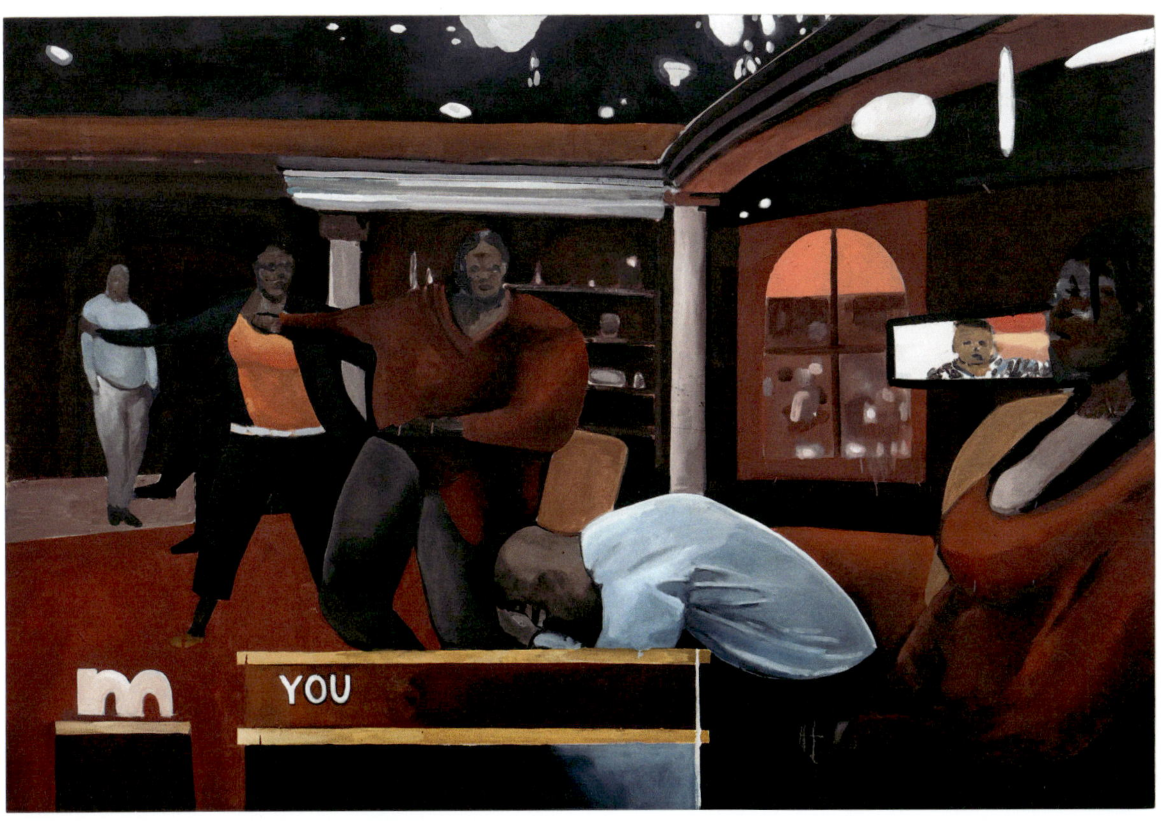

 You Are..., 2012

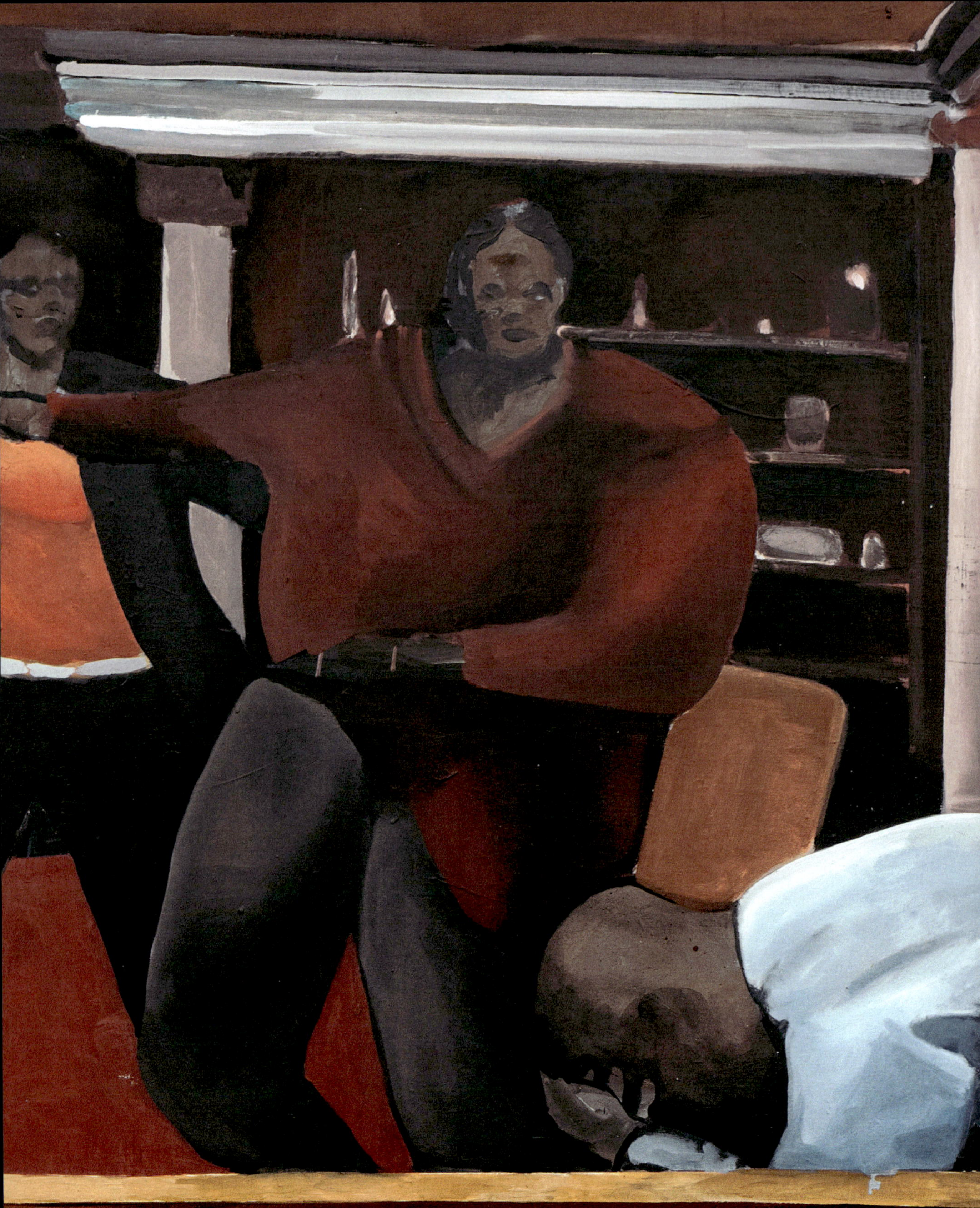
YOU

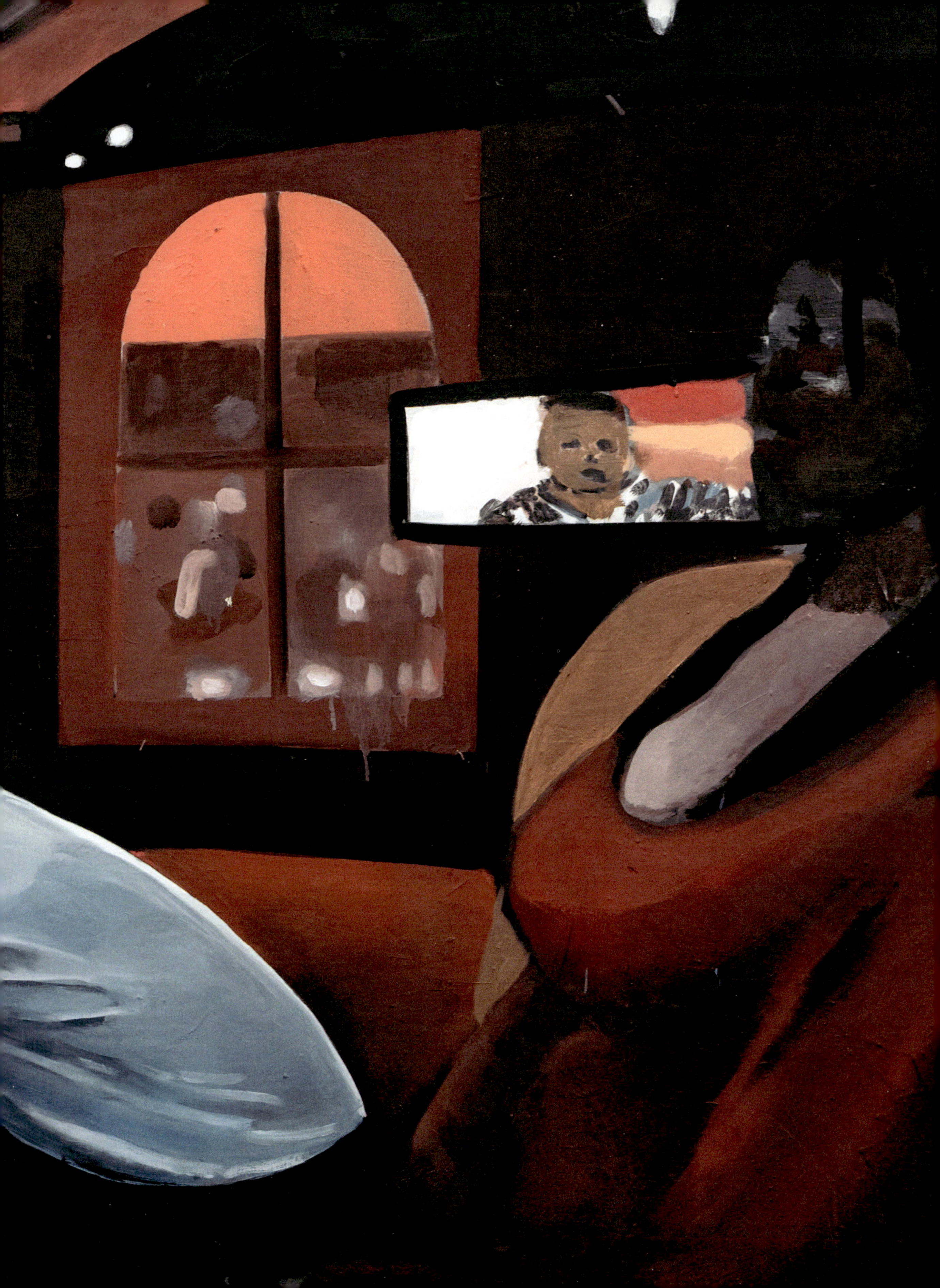

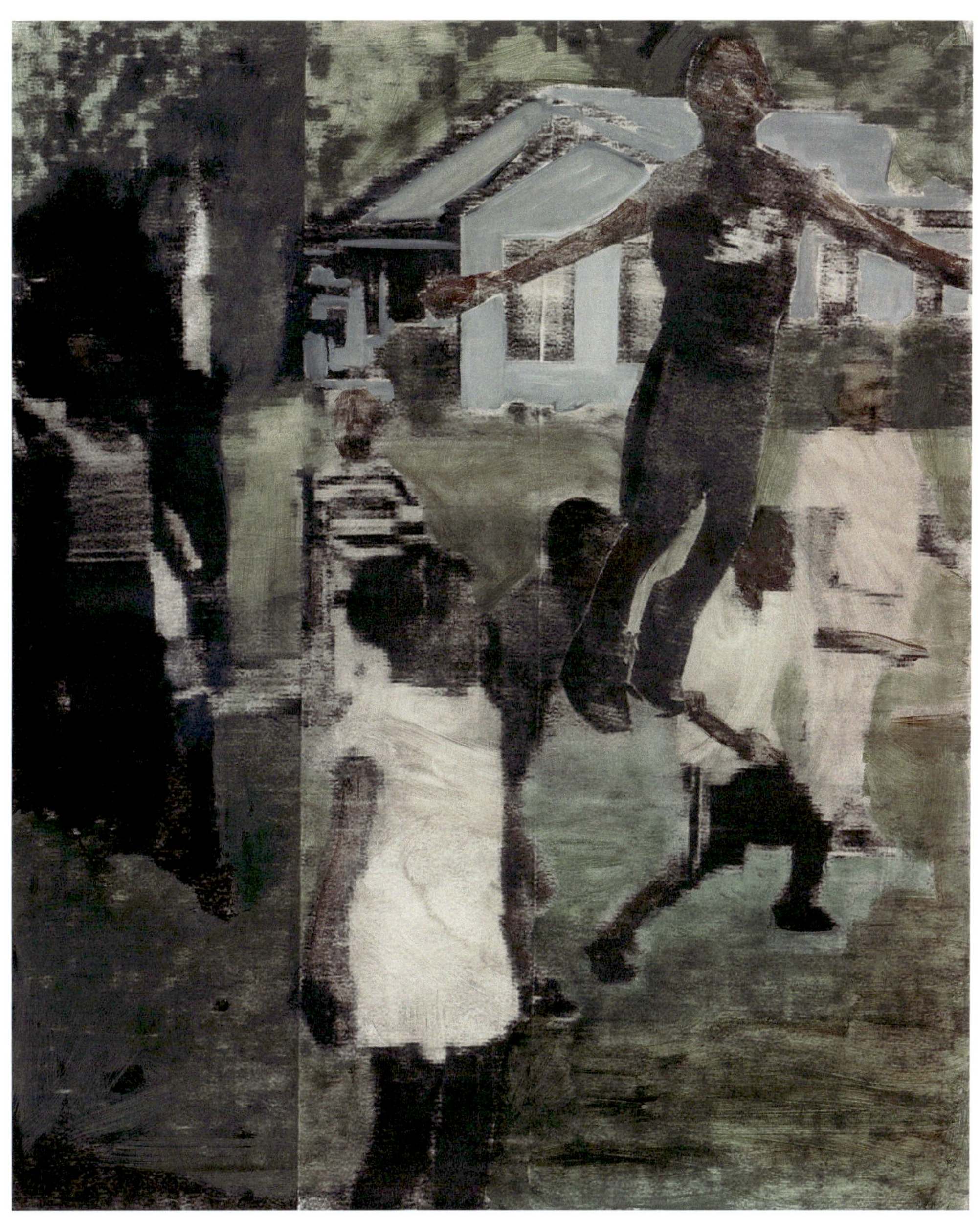

 The Missing Link 1, 2013

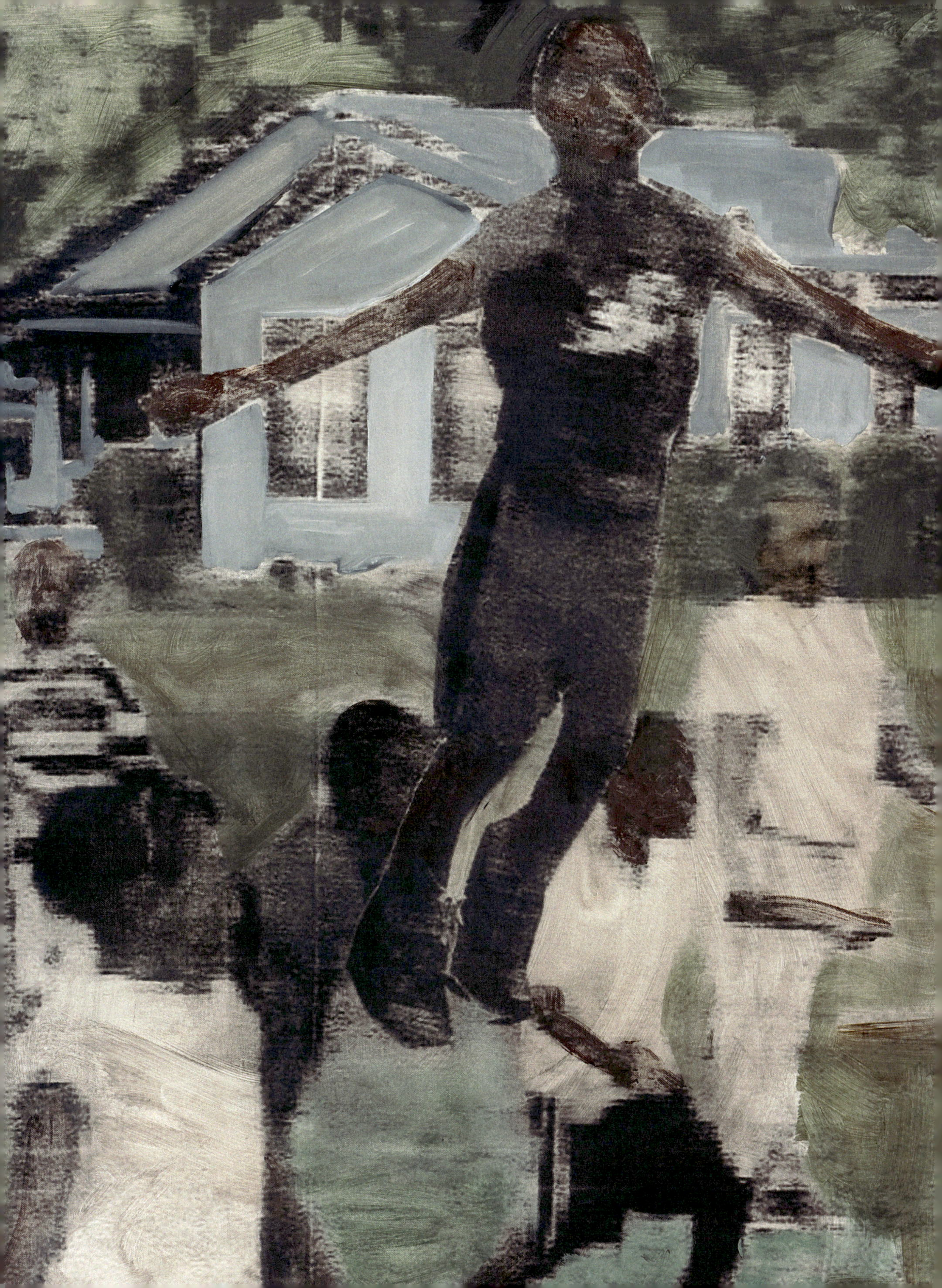

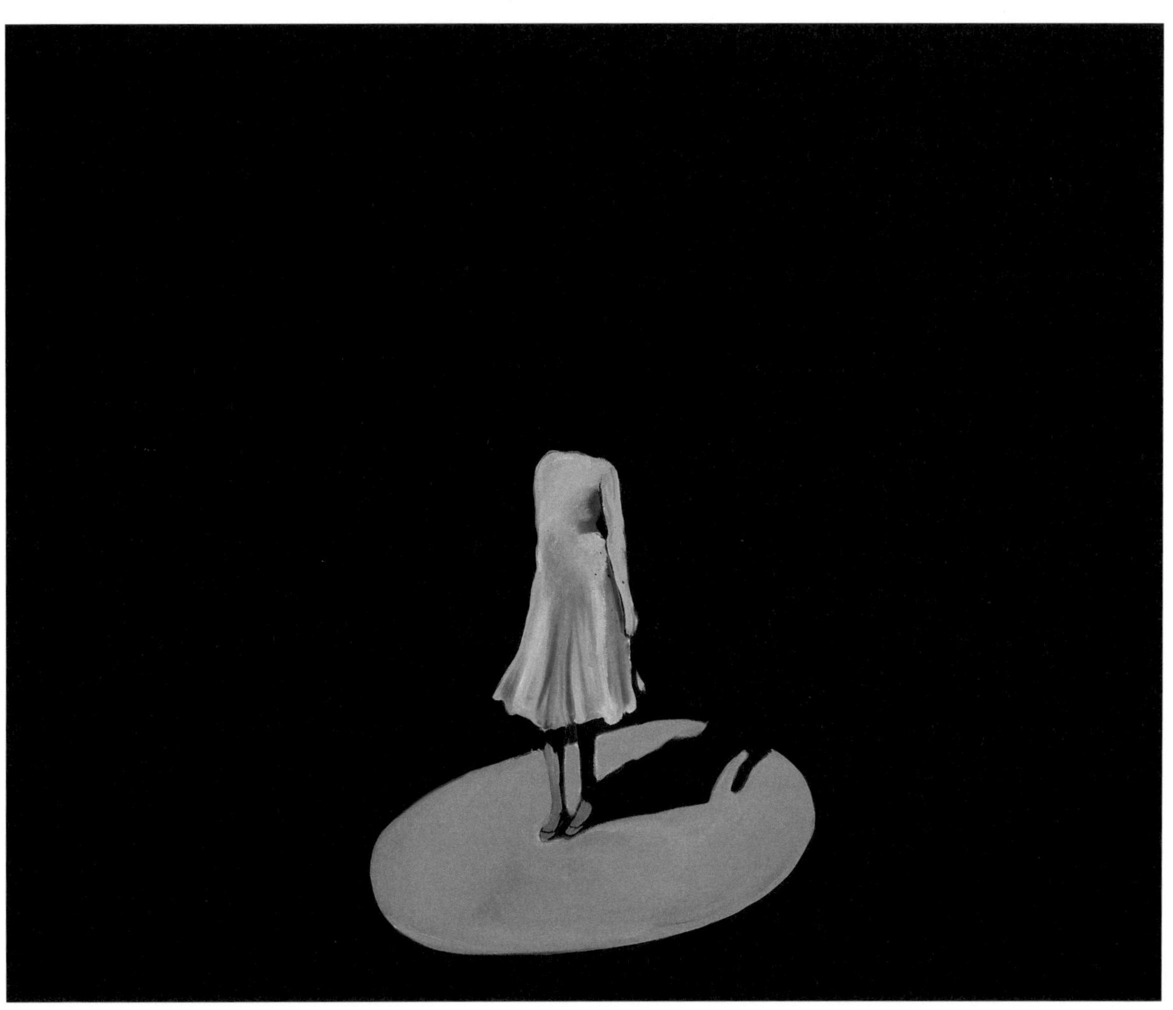

 The Missing Link 2, 2013

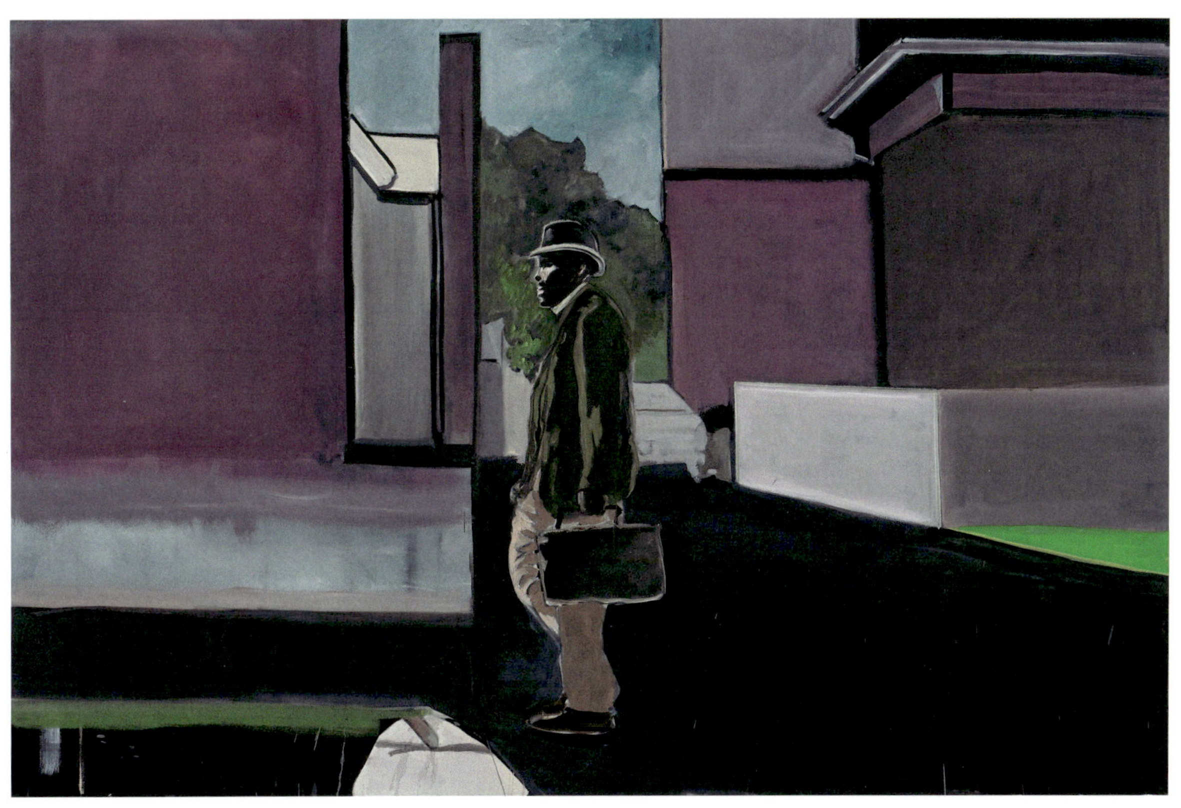

 The Missing Link 3, 2013

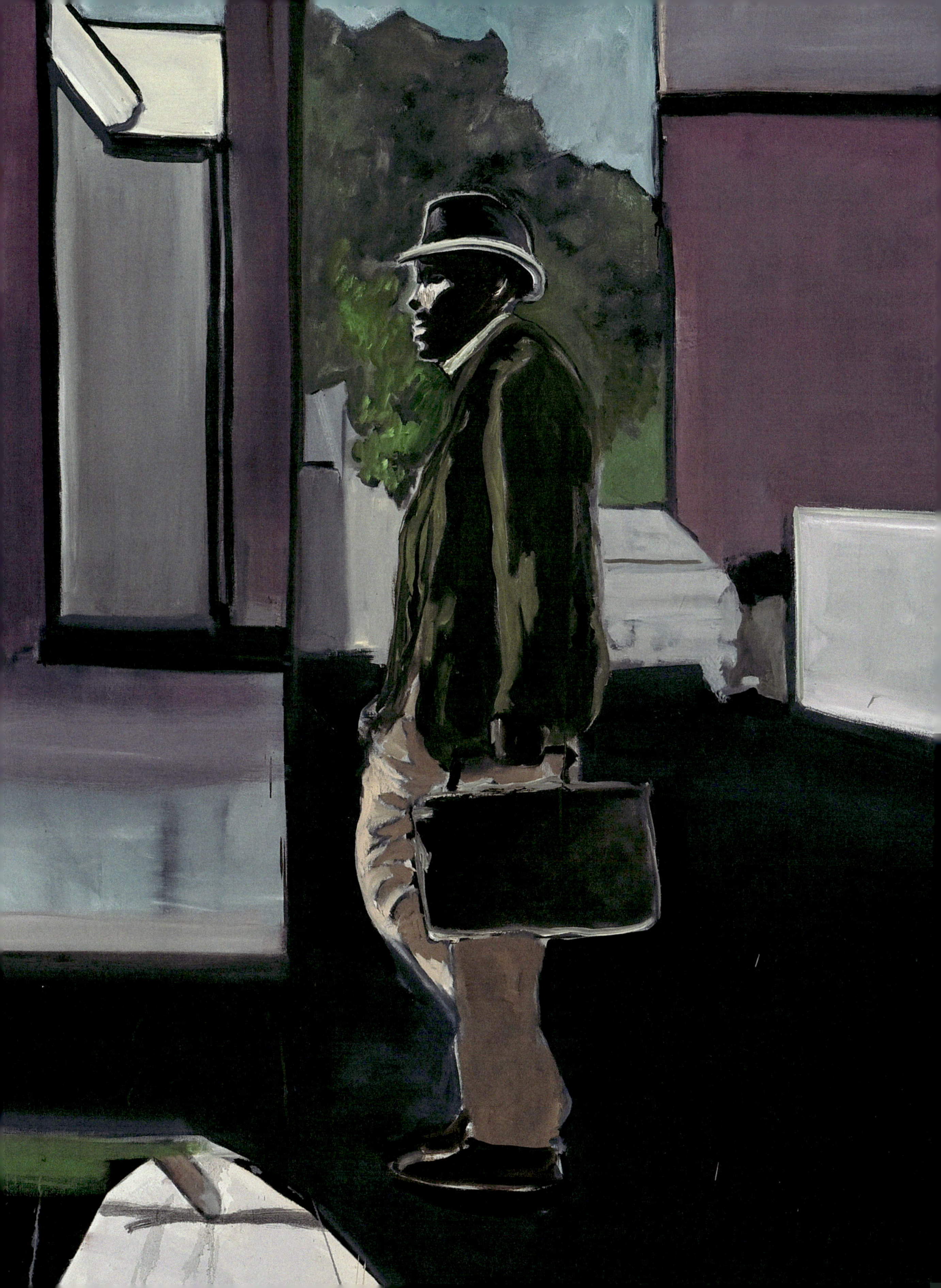

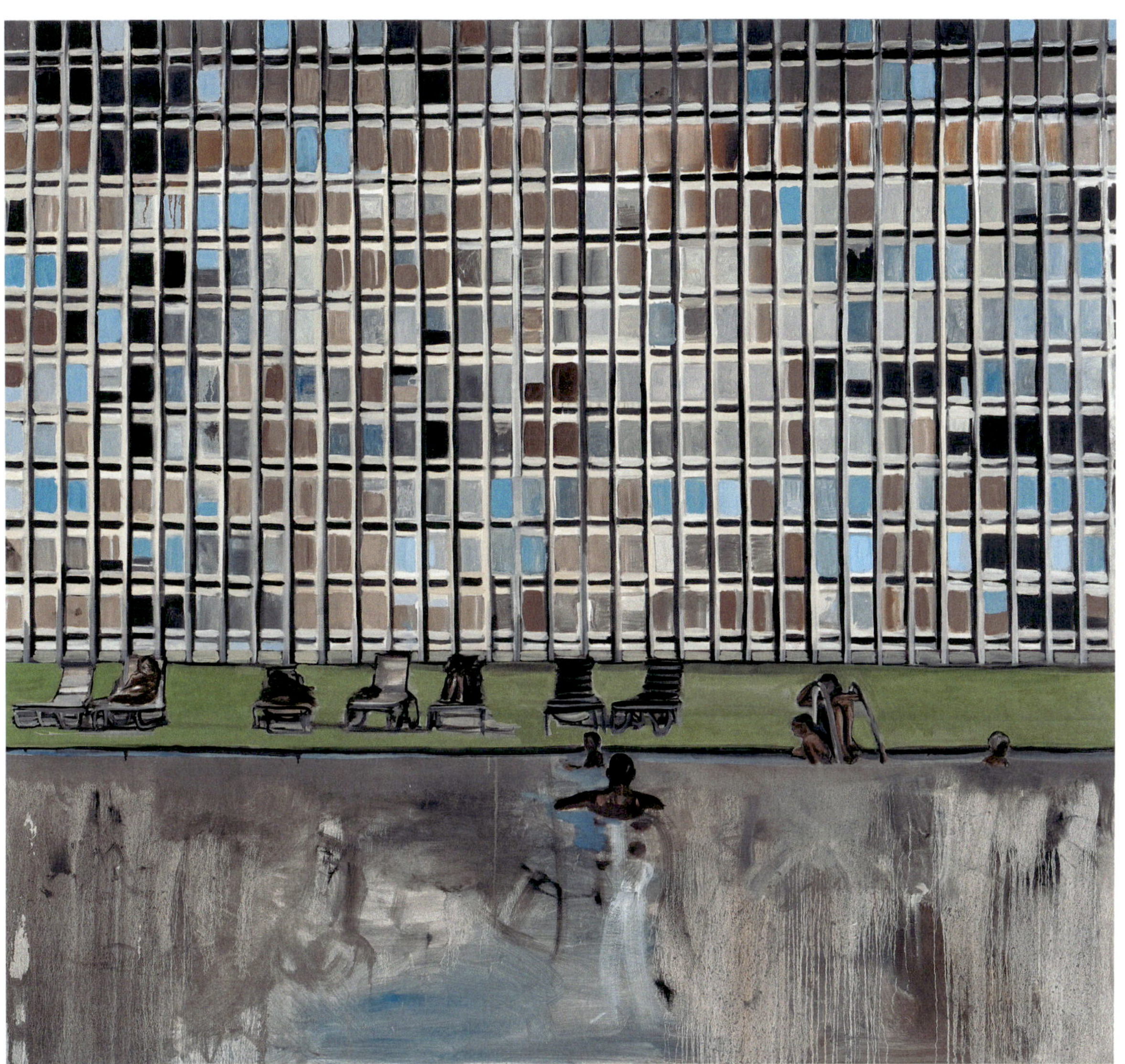

 The Missing Link 4, 2013

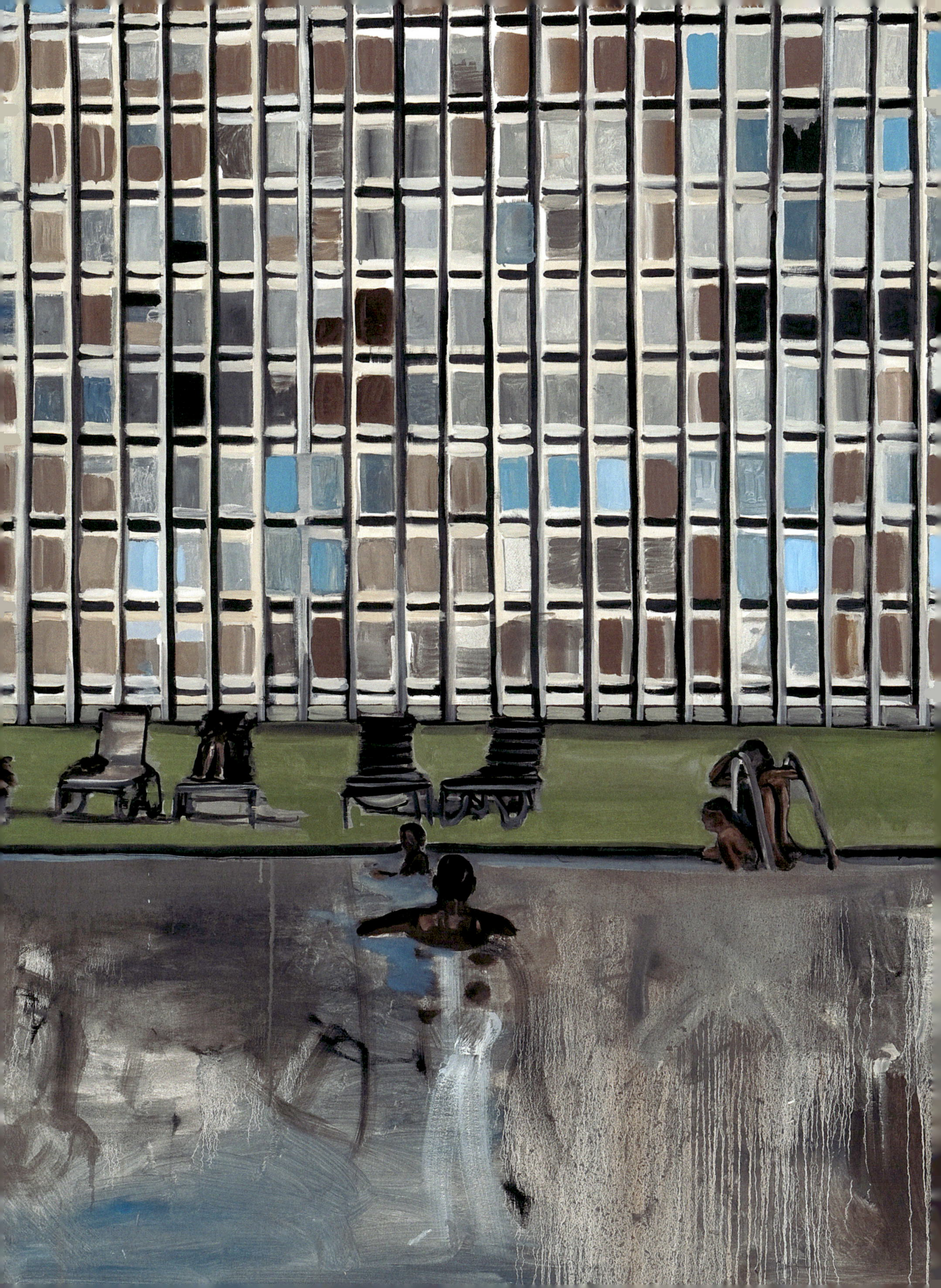

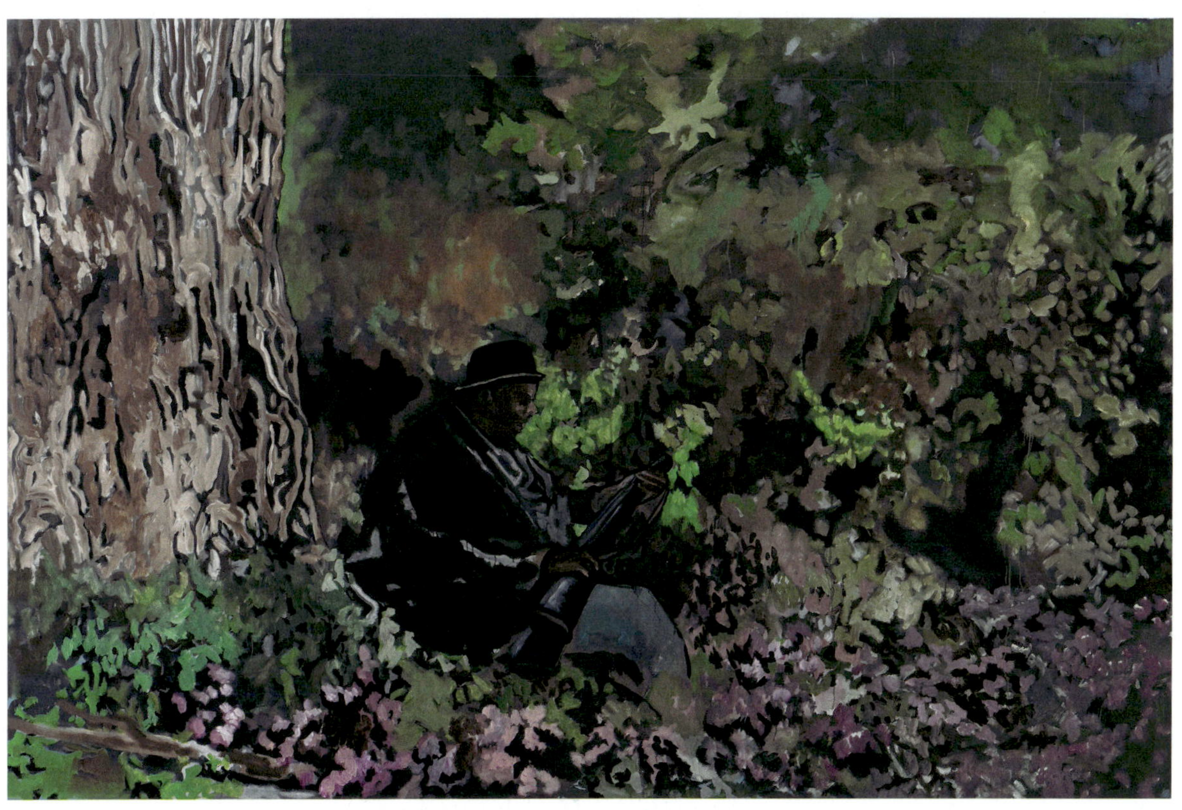

 The Missing Link 6, 2013

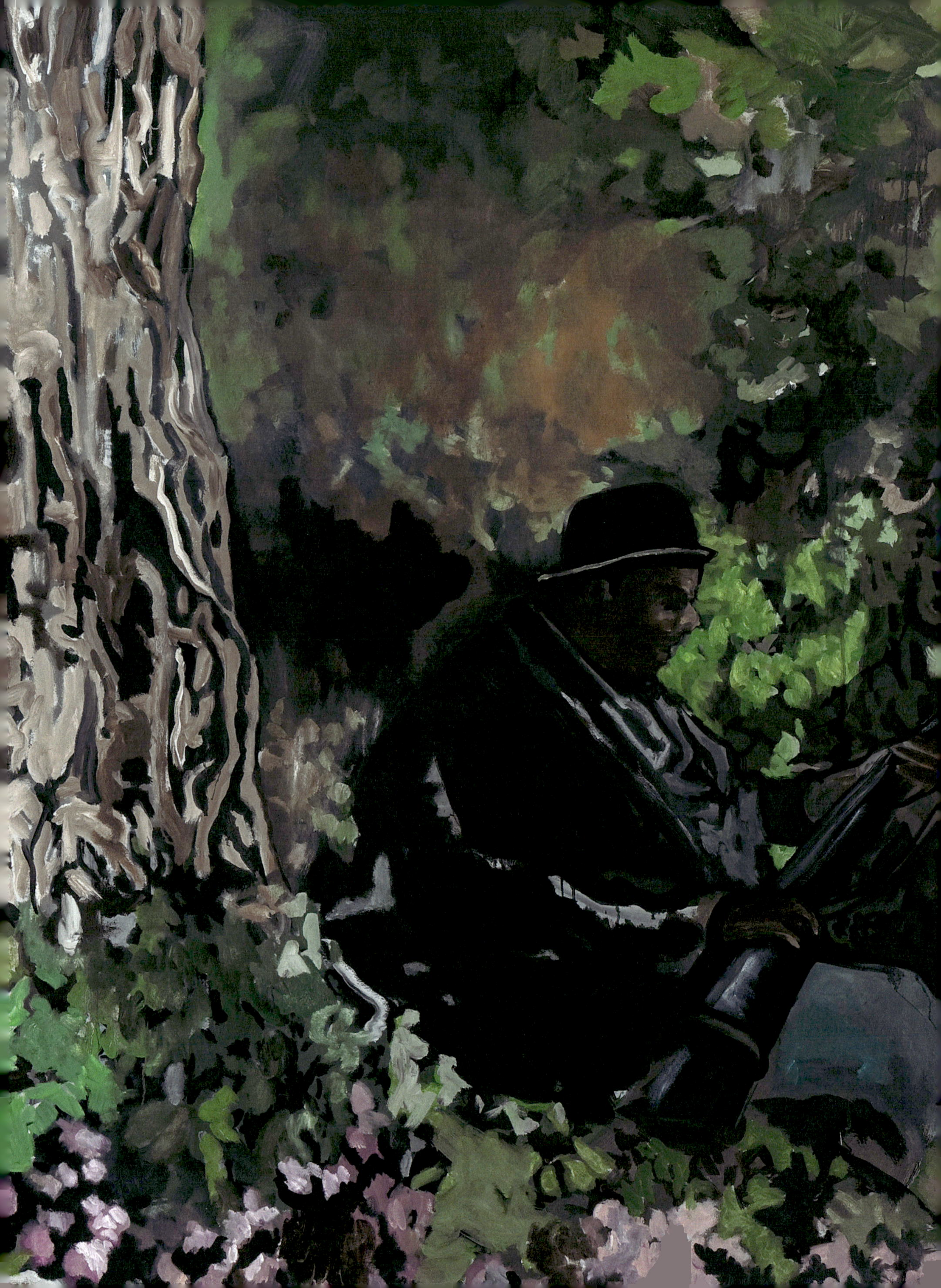

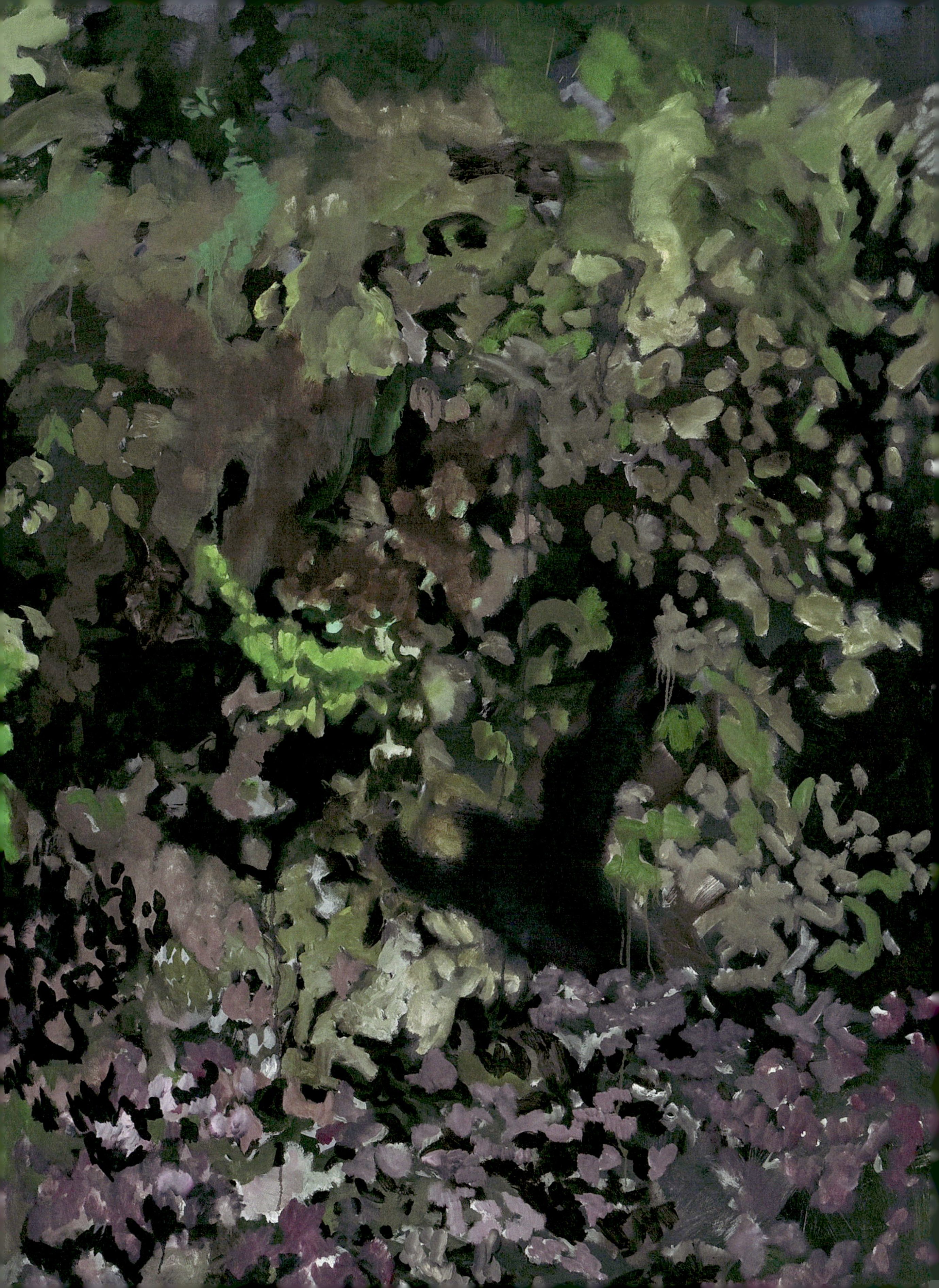

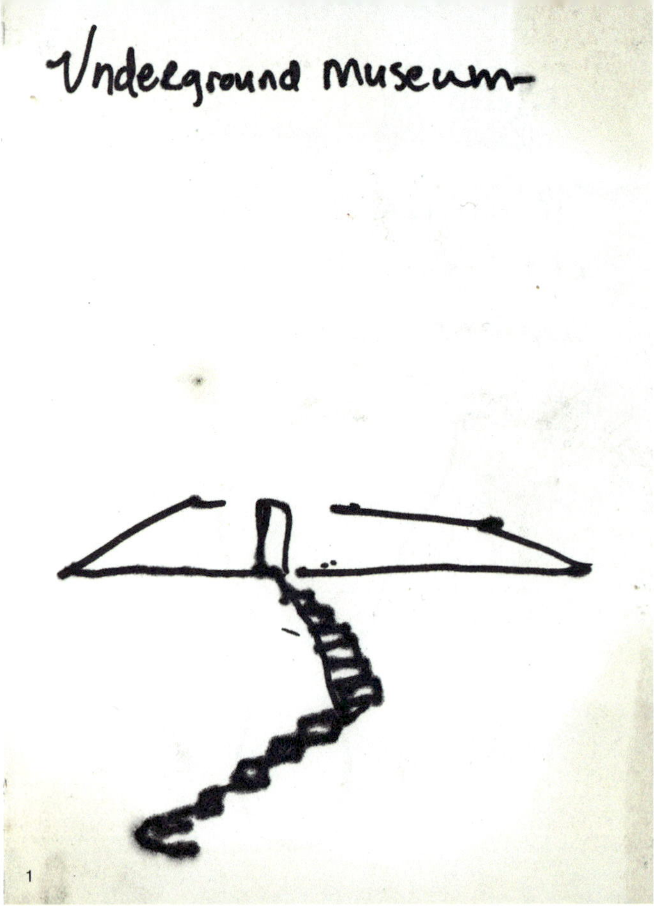

Undeground Museum

1

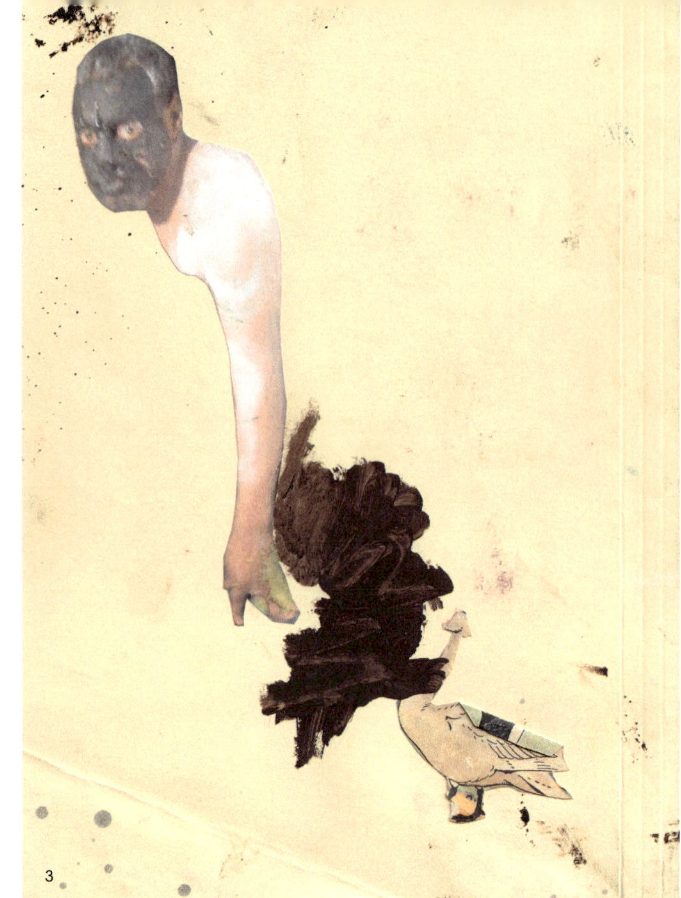

3

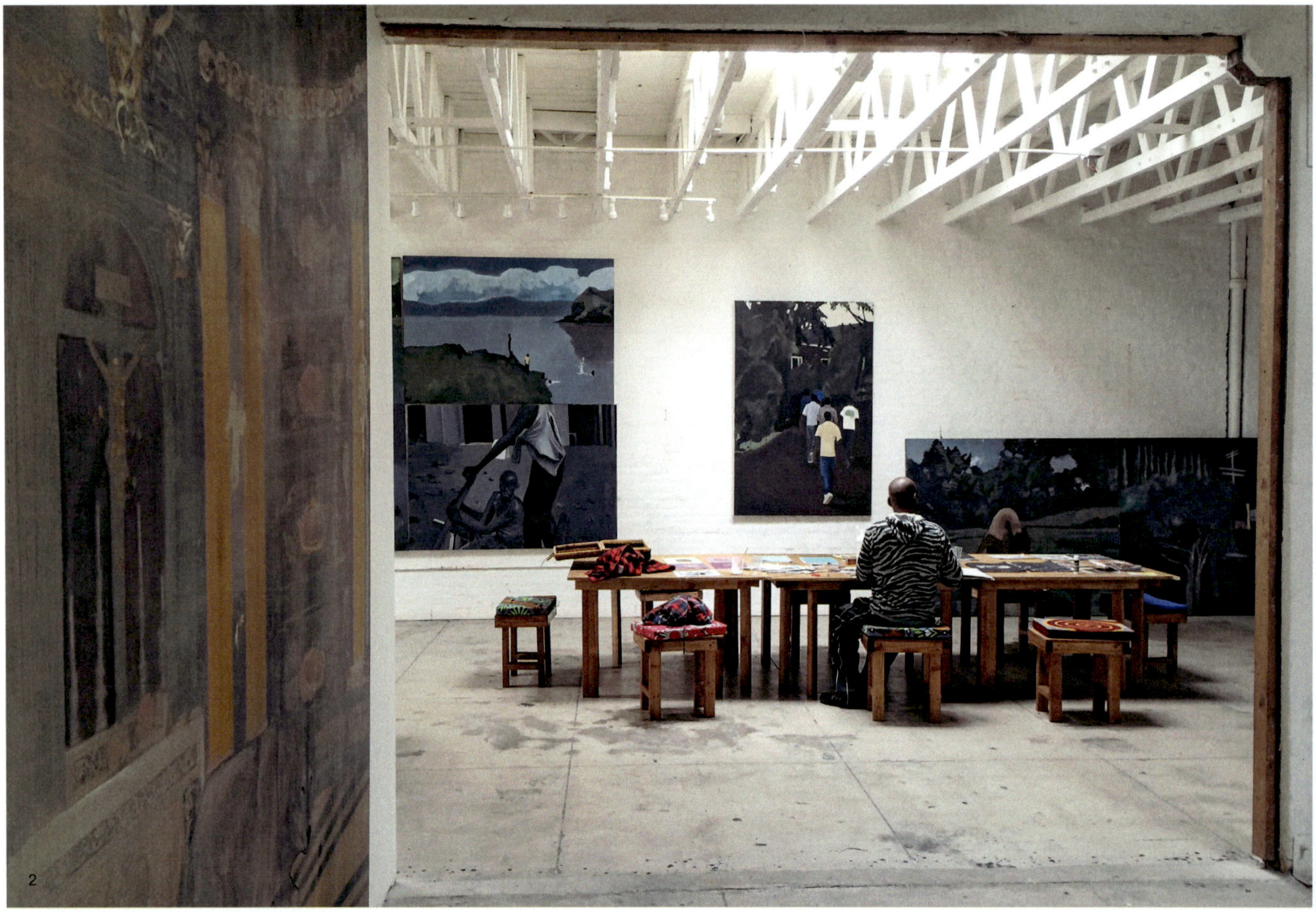

2

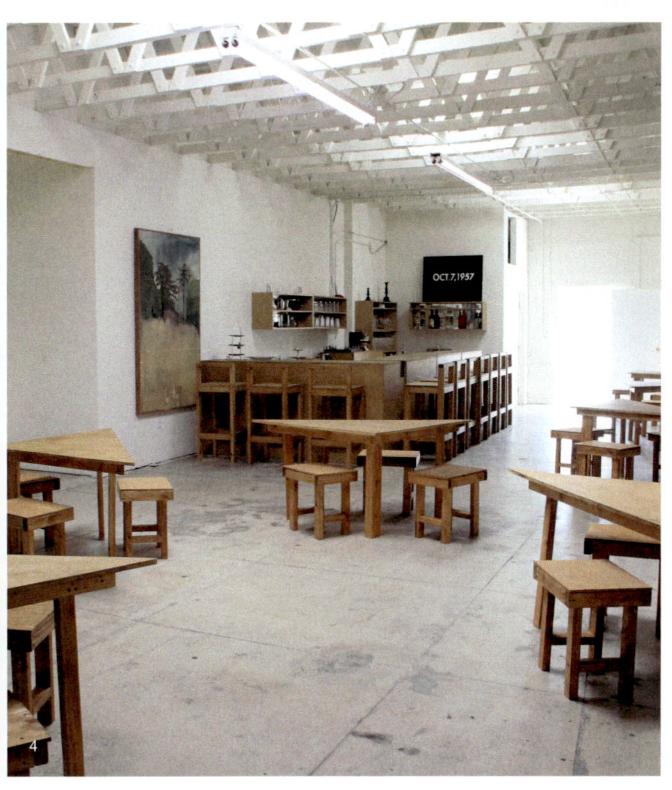

4

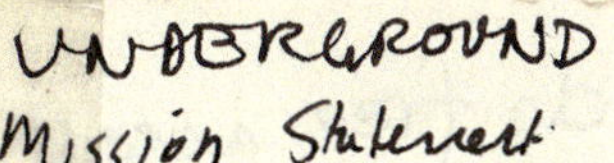
UNDERGROUND
Mission Statement

To exhibit world class art /
to a community that does not
have access to such resources.

5

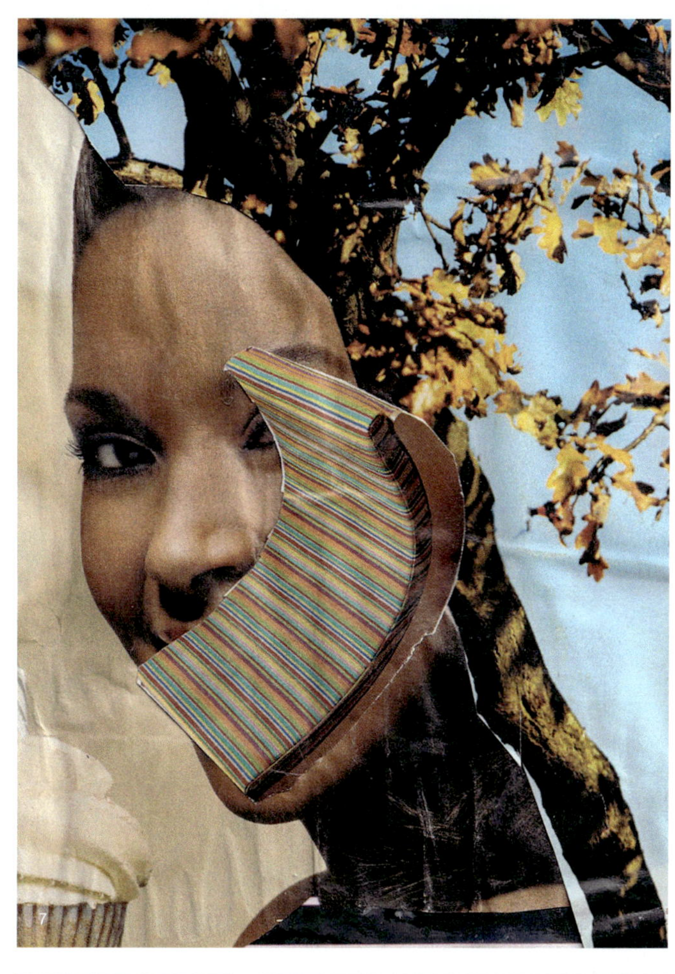

7

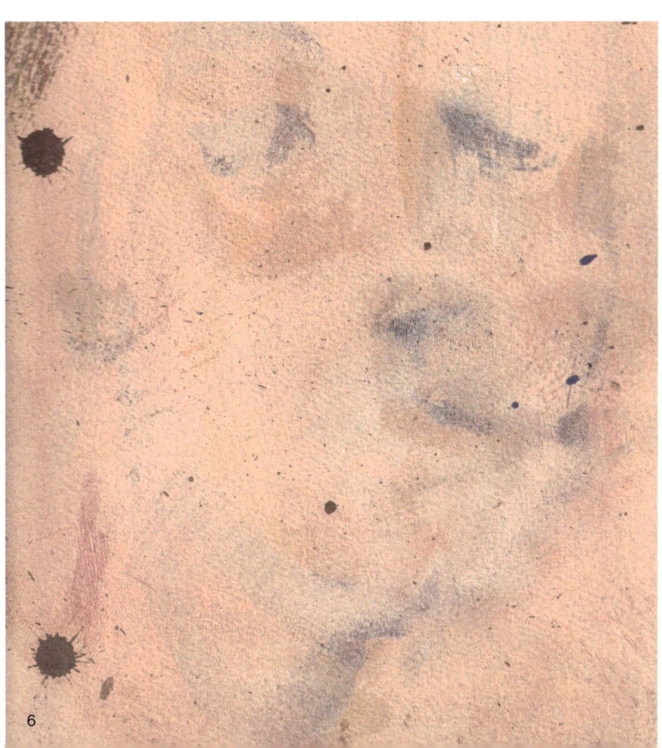

6

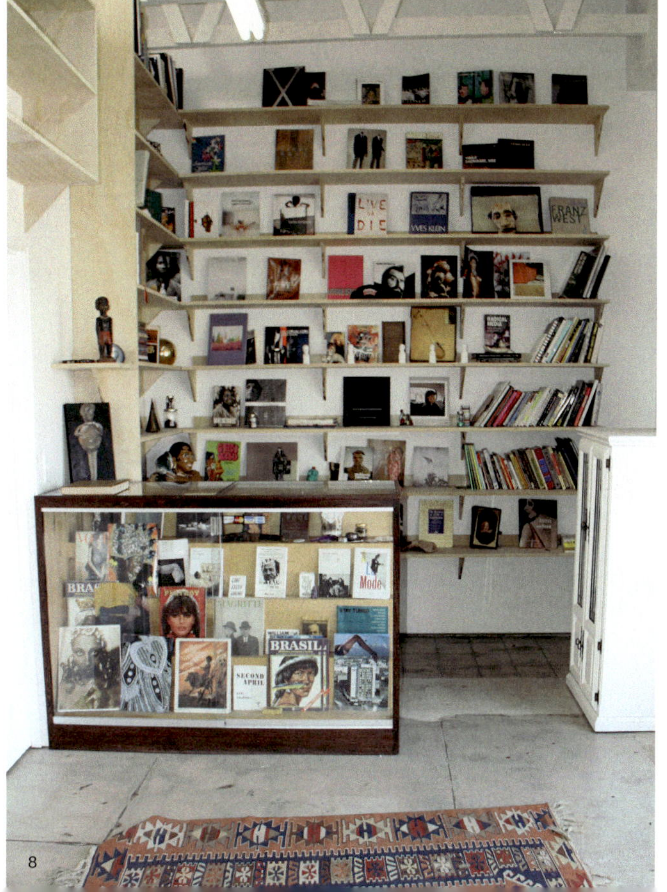

8

To provide free access to worldclass art ~~to~~ ~~communities~~ on ~~a~~ on a ~~in a~~ community ~~that~~ ~~is not ready available~~ level.

~~To provid free access~~ to ~~world-class art~~ ~~to a~~ ~~community based level~~ ~~to communities~~ to neighborhoods without museums.

To provide inner-city neighborhoods with free access to world-class art.

9

10

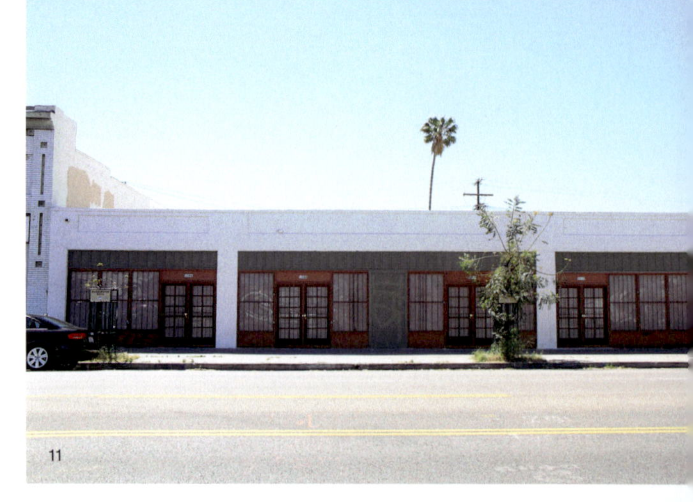

11

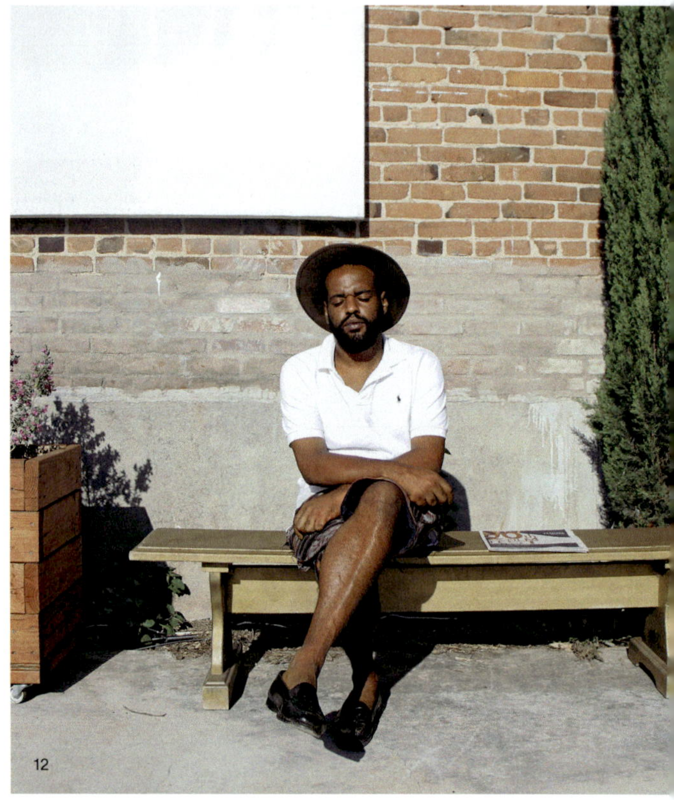

12

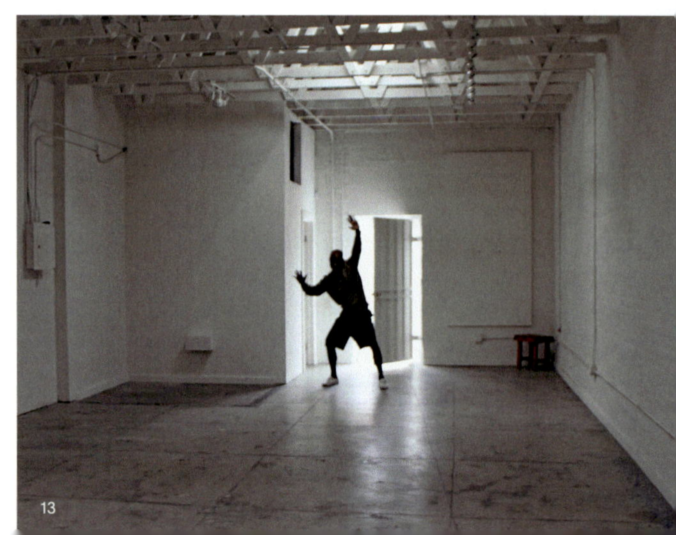

13

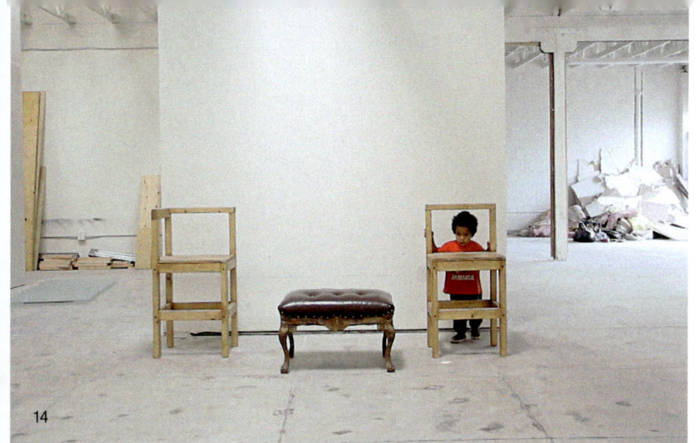

14

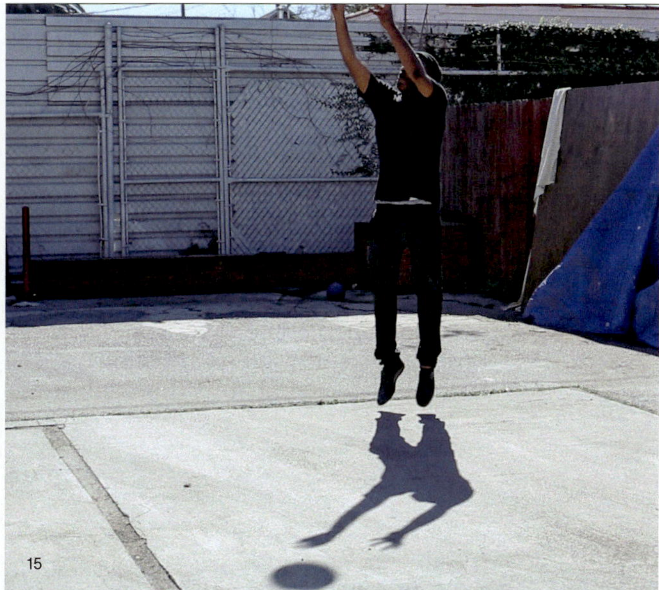

15

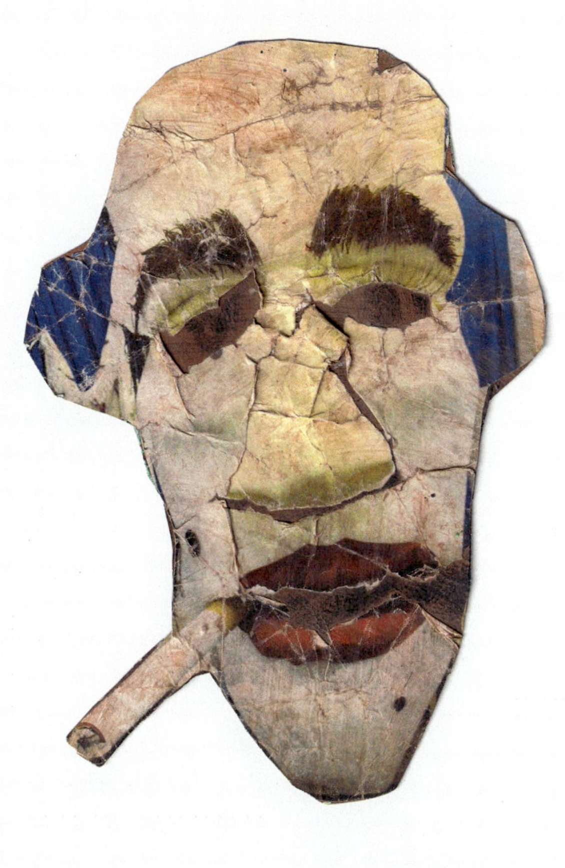

17

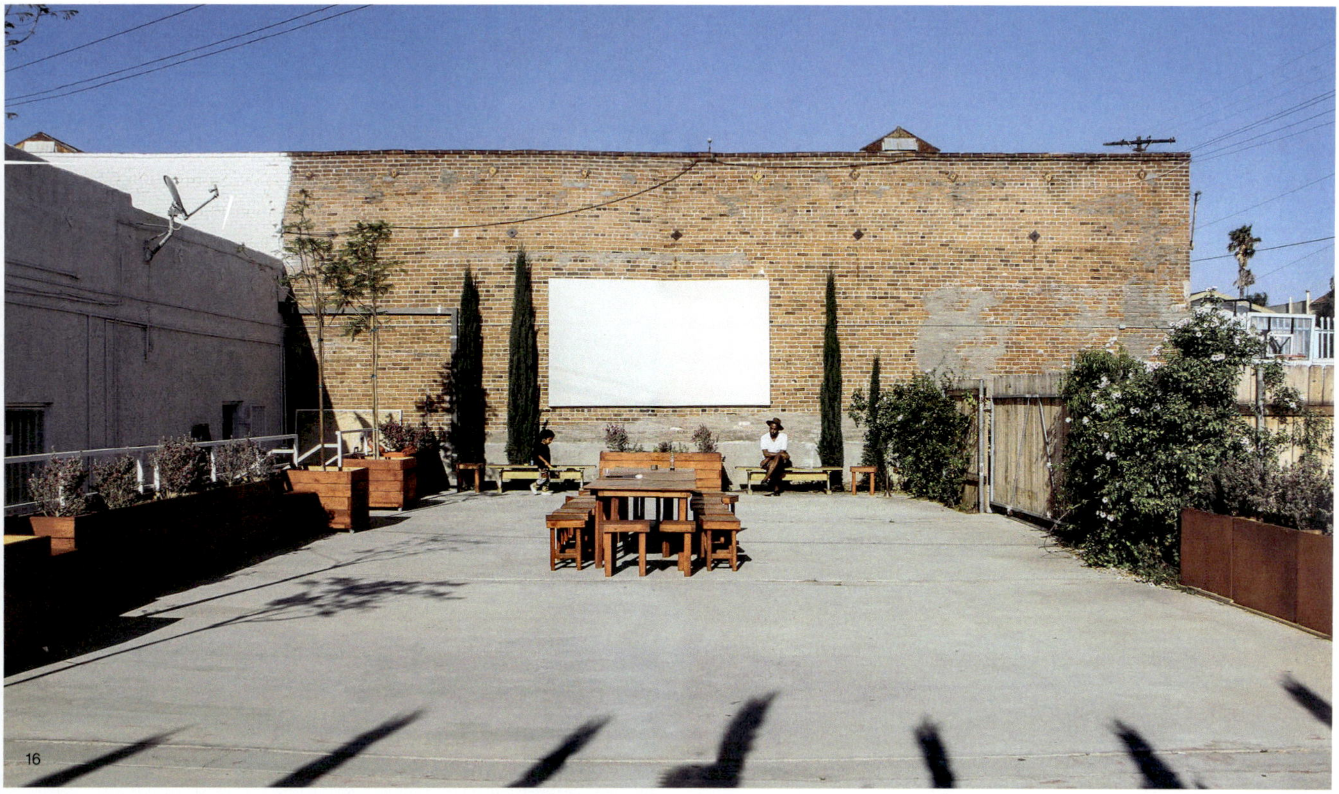

16

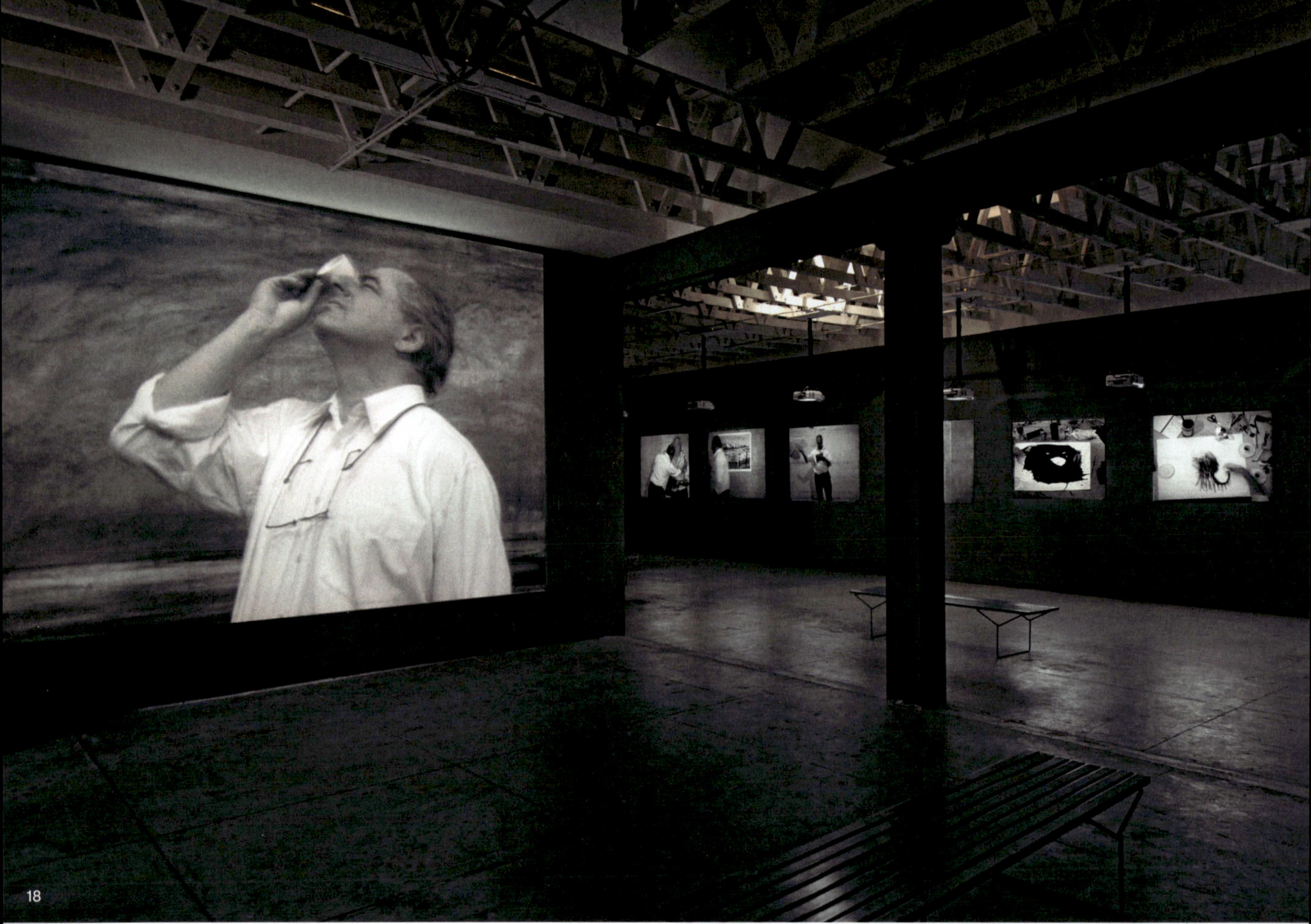

18

BRUSH
YO
TEETH

19

NOAH DAVIS

SEVENTY WORKS

20

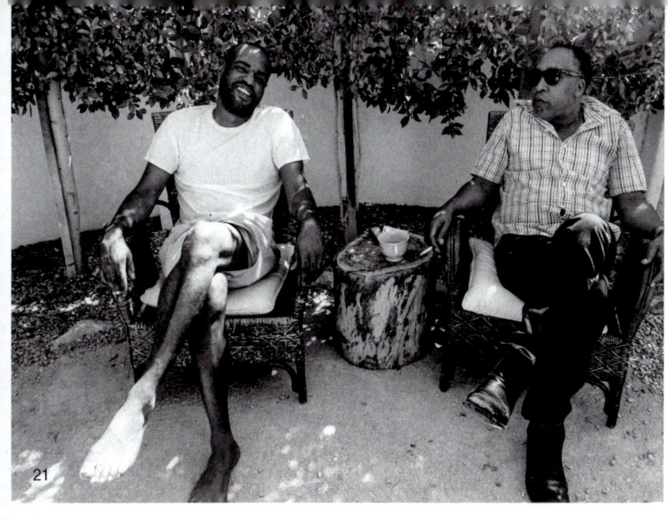

21

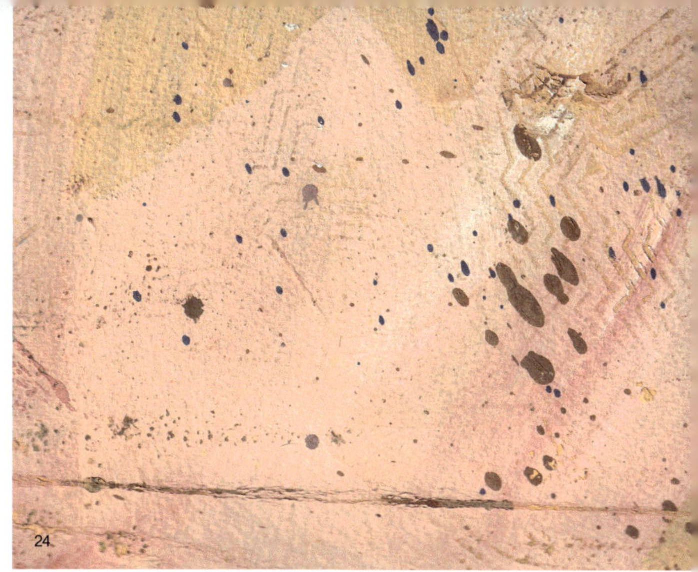

24

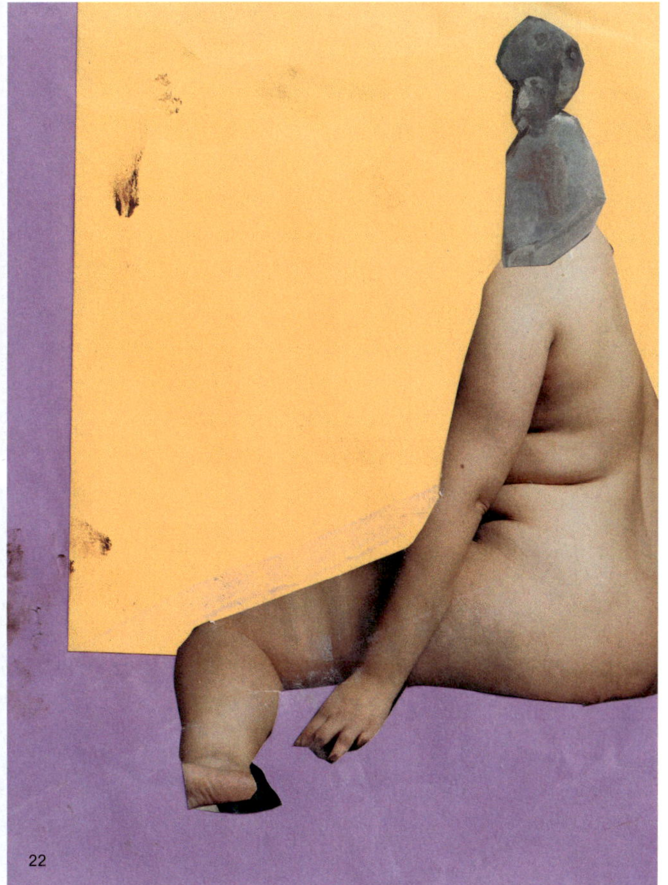

22

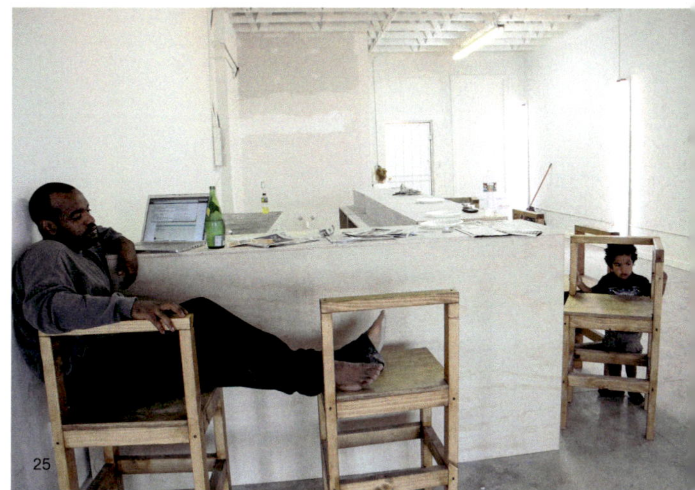

25

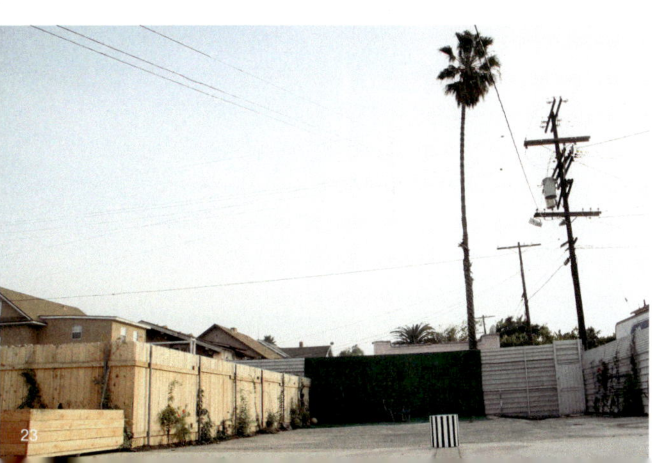

23

Why should anyone care?

what is your end game.

- Do you only want to be a painter forever. Do you make other. things.

  - Creating your own visual language.

Painters are asked to move beyond refrences, and. draw things that are created by themselves from start to finish.

- Whether that means film/photo/ still life. The documentation for a painting must be unique.

26

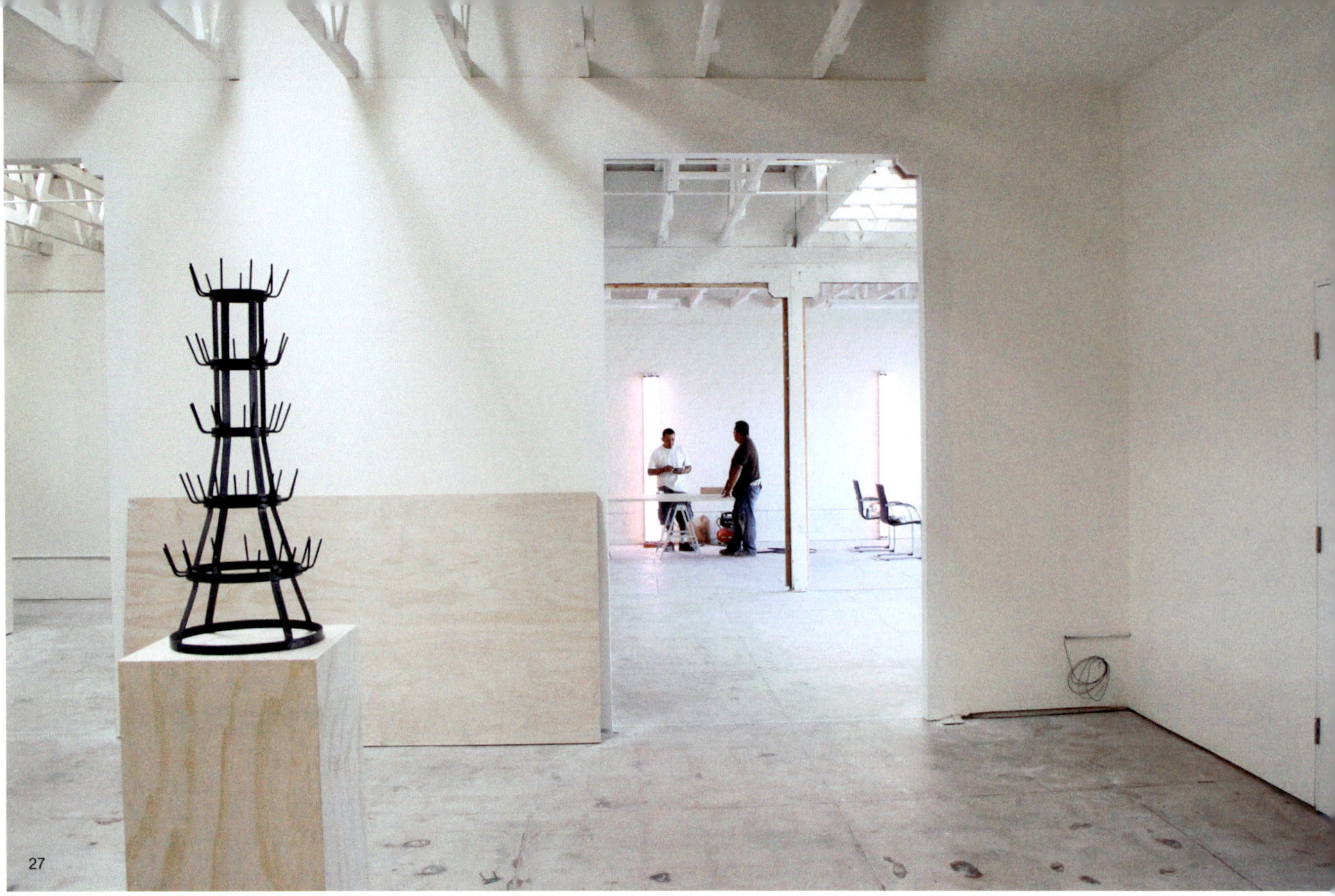

27

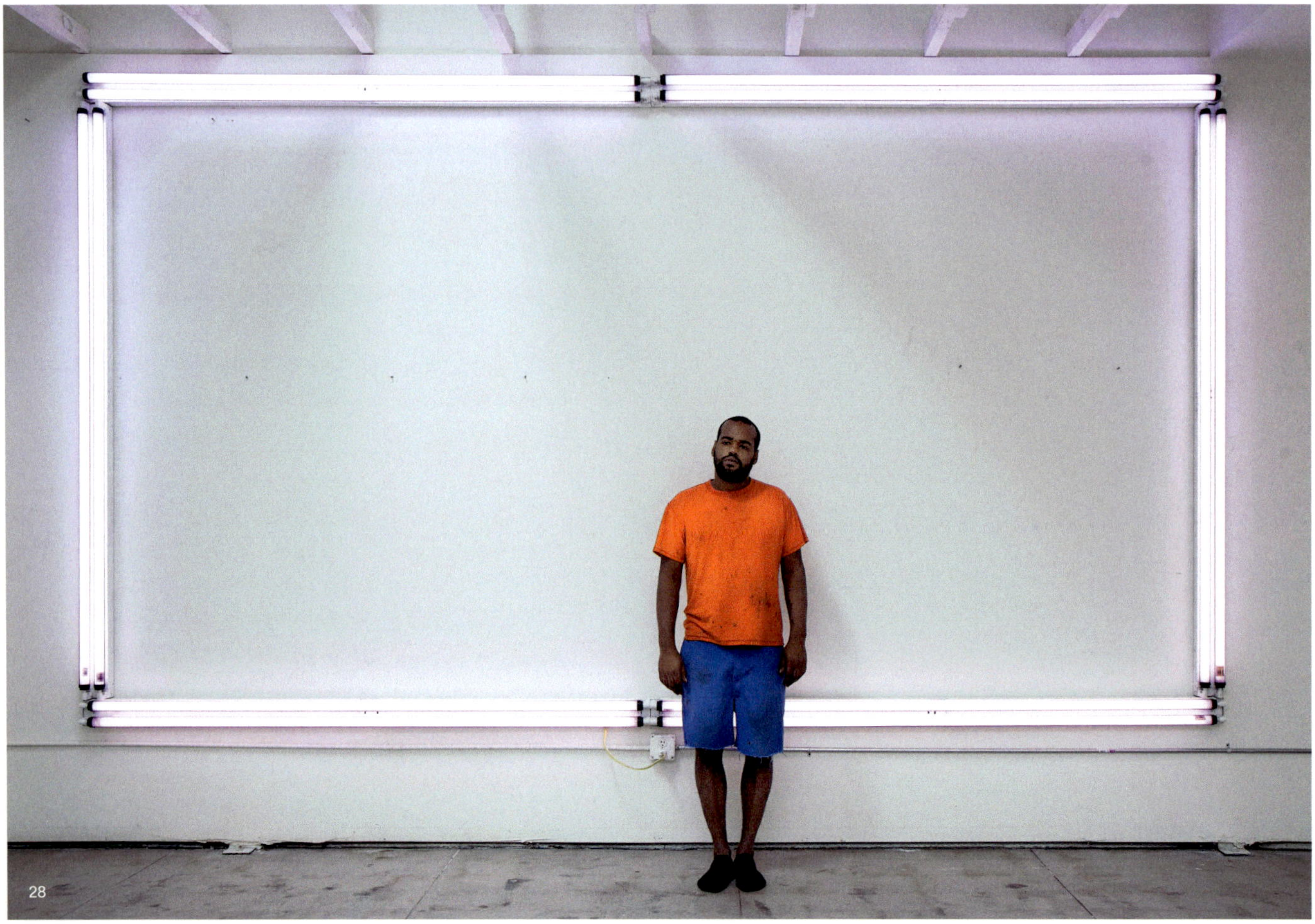

28

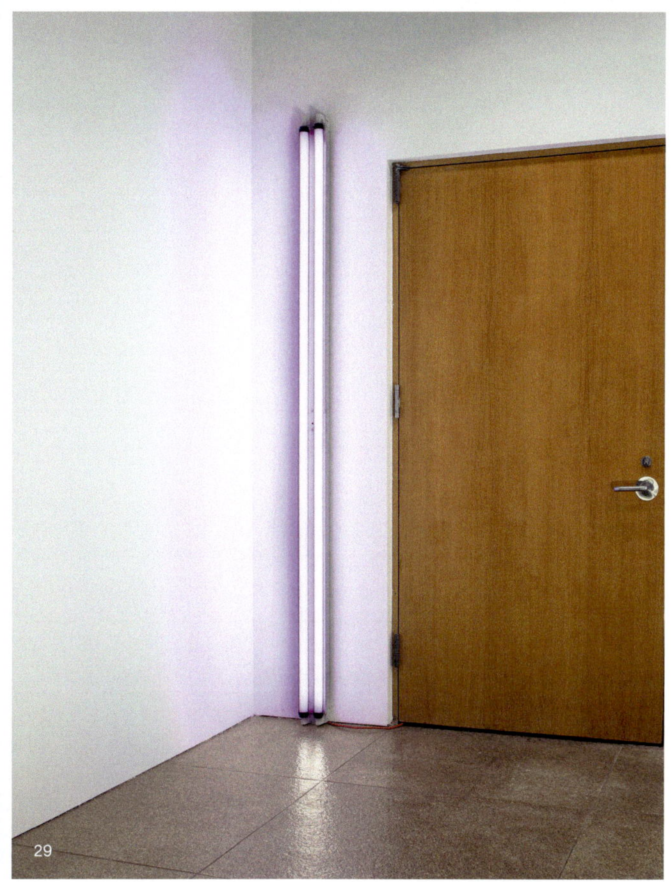

29

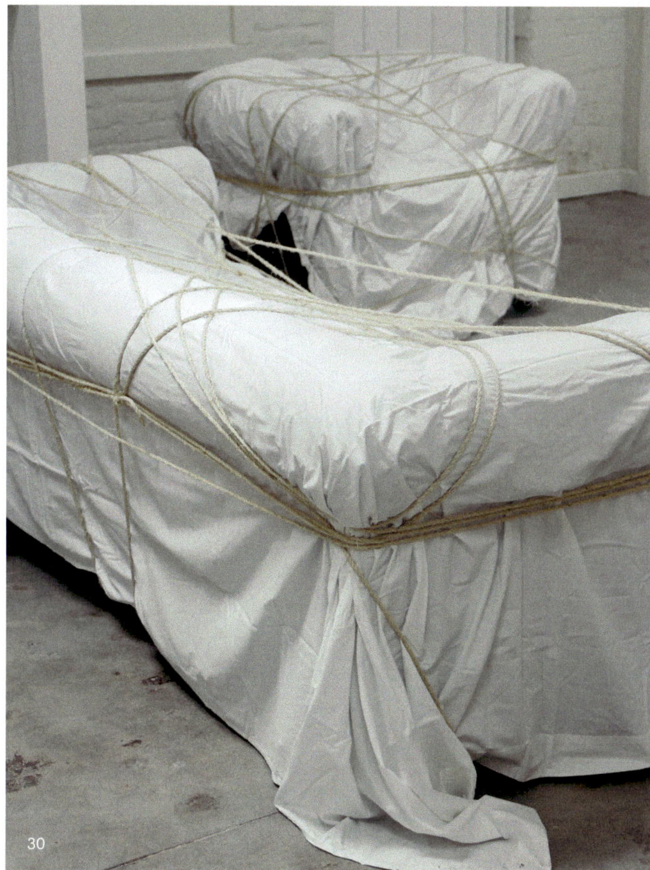

30

'*Imitation of Wealth* developed out of necessity. We had no money to put on a show, and no museum or galleries would lend us work. The Dan Flavin lights were the first. [Noah] saw these ugly fluorescent lights hanging in our space. At the time we were actually living there and building it out at the same time. He said, "What if we just use what we have like these ugly ass lights?" A light bulb literally went off in his head: "We can take these lights down and make our own Dan Flavin. We can show people you do not need to be a millionaire to enjoy these works, or even better, that you can create them yourself."

Noah was keen on working with the community and involving [locals] in his ideas. Two doors down, there is a vacuum repair shop, and he saw that they had vintage vacuums. He kept asking for the particular model used in the Jeff Koons piece. They couldn't find one. So I looked on Craigslist and found the exact one in the Valley for fifty bucks. The rest is history.'

Karon Davis as told to Tracey Jeanne Rosenthal, 'Imitation Suite', *Art Los Angeles Reader*, January 2016.

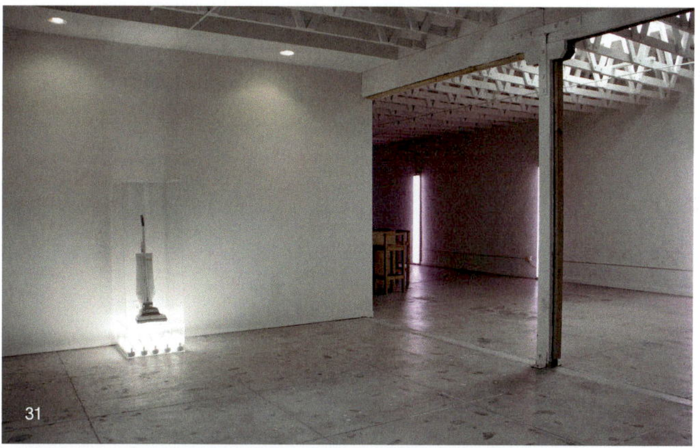

31

OCT.7,1957

32

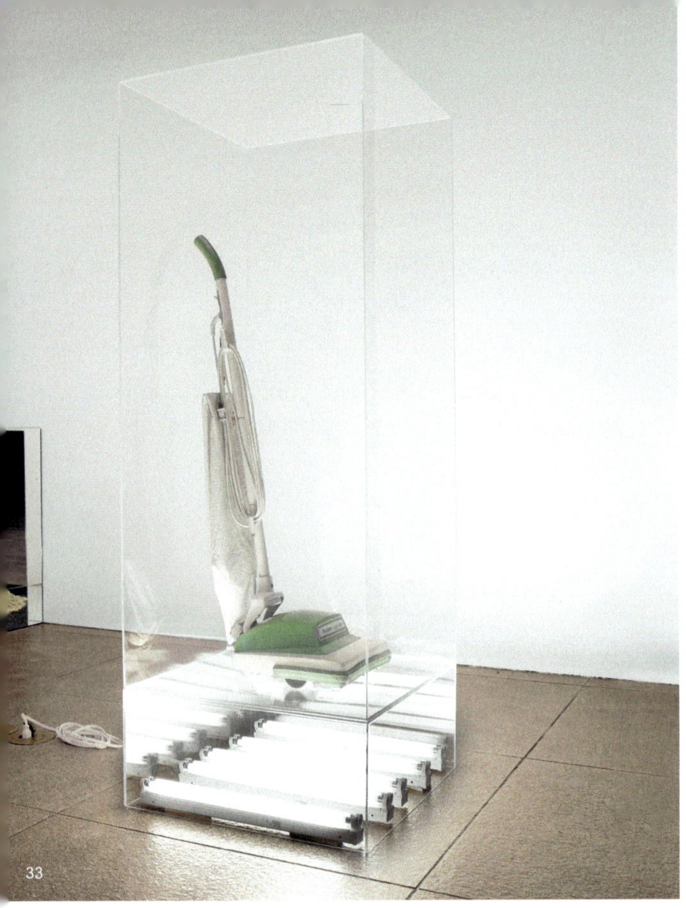
33

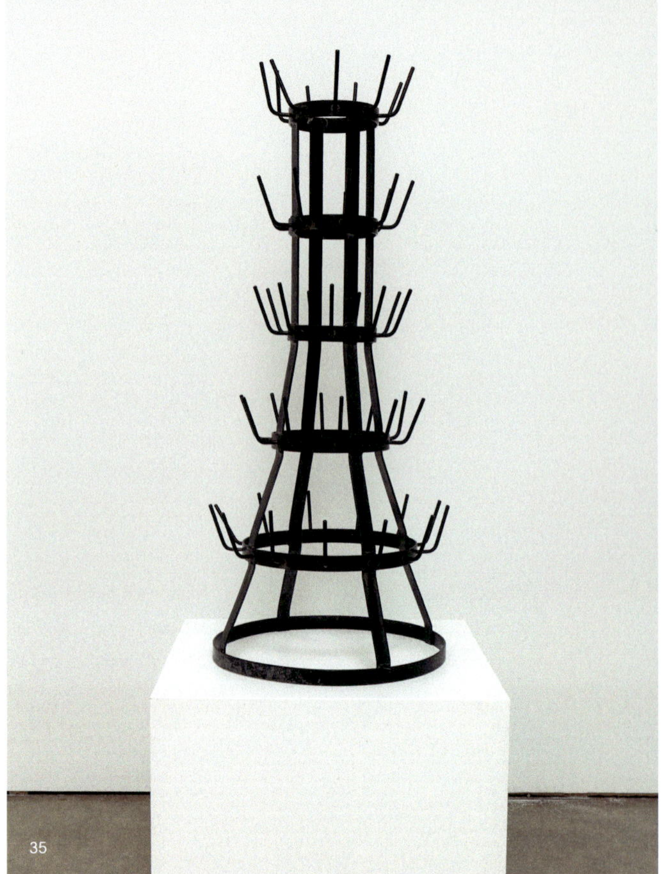
35

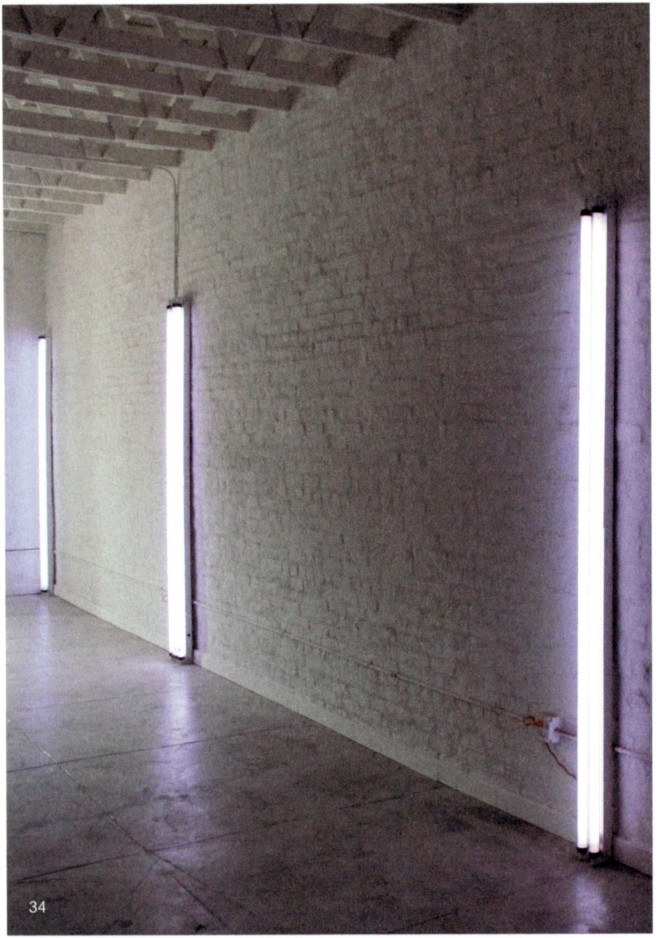
34

'Part of the critique of the *Imitation of Wealth* is a critique of museums, but it is also a critique of the art world in general. It demonstrates the fetishization of the avant-garde's impulse to broker a deal between art and life. Instead of brokering that deal on the side of life, we brokered that deal on the side of art. We did so by creating a condition of scarcity for art where there isn't one. You can go to the hardware store, buy sand and buy mirrors, and make a Robert Smithson. It's the museum and the market that have created the condition of scarcity around that object, meaning that the art world defaulted on the avant-garde's original arrangement, which was more on the side of life and the everyday, than it was on the side of art. For me, that's part of the extraordinariness of Noah's gesture.'

Helen Molesworth as told to Tracey Jeanne Rosenthal, 'Imitation Suite', *Art Los Angeles Reader*, January 2016, on the occasion of the presentation of *Imitation of Wealth* at MOCA's *storefront* in 2015–16 (quote edited by Molesworth, June 2024). *Imitation of Wealth* was originally shown at the Underground Museum in 2013.

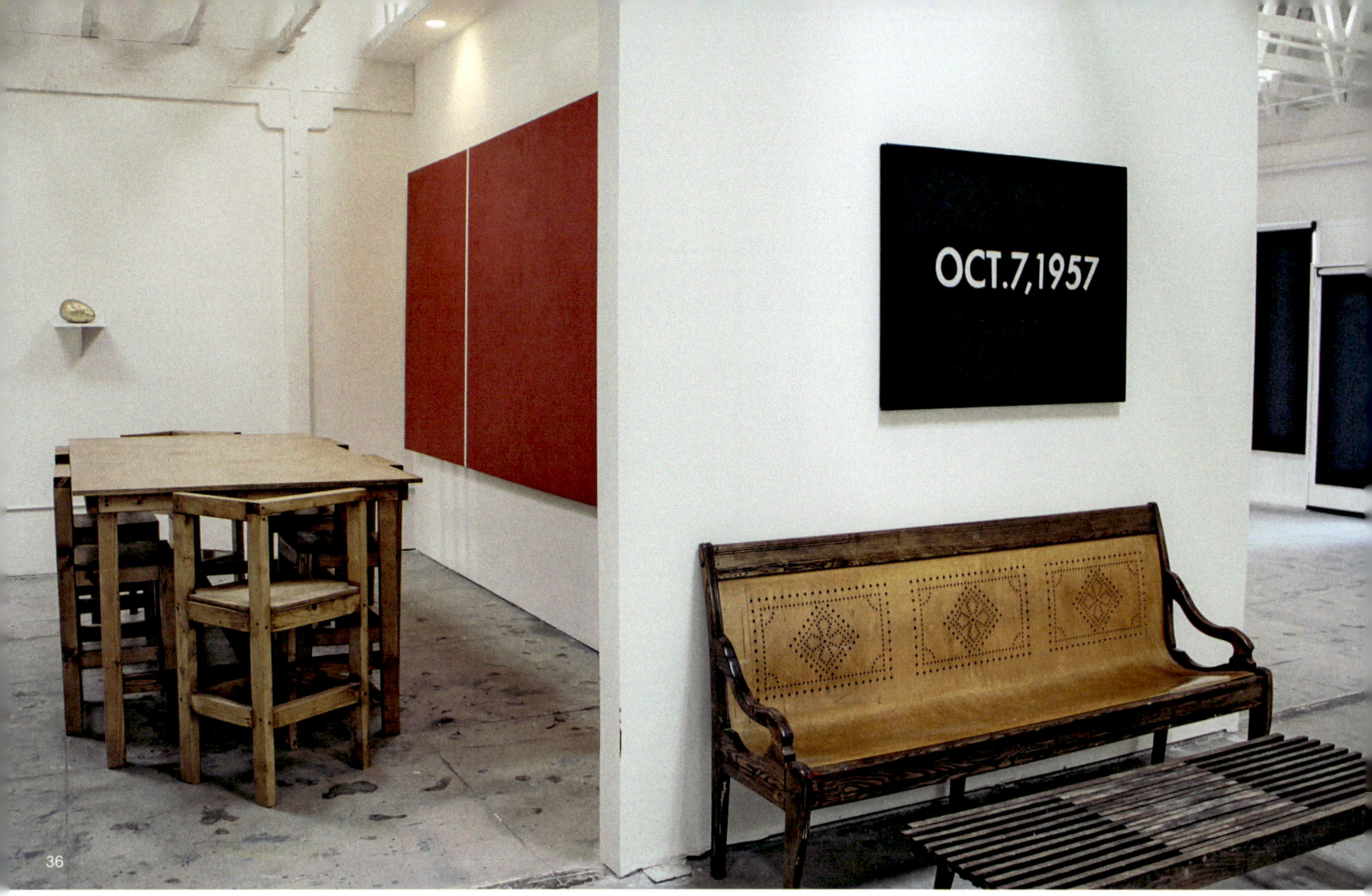

36

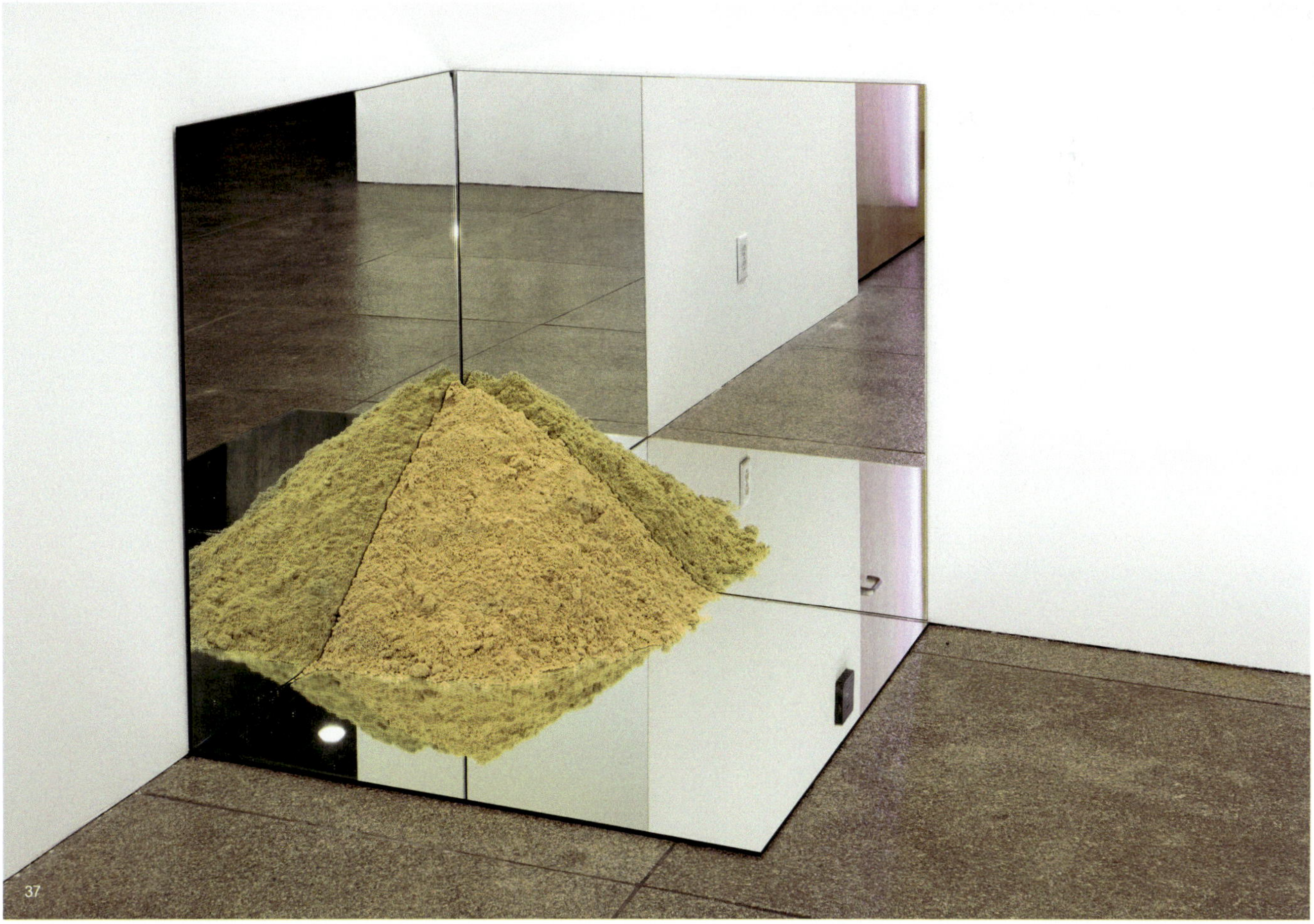

37

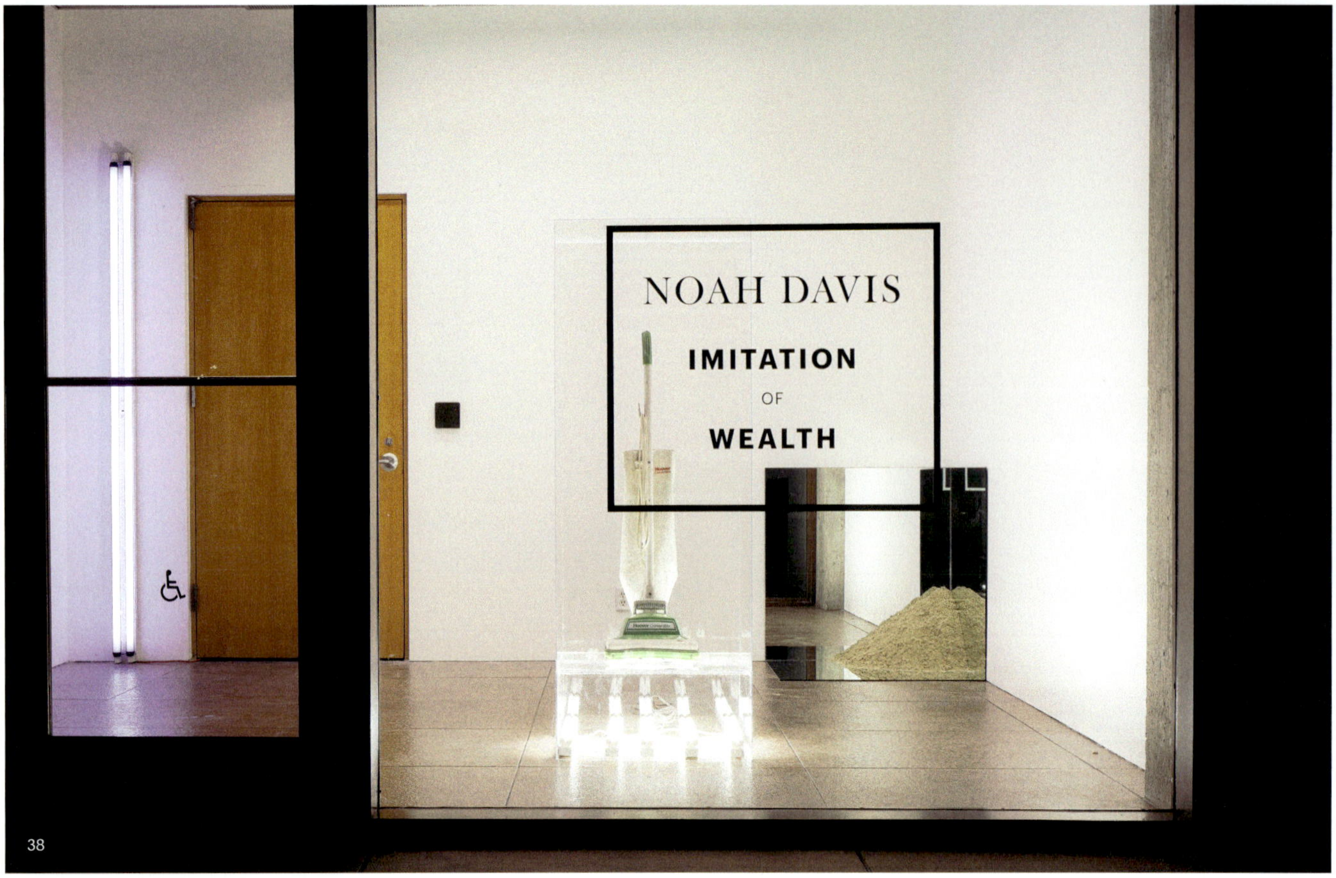

38

39

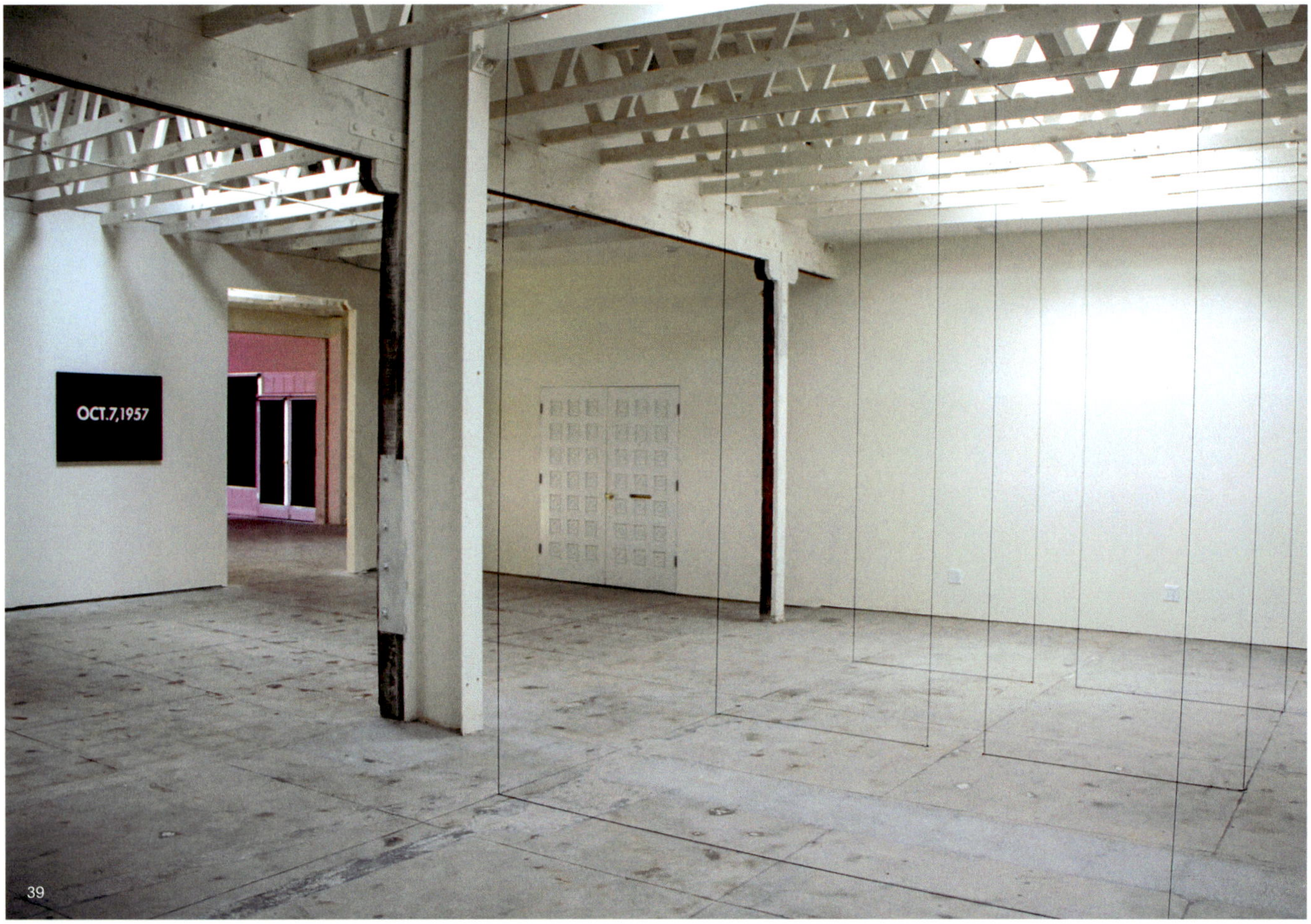

1 Notebook page, 2014
2 Davis at the Underground Museum, 2014
3 *Untitled*, 2013, mixed media on paper, 29.9 × 24.1 cm (11¾ × 9½ in)
4 The Underground Museum's bar, inspired by Donald Judd, 2013
5 Notebook page, 2014
6 *Untitled* (detail), 2015, mixed media on paper, 30.5 × 22.9 cm (12 × 9 in)
7 *Untitled*, 2014, mixed media on paper
8 The Underground Museum's lending library, 2012
9 Notebook page, 2014
10 *Untitled* (detail), 2015, mixed media on paper, 32.1 × 23.2 cm (12⅝ × 9⅛ in)
11 Exterior of the Underground Museum, 2012
12 Davis at the Underground Museum, 2012
13 Davis at the Underground Museum, 2012
14 Moses Davis at the Underground Museum, 2012
15 Still from *Untitled, in Process: A Documentary of Noah Davis*, 2016, directed by Nicole Otero, produced by Kahlil Joseph
16 Noah and Moses in the Underground Museum's Purple Garden, 2012
17 *Untitled*, 2009, mixed media on paper, 26.4 × 19.1 cm (10⅜ × 7½ in)
18 Installation view, *William Kentridge: Journey to the Moon*, the Underground Museum, 2015
19 Notebook page, c. 2010–14
20 *Noah Davis: Seventy Works* (Los Angeles: The Underground Museum, co-published with Omid Fatemi, 2014)
21 Davis and Henry Taylor, Palm Springs, 2014
22 *Untitled*, 2015, mixed media on paper, 30.2 × 22.9 cm (11⅞ × 9 in)
23 Parking lot at the Underground Museum before it was transformed into the Purple Garden, 2012
24 *Untitled* (detail), 2015, mixed media on paper, 31.8 × 23.5 cm (12½ × 9¼ in)
25 Noah and Moses at the Underground Museum, 2012
26 Notebook page, c. 2010–14
27 Installation view, *Imitation of Wealth*, the Underground Museum, 2013
28 Davis in front of *Imitation of Dan Flavin*, 2013, the Underground Museum, c. 2012
29 *Imitation of Dan Flavin*, 2013; installation view, *storefront: Noah Davis: Imitation of Wealth*, MOCA Grand Avenue, 2015–16
30 *Imitation of Christo*, 2013; installation view, *Imitation of Wealth*, the Underground Museum, 2013
31 Installation view, *Imitation of Wealth*, the Underground Museum, 2013
32 *Imitation of On Kawara*, 2013
33 *Imitation of Jeff Koons*, 2013; installation view, *storefront: Noah Davis: Imitation of Wealth*, MOCA Grand Avenue, 2015–16
34 *Imitation of Dan Flavin*, 2013; installation view, *Imitation of Wealth*, the Underground Museum, 2013
35 *Imitation of Marcel Duchamp*, 2013
36 Installation view, *Imitation of Wealth*, the Underground Museum, 2013
37 *Imitation of Robert Smithson*, 2013; installation view, *storefront: Noah Davis: Imitation of Wealth*, MOCA Grand Avenue, 2015–16
38 Installation view, *storefront: Noah Davis: Imitation of Wealth*, MOCA Grand Avenue, 2015–16
39 Installation view, *Imitation of Wealth*, the Underground Museum, 2013

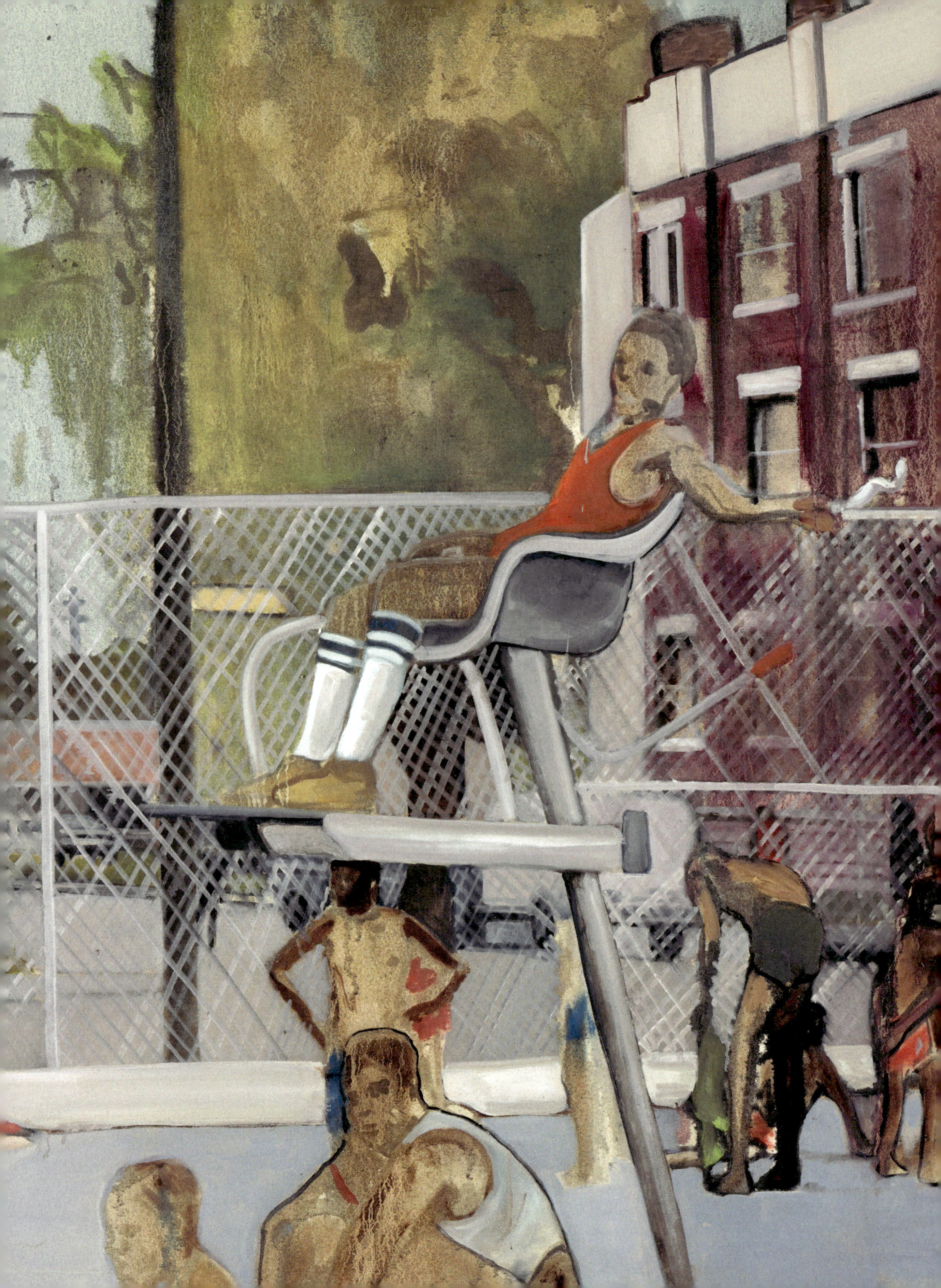

DAWOUD BEY on *1975*, 2013

I first saw Noah Davis's paintings in 2016, at Stony Island Arts Bank in Chicago, where I currently live. The paintings were from his series *1975*, which was inspired by photographs that his mother, Faith Childs-Davis, had taken while she was a high school student on the South Side of Chicago. Forty years later, her undeveloped rolls of film were found by Davis's brother, Kahlil Joseph, at their father Keven Davis's apartment in Harlem shortly after his death. Davis re-imagined his mother's photographs in his *1975* paintings, materially transforming the photographic colours into a palette that does not naturally exist in the known world.

Beyond the paintings themselves, I was struck by the series title, which immediately resonated, as 1975 was when I first began to travel from my home in Jamaica, Queens, to the streets of Harlem, making photographs inspired by my family's history in that storied community. Similarly, Davis, who grew up in Seattle, seemed to be painting his mother's photographs as an act of historical retrieval and a process of self-immersion into her history on the South Side of Chicago. The intertwining narratives of these Black cultural centres and the work that came from two young artist sons who connected with (but never lived in) these mythic urban spaces are what I want to briefly examine here.

Much has been written about the roles that Chicago and New York played in the formation and nurturing of Black creative expression in the early decades of the twentieth century. Bronzeville on Chicago's South Side and the main thoroughfares of 47th and 125th Street in Harlem were major centres of art and music, with clubs and theatres showcasing the most famous Black performers of the day. Each community also had their renowned poets-in-residence: Gwendolyn Brooks on Chicago's South Side and Langston Hughes on 127th Street in Harlem.

But by the time Childs-Davis and I had both started making photographs, the South Side and Harlem had become very different neighbourhoods from what they had been a few decades earlier, with communities decimated by social and economic neglect, and the dysfunctions this gave rise to. Childs-Davis alludes to this decline when she recounts, 'The one photography class that I took in my senior year at South Shore High School is probably the one class that saved my life. While my peers were dodging drug dealers and stray bullets, I was the lucky and proud owner of a 35mm.'[1] This deterioration is little evidenced in either of our early work, since we were both using our cameras to document the features of these Black spaces that held our particular interests, which did not include their degradation or social decay. I was searching for the Harlem that exuded aspects of its once-celebrated past, while Childs-Davis was capturing the vibrant lives of those around her, as represented in Noah's paintings *1975 (8)* and *1975 (9)* (both 2013) (pp. 158–59). Like Davis could only observe his mother's young experiences of her community through her photographs, I could not travel back to the time of my parents' life in Harlem. But with a camera, I could visualise aspects of its present informed by my sense of its lingering past.

Davis's connection to community was a major element of his practice beyond his paintings. In 2012, he co-founded the Underground Museum (UM) with his wife, the artist Karon Davis, in Arlington Heights, a historically working-class Black and Latinx neighbourhood in Los Angeles. This ambitious space was conceived to make 'museum-quality' art accessible to its immediate community (which was not unlike the troubled community his mother encountered in Chicago almost forty years prior). The UM succeeded in its mission, with exhibitions and events that fostered both a thriving artistic life and a renewed cultural vitality in a socially marginalised neighbourhood.

In his *1975* paintings, Noah Davis made art that engaged with his mother's past while he worked with his family to reshape a different kind of reality in the present. This is what gave his work such a deeply personal impetus along with its real social urgency. In so doing, he made clear, as a young artist, the profound role that family history can play in the shaping of a vision that is at once familial, aesthetic and communal in its implications.

1 '1975 Paintings', mutualart.com/Exhibition/1975-Paintings/A6CD57448EBF0900.

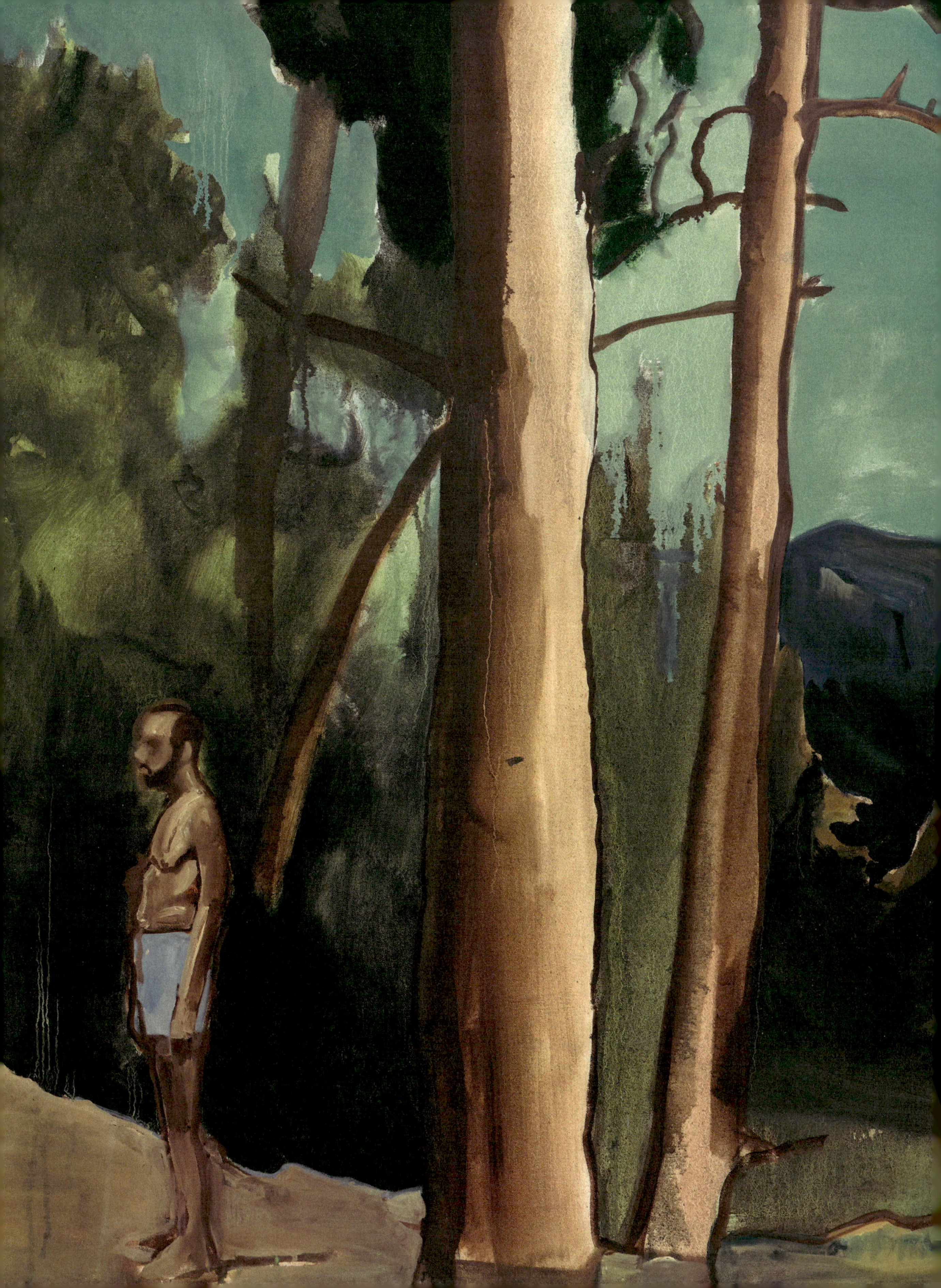

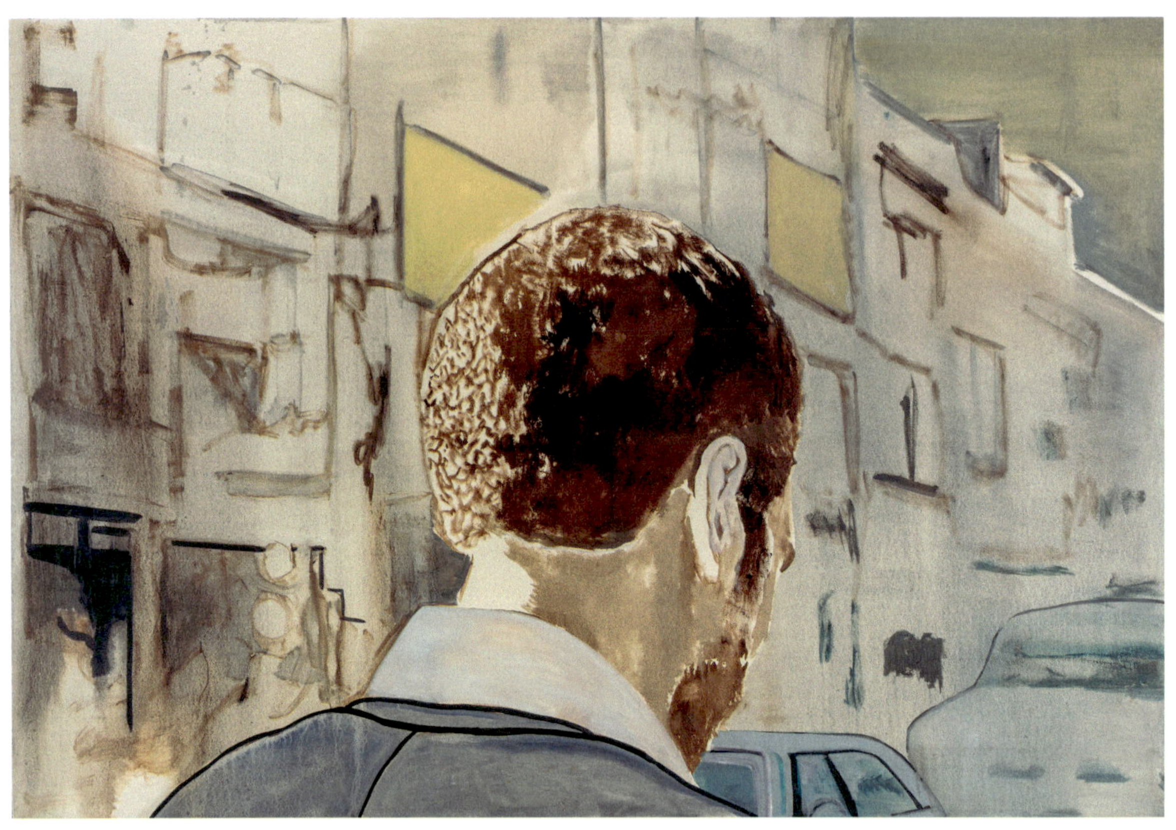

1975 (1), 2013

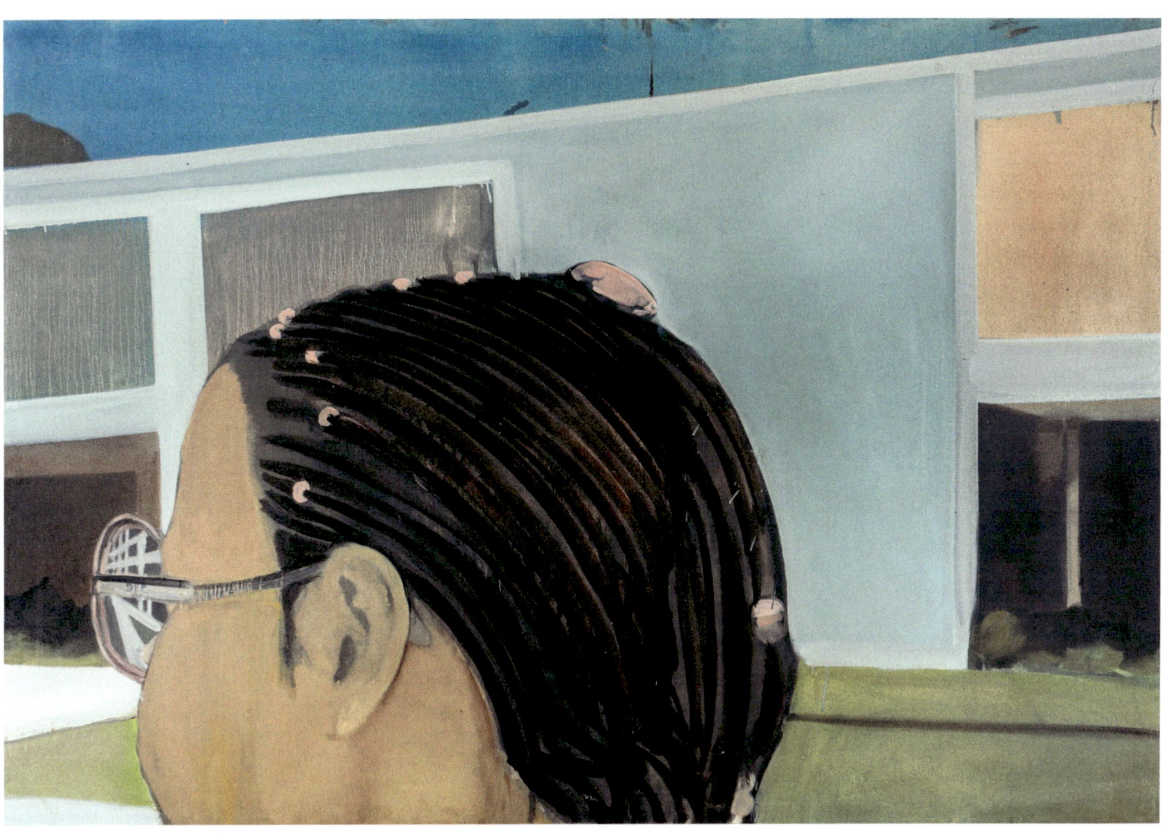

 1975 (2), 2013

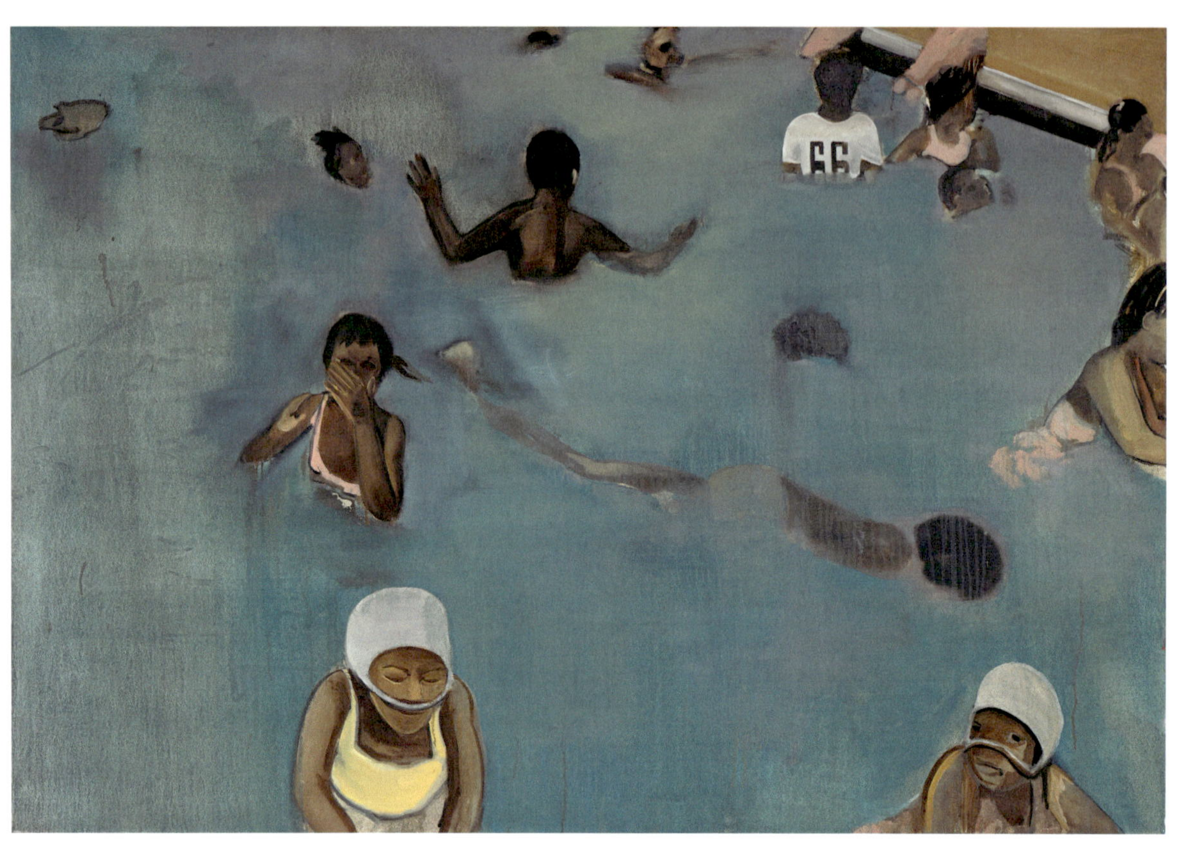

1975 (3), 2013

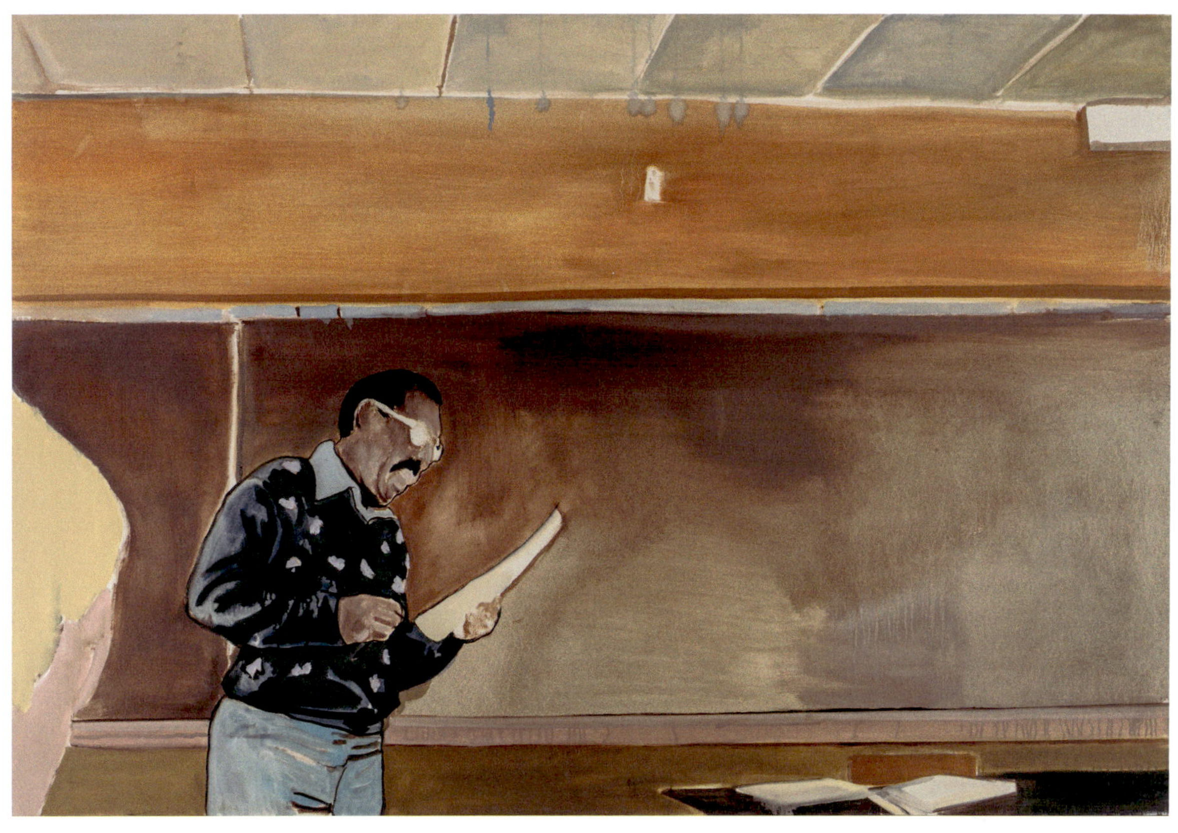

 1975 (4), 2013

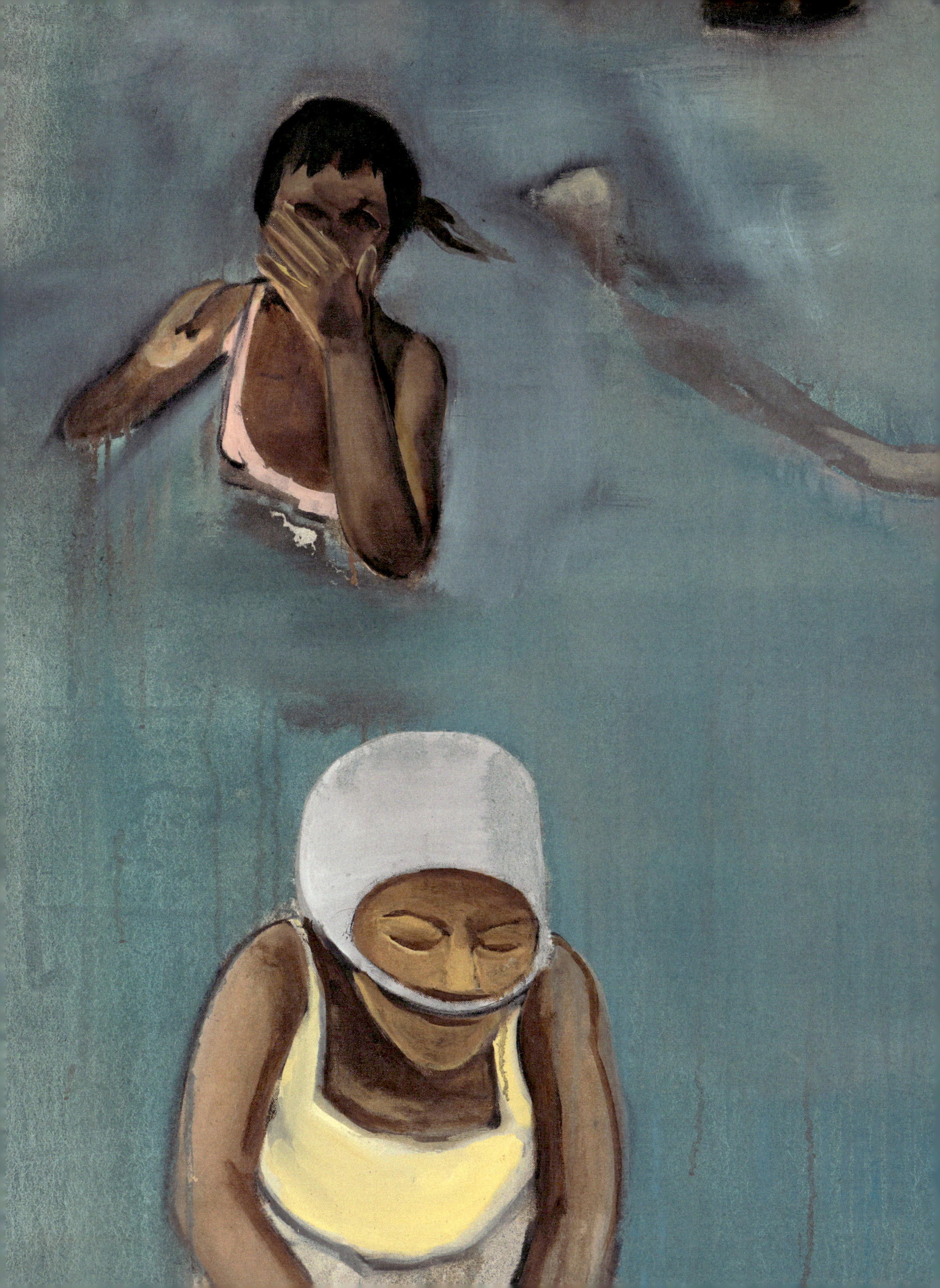

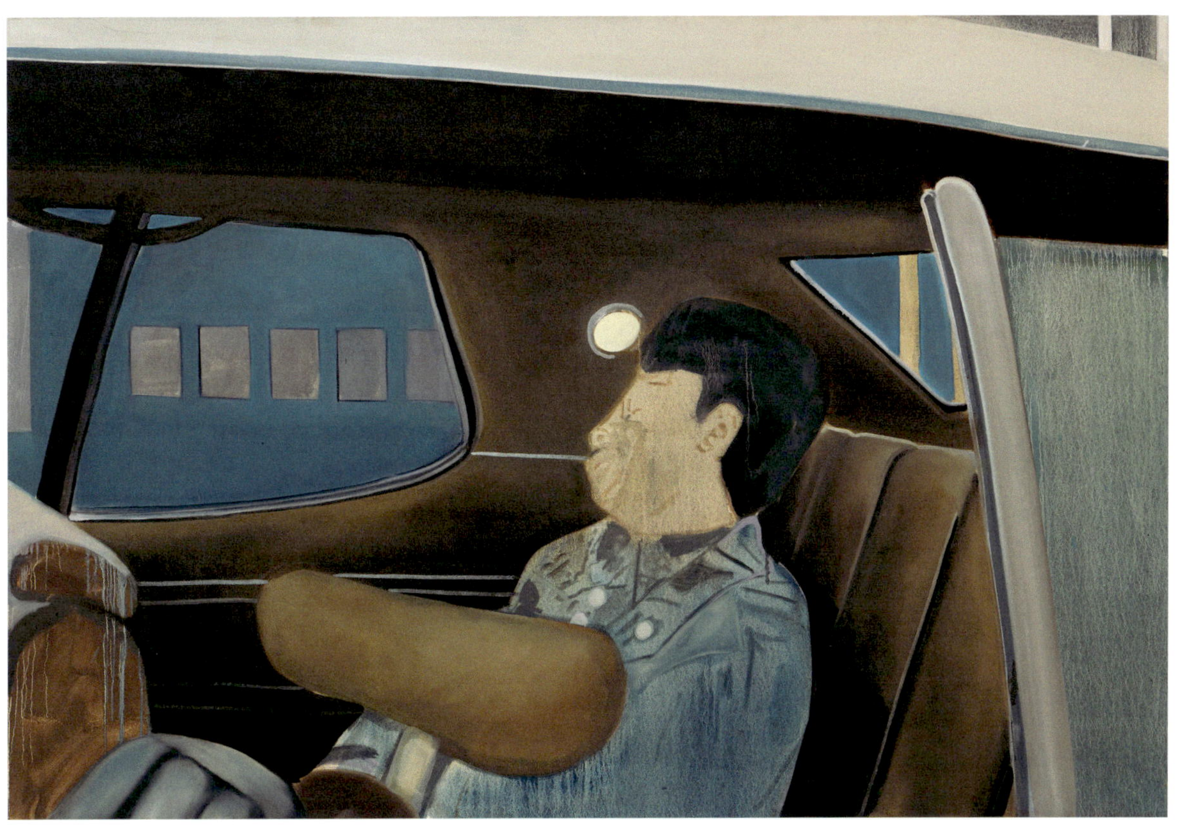

 1975 (5), 2013

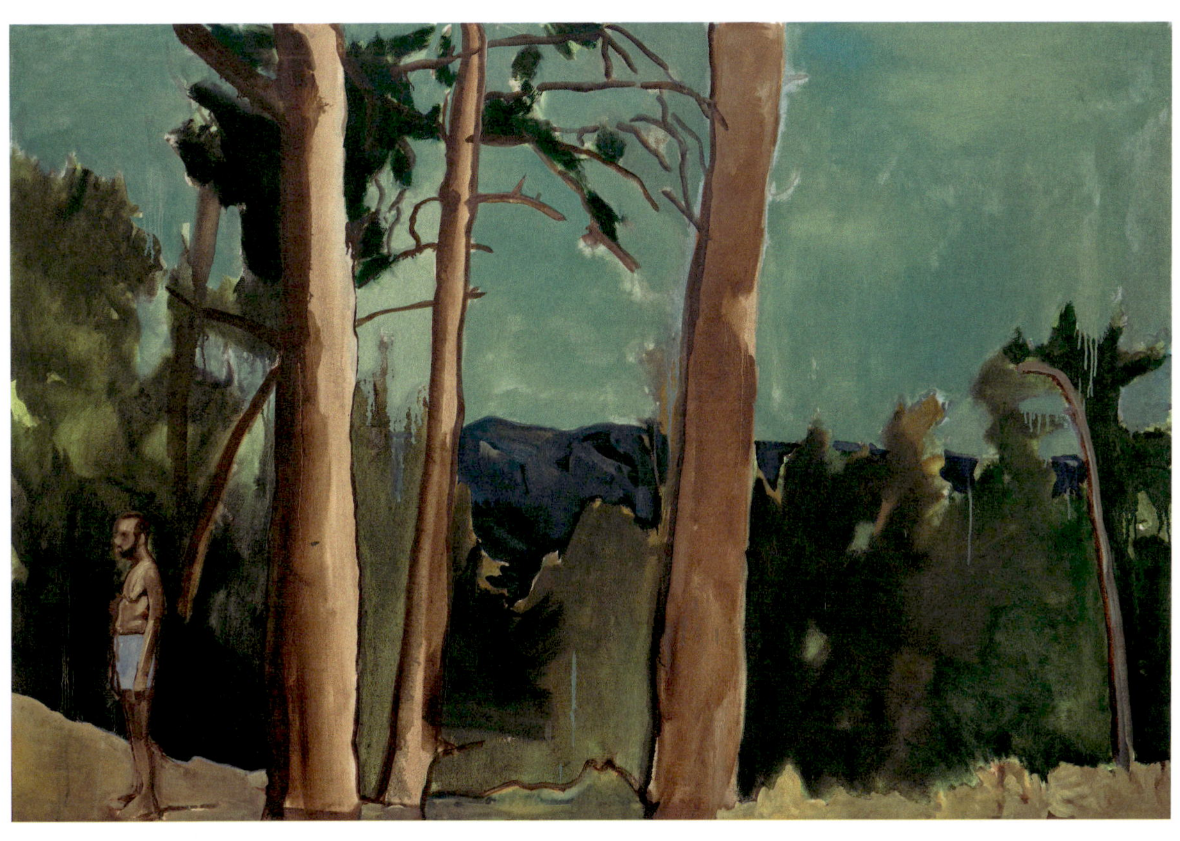

 1975 (7), 2013

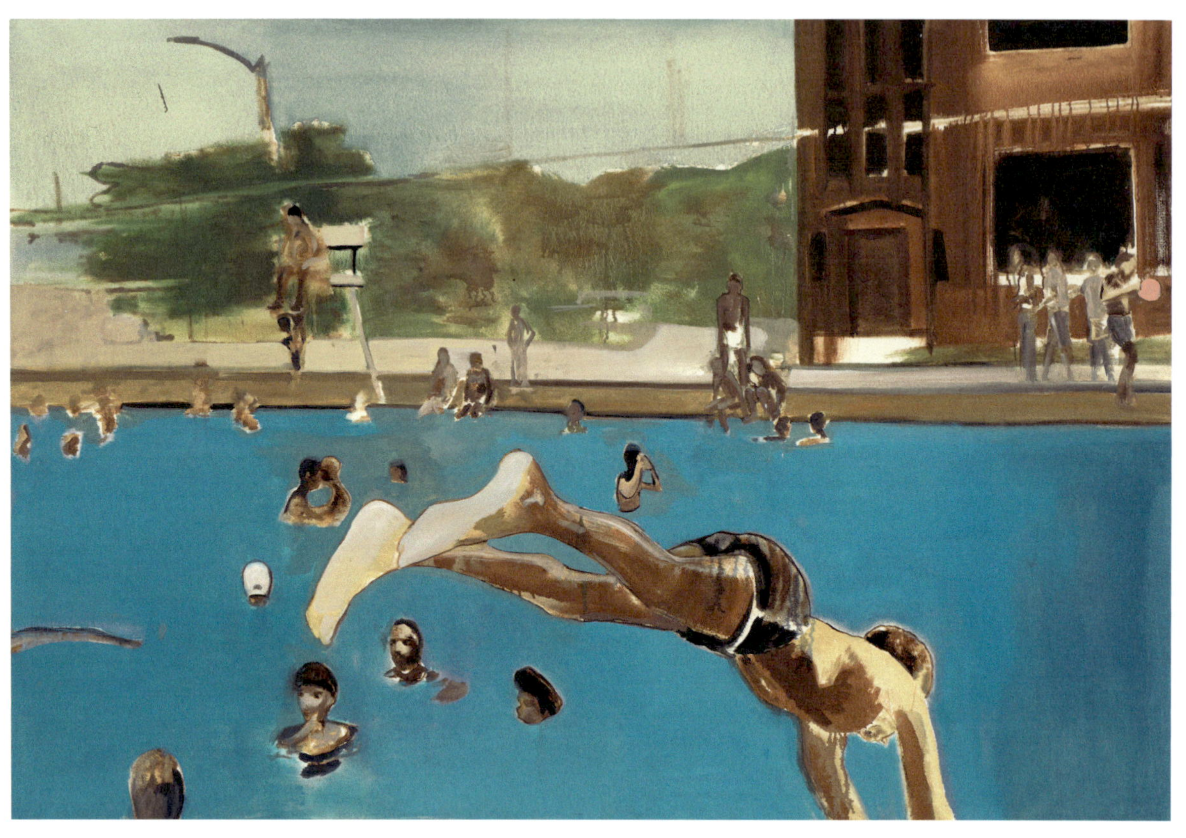

1975 (8), 2013

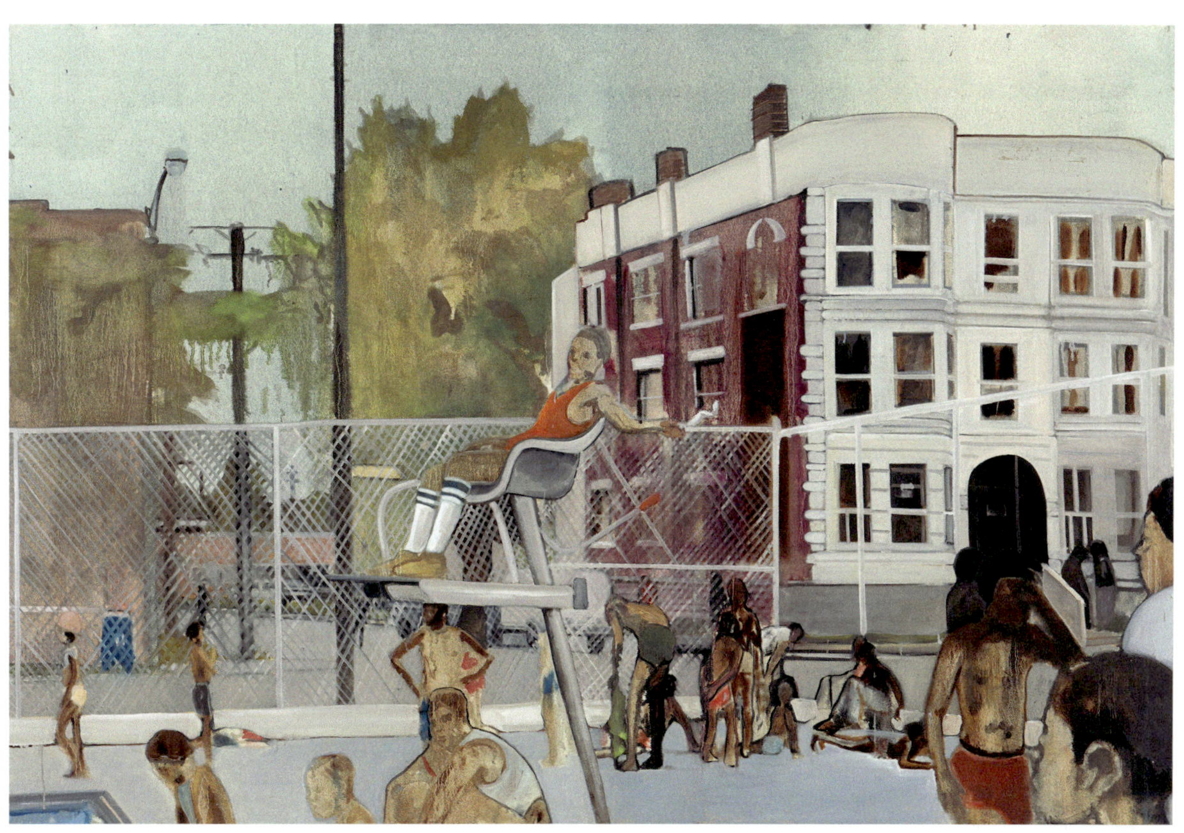

 1975 (9), 2013

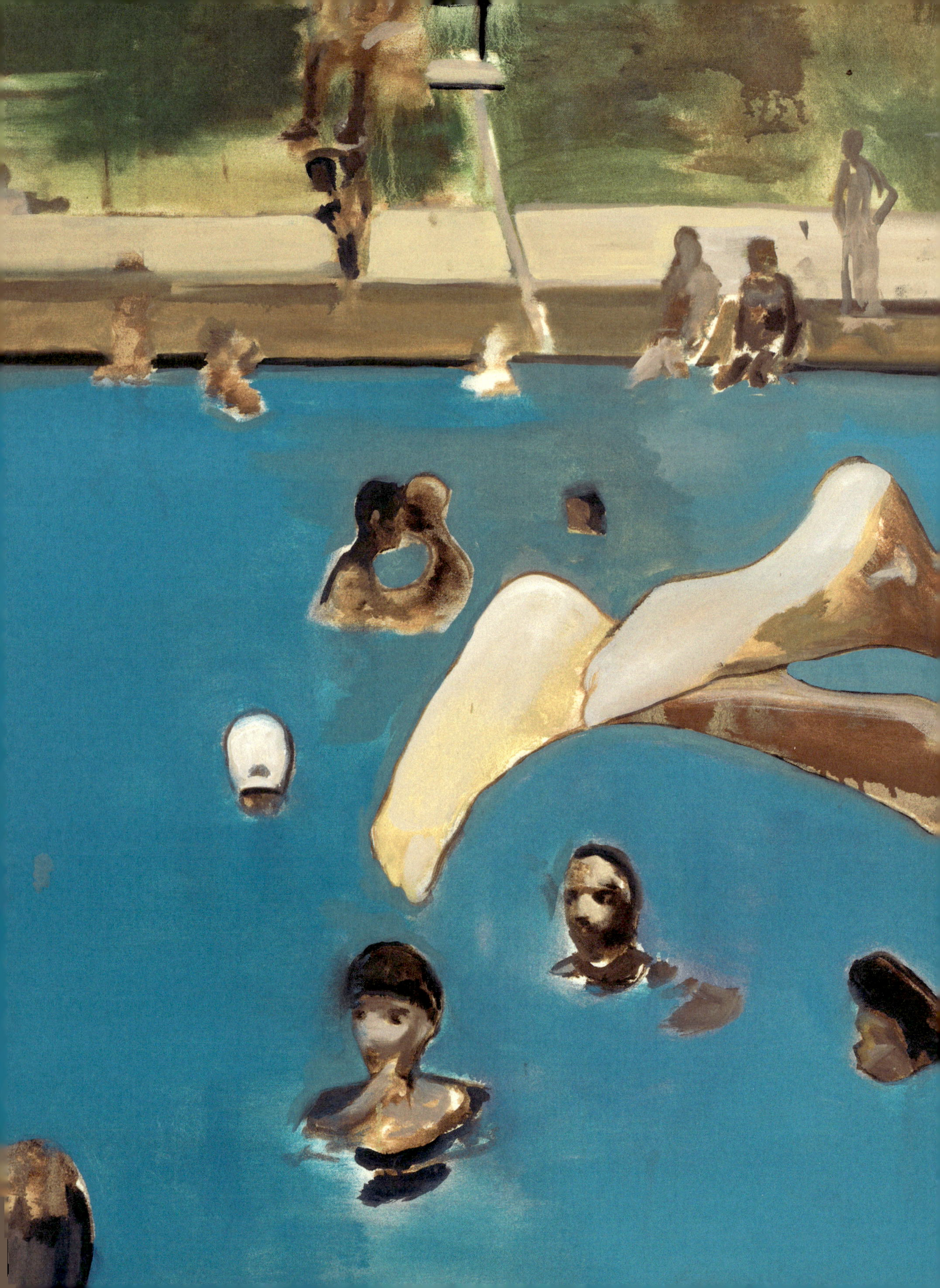

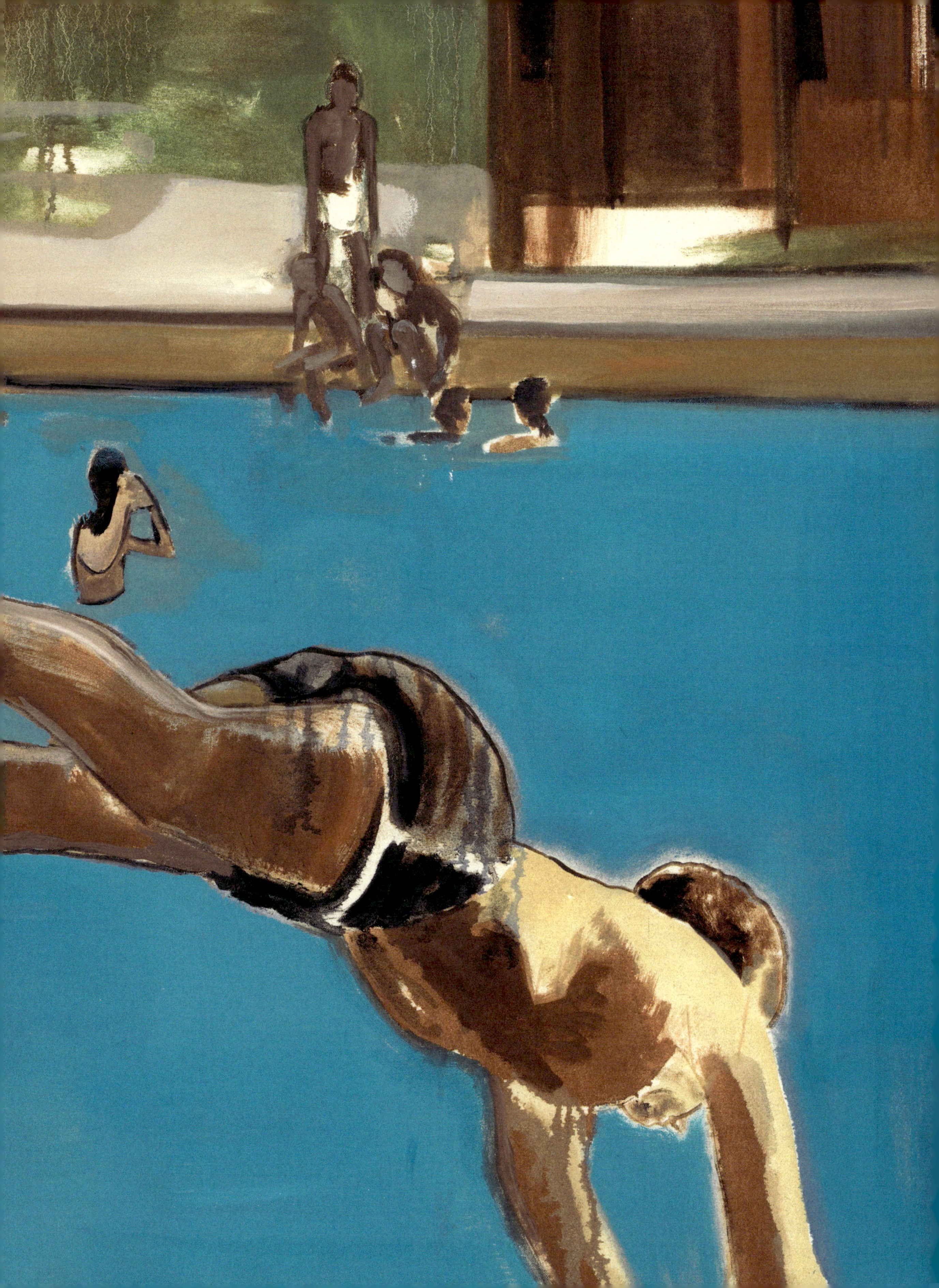

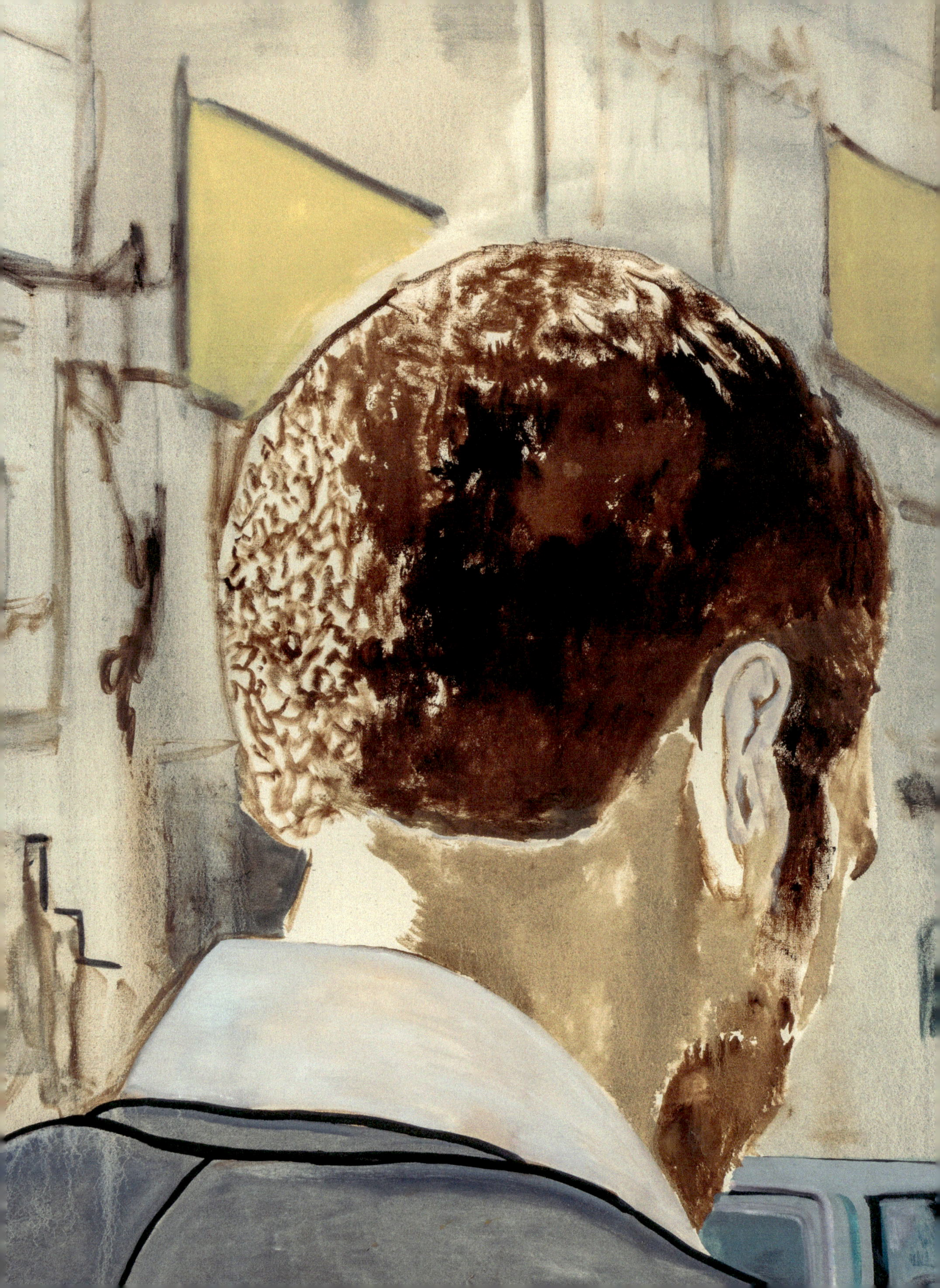

BLACK-GROUND: NOAH DAVIS AND THE SPATIAL FREQUENCIES OF THE BLACK EVERYDAY

Tina M. Campt

Race plays a role in as far as my figures are Black. The paintings aren't political at all though. If I'm making any statement, it's to just show Black people in normal scenarios, where drugs and guns are nothing to do with it. You rarely see Black people represented independent of the civil rights issues or social problems that go on in the States. I'm looking to move on from that stage...[1] Noah Davis

It is a scene of lounging and lingering.
A scene full of motion despite the stillness of its painted figures.
The sharp outlines of a brick or stone domicile form its visual frame.
The lines are accentuated by mottled green-brown trees that hover like low-hanging clouds.
Dappled, draping greenery extends across telephone lines traversing the street.
It is a backdrop we view through the criss-crossing pattern of a chain-link fence.
Its tight links delineate a space of leisure from a place of residence.
But their connection is confirmed by the assembly that unfolds on our side of the fence.

Two lanky brown boys amble in opposite directions.
Another stands, arms akimbo, peering into a pool made visible only by a small blue corner.
Groups of brown bathers – large and small, young and old – gather seated, standing or stretched out.
They fellowship together in animated conversations.
Cropped faces direct their attention towards the gathering behind them.
Meanwhile, another lanky boy approaches, a shadow falls across his face.

At the pool's edge, two brown figures sit bathed in the glow of sunlight.
They are transfixed by the water that laps at their feet.
Just behind them, a boy crouches beneath a lifeguard's chair.
Both he and his elevated brother discern the camera and return its gaze.
They are the only ones who seem aware of their capture.
One is tentative in the face of it.
The other extends a bragging, beckoning arm.
It is a gesture of invitation and embrace.

•

Noah Davis is undoubtedly a master of figuration, though his command of his medium transcends stylistic boundaries by seamlessly integrating abstraction and the surreal. His influences ranged widely, from painters like Kerry James Marshall, Henry Taylor, Luc Tuymans, Marlene Dumas, Lucian Freud, Francis Bacon and Mark Rothko to the Leipzig School and architects like Paul Revere Williams. Yet Davis's artistic virtuosity perhaps reigned most supreme in his ability to reconfigure our sense of space through paintings that entangle viewers in an almost three-dimensional, multi-sensory immersion in Black space.

Davis's canvases capture spaces of Black domesticity and domicile, labour and leisure. His paintings invite us into spaces of Black pleasure and enjoyment, respite and repose. They feature solitary figures in moments of reflection or group constellations in dialogue. They stage unexpected encounters with the young, the vulnerable, the innocent. Those who would normally recede from view or be overlooked in a crowd come into a different kind of focus in the Black spaces that unfold within Davis's paintings. They come into view through richly textured depictions of Black sociality that weave intricate tapestries of the Black quotidian and reflect our community's humanity and humility.

The unmistakable throughline that runs throughout Davis's work is that they capture anything but spectacular scenes. They are not depictions of precarity or dispossession.

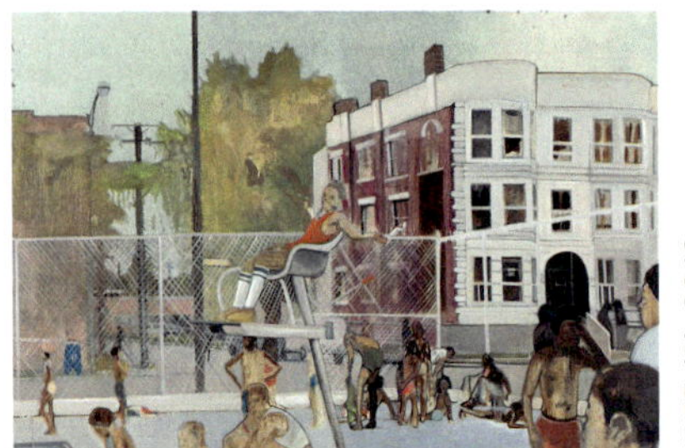

1975 (9), 2013

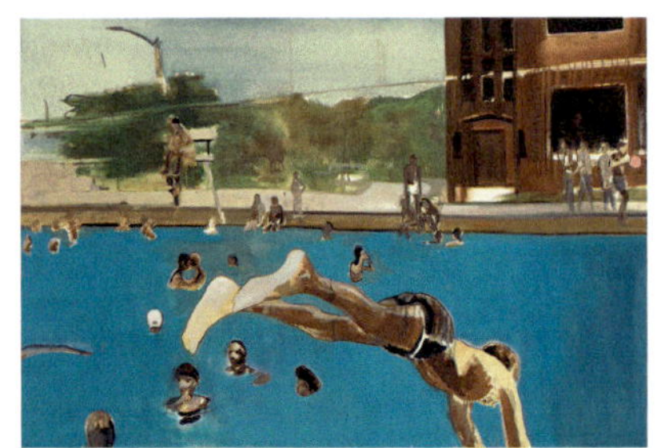

1975 (8), 2013

They are paintings that invite us to partake in the sublimely unspectacular space of the Black everyday. They are paintings that map the contours of Black world-making.

•

Brown figures immersed in a luminous palette
of cerulean blue.
Head touches head in an ambiguous embrace.
Heads and shoulders bob alone, in pairs or
in triplets.

Bodies perch at ground level or aloft.
They fade into then re-emerge from a backdrop
of fuzzy foliage smudging the horizon.
Silhouettes assemble along a brown border that
bifurcates the canvas.
Above it, earth-toned strokes, daubs and streaks
set the stage for a scene of summer revelry.
Beneath the border, the scene transitions from
terrestrial to aquatic.
It returns us to the cerulean basin and those who
frolic within it.

But our position as viewers is ruptured by a long
brown body in suspended forward motion.
It is a leap that anticipates the sound of his
aquatic entry: a splash.

His body lingers on the precipice of entry as
he plunges into the depths of this
motionless blue.
His stilled motion merges our space with his as
he dives from our plane into his pool.
His dive punctures the relation between canvas
and viewer.
It is a puncture that suspends us in the Black
space that emerges in their interstices.
It is a puncture that girds us for a gush of water
out of the canvas and onto us.

•

These are paintings number eight and nine in a group of eleven; two pieces in a body of work that bears no descriptive title. They are identified only by a date: *1975*. It is not a date of commemoration. It is not a birthday or anniversary. It is a date that announces an archive and initiates a backward gaze on memories twice removed. Although these works are by no means Davis's most iconic paintings, they reference a seminal element of his practice: his commitment to the power of community. In the *1975* paintings, it is a commitment articulated in a very different idiom than the landmark Los Angeles institution he founded in 2012 with his wife and fellow artist, Karon Davis. While the Underground Museum was a beacon to so many and a singular accomplishment in Davis's career, I want to foreground the subtle and sophisticated ways his dedication to community finds formal – and what I would describe as 'frequential' – expression in his artistic practice. Here, the *1975* paintings provide a uniquely generative site of engagement.

The one photography class that I took in my senior year at South Shore High School is probably the one class that saved my life. While my peers were dodging drug dealers and stray bullets, I was the lucky and proud owner of a 35mm … through the lens of that Canon, I discovered my future self and captured my own personal journey from the South Side of Chicago.[2] Faith Childs-Davis

The date references a set of images found in the home of Davis's father, Keven Davis, shortly after his death in 2011 – a collection of undeveloped film rolls shot by Davis's mother, Faith Childs-Davis. They were photos taken by her as a girl coming of age in Chicago and later as a young woman travelling in California and abroad. In 1975, Childs-Davis's camera was a refuge and a fugitive pathway beyond the South Side. It was a conduit for the discovery of a future self and the promise of Black possibility. And it was through this same lens that Noah Davis visualised the intimacies of Black possibility in the series of paintings he titled *1975* (2013). They are works that draw inspiration from the photographs his brother, Kahlil Joseph, subsequently developed from their mother's reclaimed archive.

While it may seem counter-intuitive, Davis's *1975* paintings digitise his mother's photographs, albeit not by way of digital technologies. Rather, it is a haptic 'digitisation' that transposes his mother's gaze from the alchemy of photography to the tactility of oil on canvas; a visual-tactile transfer between eye, hand and brush. What emerges in these intimate (re)compositions is a distinctively doubled and, at times, triangulated *Black gaze* – one that recentres the quotidian as a site of care, possibility and Black worlding. In Davis's paintings, the afterlife of his mother's images registers as a refracted Black gaze that activates the visual frequencies of the Black everyday.

In *A Black Gaze: Artists Changing How We See* (2021), I describe a Black gaze not as a Black point of view but as a position of implication in relation to the precarity and potentiality inherent to Black life. It is not seeing *as* or *through the eyes of* a Black person; it is a positioning *alongside*, as a witness. It is a viewing practice that makes demands of us not only because it brings us into proximity with the fraughtness of Black being but because it requires that we exert the labour necessary to understand Blackness on its own terms. The Black gaze that emerges in Davis's paintings is a disordering gaze, where Blackness is neither figure nor ground, neither foreground nor background. What his works compose instead is a *Black-ground*, where Blackness is the starting point for what can be thought. It is Blackness *as ground* – Blackness taken on its own terms and not set in relation to an assumed white ideal.

Davis's rendering of *Black-ground* in his *1975* paintings is a striking enactment of a broader dynamic that is at the core of his creative practice. Like the stylistic multivocality we see in *1975 (8)* and *1975 (9)*, his paintings merge the figurative with the abstract and the surreal in ways that destabilise the optic relations between background and foreground, compelling viewers to toggle back and forth between figure and ground. Taking the Black everyday as the foundation of his aesthetic intervention, Davis's richly textured canvases conjure vivid spaces where the Black figure becomes *Black-ground.* While painting from photographs certainly contributed to the depth of Davis's representations of Black spaces, his works are neither reproductions nor replications; they are enlivened, affecting counterparts/-points to their photographic originals.

The *1975* paintings push this practice a step further, as Davis positions both himself and his viewers behind and alongside his mother's lens. These works allow us to poignantly inhabit Childs-Davis's forward-looking gaze of self-discovery through community, even in the absence of her original photographs (which Davis and Kahlil Joseph first published in their experimental online photoblog *FEB MAG*). It is a gaze that bridges multiple temporalities, allowing us to see the Black everyday of the 1970s through the backward glance of his mother's photographic archive.

In *1975 (1)* and *1975 (2)*, we are fellow travellers accompanying a young girl on the block and a man on the street. What we witness is unremarkable, but it is their unspectacularity that creates the space for us to linger and dwell in a *Black-ground* that registers the durational frequencies of Black life in which Davis's paintings are so firmly embedded. Yet, to appreciate the resonant Black space Davis creates in these canvases, we must not only walk alongside Davis and his mother's gazes. We must listen as well as look – attuning ourselves to the complex frequencies of Davis's *Black-ground.*

When we attend to the ambient sounds of a street scene, do they distract us and shift our view? When we lose ourselves in these mundane urban frequencies, perhaps our vision loses focus, and we see only the washed-out fuzzy blur of storefronts and parked cars. Our focus might shift to the sound of the footsteps of the Black man we walk alongside. His downcast eyes suggest that we accompany him on a path he knows by heart. Might the pace of his steps signify the ease he feels in a social landscape that embraces him? Or might we hear instead the accelerated pace of someone feeling out of place and passing through quickly on his way to more welcoming territory? Listening to and walking alongside, we mirror his steps to stride more quickly or slowly in tandem with his pace. We synchronise our steps in kinship with our companion, reassured by his presence of our arrival at our destination.

When we look alongside and over the shoulder of a friend, when we gaze with her through the refracted magnification of her glasses, we view the angular geometry of a green lawn framed by an asphalt driveway

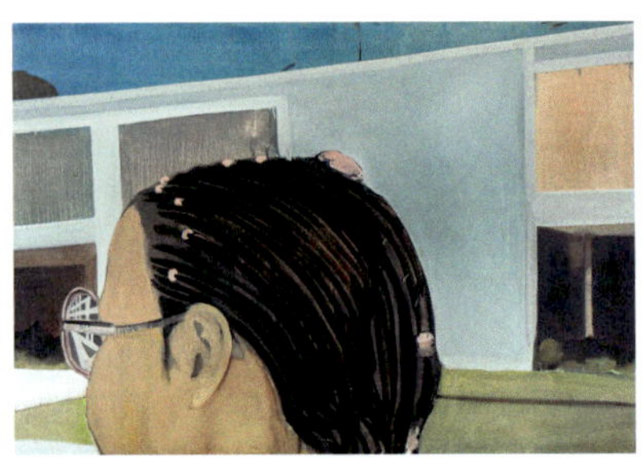

1975 (2), 2013

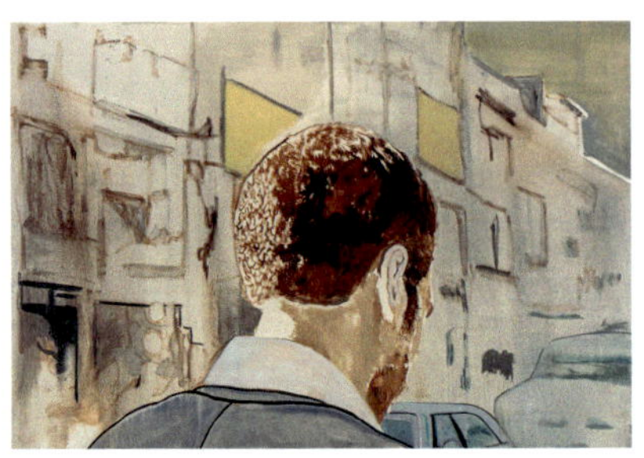

1975 (1), 2013

and concrete sidewalk. But what do we hear? Do we hear music streaming from an open window? Do we hear lawnmowers cutting the grass? Do we hear a mother, a father or neighbours greeting us along the way? Listening to these canvases and attending to the sounds we encounter that were their source of inspiration, what registers in Davis's careful *Black-ground* are the sonic frequencies of a Black sociality rooted in the creation of shared community spaces.

What do we hear when we attend to the sound of a classroom as we look out from behind or alongside a fellow pupil whose features are abstracted from our view? The painting directs our gaze past him to fix on a bespectacled Black teacher in a patterned pullover, studying his notes intensely. While our attention is drawn to the textured brushstrokes that suggest a freshly erased chalkboard, the earnest gaze in which we are captured insists that we attend to the teacher's words and the tone of his instruction. Is he a revered mentor? Is he stern and intimidating? Is he charismatic and beloved? Is he all these things at once?

We must attune ourselves to the timbre of his voice and the tenor of his enunciations. They co-mingle with the call and response of a teacher's questions and his students' replies. They, in turn, tussle with the bold backchat and comical side comments of sassy student recalcitrance we imbibe in the daily banter of the classroom. What also resonates in Davis's warm palette and textured strokes are the ambient sounds of our fellow classmates that we cannot tune out: the involuntary coughs and sneezes, the rustling of bodies shifting in chairs, the fidgety clicks of pens or the scratchy scrape of pencils taking notes.

When we listen with attunement to Davis's *Black-ground*, his paintings make the visual frequencies of Black life audible and legible. In his *1975* series, we discern multiple layers of Black potentiality through a tripled Black gaze: a mother's gaze amplified by a son's backward view of Black sociality captured by her camera and reactivated in paintings of oil on canvas. Davis reanimates the visual archive of 1970s Black possibility captured in his mother's photographs through the relay between a son's refraction of his mother's gaze on the beauty of the Black quotidian. It is a visual correspondence that resonates at the lower frequencies of the *Black-ground* in *1975 (8)* and *1975 (9)*. In these paintings, it resounds in the cacophony of a neighbourhood pool that was not only the site of leisure and community. It resurfaces, as well, the history of the not-so-'public' neighbourhood pool, which, only a few years before, was a site of Jim Crow segregation and policing.

What does it mean to inhabit Blackness *as ground*? What does it look, sound or feel like to ground our view of the world in Black life? In Davis's *1975* series, *Black-ground* makes space for a Black gaze that positions viewers at the pinnacle of a triangulated correspondence between a mother and son – the triangulation of walking alongside your mother as a belated witness to the simultaneity of Black precarity and possibility in 1975. It is the labour of walking with a son walking with his mother, as her witness. It is the labour of bearing witness to the *Black-ground* and the overlapping sonic, visual and temporal correspondences of Black potentialities in 1975, 2013 and 2024.

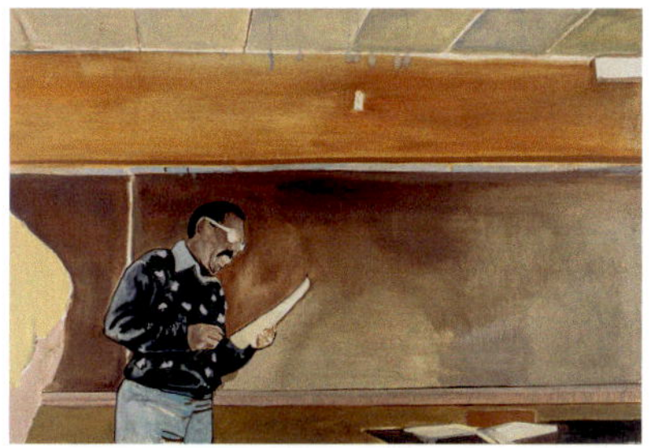
1975 (4), 2013

1 Ben Ferguson, 'Noah Davis', *Dazed Digital*, 9 February 2010, dazeddigital.com/artsandculture/article/6483/1/noah-davis.

2 '1975 Paintings', mutualart.com/Exhibition/1975-Paintings/A6CD57448EBF0900.

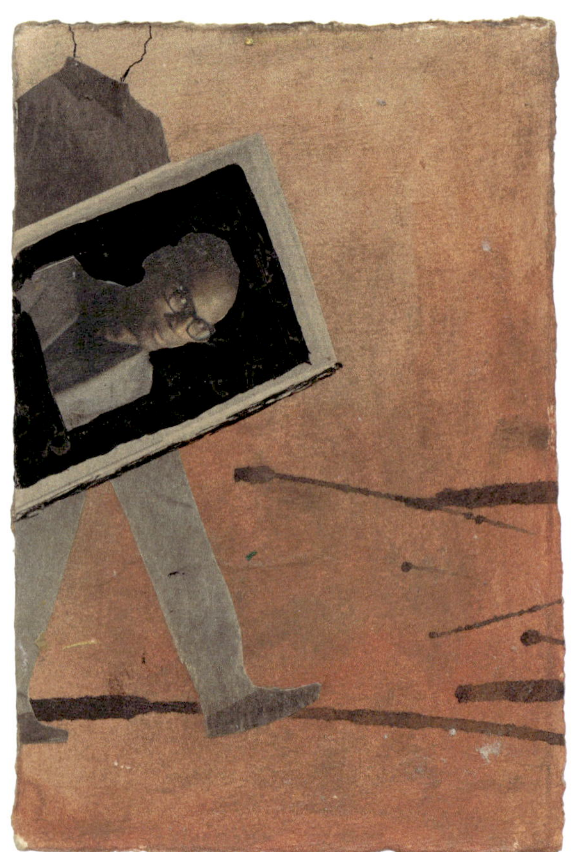

Left *Untitled*, 2014
Right *Seventy Works (9)*, 2014

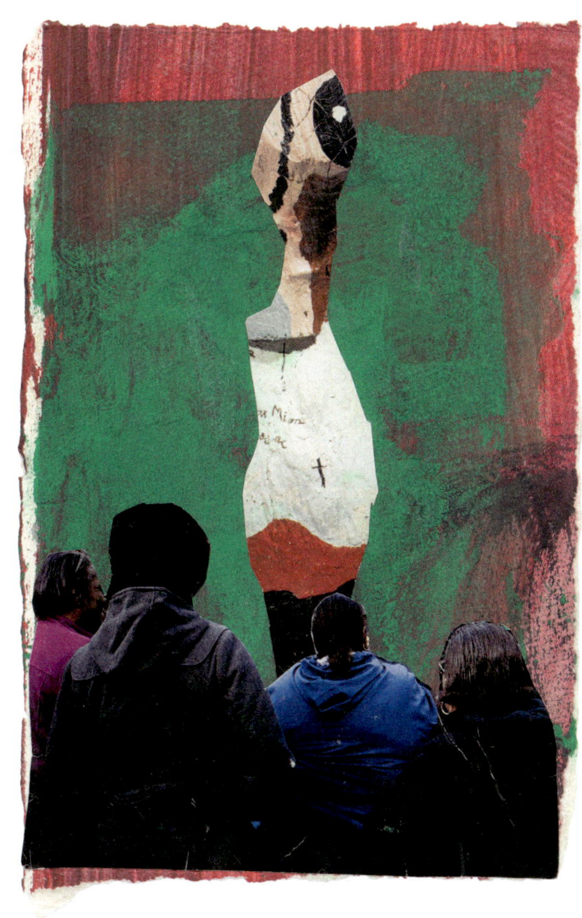

 Untitled, 2014

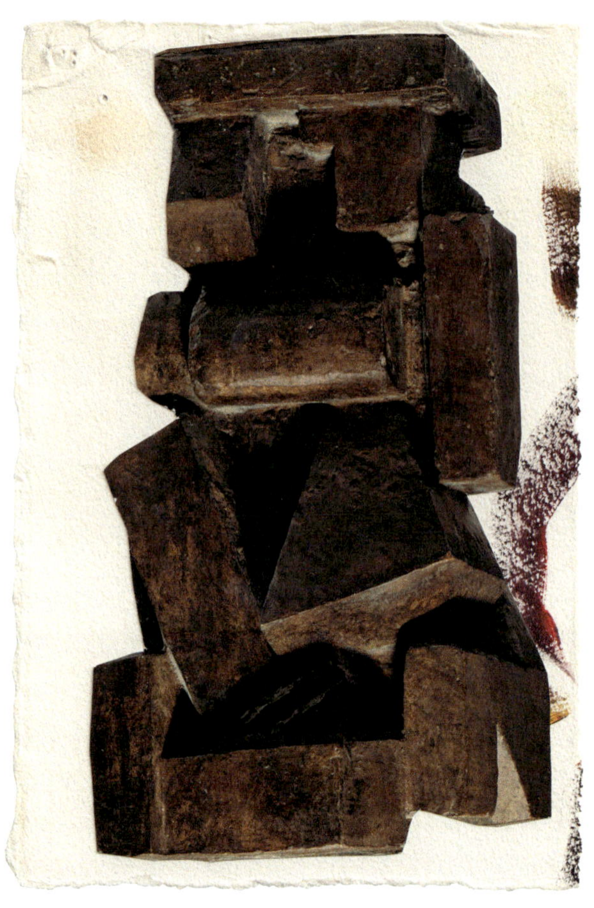

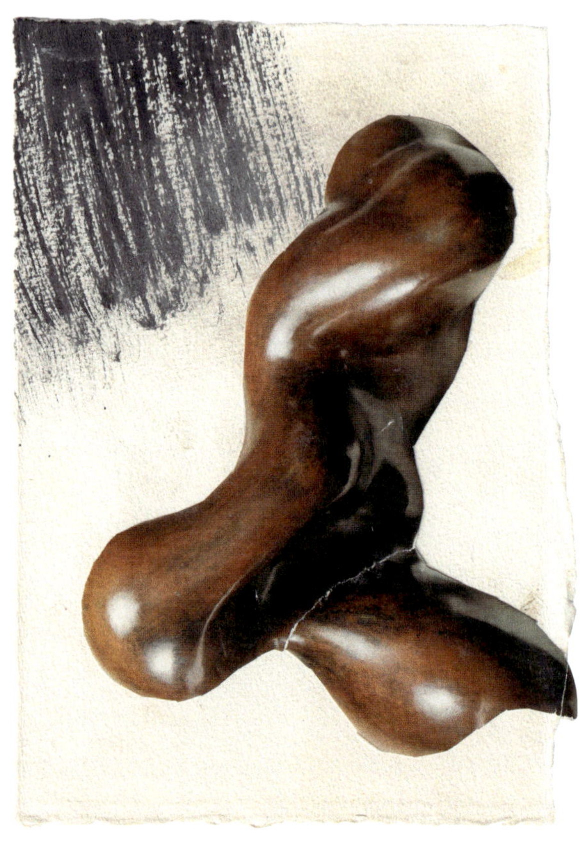

Top *Untitled*, 2014
Bottom *Untitled*, 2014

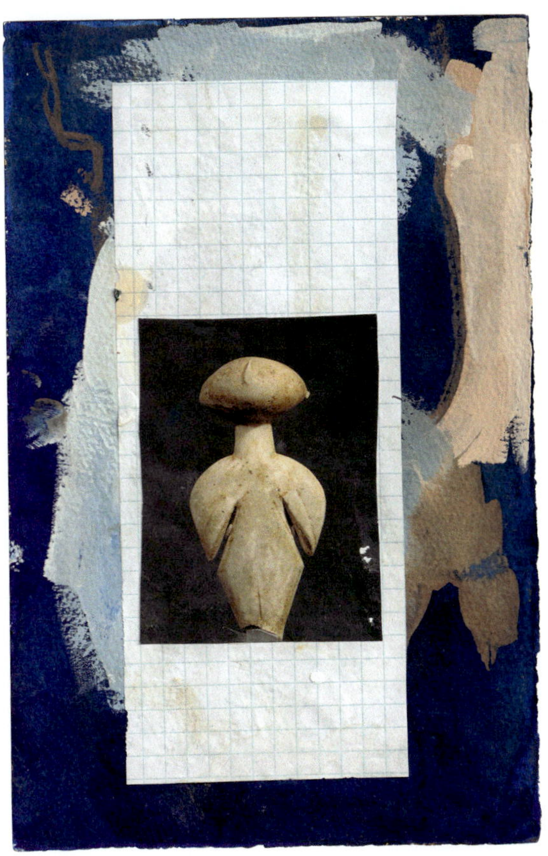

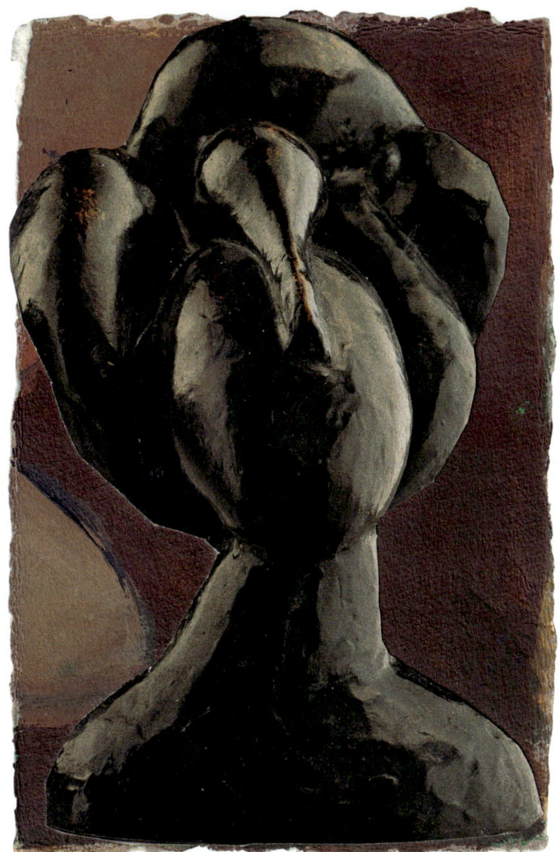

Left *Untitled*, 2014
Right *Untitled*, 2014

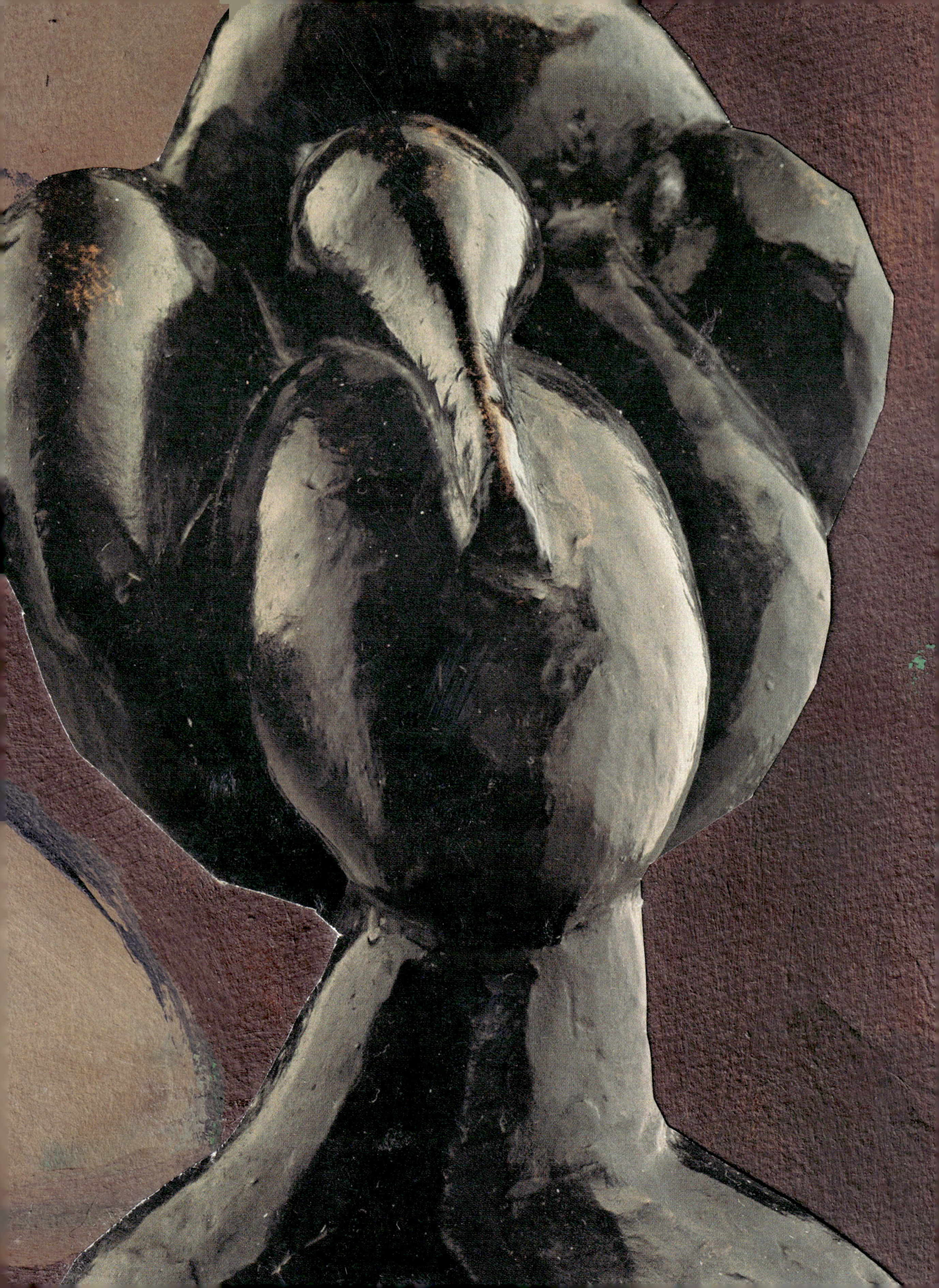

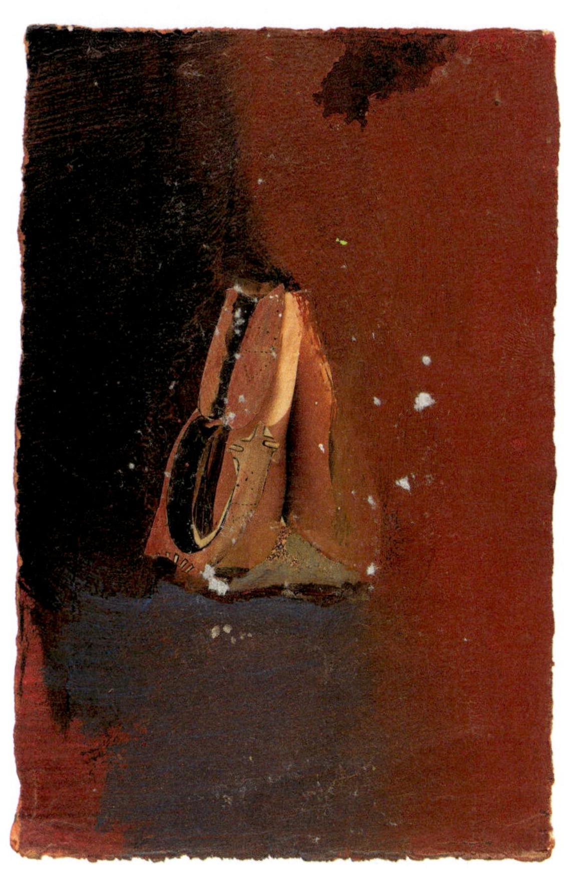

 Seventy Works (17), 2014

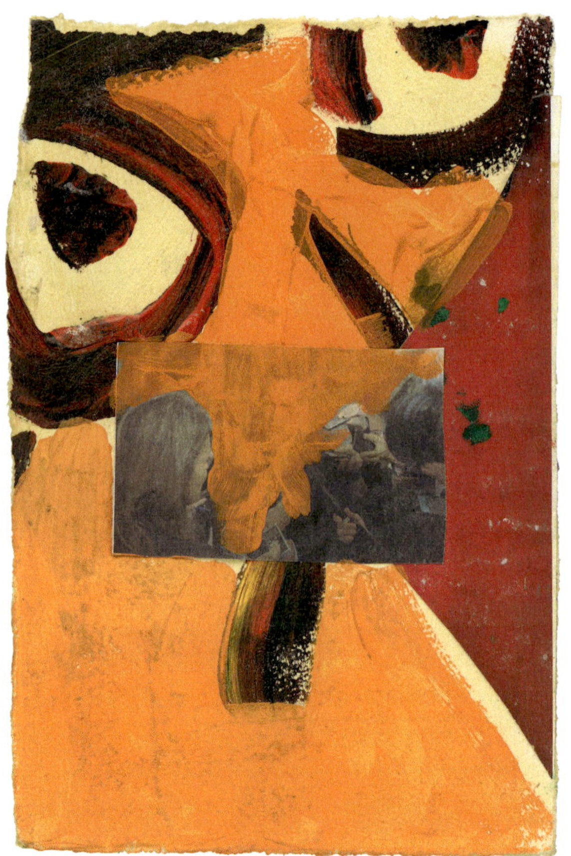

Left *Seventy Works (30)*, 2014
Right *Seventy Works (15)*, 2014

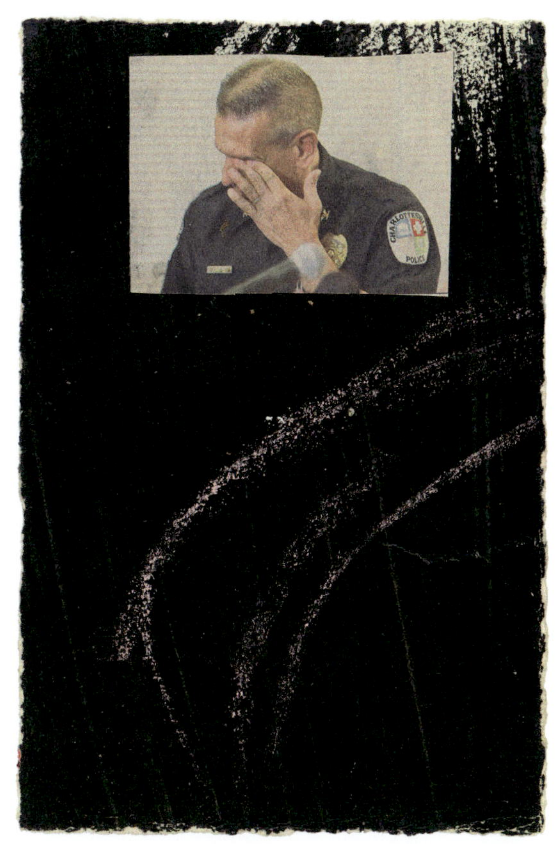

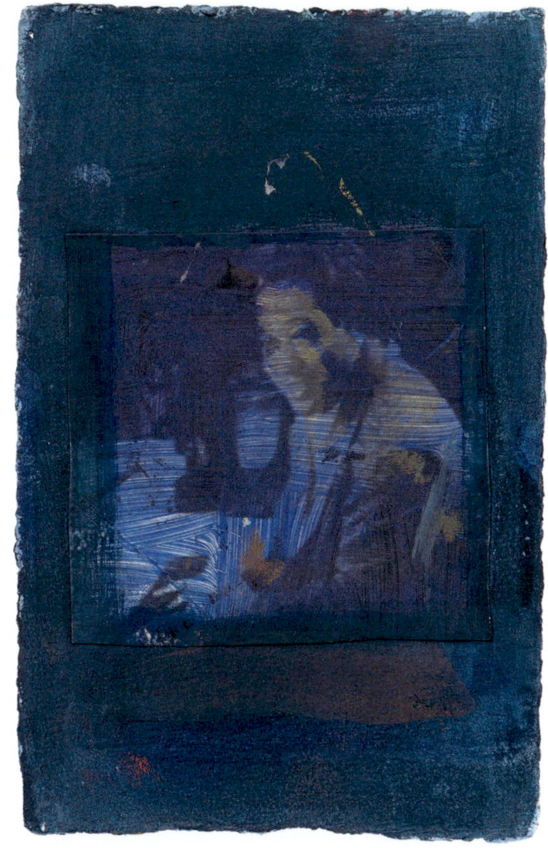

Top *Seventy Works (28)*, 2014
Bottom *Seventy Works (45)*, 2014

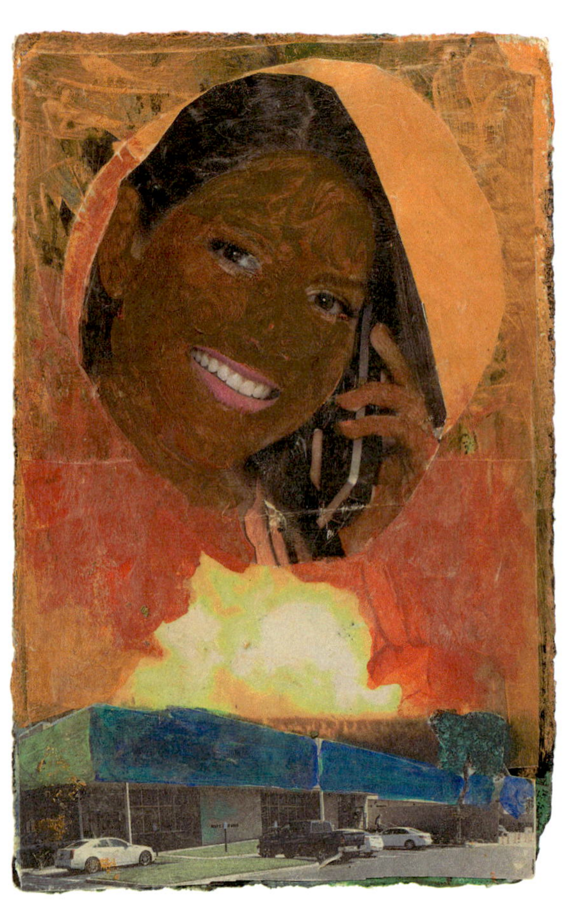

Top *Seventy Works (61)*, 2014

Top *Seventy Works (36)*, 2014
Left *Seventy Works (50)*, 2014
Right *Seventy Works (43)*, 2014

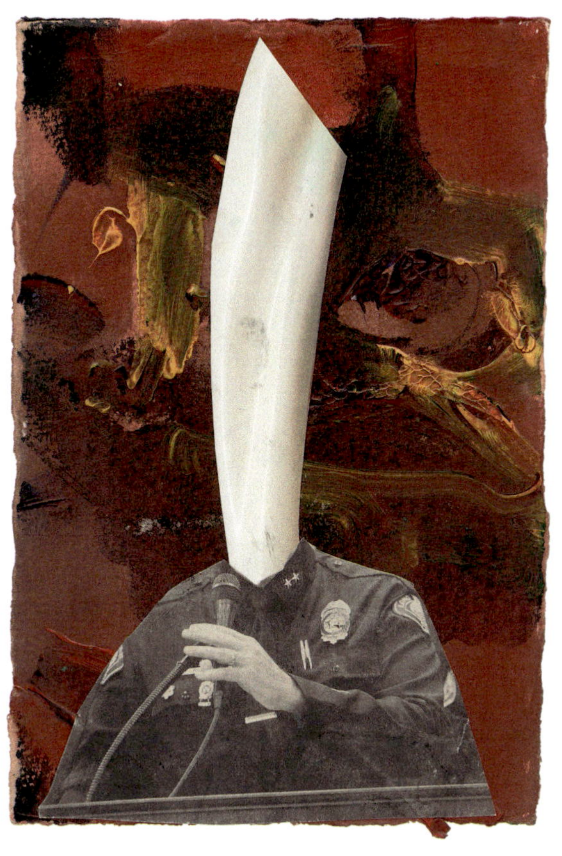

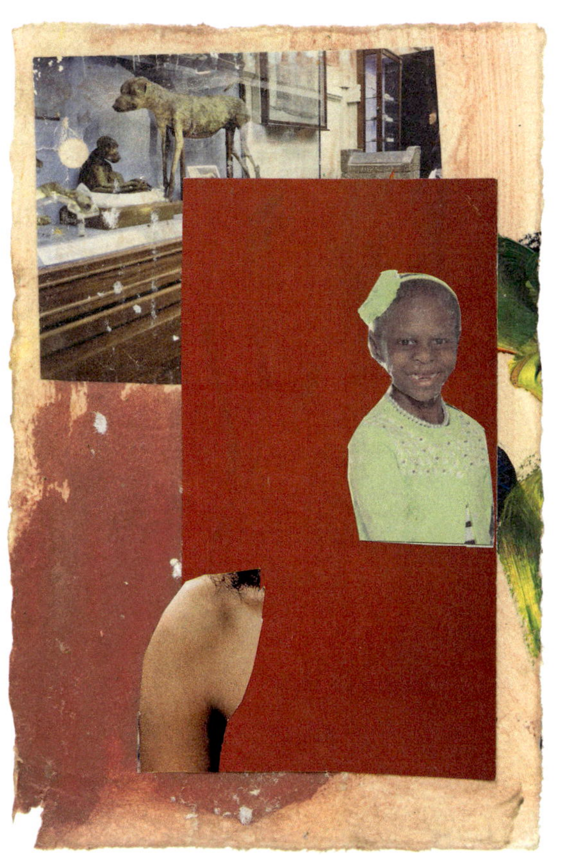

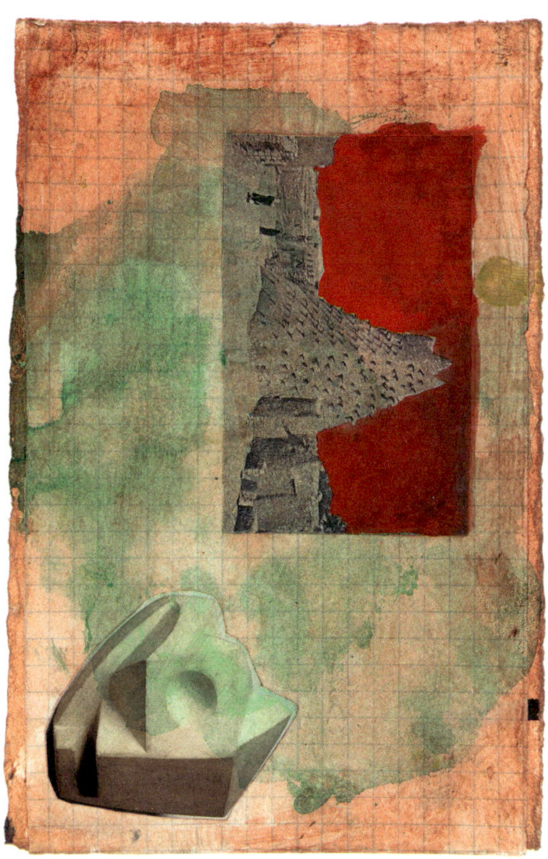

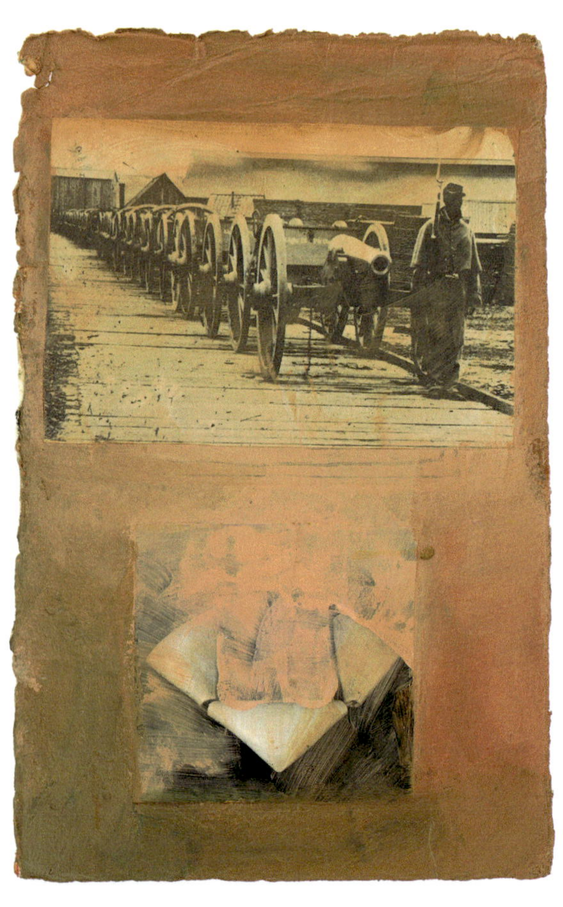

Seventy Works (64), 2014

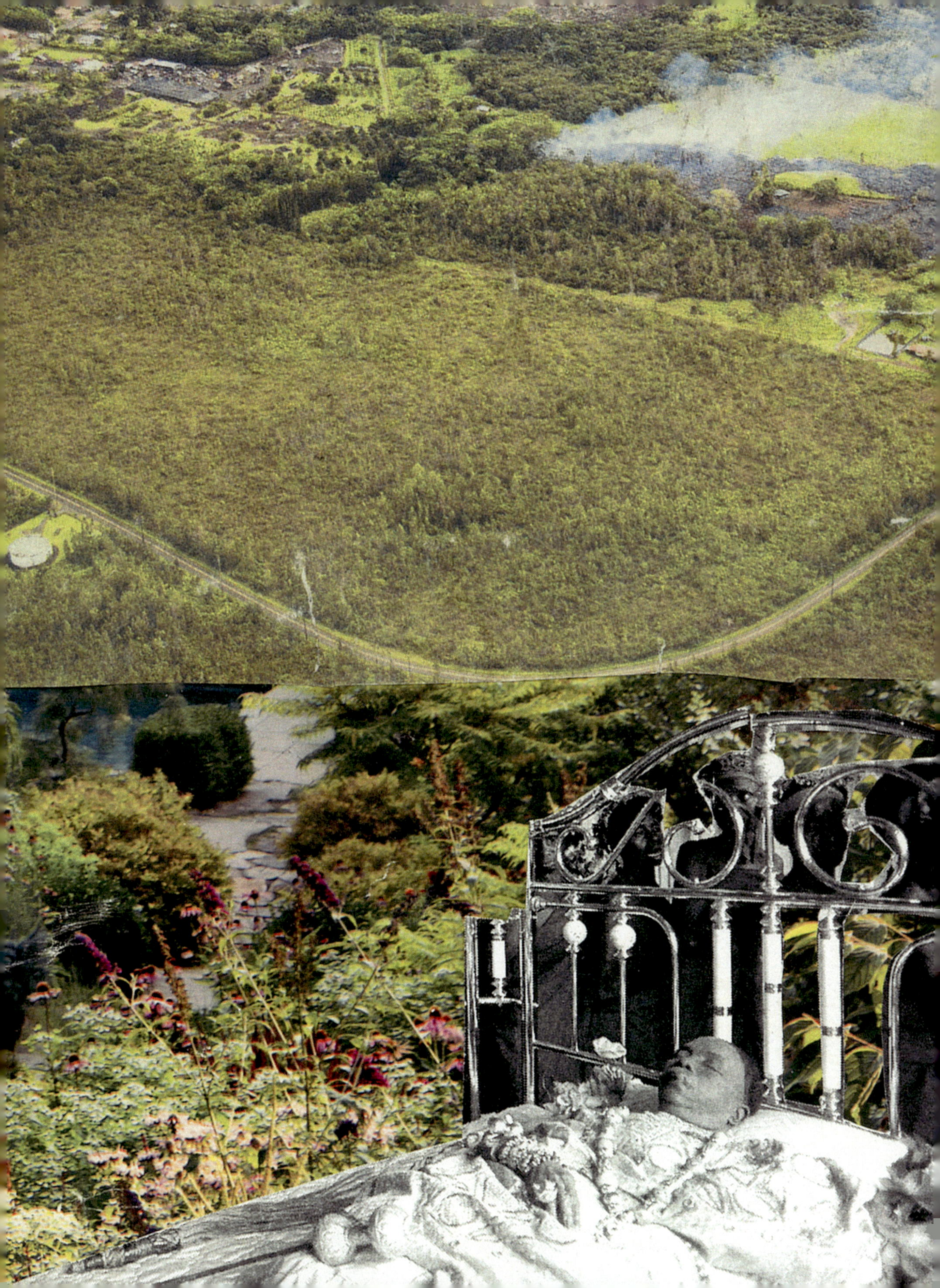

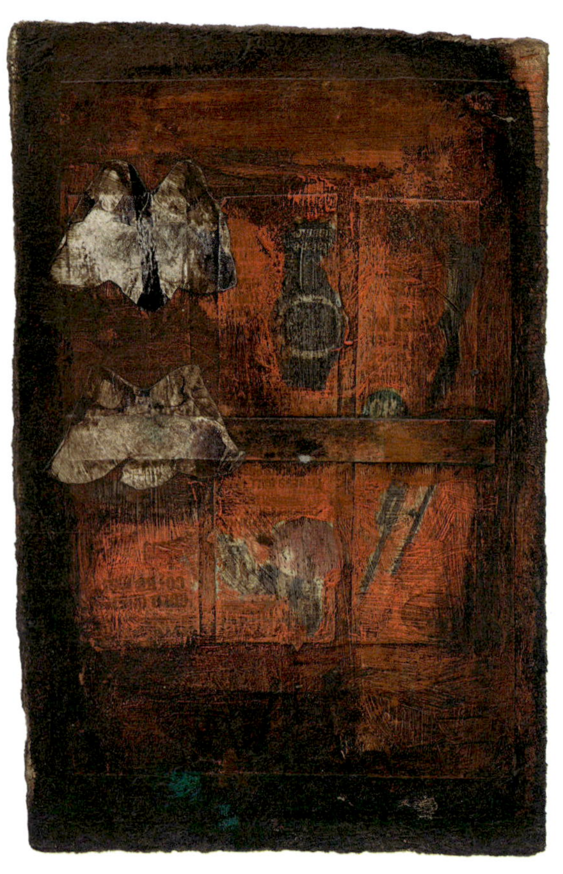

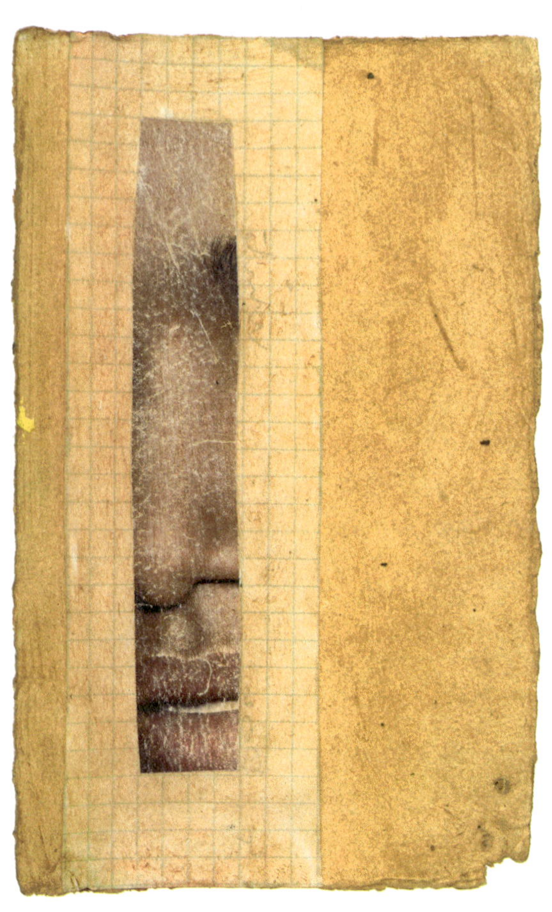

Top *Seventy Works (68)*, 2014
Bottom *Seventy Works (67)*, 2014

Left *Seventy Works (70)*, 2014
Right *Untitled*, 2014

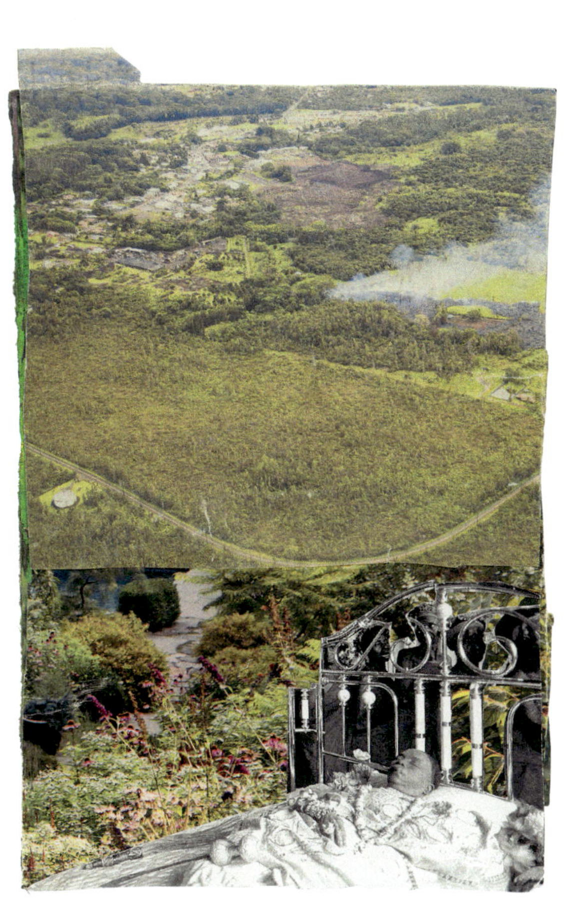

JASON MORAN on
Pueblo del Rio: Concerto, 2014

If you see a piano on the street, someone painstakingly moved it there. Grand pianos have three legs, weigh a tonne, and are notoriously difficult to manoeuvre. In homes with a piano, the instrument is a symbol of permanence, a sculpture that sits in the same living room corner for decades, often used as a surface to display tchotchkes and family photographs.

In Noah Davis's *Pueblo del Rio: Concerto,* a concert grand piano is outside in the street, removed from the home that framed its sound. It is in the wild, unrestricted by walls. Davis's pianist sits before sheet music resting on the piano's music desk and appears to be glancing slightly to their right as if the focus of their vision is just out of view. They casually hunch over the keys, both hands positioned below middle C, manipulating the piano's longer strings for lower tones. Pianos of this calibre can be found in the world's most prestigious concert venues; if one is in the street (in this case, beneath an overcast sky at the iconic Pueblo del Rio Los Angeles housing project designed in part by architect Paul Revere Williams), it is for a reason. Maybe the pianist is accompanying the ballerinas Davis depicts in one of the other works in his *Pueblo del Rio* series (p. 187). Or maybe not. Either way, Davis definitively places this evening of concertising 'in the hood'. This is a concert that is open to all. It requires no reserved ticket, no paid parking, no turning off cell phones. As the work gently implies, it is the music that emerged in spaces like this housing project that formed the roots of what became canon.

This painting reminds me of a story I once heard from the legendary horn player Robert Northern, a.k.a. Brother Ah, who played on major recordings with John Coltrane, Thelonious Monk and Sun Ra. We met in Washington, D.C., and as we discussed his work with Monk, Brother Ah told me the incredible story of how Monk found rhythmic inspiration for his 1957 composition 'Evidence', which mostly consists of surprising and unpredictable notes that seem to jut out of thin air. But before the story, some context: Monk is of the

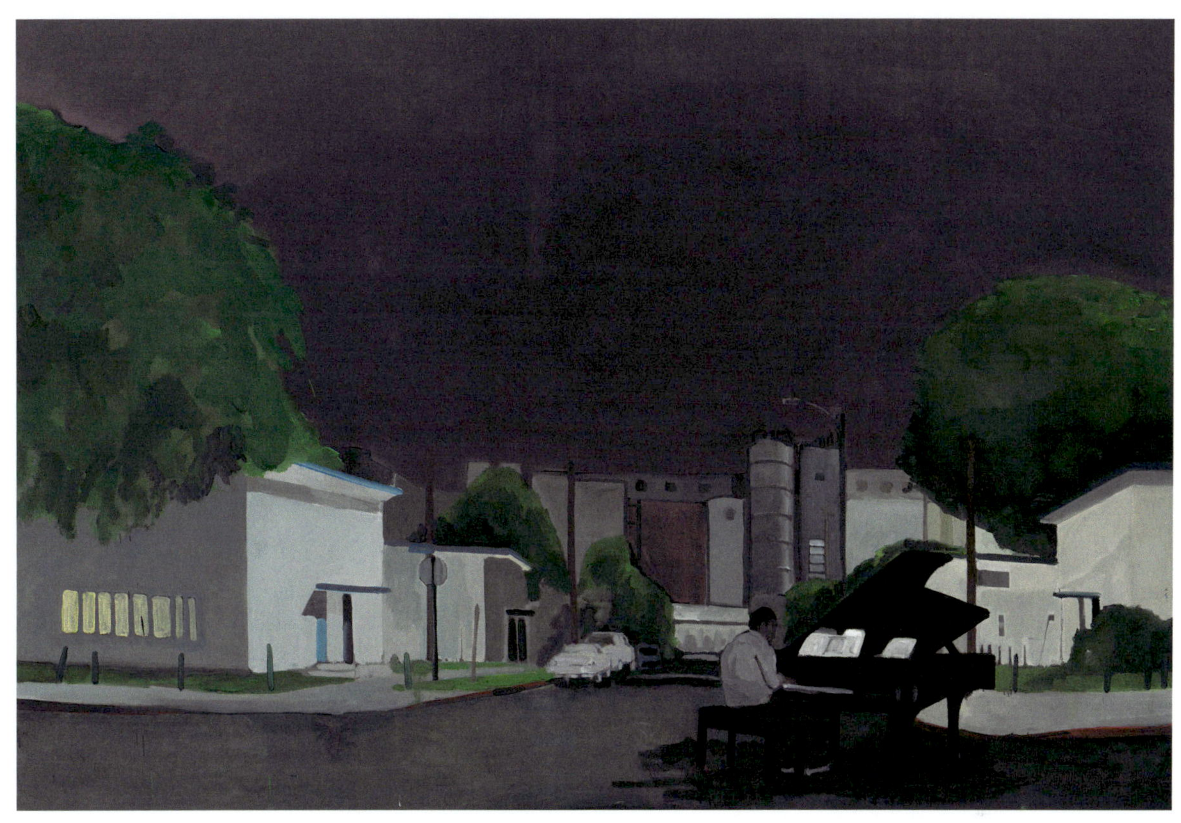

 Pueblo del Rio: Concerto, 2014

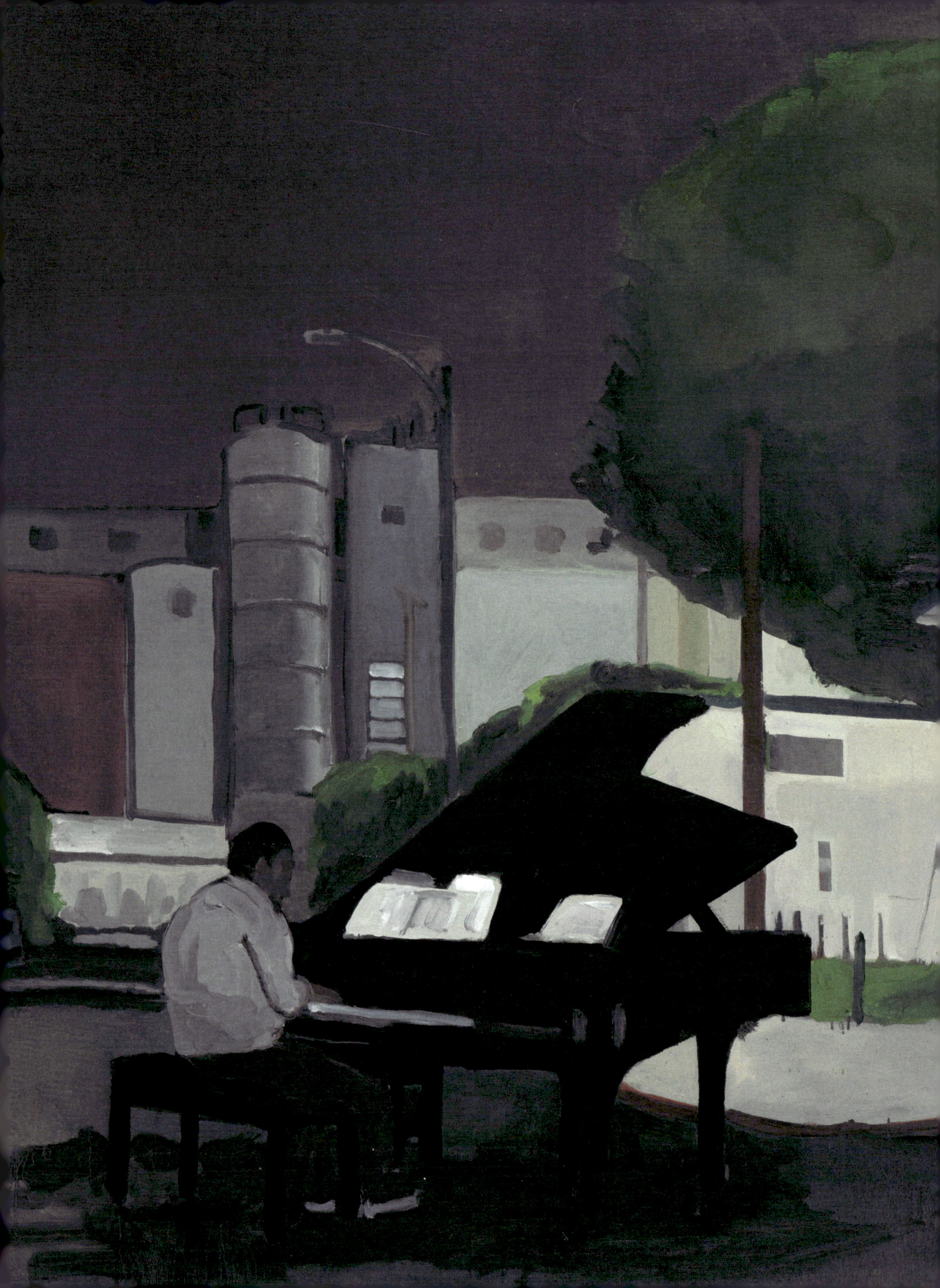

bebop generation, which helped brand an entirely new strand of syncopation. Along with Charlie Parker and Mary Lou Williams, Monk departed from the danceable riffs of the big-band era in favour of a smaller and more nimble choreographic approach, like birds chasing one other through the air. Brother Ah told me that Monk would often drag an upright piano to the basketball court at a New York City housing project on his block, where he would sit down and play while kids played basketball around him. The rhythm of 'Evidence' is the rhythm of the kids playing ball. All the pump fakes, behind-the-backs, no-look passes evolved into a melody. (Brother Ah demonstrated this to me by singing the melody while mimicking basketball moves.) Monk was outside – part of the game – composing from life. The neighbourhood basketball court provided him with a space for these kinds of explorations. Monk's music didn't need to be contained in private spaces (like living rooms and concert halls) but could exist outside, become part of life in the street. The story amplifies the necessity of these interactions.

Davis paints this.

Evidence. Non-Fiction.

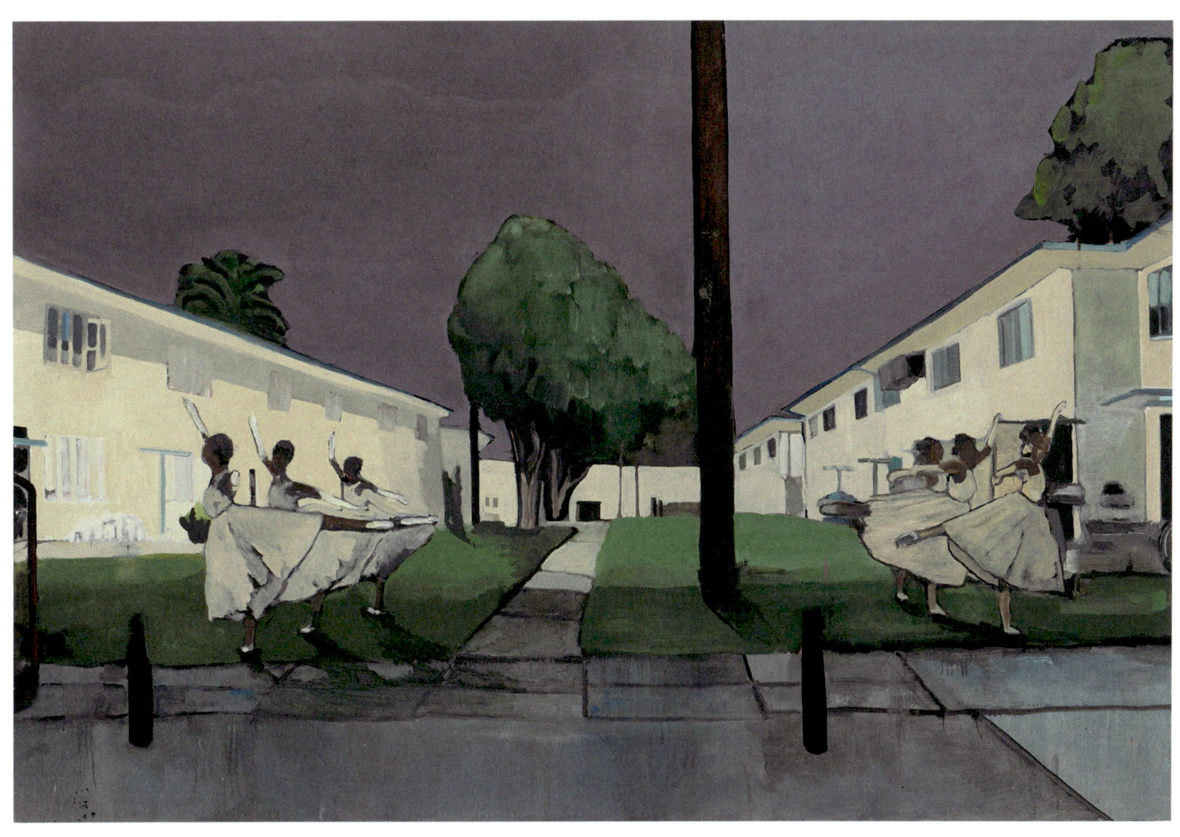

 Pueblo del Rio: Arabesque, 2014

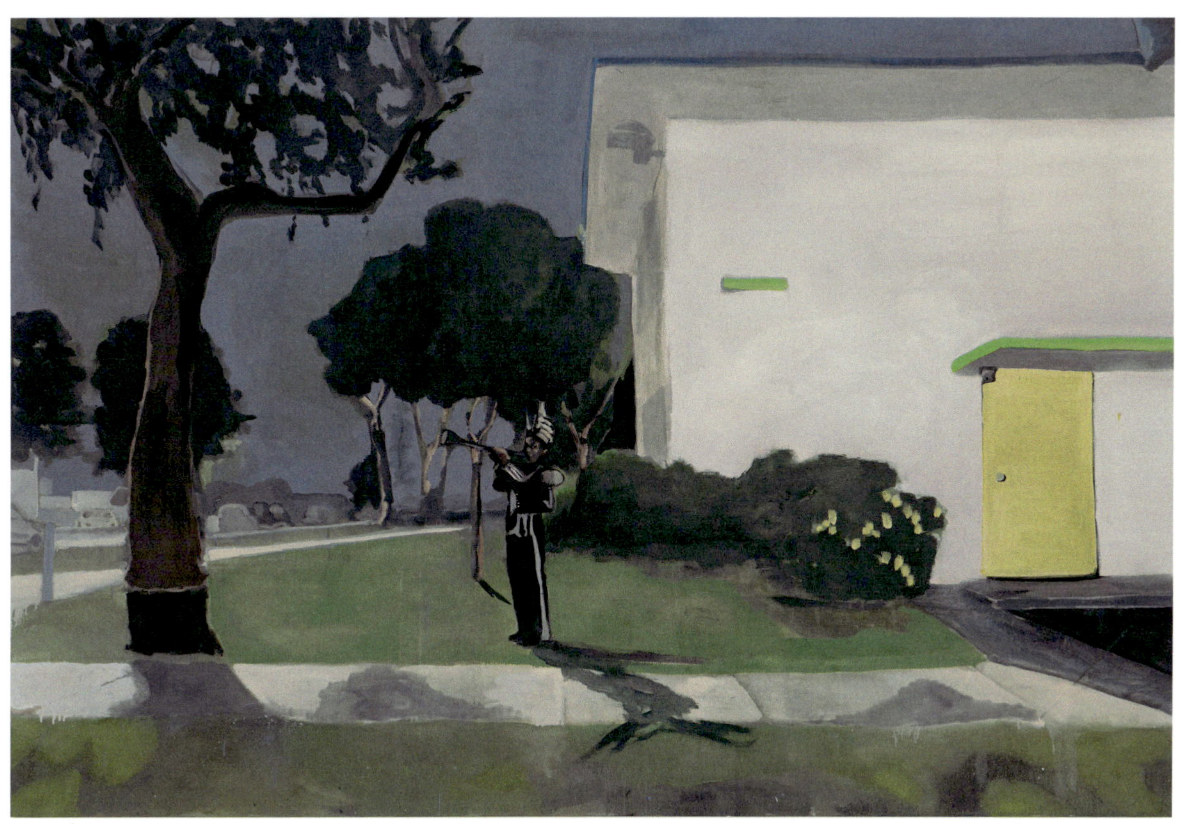

 Pueblo del Rio: Prelude, 2014

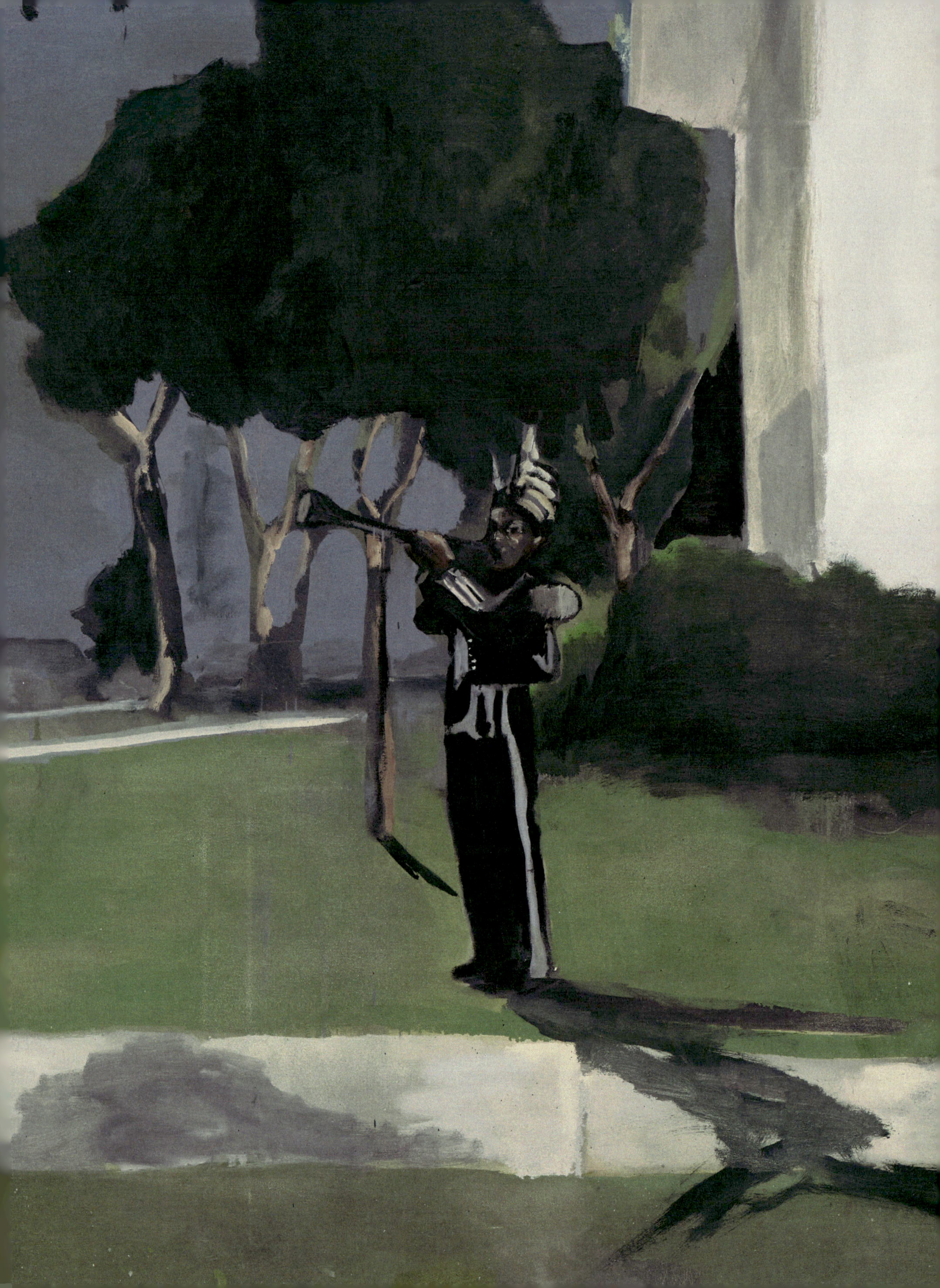

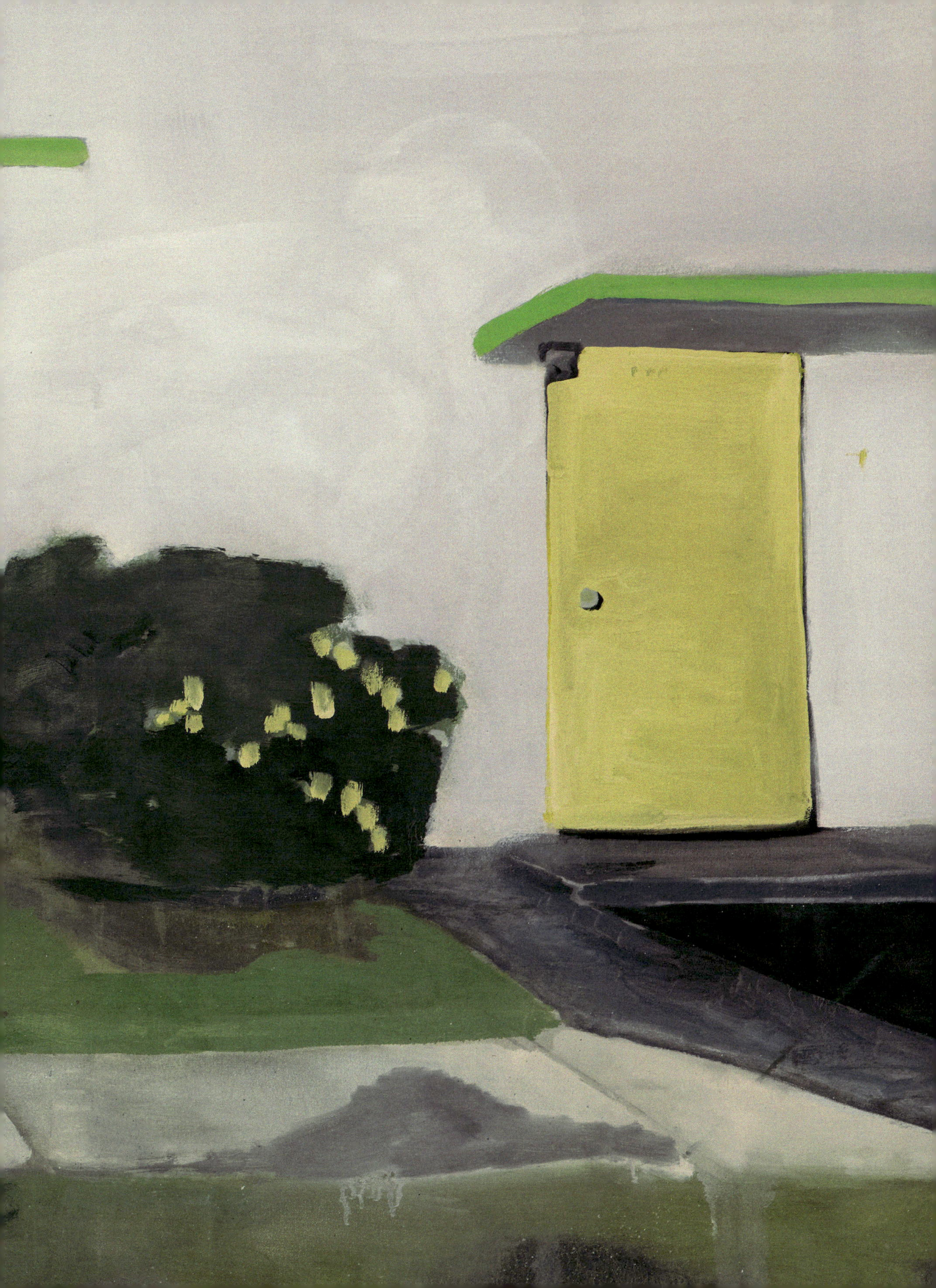

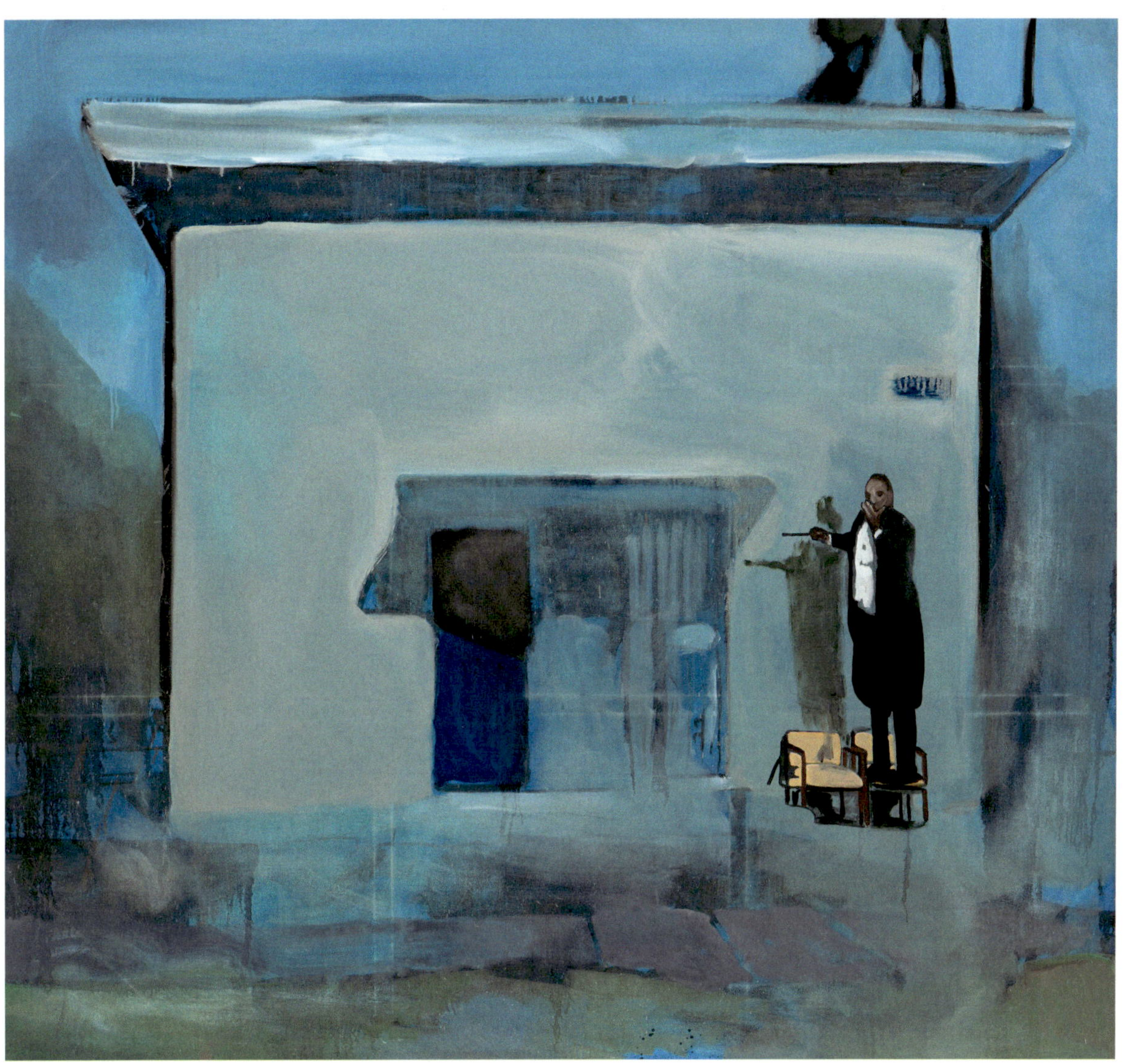

 The Conductor, 2014

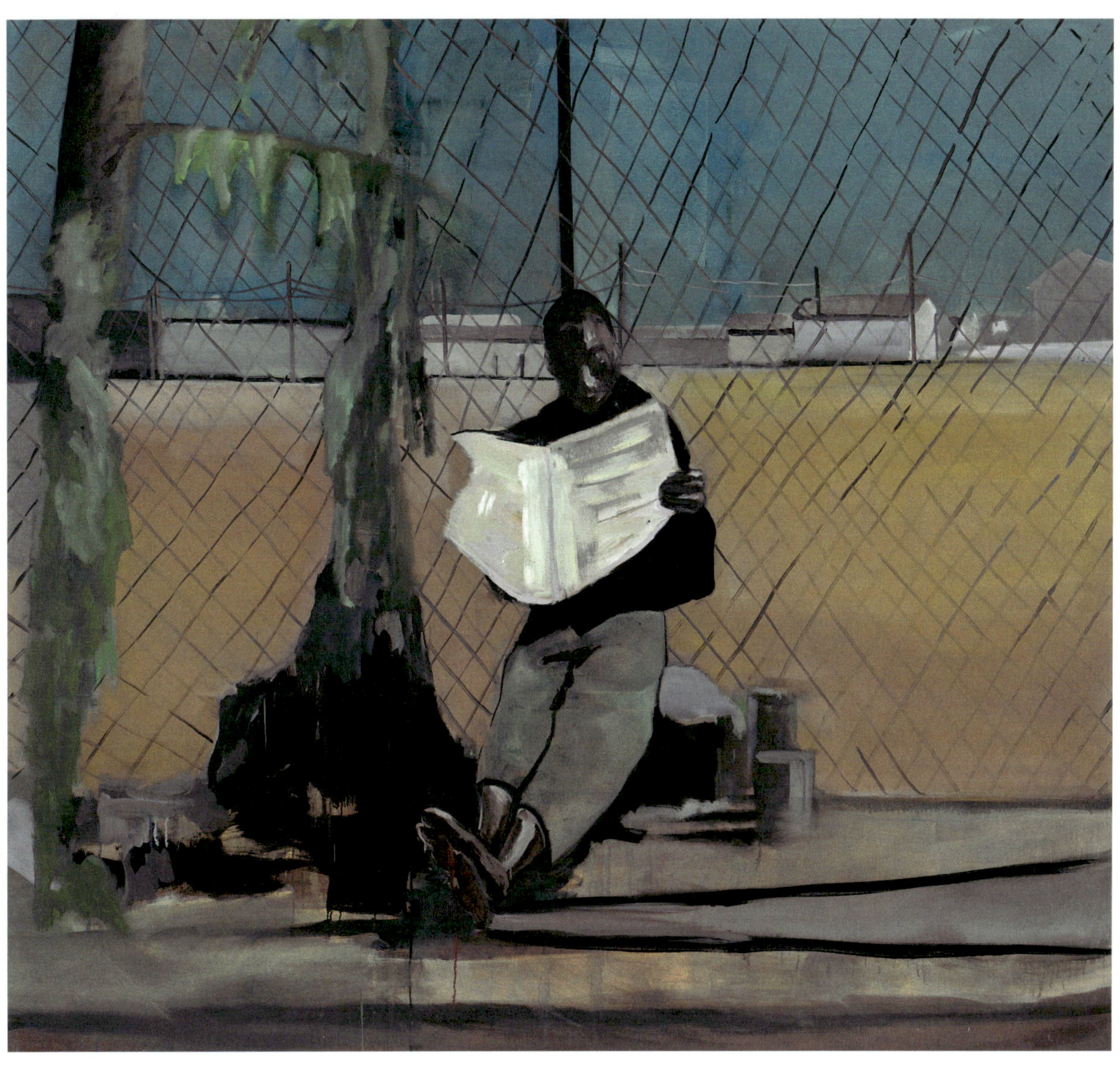

 Pueblo del Rio: Vernon, 2014

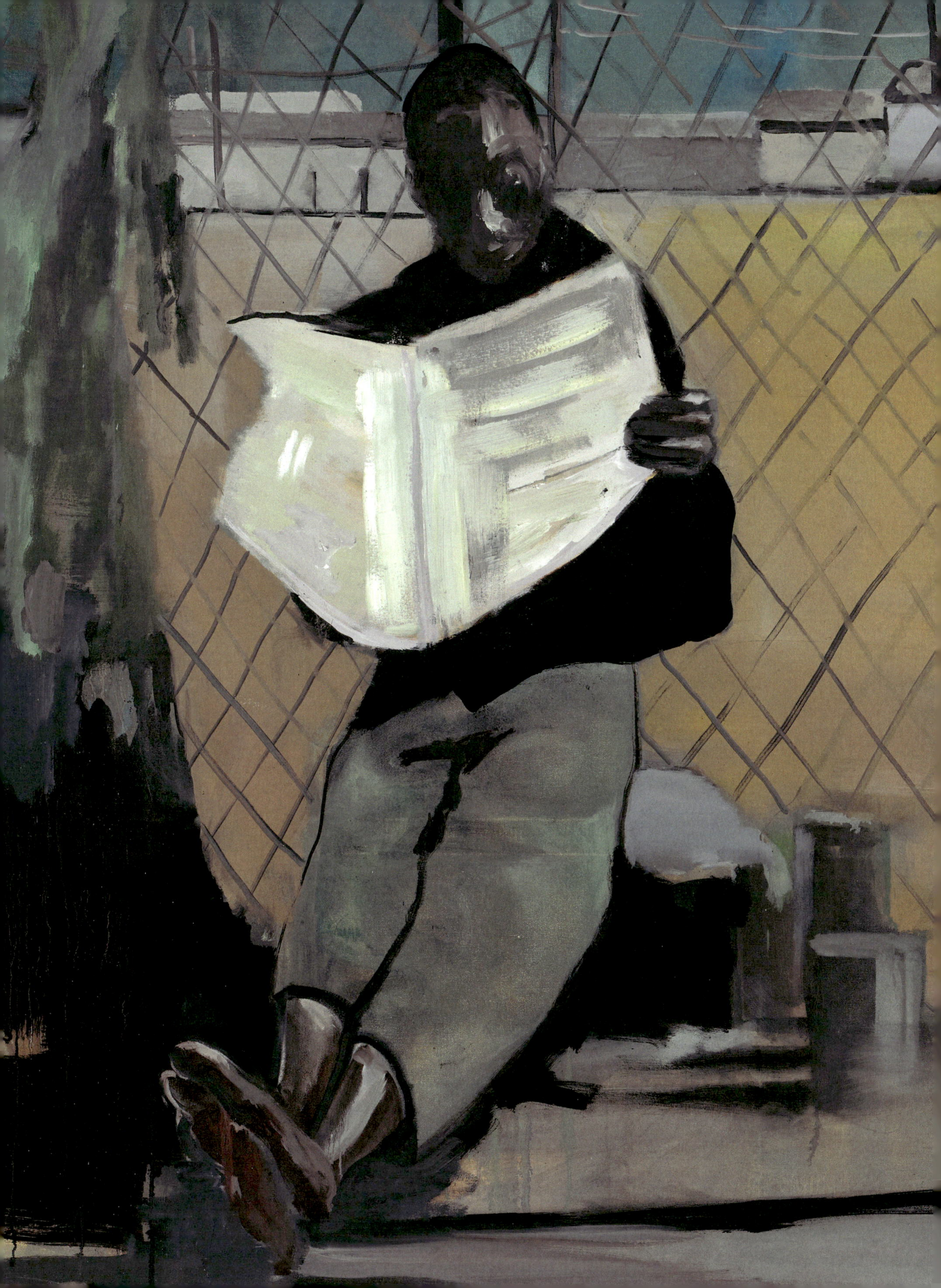

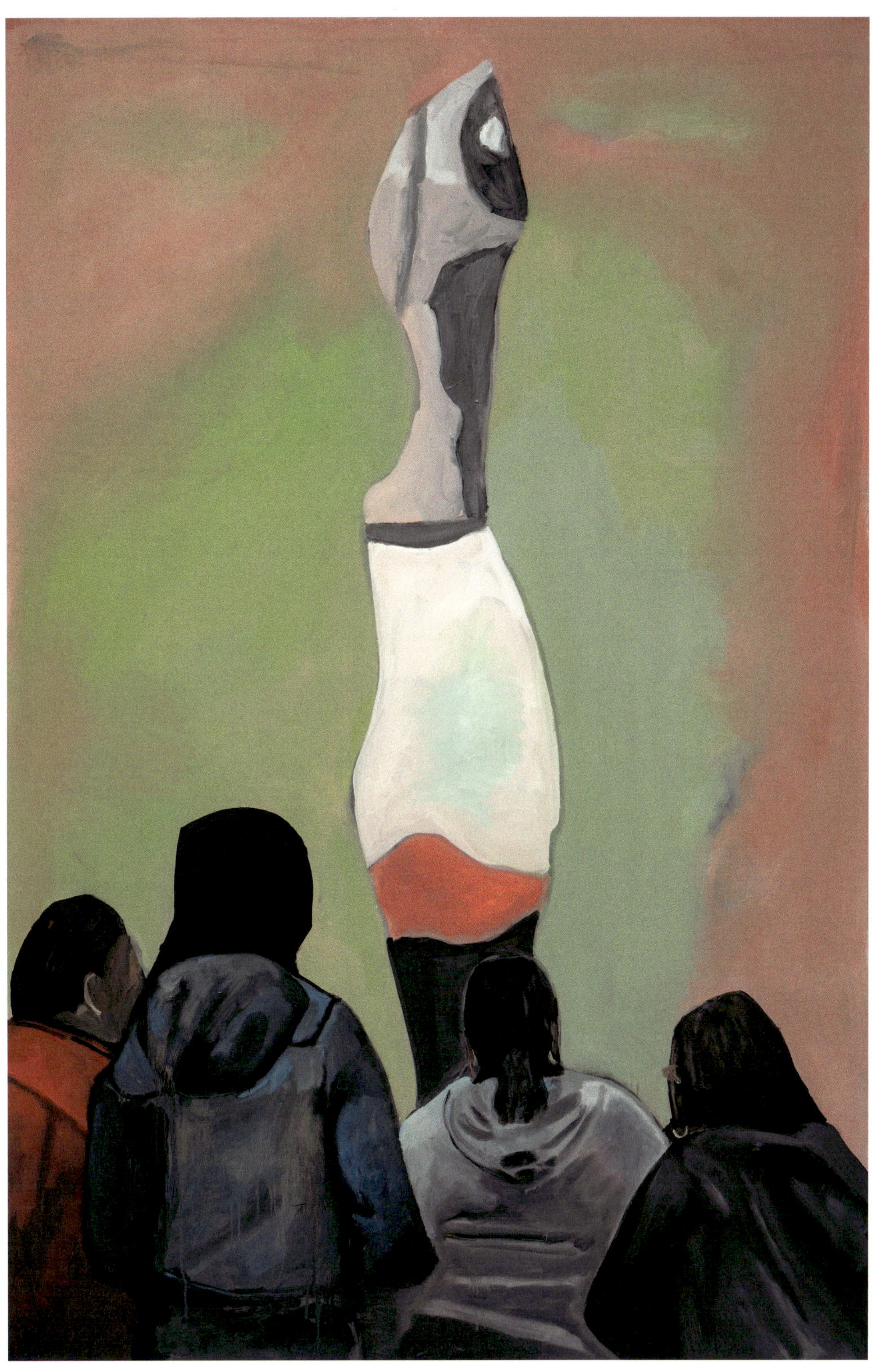

 Pueblo del Rio: Public Art Sculpture, 2014

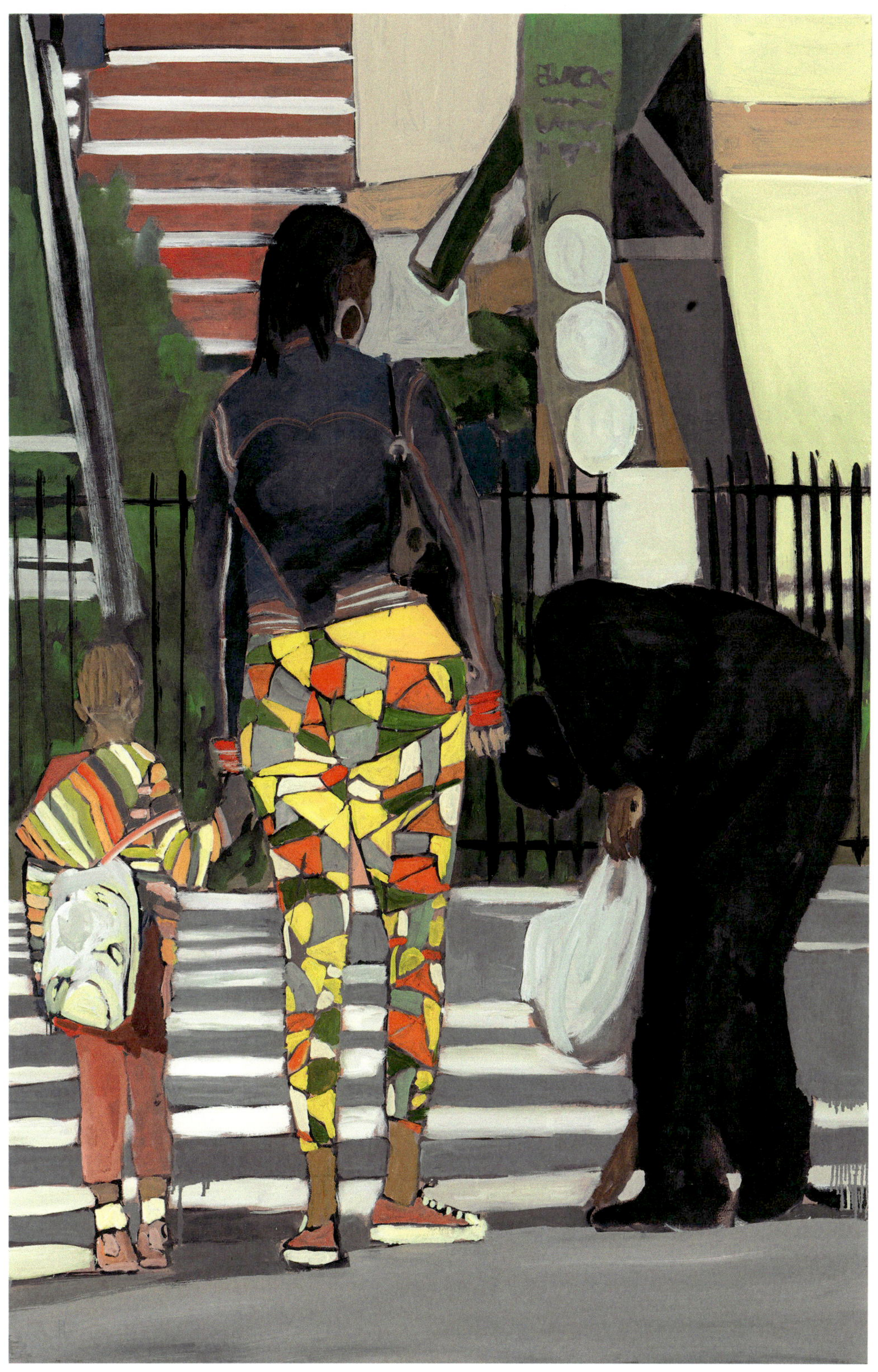

 Pueblo del Rio: Stain Glass Pants, 2014

NOAH DAVIS, THE ARCHITECT
by Wells Fray-Smith

In a filmed interview at the opening of his first solo exhibition in New York, at Tilton Gallery in 2010, Noah Davis singled out *The Architect* (2009) (p. 69) as his favourite work in the show. In the painting, a Black man in a suit sits facing an architectural model with the trademarks of twentieth-century modernist simplicity: a pyramid-like structure surrounded by intersecting planes of pure, rectangular forms. Magnanimous and God-like, he delicately stretches one hand over his creation as though slightly tweaking it, making it just right. With the interviewer's hand-held camera close to his face, Davis explains:

> 'To me, on a personal level, it's about the architect...in the arts, it seems like you start off as a painter, and then you kinda see your place in society as kind of like this urban development. To me, this [painting] is the culmination of the whole story. A lot of Egyptian texts are about architects, a lot of the great pharaohs are great architects, so that's kind of what it's about – it's reinforcing the fact that this really high position is, you know, it's extremely important, you know? And for a long time, there's been Black architects...'[1]

As Davis goes on to clarify, the architect in the painting is Paul Revere Williams, an astonishing figure in the history of Los Angeles and twentieth-century American architecture. Beginning his career at a time when almost all architects were white men, Williams designed more than 3,000 buildings across the city between the 1920s and 1970s. His work ranged from a space-age building at LAX to middle schools, churches to public service buildings, affordable housing projects and luxury homes. Nicknamed an 'architect to the stars', Williams designed countless Hollywood mansions for the rich and famous and the crescent wing of the now-iconic Beverly Hills Hotel, a dark irony given that he was not allowed to eat in the hotel's restaurant, which was a 'whites-only' establishment.

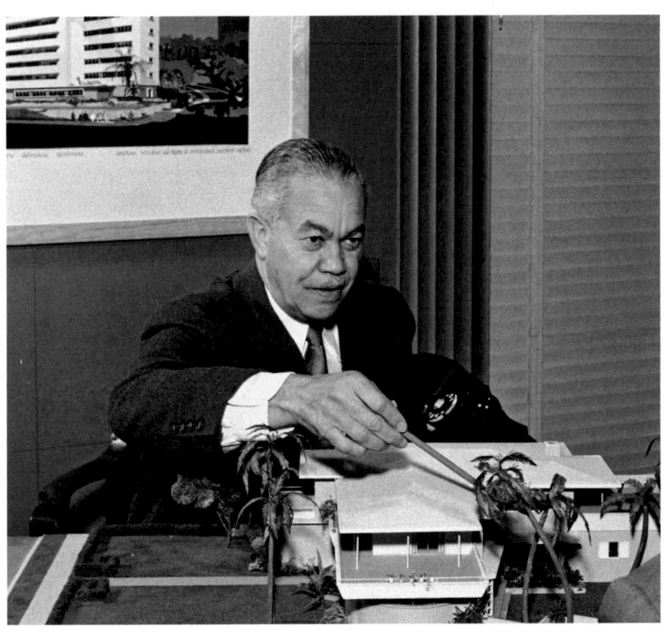

Paul Revere Williams, 1952

Davis was obsessed with Williams. He presumably had an early introduction to his work, as his father, Keven Davis, was best friends and frat brothers with Williams's grandson Glenn Harvey. Later, when Davis moved to Los Angeles, he was suddenly surrounded by Williams's architecture, an unavoidable element of the city's urban fabric. Beyond *The Architect*, Davis featured Williams's buildings in his *Pueblo del Rio* series – a suite of seven paintings set within the vast LA housing project Williams co-designed. In one of Davis's final paintings, made in 2015, he ditched figuration altogether and painted Williams's name across a green, abstract ground. When Davis moved to Ojai in July 2015, one month before he died, he gathered his closest companions and collaborators to discuss the future of the Underground Museum in a friend's house originally designed by Williams.

Williams's biography provided a model of possibility for Davis, whose dream was to 'create a world in which you can express your own ideas'[2] and aimed for an artistic legacy 'that not only transcends Blackness but confluences and impacts all cultures'.[3] Despite segregation, prejudice and racism, Williams slid fluidly between worlds, belonging to Black communities but entering and impacting the white world.[4] He also gave back to his community, becoming a founding board member of the Black-led Broadway Federal Bank, which gave loans to minority consumers who otherwise would not have been eligible. In the writing of history, however, Williams has been eclipsed by his white contemporaries. He is both the forgotten hero and the god who succeeded. He built his own world, and he did it with flair, always impeccably dressed (a detail which perhaps also resonated for Davis, who painted in dress shoes).

Beyond Williams, Davis was more broadly interested in modernist architecture. He was captivated by its aesthetics and its failures, by the ways in which modernist buildings were invested with hopeful futures that sometimes materialised but which, more often, did not. With crisp lines and essential forms, the built world

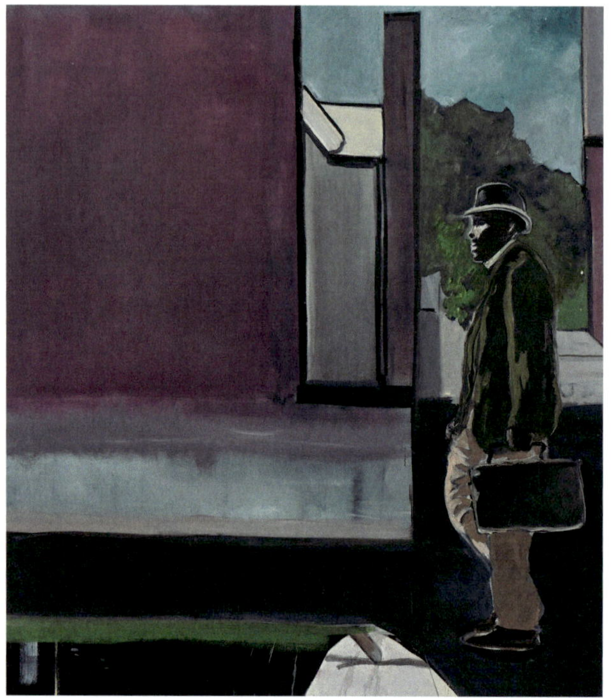

The Missing Link 3 (detail), 2013

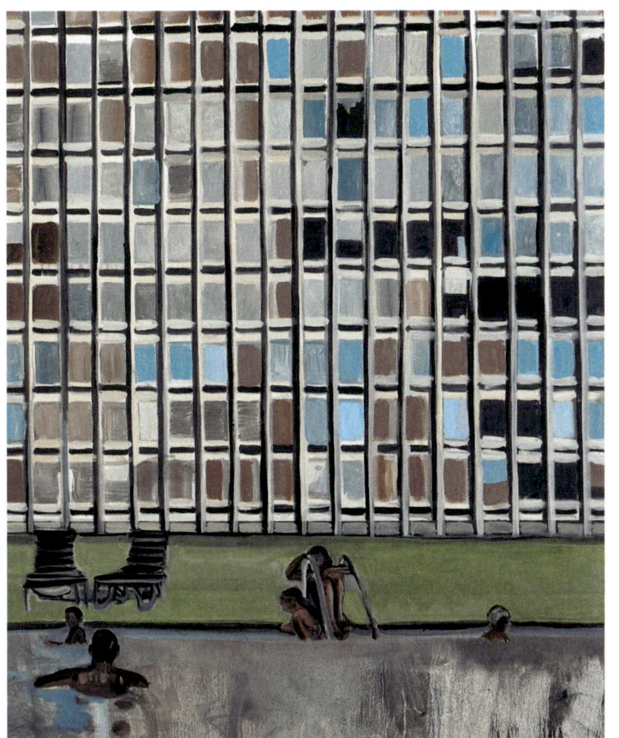

of modernist design provided a basis for Davis to explore the formal connections between architecture and painting, the three-dimensional and two-dimensional, the real and the abstract. Davis would walk around the streets of Los Angeles and take photos of what he called 'hood Rothkos', patches of exterior walls where graffiti was painted over so that it looked – to Davis's eye – like Rothko's hazy edges, as in *The Missing Link 3* (2013). Is what we see on the left of this work a representation of a wall, a painted wall or a painting? Davis pushes his abstract projections on the built world even further in *The Missing Link 4* (2013), in which the steel and glass façade of Mies van der Rohe's modernist housing development in Detroit's Lafayette Park glimmers in a chequered pattern of blue, brown, black and grey marks. The abstracted façade dominates the painting, while in its lower third, Black children play in the development's swimming pool.

Beyond his visual inspiration, Davis also drew on modernist architecture for conceptual and philosophical material, using it to investigate the intersection of race, class and urban development. Mies's Lafayette Park was an epic endeavour intended to provide new housing for the middle classes in downtown Detroit. But to make the development's three 22-storey tower blocks and 186 houses, a predominantly Black working-class neighbourhood named Black Bottom was razed. Demolishing poor, mostly Black neighbourhoods was a common practice at the time, forming an essential part of federally funded urban renewal programmes that displaced more than 300,000 families across the US from the 1950s to the 1970s. Whereas in other cities, the racist ideologies underlying mass development on this scale engendered further segregation, in Detroit, the opposite happened. In 2013, when Davis turned his attention to Lafayette Park, the development was one of the most racially integrated neighbourhoods in the city.[5] It was, he said, 'an interesting example of urban renewal and the advent of housing projects… I guess you

The Missing Link 4 (detail), 2013

could say I am fascinated with instances where Black aesthetics and modernist aesthetics collide.'[6] And collide they do – in this work, Davis's palette of blues, browns, blacks and greys encompasses the building, the pool and the people, as though the building is both a container for and mirror to life.

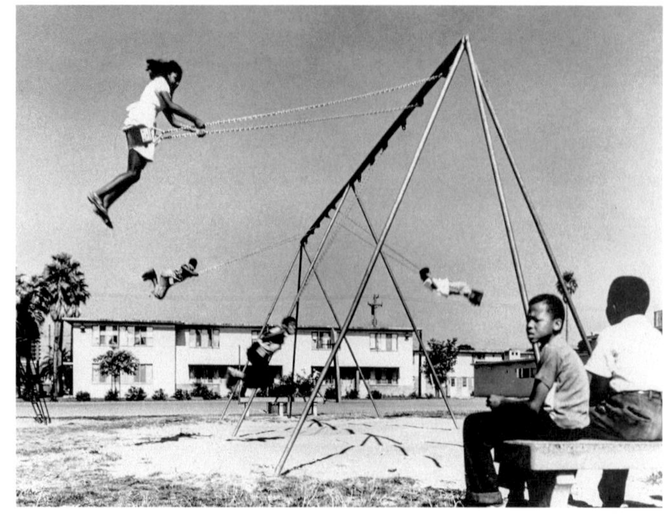

The confluence of 'Black aesthetics' and 'modernist aesthetics' that Davis noticed in Detroit is also present in LA, where mid-century housing projects – many of them designed specifically for African Americans as a hangover from enslavement and segregation – ripple across the city. There, modernist buildings and racially zoned neighbourhoods provide settings for countless Black lives to unfold. A year after painting *The Missing Link 4*, Davis turned his attention to one of the oldest and largest public housing developments in the city, designed by Williams alongside Richard Neutra, Gordon B. Kaufmann, Adrian Wilson and the firm Wurdeman & Becket. Opened in 1942, Pueblo del Rio was built for defence-industry workers, the majority of whom were Black. It was specifically intended to provide affordable housing for 'families of pinched income' and trialled cheap masonry construction with no frills.[7] Designed as a garden city, the houses were built around open, grassy spaces for leisure and play. The project was ill-fated from the start – within a decade, white families started moving out, local factories closed, money ran short, and Pueblo del Rio became a racially segregated and impoverished neighbourhood. In 2009, the *Los Angeles Times* reported that from the 1970s, 'violent outbursts became routine' and declared it 'a place beset with crippling poverty'.[8]

Davis used Pueblo del Rio as the setting for seven paintings (all painted in 2014), using the architecture to explore the assumed majesty of what Pueblo del Rio once was and to imagine what it could have been. In Davis's vision, the housing development is pregnant with possibility, holding and gestating the aliveness of Black people – their creativity, their noise, their movement, their quietude, their contemplation, their rest. Some of these paintings seem strikingly real, as though we are the audience to everyday life unfolding. A man reads a newspaper; a woman

Children play in Pueblo del Rio housing project playground

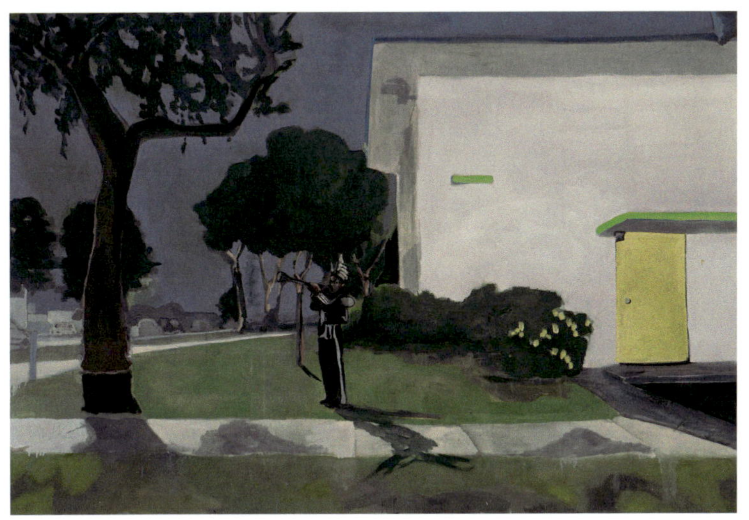

in brightly coloured trousers and her young daughter prepare to cross the street; a group of four teenagers in hoodies stand in front of a totem-like public sculpture. Others are surreal, strange, magical, unbound by time. A conductor in a tailcoat gestures to an unseen orchestra; a group of ballet dancers extend their arms and legs in perfect formation; a lone horn player in marching band regalia locks eyes with the viewer; a pianist sits at a grand piano in the middle of an intersection (pp. 183–201). In this setting, amid the bricks and mortar, these figures look like they have been dropped in or superimposed. In these works, the architecture is cold and restrained, the mauve sky is bruised with yellows and greens, but the canvases are charged with the magic of creativity; with music, with song, with dance. As Davis summarised: 'the paintings represent the potential of art and performance in a low-income community.'[9] Forget the poverty, forget the failure. Anything is possible in the Pueblo del Rio.

How do you 'create a world in which you can express your own ideas'? You paint it. You build it yourself. As Davis was making magic in paint, so too was he creating it in life. By the time he painted the *Pueblo del Rio* series, the Underground Museum had found its purpose to provide 'inner-city neighbourhoods with free access to world-class art'.[10] Having been through different iterations as a studio, a place for Noah and his wife Karon and their son Moses to live and a site for residencies (under the name Inner City Avant-Garde), the

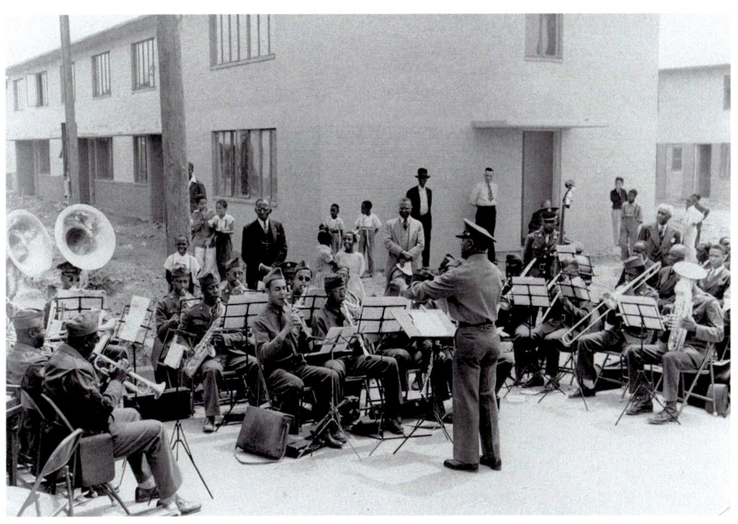

Top *Pueblo del Rio: Prelude*, 2014
Bottom Band performs at Pueblo del Rio

museum manifested the potential of art and performance in a low-income community. Based in Arlington Heights, a neighbourhood without other cultural outlets, the Underground Museum was borne from Davis's drive to 'just make this shit ourselves'.[11] In Davis's imagination, it was an 'experimental space open to community', which is to say, it was radically free from institutional pressure to do things a certain way, and radically inclusive to anyone and everyone who walked through its doors.[12] Formerly a pupusería and a church, the converted storefronts carried resonance as places of gathering (over food or faith).[13] Davis honoured this history, dreaming of a space for people's lives and stories to be held, represented and reflected. 'You start off as a painter and then you kinda see your place in society as... this urban development. To me, this is the combination of the whole story.' There he is. Noah Davis, the architect.

1 'Shelley Wade interviews Painter Noah Davis', Tilton Gallery, New York, 8 April 2009, youtube.com/watch?v=dVgVkMUNejk.

2 'Educators' Night Out' at the Corcoran School of the Arts & Design, 4 October 2011, online recording, vimeo.com/31541073.

3 The Underground Museum, theunderground.museum/about/.

4 Though this was not without concession. As mentioned in T. J. Clark's entry in this catalogue (pp. 68–71), Williams was famous for learning how to sketch upside down so he could sit across from – rather than next to – his white clients while still showing them his vision.

5 'Home Sweet Architectural Masterpiece', *New York Times*, 3 October 2012, https://www.nytimes.com/2012/10/04/garden/a-new-book-celebrates-mies-van-der-rohes-lafayette-park-complex-in-detroit.html?unlocked_article_code=1.9E0.a01o.aOM48msyWf76&smid=url-share. The most famous failed housing development in architectural history is the Pruitt-Igoe development in St Louis, Missouri. With 33 highrises, it was one of the largest public housing developments in the United States when it was built in 1954. From the outset, the apartment buildings were segregated, and when white families did not move in, it became an almost exclusively Black dwelling for largely impoverished residents who could not afford to move elsewhere. Poor facilities and lack of funding and maintenance created sub-par living conditions that disproportionately affected Black residents. In 1972, the complex was deemed a failed experiment, and two of the 33 buildings were demolished live on television.

6 Yael Lipschutz, 'Q+A with Noah Davis', *Art in America*, 7 March 2013.

7 *Architecture and Engineer*, February 1937, reproduced in 'Pueblo del Rio Housing Project, Los Angeles, CA', Paul Revere Williams: American Architect, paulrwilliamsproject.org.

8 Scott Gold, 'At an impoverished housing complex, a reflection of South L.A.', *Los Angeles Times*, 14 July 2009, latimes.com/local/la-me-southla-pueblos14-2009jul14-story.html.

9 Noah Davis quoted in the press release for *Noah Davis: Garden City*, Papillion, Los Angeles, 2014, papillionart.com/photo-gallery/noah-davis-garden-city.

10 Noah Davis's notebook, 2014, n.p.

11 Helen Molesworth, 'Some Years Count as Double', Helen Molesworth (ed.), *Noah Davis*, exh. cat. (New York: David Zwirner Books/The Underground Museum, 2020), p. 165.

12 Yael Lipschutz, *Art in America*.

13 A pupusería is a vendor of pupusas, a popular stuffed flatbread similar to a tortilla from El Salvador, Honduras, Nicaragua and Guatemala.

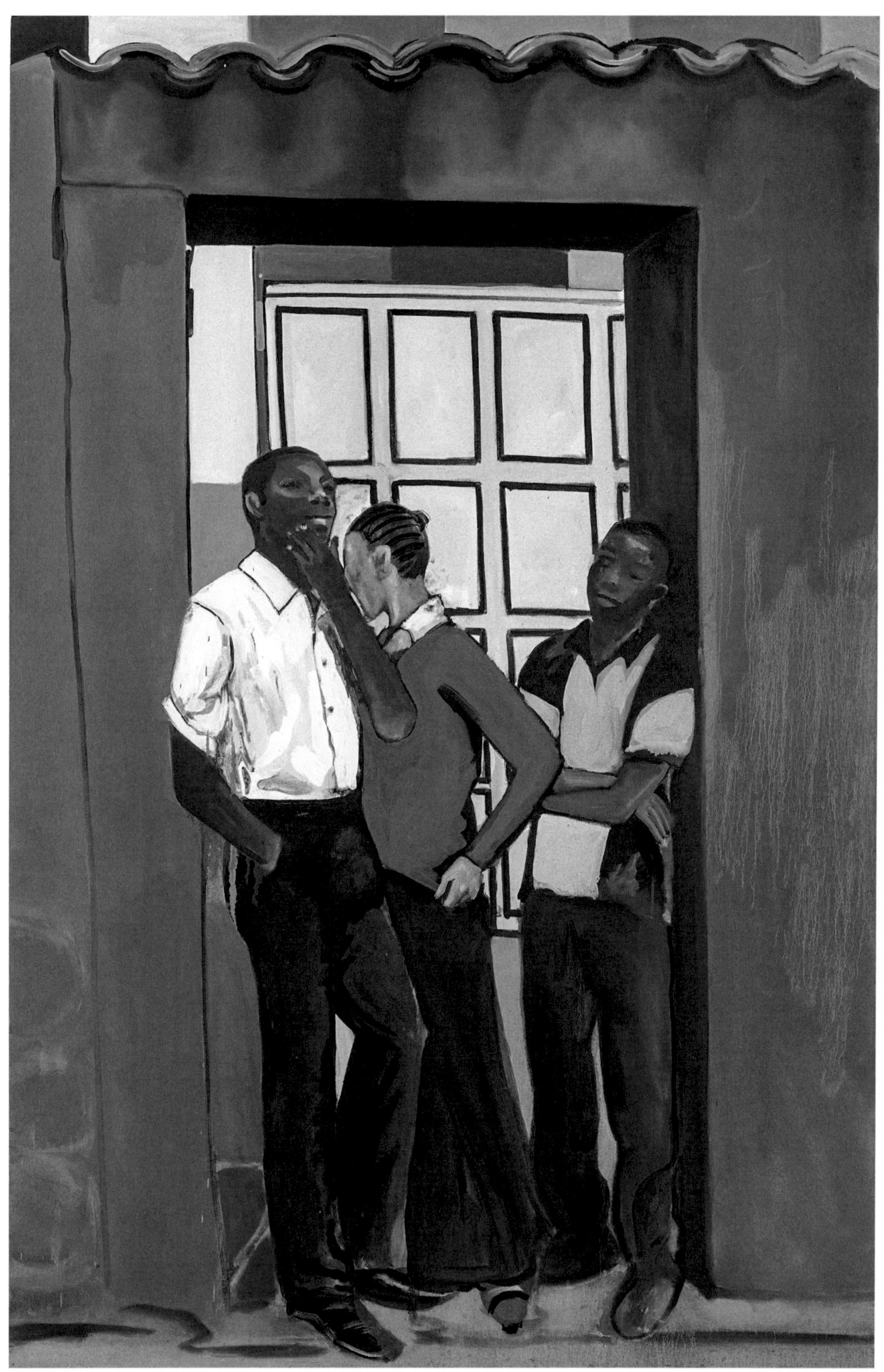

211 *Congo #7*, 2014

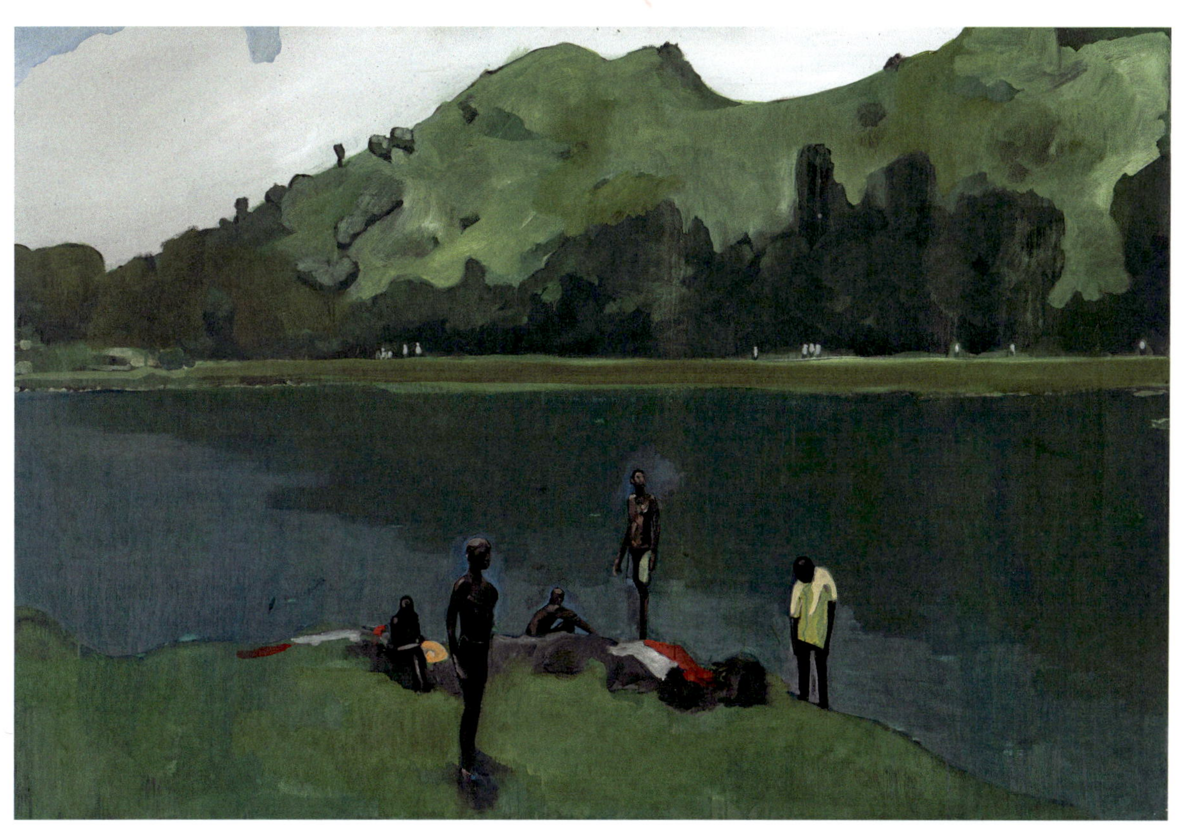

 Congo, 2015

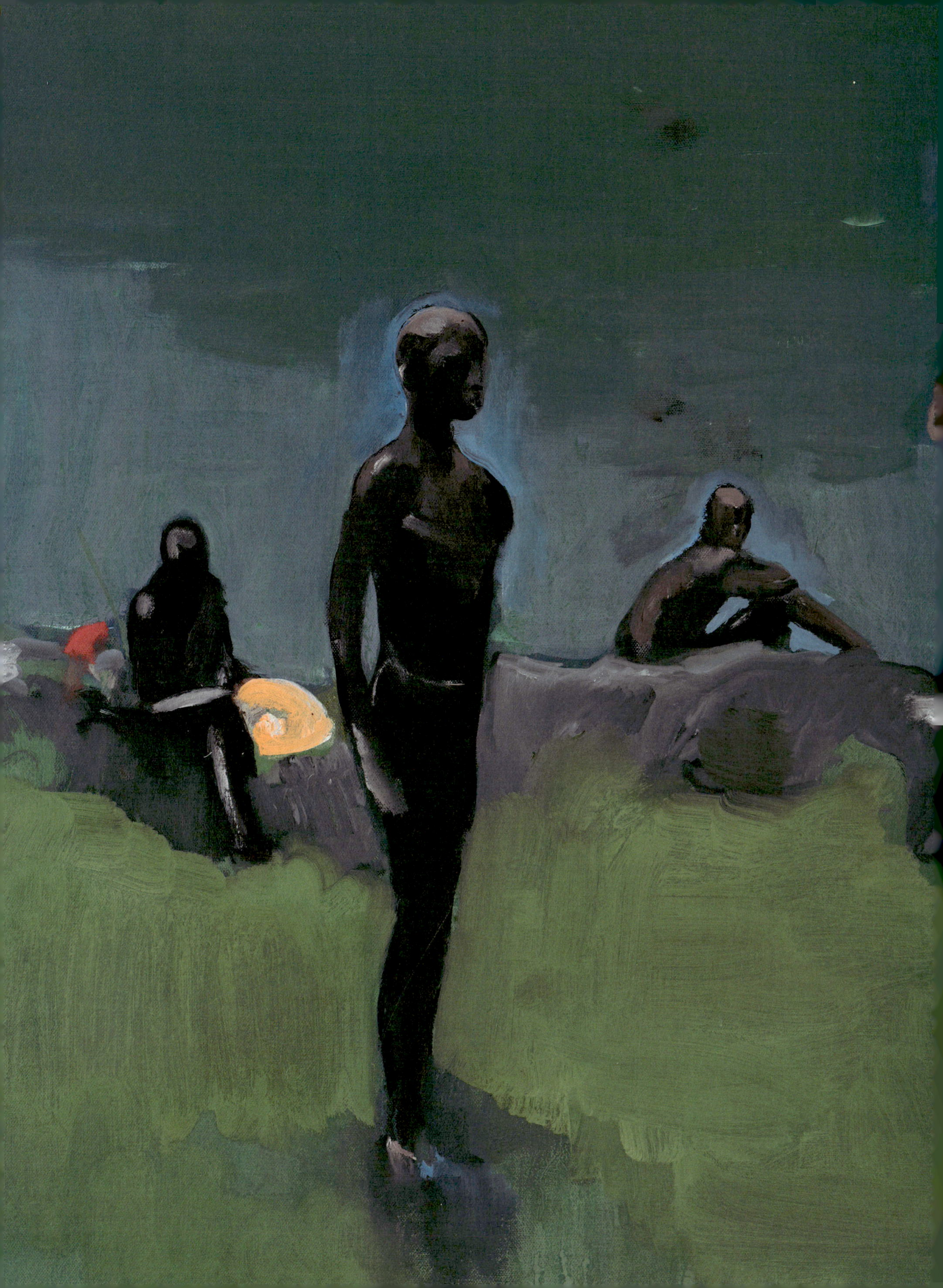

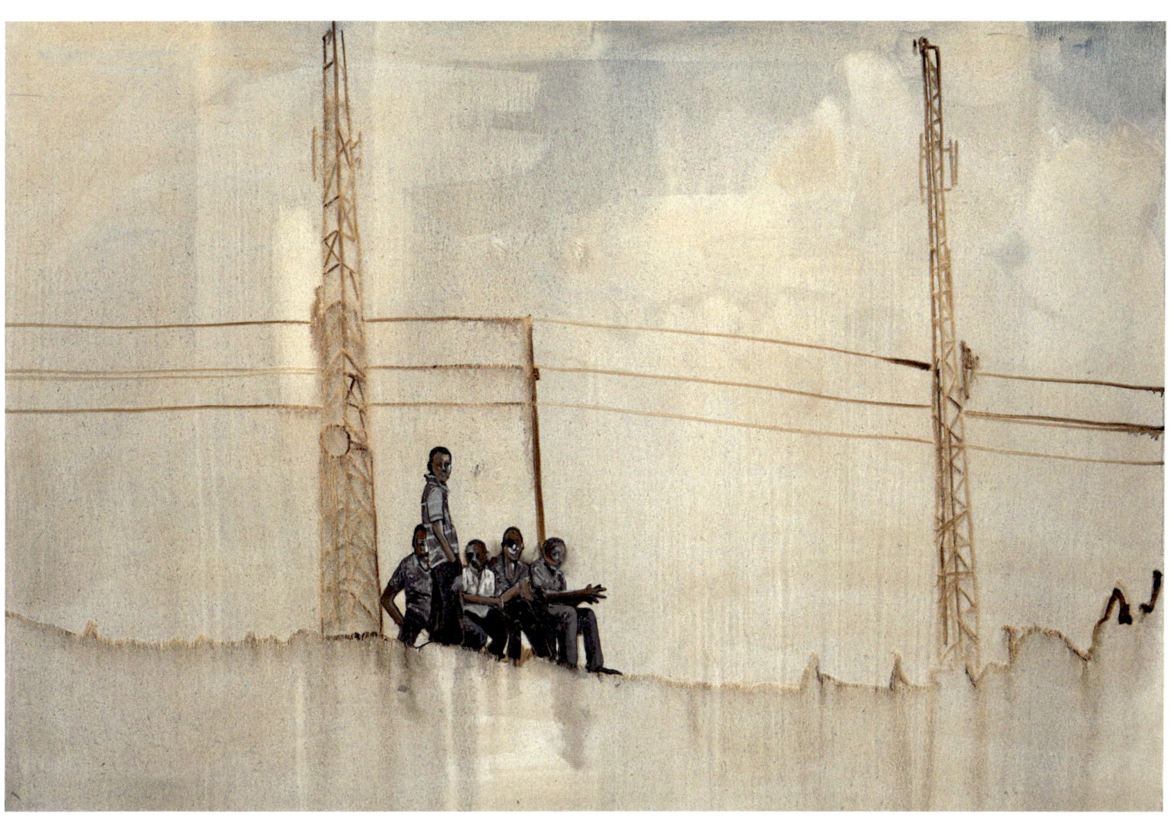

 Congo #2, 2015

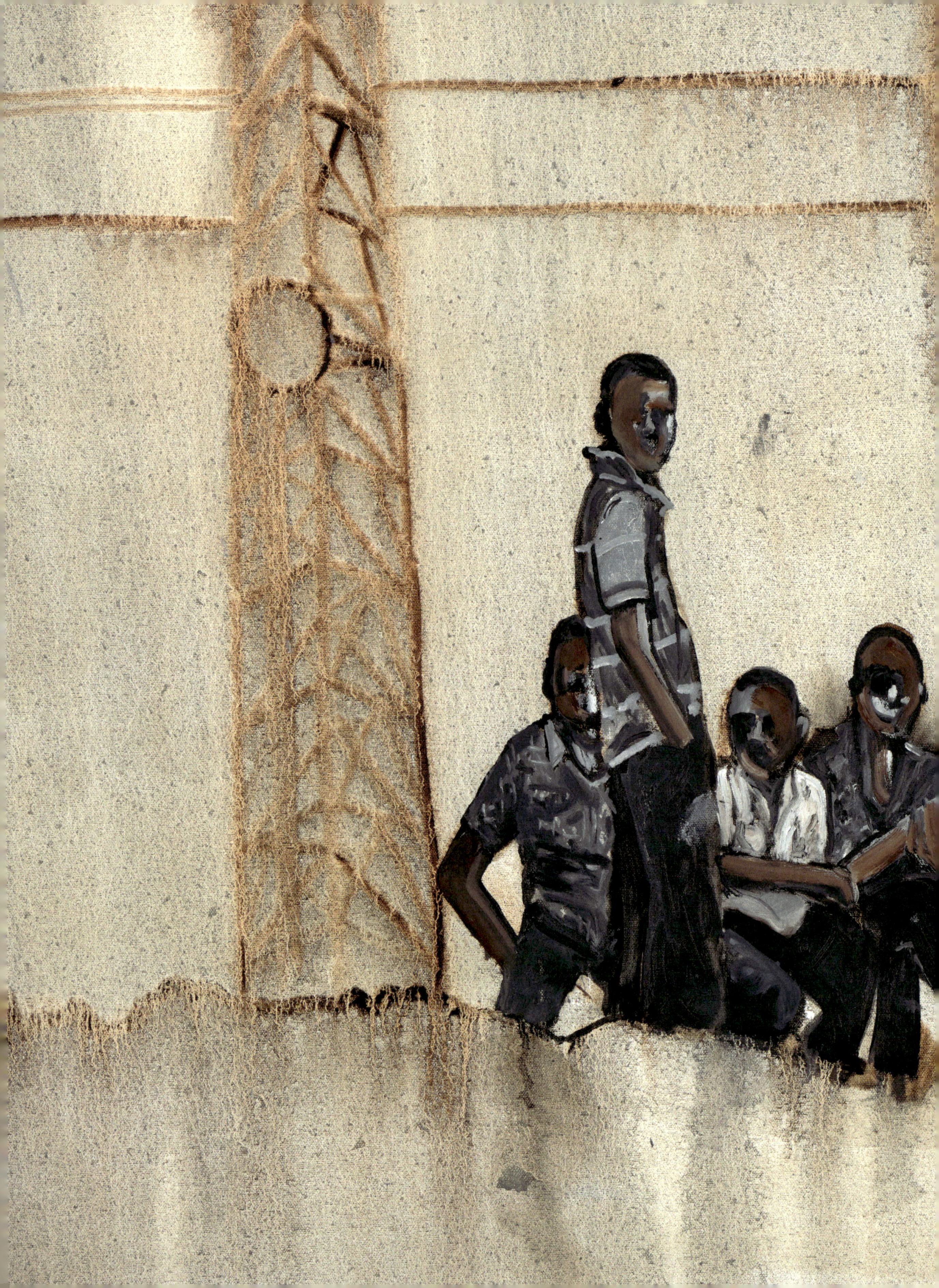

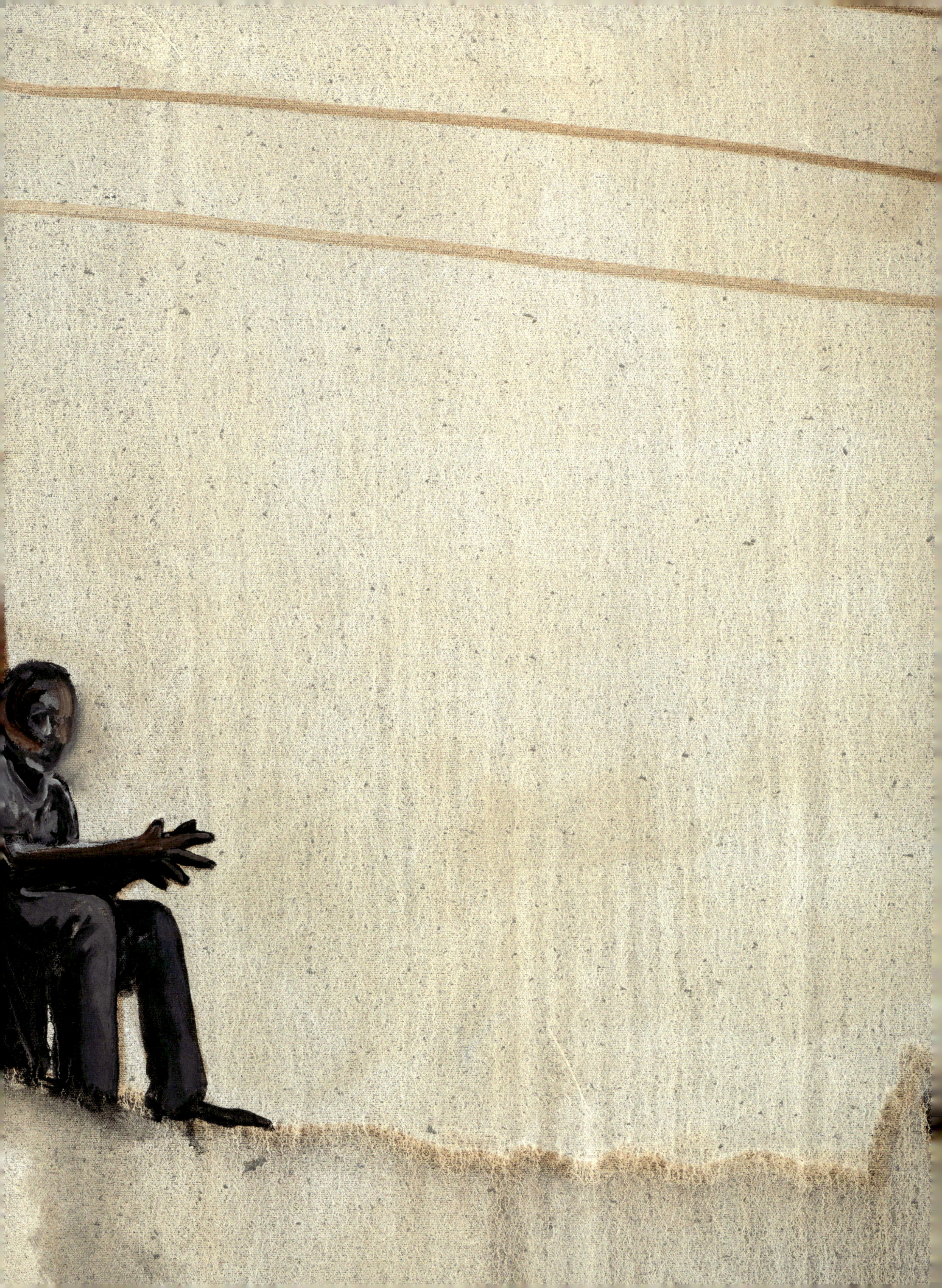

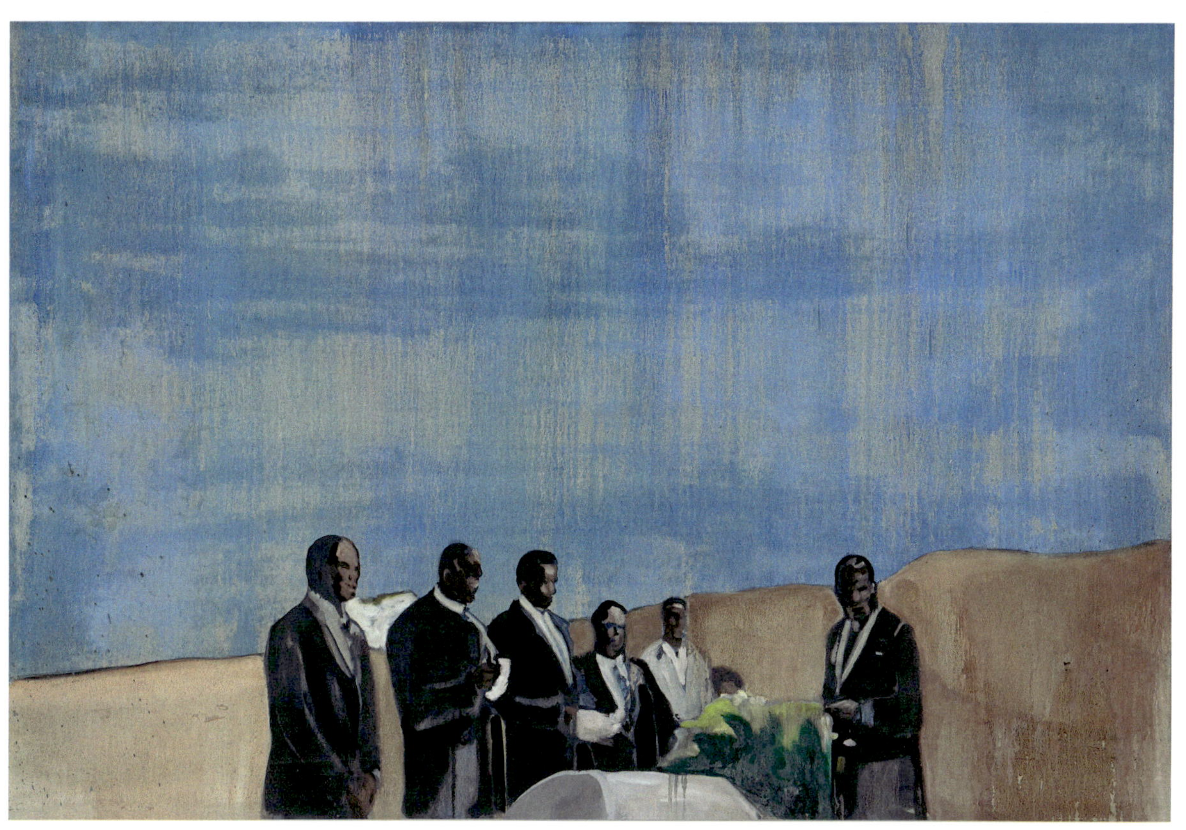

 Untitled, 2015

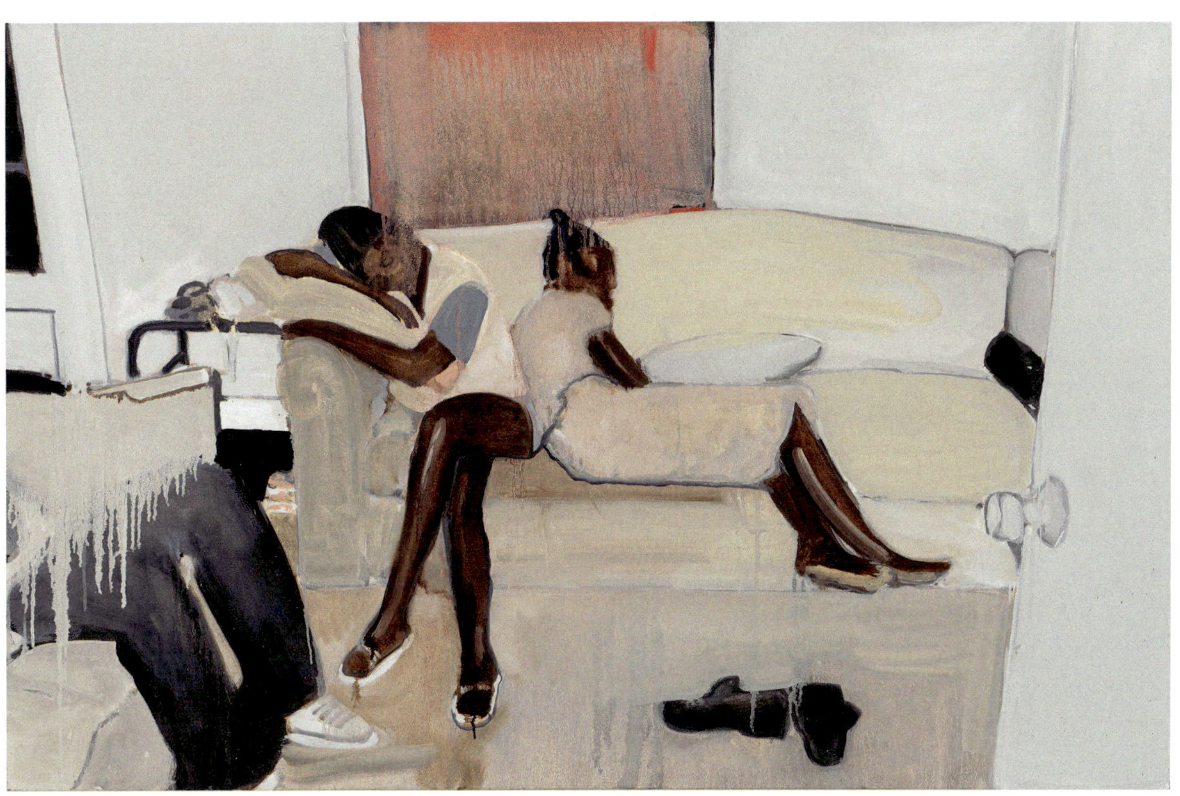

 Untitled, 2015

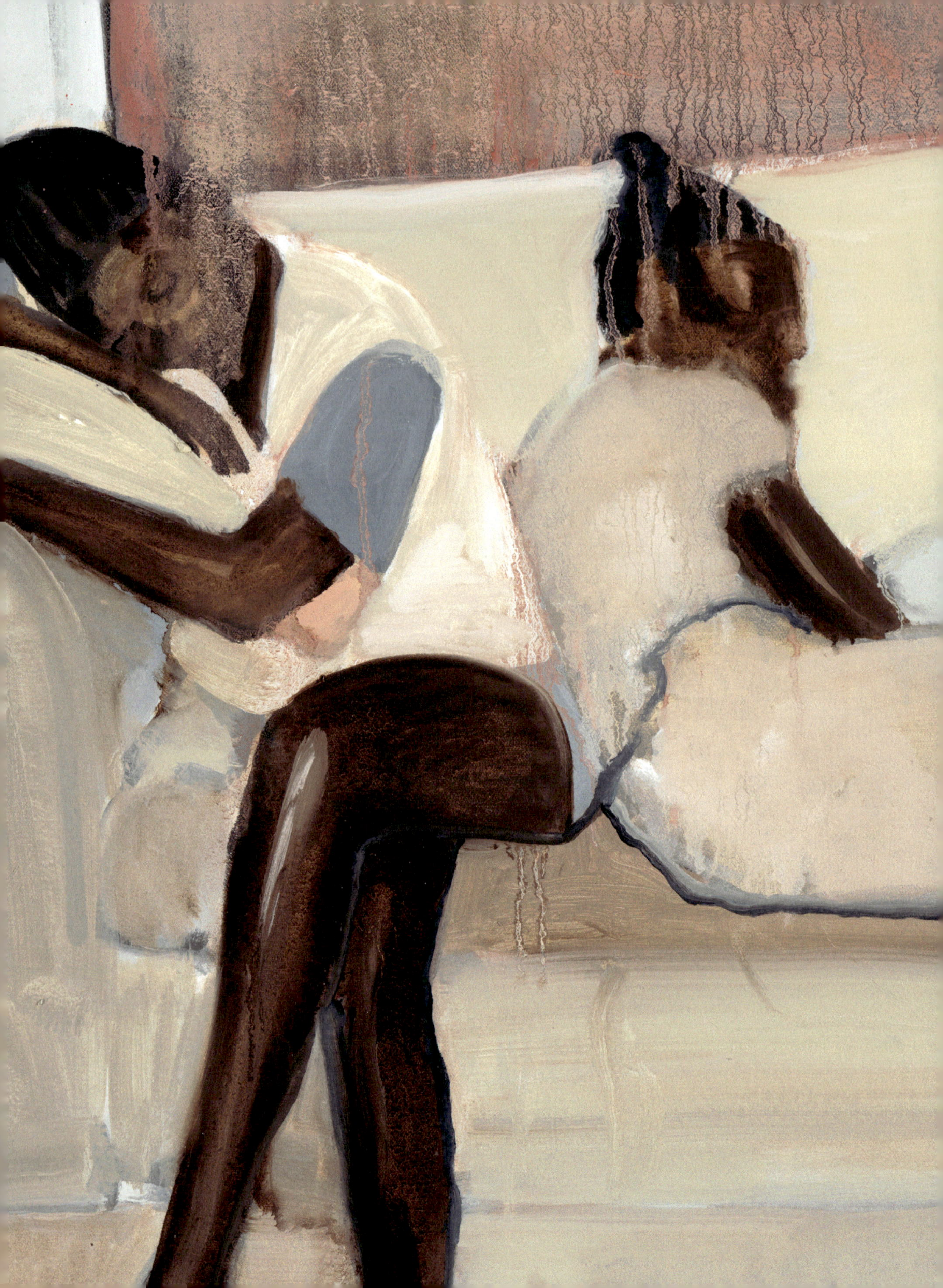

UNTITLED, 2015

Claudia Rankine

In the 2015 oil and canvas painting entitled *Untitled*, two central figures of indeterminate age, teenager to adult, nap on a couch side-by-side. They have collapsed into the right corner of the yellowing fabric; their backs are touching. Their positioning suggests familiarity with each other, intimacy. Sisters, cousins, close friends, mother and daughter? They are Black love in repose. It's late spring or early summer, as one figure's grey-blue cap sleeves, shorts and sandals suggest. She has repositioned a cushion to lay her head on. Her long, thin arms cradle the cushion and the arm of the couch as if they, too, are friends. Her fingers are not clenched but extended, relaxed or wholly exhausted, and without definition. A single closed eye and the suggestion of a mouth are discernable, but this is not that form of portraiture. Definition is not the goal. The collective, suggestive mood might be more the intention. The figure by her side has removed her shoes and readied herself for a moment of rest. We see the soles of her feet, but they remain close to the ground; she has not pulled them up onto the couch. She is not completely at home, it seems. This is not a home. They are not at home. Her partial collapse into the couch – with her head and upper body reclining against the backrest – is what she allows herself. The figures buttress each other on one half of the couch while the remaining space seems as if it's awaiting another.

These two figures, though they command our gaze, are not alone. A person in white sneakers and black pants sits on an adjacent couch, co-existing with them in the room, but barely. The couch this other figure sits on bleeds its greyness into them, covering their torso and face, though their legs, once noticed, remain clear. There is enough space next to this figure for another, as well. But given the grey wash erasing them, it's hardly an invitation. Are we, as viewers, intruding? Still, and importantly, the door through which we view this scene is open. *Come. Come in. Join them. Rest. Whatever form it takes, rest. All feeling belongs here. The exhaustion belongs to everyone. Time is timeless.*

What does it mean to write into the living memory of a person you have never met but whose works carry forward a feeling of community long after their passing? Noah Davis created the spaces he imagined, even as he left those spaces behind. In 2012, three years before his death from cancer at the age of 32, Davis brought one of his imagined spaces into the culturally underserved Los Angeles neighbourhood of Arlington Heights. The space, which would become known as the Underground Museum (UM), lasted for ten magical years before closing in 2022. The genesis of the idea for the UM began with Davis's father, Keven Davis, who left his son an inheritance to invest in a space for 'the community'.[1] And so the UM defined its mission 'to ensure no one has to travel outside the neighbourhood to see world-class art, or learn from leading thinkers, educators, chefs, and artists'. On the doors of the UM, it reportedly read: 'This is a Black space, but all are welcome.'

In 2021, the curator Helen Molesworth conducted a roundtable discussion dedicated to the UM, in which the scholar Fred Moten made the insightful claim that the UM was 'a quintessentially Black space because it wasn't exclusive. It was aggressively not exclusive.'[2] This lack of exclusivity is the gift Davis offered to the concept of community within Black spaces, in the convening, in the community called together. As open as the doors remained, he still communicated that we have all we need right here among us, between us. *Come. Come in. Join us.*

To stand in front of work made by Davis is to feel held by a carved-out space. Or maybe not just held but encircled by a realm of quiet, quiet joy, quiet sorrow or ordinary acceptance of our quotidian. Each day's possibilities are on offer, as well as their limits. *Murmurations* – a word and image I encountered in John Akomfrah's 2021 multi-channel video response to the murder of George Floyd – comes to mind. The fullness of our daily murmurations, as we exist in unison, with and for each other, like starlings in formation. The word seems apt when taking in the whole of Davis's oeuvre. Sometimes, the quiet in his figurative paintings communicates rest; sometimes, it holds contemplation. Sometimes, there are questions being asked for which we have no answers, but we hold their indeterminacy anyway – together and alone.

Even within paintings depicting private, intimate moments that are unknowable, bordering on the *sur*-real, there remains an invitation to counter the chaos (or is it the cosmos?) with stillness. *Repose here, Pueblo del Rio*, they seem to suggest. (Pueblo del Rio is a public housing project Davis portrayed in a 2014 series of the same name.) In painting after painting, a blurry figure has paused, but whatever is behind the eyes (when seeing is allowed) has not. There are thoughts held or dreams occurring in conversation with others; maybe even a call to move over, to make more space, so another can join. Davis was known to paint over paintings, to reuse canvases, creating shadows that ghost within the paintings themselves. There was always room for more. The space that holds somehow always makes extra space for the viewer, too. It's the action of community-building built into an artistic practice. In Davis's work, there's sometimes a room or a street that we enter to exist alongside others. Sometimes, there exists an actual space in the world, and sometimes, the space resides in a questioning gaze within a painting. *There is room enough for all of us* is the mood Davis orchestrated so that we may inhabit, take in, share. *Come. Come along. Join in. Rest.*

The UM's inaugural exhibitions in early 2013, *Imitation of Wealth* and *Karon Davis: new sculptures and photographs*, were, in a sense, an improvisational adjustment after Davis wasn't able to secure institutional loans for the pieces he originally wanted to display. How do you approach the signified destination without ever reaching it? In this case, Davis's boot-legged Dan Flavin or Jeff Koons pieces signified more about wealth than art, given that had they been about art, they would have been shown as themselves. *Karon Davis: new sculptures and photographs* stood as signified, as art.

By the time two years had passed, Davis had secured a loan agreement with MOCA facilitated by Molesworth, and in June 2015, the UM exhibited works by William Kentridge, another community-based artist with a profoundly integrated practice.[3] *William Kentridge: Journey to the Moon* showed *7 Fragments for Georges Méliès* (2003), a series of animated films concerned with process and artmaking that were a tribute to the titular French filmmaker and magician. One might see these films (with their use of slow motion and reverse cuts and dissolves) as paying homage to the power of the imagination and the ways it opens us out both to the world and the vast possibilities inherent in our interior lives. The imagination doesn't solve; it enables. Davis knew this. *Come in.*

The complex, layered nature of our individual interior lives deepens through our interactions with who and what we encounter and absorb. Davis's understanding and deep belief in this form of synergy allowed his constructed spaces to help others, through art and community, to open outwards, to find the spaces within themselves that allow them to continue on. This might be one of the highest forms of activism. We enter these spaces to relax into, to leave behind, to accumulate, to join in, to be more.

I first encountered the UM when I attended the opening of *Non-fiction* in 2016, the first show to open at the museum after Davis's death. He'd left behind precise instructions for this exhibition and a number of other shows (18, to be exact). By the time the museum closed in 2022, four had been realised. On the night of the opening, I passed through the museum's bookstore into the show, and though I could hear voices coming from somewhere, there remained a period when I felt I was almost alone with the art. I stood in front of Robert Gober's 1989 *Hanging Man/Sleeping Man* wallpaper piece for a very long time. The pastel colour scheme and repetitive patterning brought to mind American wallpaper from the 1940s and '50s. The two images, one of a lynched Black man and the other of a sleeping white man, brought the horror of Jim Crow into the domestic, quotidian spaces affected by it. I'd not seen it before, and at the time, I was thinking a lot about how to uncover what we carry so it can be seen, identified and articulated within the ordinary negotiations of Black living, Black life. Daily tragic occurrences all over the United States were in line with the treatment of our ancestors. The police killings of Black people were a continuance of historical and systemic violence, and our bodies knew this, remembered, in a world that treated each wound as surprising and novel. The Gober helped me to keep systemic truths active and emotionally acknowledged in the present. It reminded me to recall the intentionality of it all. We were not here negotiating precarity by accident.

There was a photograph of a Black woman installed in front of Gober's wallpaper, almost as if it was there to counterbalance the white women in Kerry James Marshall's *Heirlooms & Accessories* (2002), which hung on its own wall in its own room (the white women, pictured in lockets, were members of a lynch mob who murdered Black teenagers Thomas Shipp and Abram Smith in Indiana in 1930). Only later did I learn that the wallpaper and the photograph were two separate pieces. The photograph, taken by Marion Palfi, was of the widow of Caleb Hill, Jr., the first reported lynching victim of 1949. Davis had married the photograph to Gober's *Hanging Man/Sleeping Man.* There we were, face to face, one Black woman to another, centuries apart, understanding this place where we lived, live. Davis brought us together across time. On the adjacent wall, a Marshall piece partnered the Gober and Palfi – a bouquet of plastic flowers in a Baptist church vase, accompanied by a video still and notecard stating 'As Seen on TV' – an elegy to the 1963 Birmingham church bombing by white supremacists, which killed Addie Mae Collins (14), Cynthia Wesley (14), Carole Robertson (14) and Carol Denise McNair (11).

Later, after Davis's death, Gober reflected, 'I was on the phone with Noah about putting my wallpaper piece in the show, and I had no idea he was in the hospital.'[4] Everything would happen until it couldn't. Even near the end, Davis made room for all of life. He knew how to hold it all. He knew how to activate a future he would never share physically. As I walked through *Non-fiction*, maybe a couple of others moved through with me, but not next to me, not near me. The experience didn't feel public. We were with the art, the artists, our artists – Gober, Palfi, Marshall, David Hammons, Theaster Gates, Deana Lawson, Henry Taylor, Kara Walker. This memory is the one that stays, the feeling of being able to see the work, the feeling of being in recognition of all of it, all we've inherited, as signalled by pieces like Marshall's *Heirlooms & Accessories* or Hammons's *In the Hood (Gray)* (1993/2016) or Henry Taylor's *Warning Shots not Required* (2011), the title of which originates from signage in prison yards across the United States. I was grateful to be able to metabolise this understanding of our history without having to split my attention. Maybe a dozen incredible works of art surrounded me, and I could take them in one at a time, even as distant voices suggested another kind of communion, another form of sociality was occurring elsewhere. Knowing I wasn't going to be left alone with the violent ongoing history the show called forward reminded me that this reality was not – and could not and should not be – my everything. That reminder was necessary to my ongoing experience. Being in community was the other part of it, the rest of it. *Come. Come in.* Everyone was in the Purple Garden. It was a glorious night. I hadn't known Davis had died when I arrived. There was that reality, too, touching everything.

It would be years later that I encountered Jennifer Packer's statement regarding her painting practice: 'We deserve to be heard and to be imaged with shameless generosity and accuracy.'[5] I took that to mean, as Tina M. Campt outlines in *A Black Gaze* (2021), 'Black visuality...is necessarily something to be felt.'[6] Davis once referred to something he was making as 'honest'. Accurate, generous, honest-feeling...that seemed like something to strive for in my own considerations. Do I mean strive towards or something to claim? Maybe both. I now think Davis wanted to claim honesty because feelings live unresolved among the raw brutality of the non-fiction.

To return to the 2015 painting entitled *Untitled*: the lack of precision in the brushstrokes and the dripping, bleeding paint gives the work a sense of dissolution that opens it out to be experienced and felt rather than read as a scene replicating Blackness – not a picture, but an experience of something true, a memory truth, a future memory of a feeling. The figures and the environment within and beyond the painting – aided by this dissolving technique – become one. There exists no hierarchy between figure and environment. The resting figures more or less blend into their environment. To enter into this space as a viewer is to give yourself over to a sense of a place rendered, a sense of exhaustion, a spirit of rest, unrest. The painting's Rothko-like image on the back wall (Davis was taken with Rothko's work) introduces a different palette of reds and pinks into the room without shifting the already established muted tones. Resistance here is rest. The need for rest in the face of anticipated loss, perhaps, but also on account of true exhaustion. Nothing, not even an open door, will disturb that.

The discoloured white walls, the yellowing couch, the grey subsuming the third figure return me to 2015, the year Davis painted what he left untitled. He would pass away on 29 August of that year, almost three months after turning 32 on 3 June. On that day in June, one of the longest days of the year, because he didn't want to spend his birthday in hospital, Davis left chemo with his wife, the artist and UM's co-founder Karon Davis, to return to his Purple Garden. Purple not (entirely) in homage to Prince, but because, as Karon tells us, Noah wanted everyone to feel like royalty in that space, where they could relax, read, converse, socialise, fall in love, do yoga or simply hang out.[7] There, on Davis's birthday, his friend the artist Henry Taylor surprised him with a visit from David Hammons, who wore purple shoes to the Purple Garden. I hope, for Davis, that visit extended everything, remaking the world again in love. I don't know. I remember that during my own chemotherapy, I had this feeling of being pulled into another atmosphere, drawn away from this world as cells were being attacked in my body. Only the strength of an encircling form of love can pull you back, keep you standing in the midst of appreciation of the fact that you are here now. Only love can enable the restfulness that others enable. Rest in love. Rest in community. Rest in recognition. *Come.*

This form of rest calls to mind Tricia Hersey's assertion that 'we are resting regardless of what any of the systems are doing.'[8] As she writes in *Rest is Resistance*, 'We are not waiting. We are not asking permission. We're driven by the spirit of being subversive, inventive, and disruptive. We know this will not be easy, but we trust our divinity, the power of collective care, and a laser focus on tapping into our imagination via rest to make a way for our unravelling...' For Davis, 2015 was a year of hospital rooms, pain, treatment and care from and for others. Rest was resistance, to paraphrase Hersey. These statements point to what was probable, nothing more. I make them because the routines around illness are not unfamiliar. They belong to many as ordinary, quotidian.

In July 2015, Noah, Karon and their son Moses moved to Ojai, California, where the landscape shifts to open sky and brown earth during the hot, dry summer. In the garage of their new home, Davis painted his final paintings. Perhaps among them exist the five men in black who stand as pallbearers alongside a casket. This is another of Davis's untitled paintings. Characteristically, the men's faces are unreadable. A sixth man in white, the same shade as the casket, stands a short distance away. Does a child lean against him? The atmosphere in this painting has been streamlined to blues and browns: heaven and earth. Sky and dirt. A cratered sky made of many rooms. An abstract composition close enough to what's known presents itself as an unknown state of being. A single green and white bouquet outlasts its blossom. Was Davis prefiguring? All possibilities stand. The mood is solemn. The end of August eventually arrived.

Despite the portrayal of exhaustion in these 2015 paintings, we are also proximate to mortality, vulnerability and intimacy. And to quote Campt, yet again, 'the beauty and the potentiality of a Black quotidian, where the intimacy of tender, everyday encounters creates a path to a different kind of sociality – one where our future is realised not only through tenacious struggle but through the reparative and restorative power of intimacy.'[9] Maybe by opening doors, by keeping a door open, by doing away with exclusivity, Noah Davis creates the possibility of the only thing we are promised for a time: each other.

1 'On Noah Davis: Helen Molesworth, Kahlil Joseph, and Karon Davis', *Dialogues: The David Zwirner Podcast*, 1 April 2020.
2 *Noah Davis: In Detail* (New York: David Zwirner Books, 2023), p. 93.
3 Kentridge's Centre for the Less Good Idea in Johannesburg was conceived as 'a peripheral and experimental space in relation to the more centralised, global art world' (https://lessgoodidea.com/about-1).
4 *Noah Davis: In Detail*, p. 96.
5 *Jennifer Packer: The Eye Is Not Satisfied with Seeing* (Cologne: Verlag der Buchhandlung Walther König, 2021).
6 Tina M. Campt, *A Black Gaze: Artists Changing How We See* (Cambridge, MA: The MIT Press, 2021), p. 7.
7 'On Noah Davis'.
8 *Tricia Hersey, Rest is Resistance: A Manifesto* (New York: Little Brown Spark, 2022), p. 172.
9 Campt, *A Black Gaze*, p. 88.

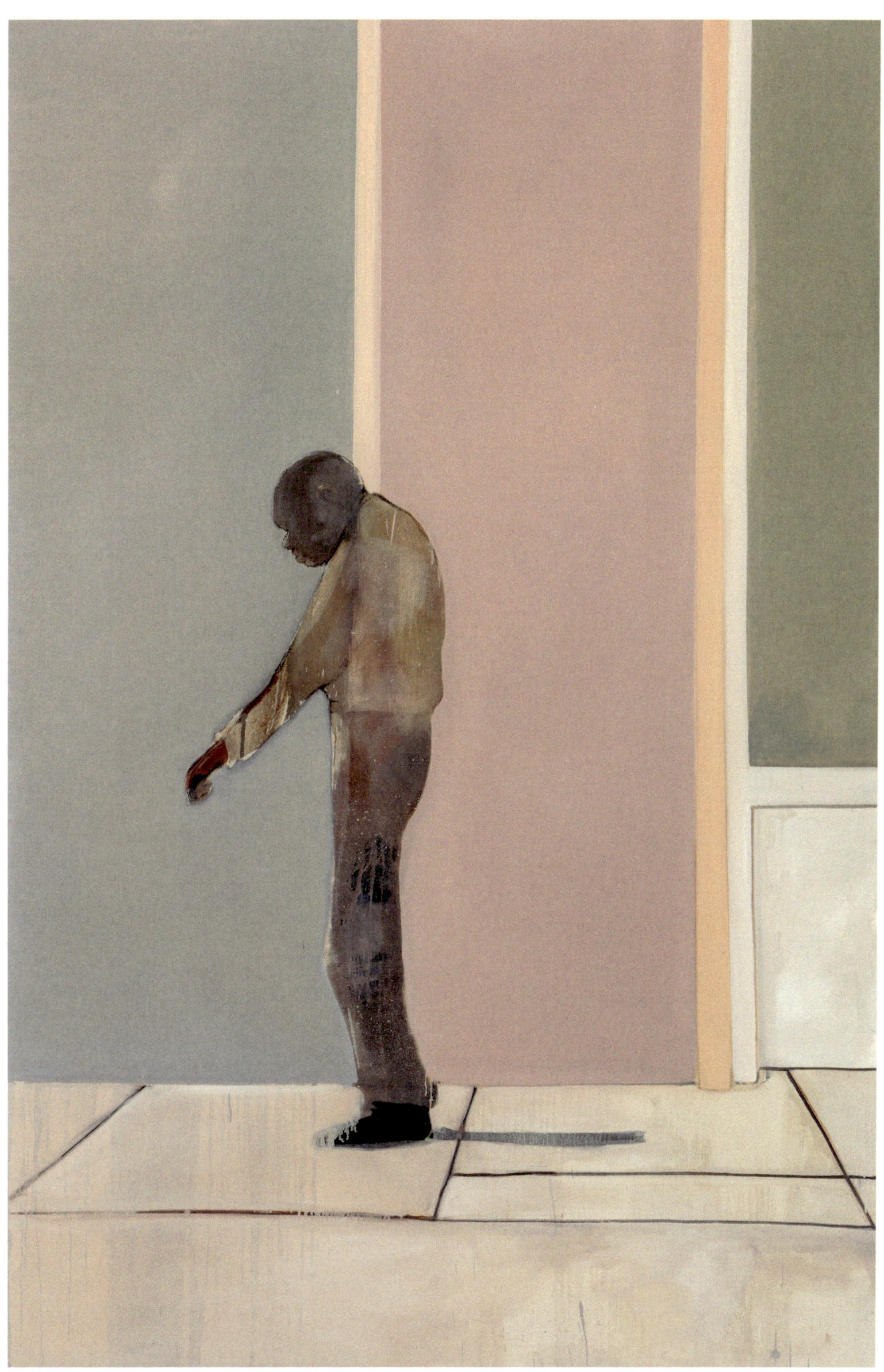

 Untitled, 2015

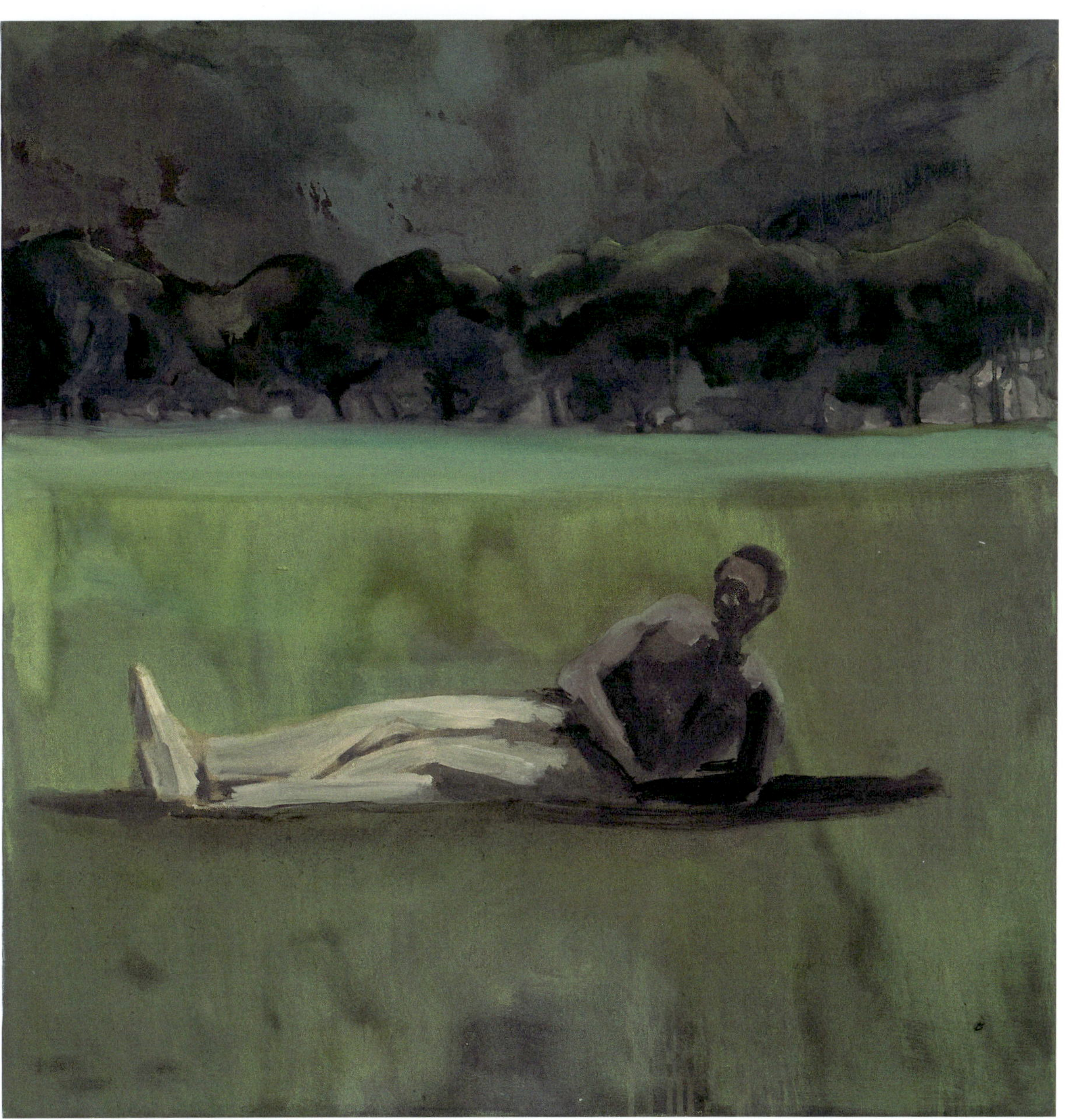

 Untitled, 2015

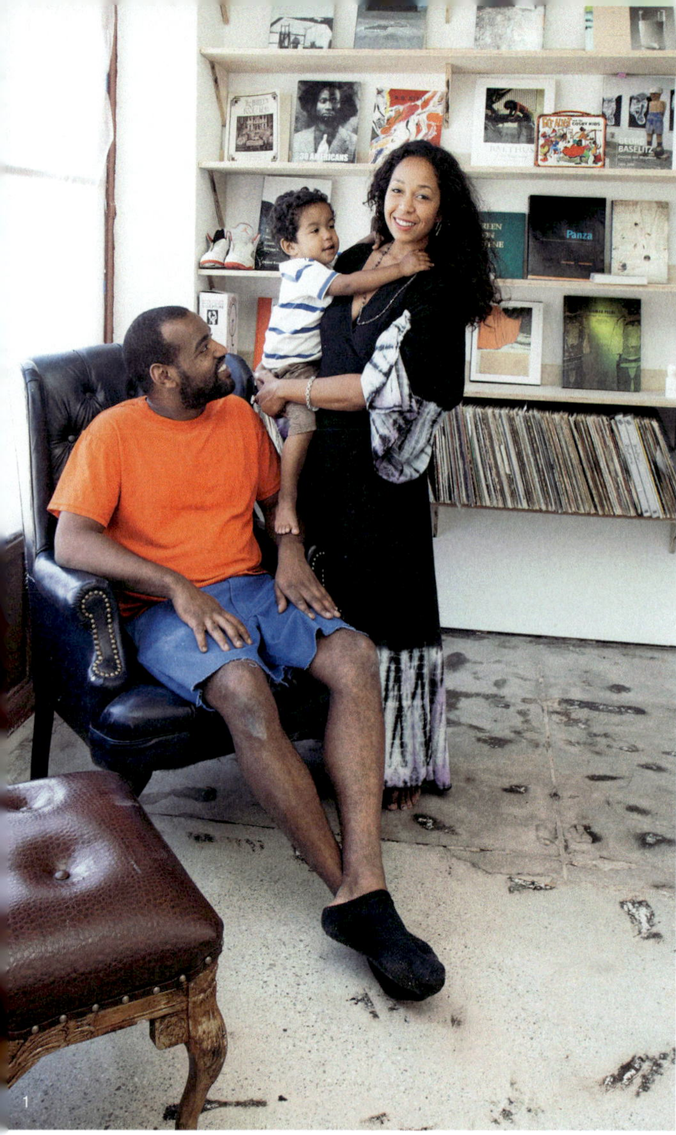

1

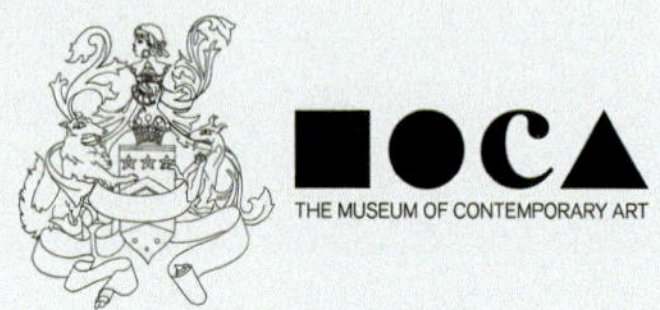
MOCA
THE MUSEUM OF CONTEMPORARY ART

THE UNDERGROUND MUSEUM
WITH MOCA

WILLIAM KENTRIDGE:
JOURNEY TO THE MOON

JUNE 25 – NOVEMBER 15, 2015

TUESDAY - SATURDAY
2-9PM
3508 W WASHINGTON BLVD
LOS ANGELES, CA 90018

2

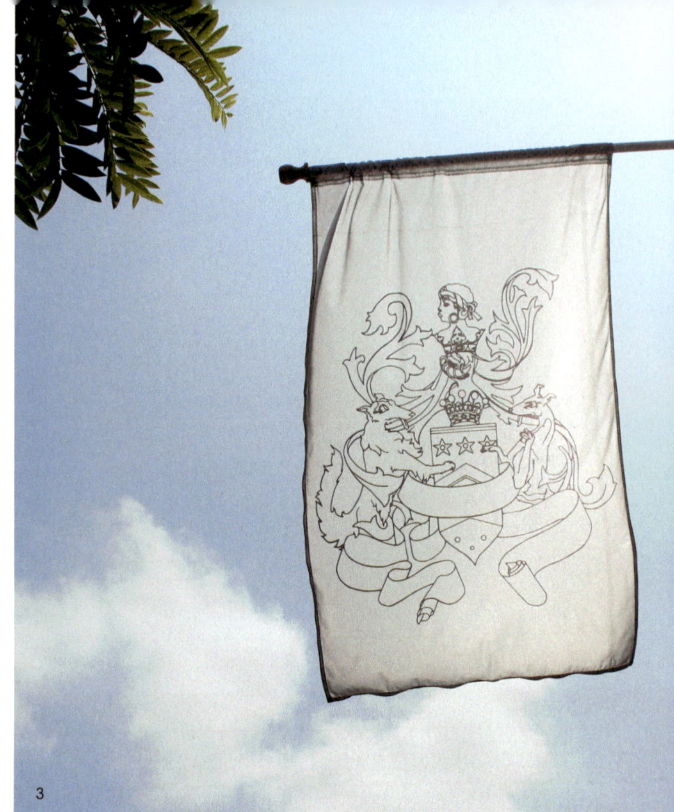
3

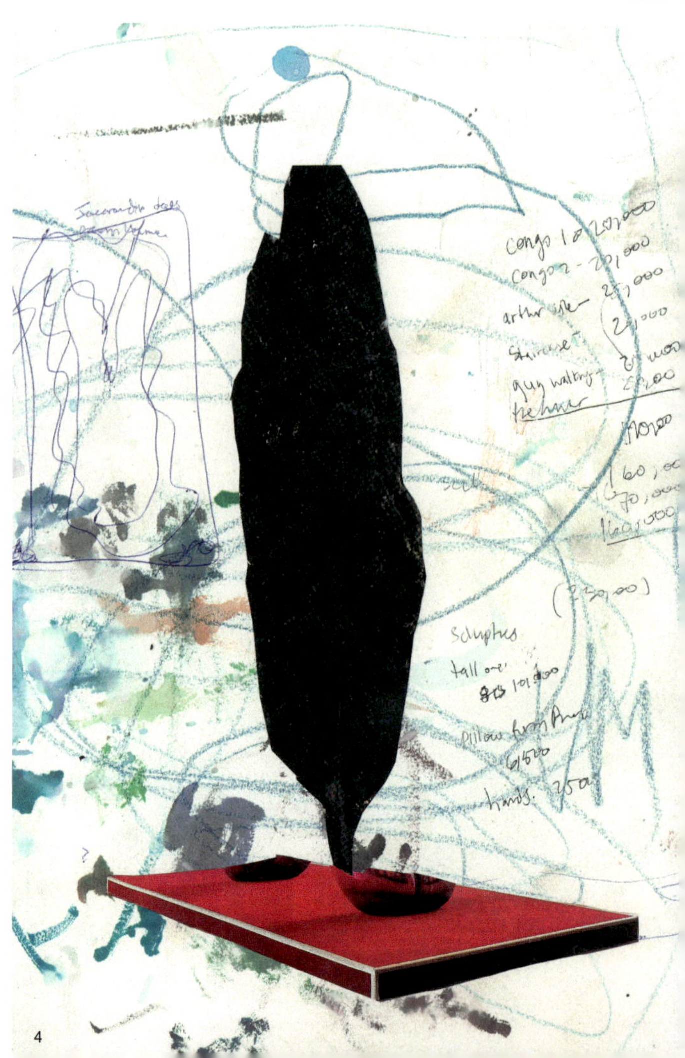
4

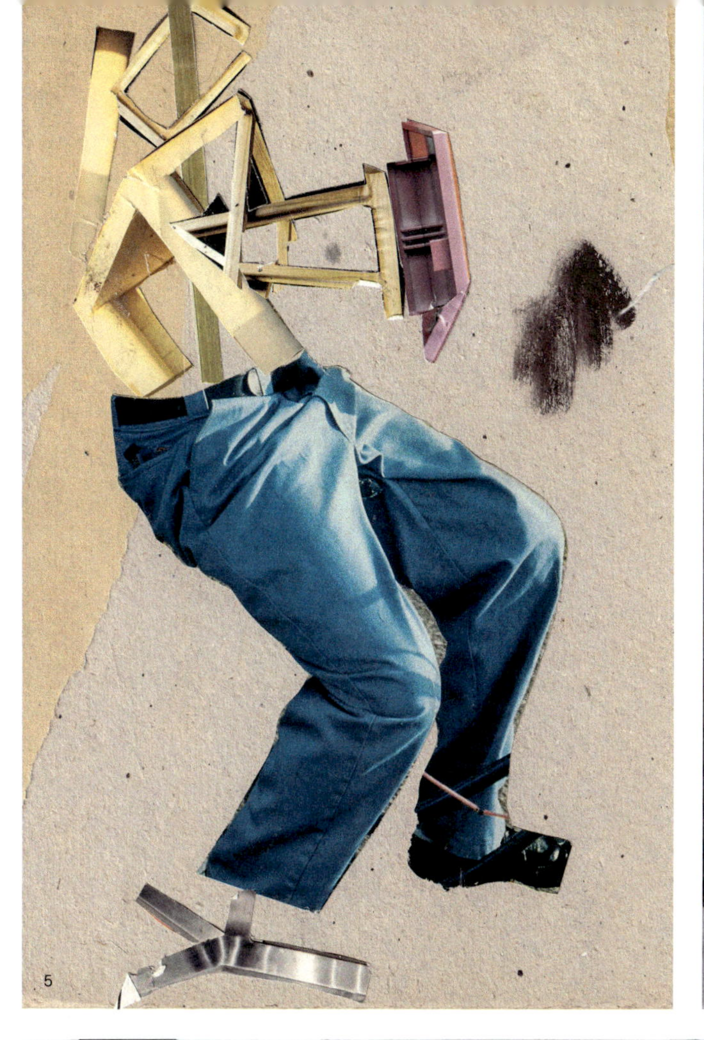

5

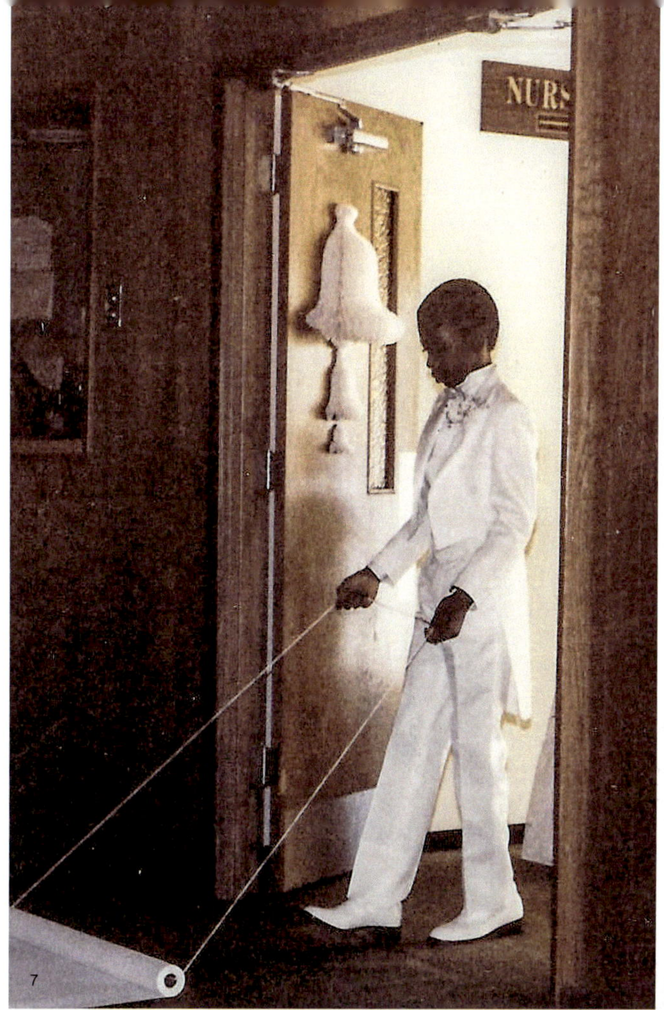

7

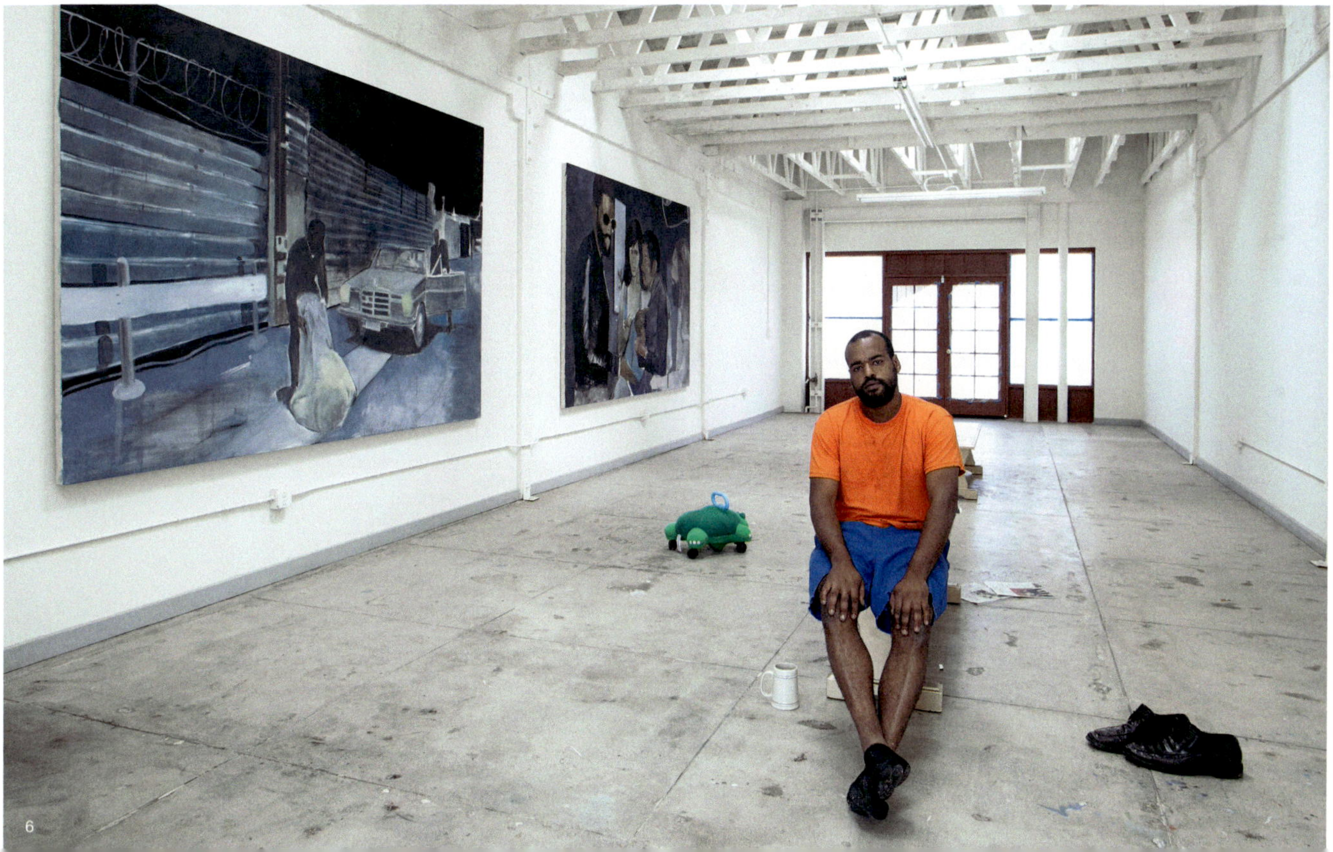

6

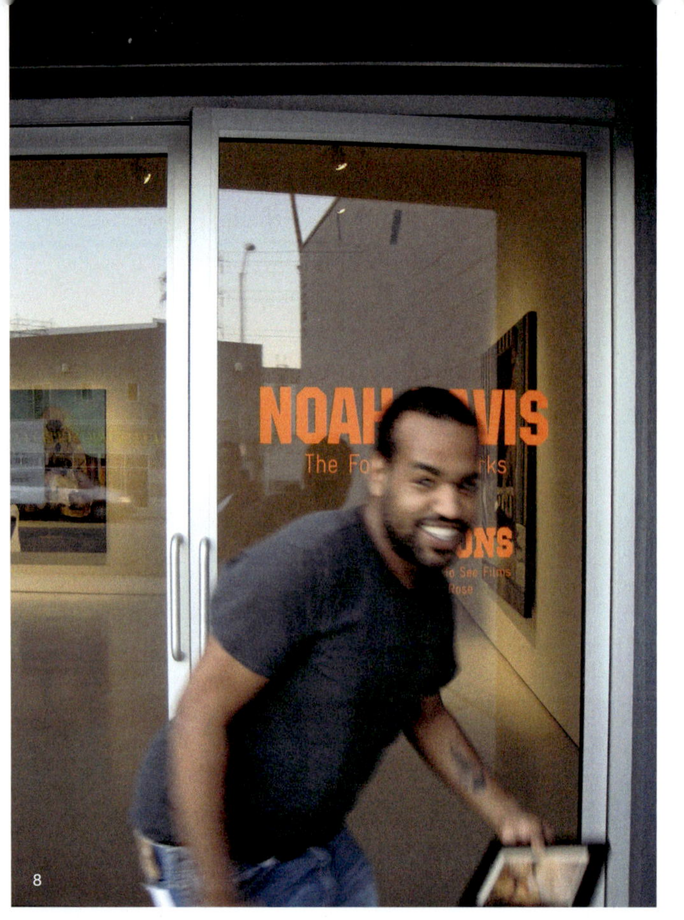

8

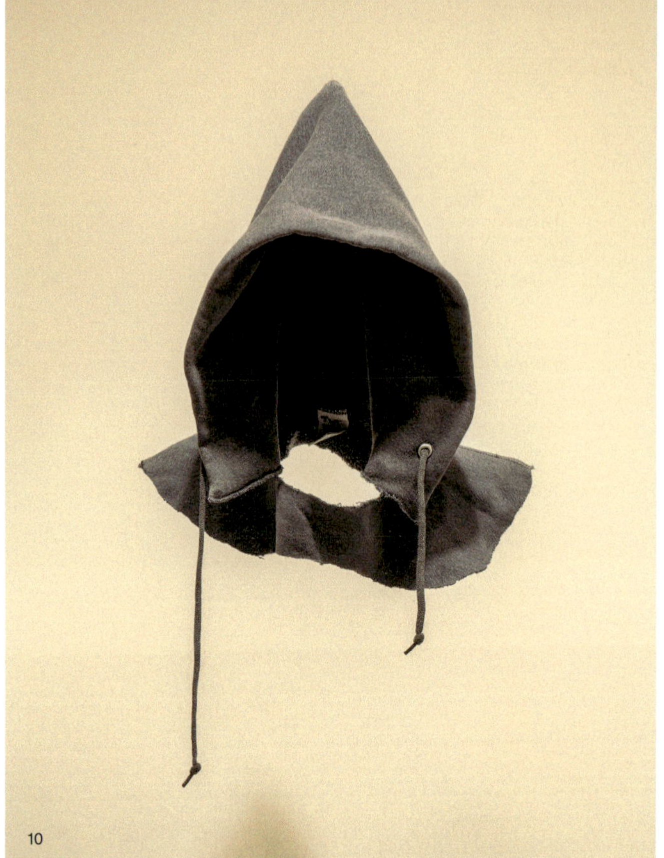
10

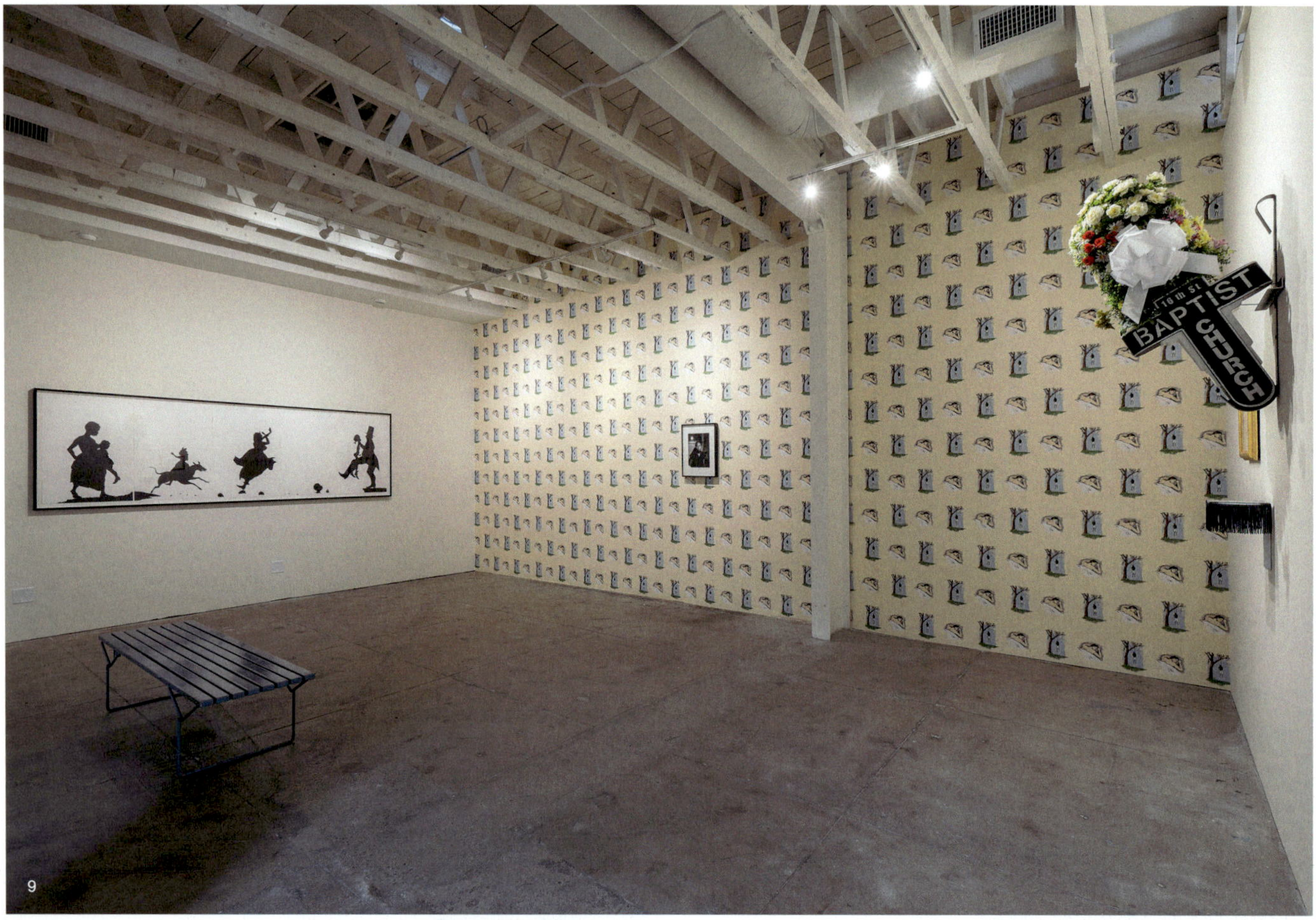

9

From: **noah davis** [redacted]
Date: Thu, Aug 20, 2015 at 12:14 PM
Subject: The Underground Museum
To: [redacted]

Mr. Gober,

Hope this letter finds you well. Thanks for entertaining this idea. I'd like to do a show called "nonfiction" that includes works by Henry Taylor and Deana Lawson (both of who are confirmed) as well as Kerry James Marshall, Theaster Gates and Kara Walker's work in the MOCA collection. All of the art will deal with the image of the black body and its relationship to history. That history—of slavery, of jim crow, of contemporary segregation and incarceration—is always also present. Right now it is very present, in light of all the murders of Micheal Brown, Trayvon Martin, Eric Garner, Dontre Hamilton, Tanisha Anderson, Christian Taylor, Sandra Bland and the list goes on.... Your wall paper forms the conundrum: does the white man dream of the black lynched figure with guilt or with desire. Can white culture wake up from this dream and deal with the nonfictional reality of the current situation? The Underground Museum is not a regular museum, its really part of a a black and Latino neighborhood and I think the community will be moved and appreciate its honesty.

Thank you for reaching out to me. I apologize that you read about it first before we had finalized it. I think everyone was excited about the partnership between the UM and MOCA that a little bit too much information slipped out. It was not my intent.

It is truly a pleasure to connect with you and I hopefully work with you as well. If you would like to discuss the show further and have any ideas you would like to share. I can be reached at [redacted].

Best,

Noah Davis

11

There is a Season
n there is a season
in the mind when the
toadstools change color.

12

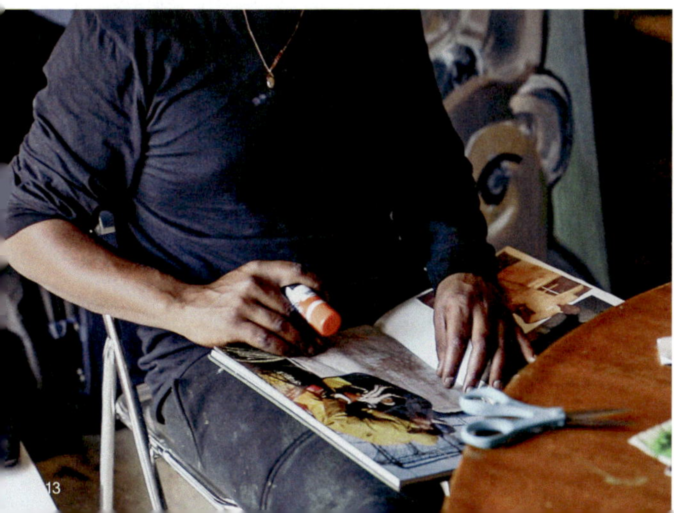

13

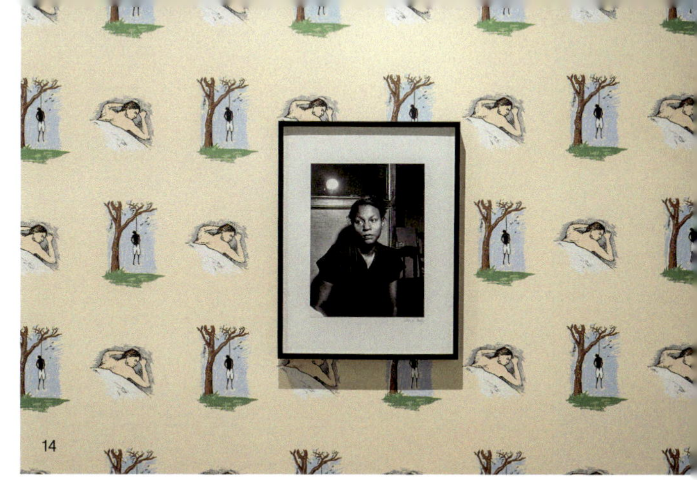

14

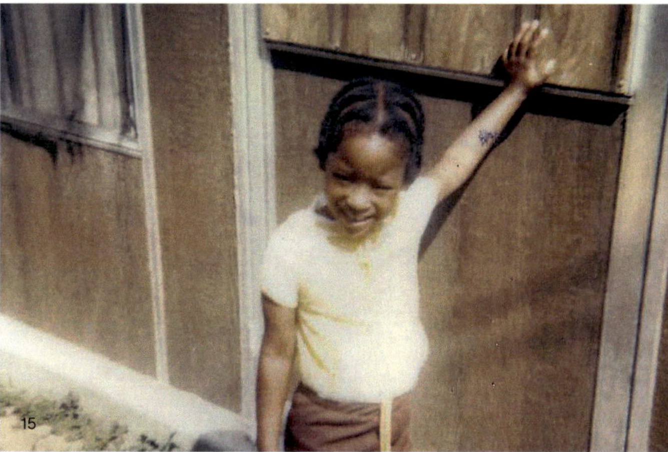

15

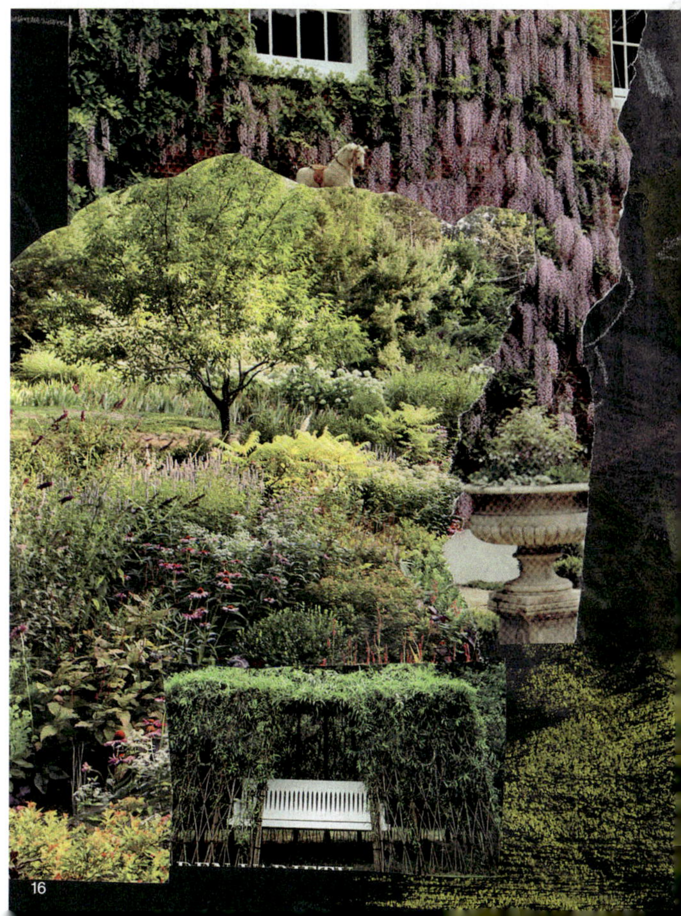

16

Why

17

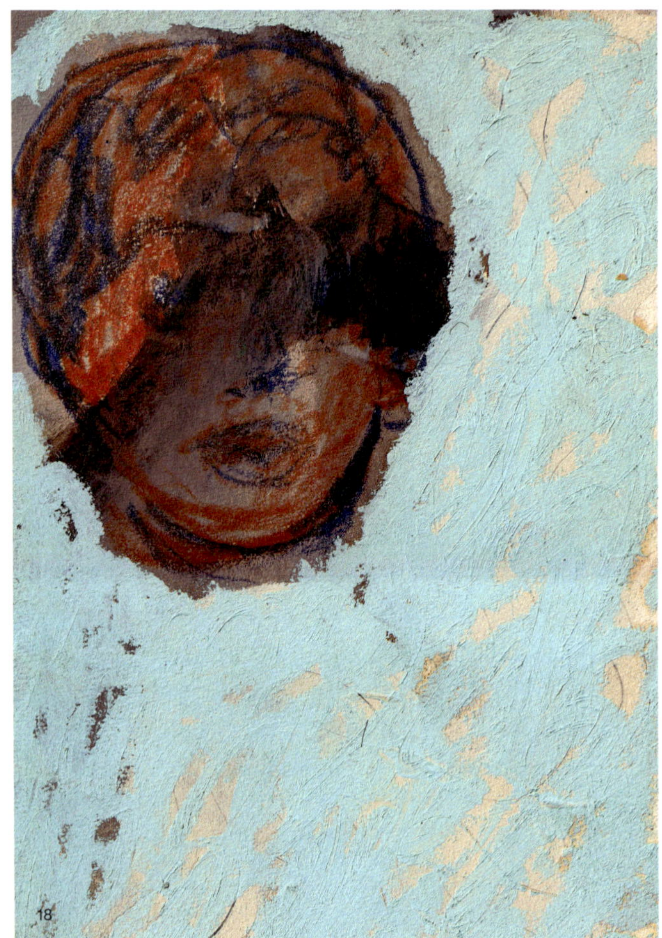

18

- ~~Eddie Murphy Paw~~
- Funeral portrait
- Artist Statement for the first 25 paintings

~~(ARTIST OF COLOR)~~

~~monograph~~

~~NOAH DAVIS~~

~~-update febmag.~~

- ~~Kahlil Joseph~~ > seattel, LA,

19

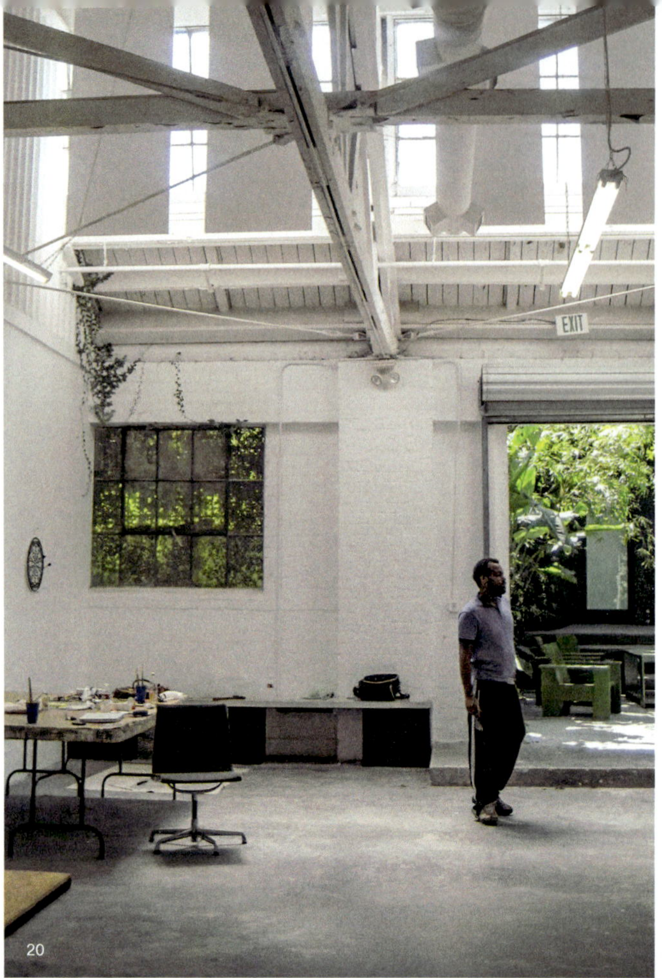

20

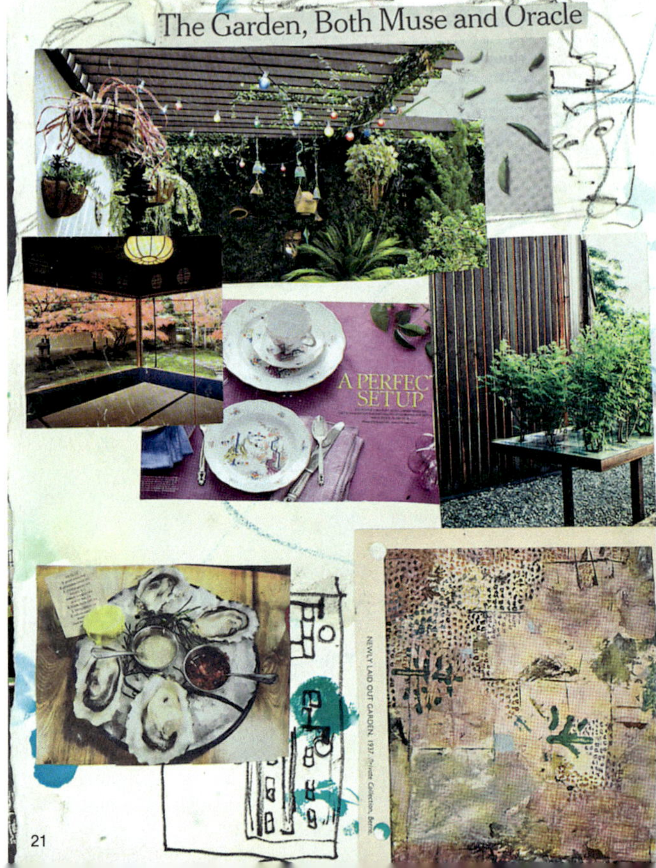

21

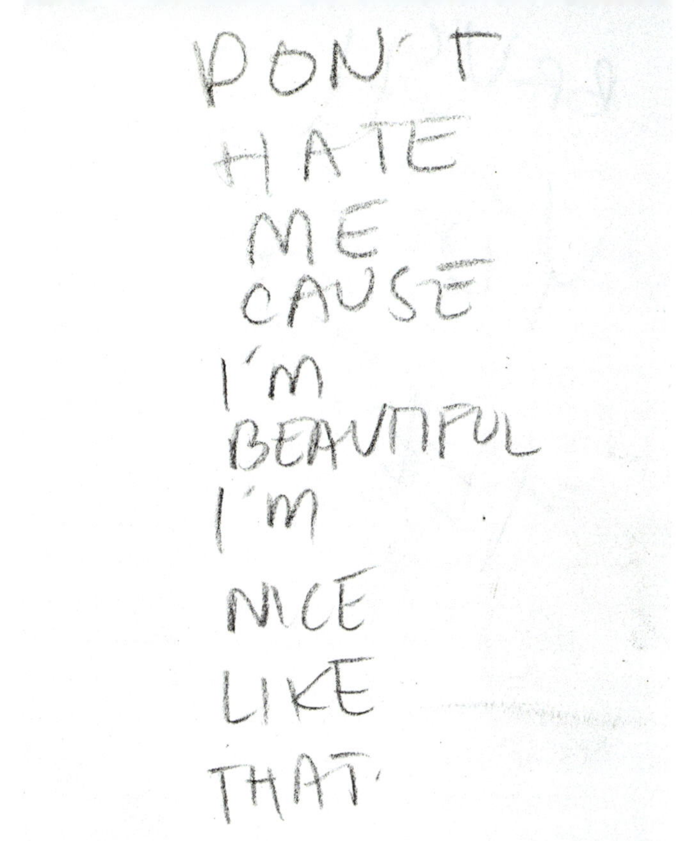

DON'T
HATE
ME
CAUSE
I'M
BEAUTIFUL
I'M
NICE
LIKE
THAT

22

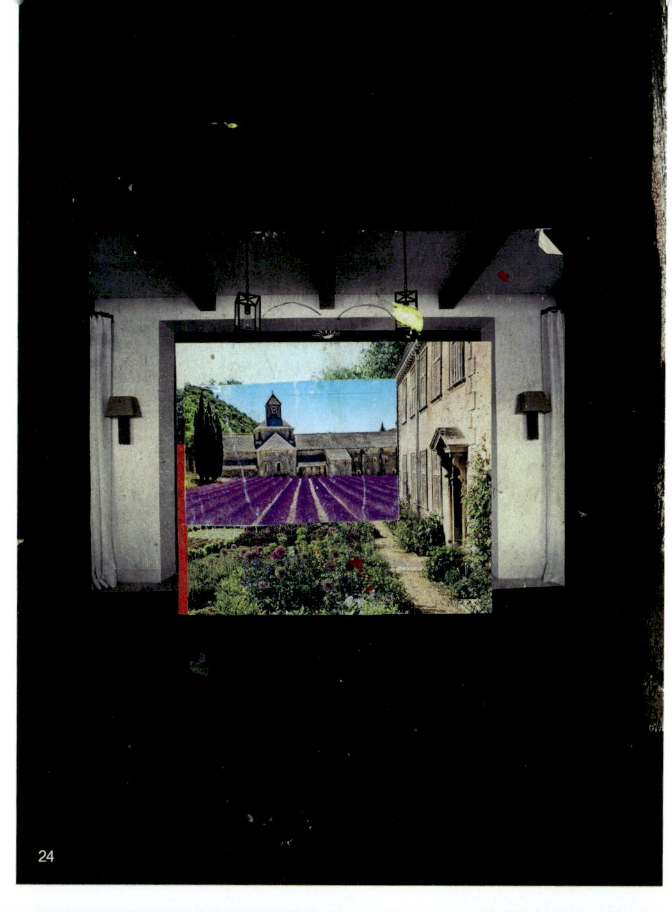

24

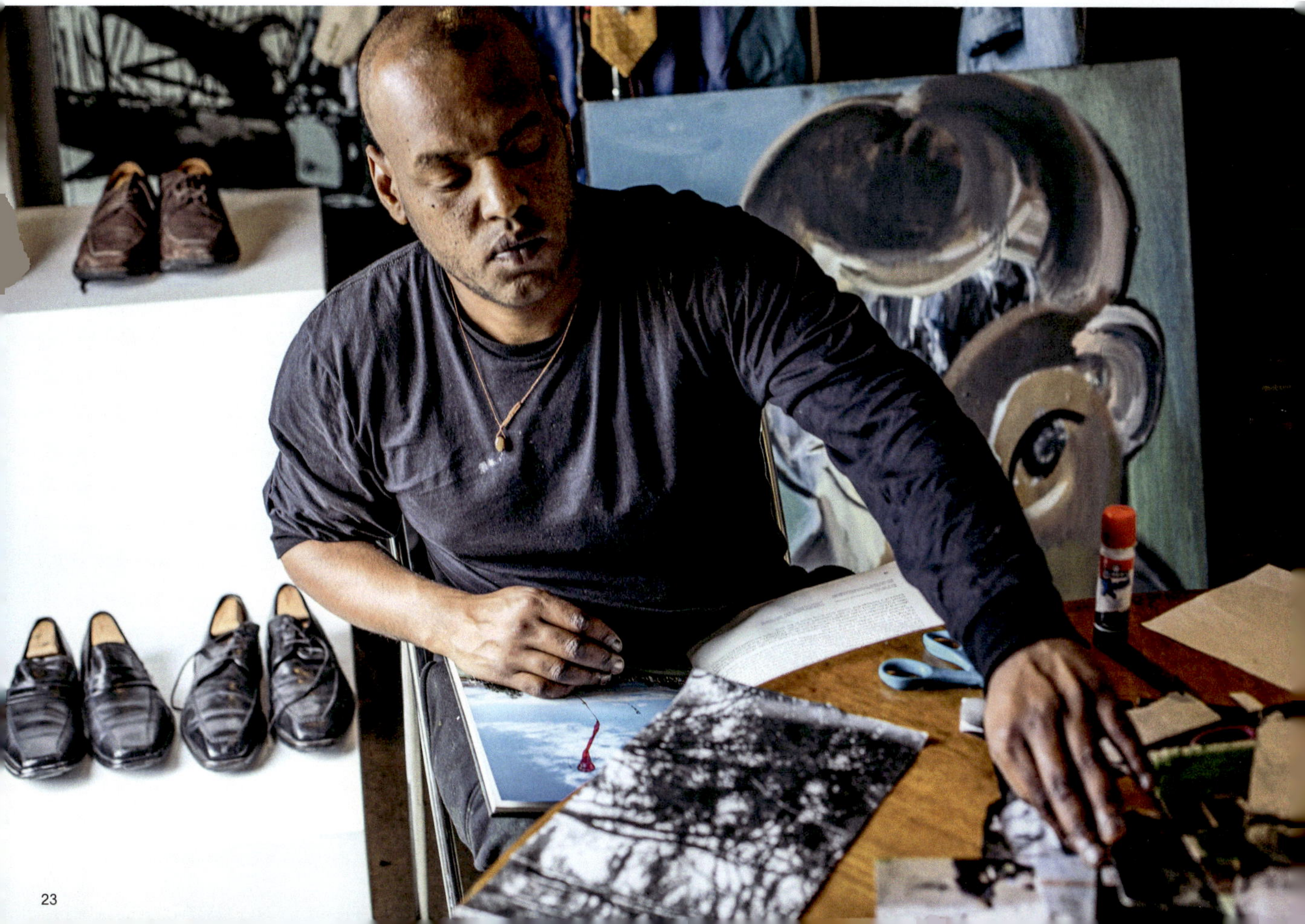

23

1 The Davis family at the Underground Museum, c. 2012
2 Draft invitation to *William Kentridge: Journey to the Moon* at the Underground Museum, 2015
3 The Underground Museum's flag with crest designed by Davis, 2013
4 *Untitled*, 2014, mixed media on paper, 38.7 × 27 cm (15¼ × 10⅝ in)
5 *Artist Of Color #2 – Collage*, 2009, mixed media on paper, 27.9 × 20.3 cm (11 × 8 in)
6 Davis at the Underground Museum, c. 2012
7 Found photograph from Davis's collection
8 Davis outside his exhibition *The Forgotten Works*, Roberts & Tilton, Culver City, 2010
9 Installation view, *Non-fiction*, the Underground Museum, 2016–17
10 David Hammons, *In the Hood (Gray)*, 1993/2016; installation view, *Non-fiction*, the Underground Museum, 2016–17
11 Email from Davis to Robert Gober about *Non-fiction*, August 2015
12 Notebook page, c. 2010–14
13 Still from *Untitled, in Process: A Documentary of Noah Davis*, 2016, directed by Nicole Otero, produced by Kahlil Joseph
14 Robert Gober, *Hanging Man/Sleeping Man*, 1989; Photograph by Marion Palfi, *Wife of a Lynch Victim*, 1949; installation view, *Non-fiction*, the Underground Museum, 2016–17
15 Found photograph from Davis's collection
16 *Untitled* (detail), 2014, mixed media on paper, 38.7 × 27 cm (15¼ × 10⅝ in)
17 Notebook page, c. 2010–14
18 *Untitled* (detail), 2014, mixed media on paper, 40 × 26.7 cm (15¾ × 10½ in)
19 Notebook page, c. 2010–14
20 Davis at Pico Studio, Los Angeles, 2010
21 *Untitled* (detail), 2014, mixed media on paper, 38.7 × 27 cm (15¼ × 10⅝ in)
22 Notebook page, c. 2010–14
23 Still from *Untitled, in Process: A Documentary of Noah Davis*, 2016, directed by Nicole Otero, produced by Kahlil Joseph
24 *Untitled* (detail), 2014, mixed media on paper, 38.7 × 27 cm (15¼ × 10⅝ in)

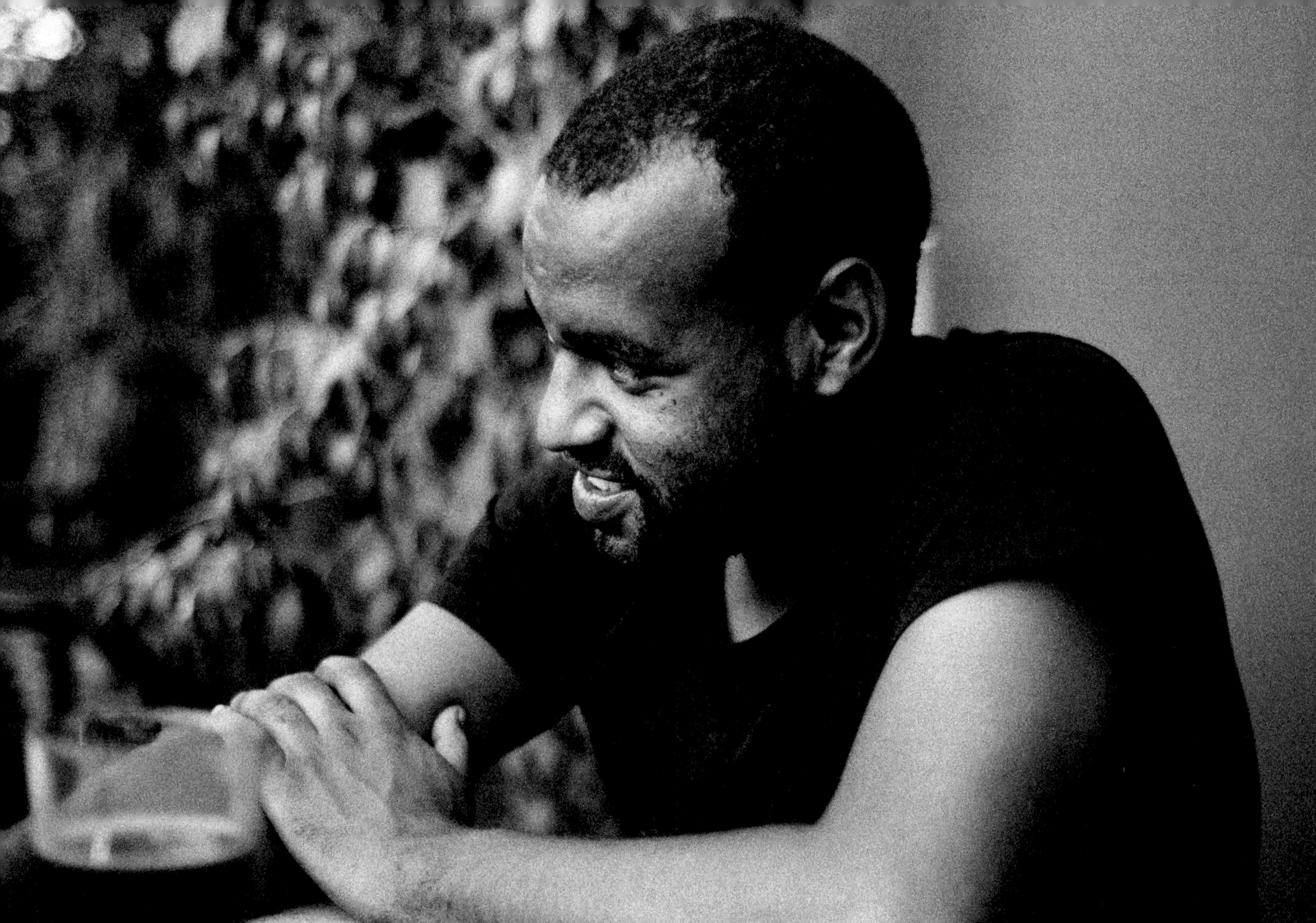

 Davis at Pico Studio, Los Angeles, 2009

CHRONOLOGY compiled by Colm Guo-Lin Peare

This text is based on and expands the first published chronology of Davis's life by Lindsay Charlwood in *Noah Davis: In Detail* (New York: David Zwirner Books, 2023).

1983

On 3 June, Noah Davis is born in Seattle, Washington. His parents, Faith Childs-Davis and Keven Davis, raise him with his older brother, Kahlil Joseph. Keven Davis works as a corporate lawyer, representing diverse clients including the rapper Ludacris, the jazz musician Wynton Marsalis, and Venus and Serena Williams. Faith Childs-Davis works as a teacher.

1997

At age 14, Davis has a formative experience visiting the exhibition *Kara Walker: Presenting Negro Scenes Drawn Upon My Passage through the South and Reconfigured for the Benefit of Enlightened Audiences Wherever Such May Be Found, By Myself, Missus K.E.B. Walker, Colored* when it travels to the Henry Art Gallery at the University of Washington, Seattle. He later reflects that it is the first truly radical art he has experienced.[1] The work was originally commissioned for the Renaissance Society at the University of Chicago by Hamza Walker, who writes in the exhibition's accompanying essay: 'Maybe the issue is not whether some imaginations are more active than others but what some imaginations are willing to wield and therefore yield...The mind can be a terrible thing, a frightening thing, only because it is a powerful thing; a thing, as Walker proves, capable of breaking the shackles of history.'[2]

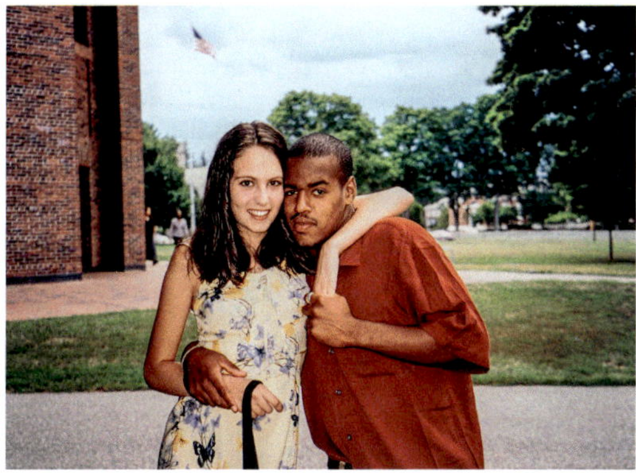

1999

Davis travels from Seattle to Phillips Exeter Academy in New Hampshire for an interdisciplinary educational summer programme. There, he becomes friends with Lindsay Charlwood (who would later become a gallery director and a staunch advocate of Davis's work throughout his career) and takes a class called 'The Art of Being Human', where students discuss art, music, literature, philosophy and psychology.

2000

During Davis's junior year of high school, his parents rent an apartment near their home in Seattle for him to use as his first painting studio.

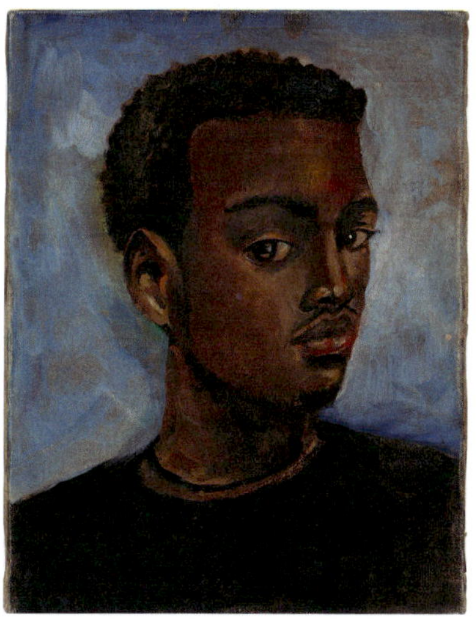

At Broadway Market shopping mall in downtown Seattle, Davis mounts an exhibition of his work in a corridor outside a former cinema, showing watercolours inspired by Francesco Clemente.

2001

Davis moves to Dumbo in Brooklyn, New York, where his father is already living. He enrols at Cooper Union School of Art in the East Village, gaining admission at the competitive institution with a concertina book in which he reinterprets Picasso's *Guernica* (1937). Davis's first term begins one week before September 11. Davis stays at Cooper Union for three years,

Left Lindsay Charlwood and Davis at Phillips Exeter Academy, 1999
Right *Untitled* (Self-Portrait from High School), undated

studying under artists including Hans Haacke and Lorna Simpson.

2004

During his time at Cooper Union, Davis works with the Bruce High Quality Foundation (BHQF), an artists' collective created as 'an alternative to everything' by fellow students Seth Cameron, Rhys Gaetano and John Kiehnhoff.[3] The first image the collective exhibit is *The Raft of the Medusa* (2004), a photographic imitation of Théodore Géricault's 1818–19 oil painting depicting the 1816 wreck of a French naval frigate, which was commanded by an incompetent aristocrat of the recently reinstated *ancien régime*. The painting's modern sympathy towards revolution makes it a fitting reference for BHQF's inaugural artwork, in which Davis stands at the helm of a raft made from urban debris.

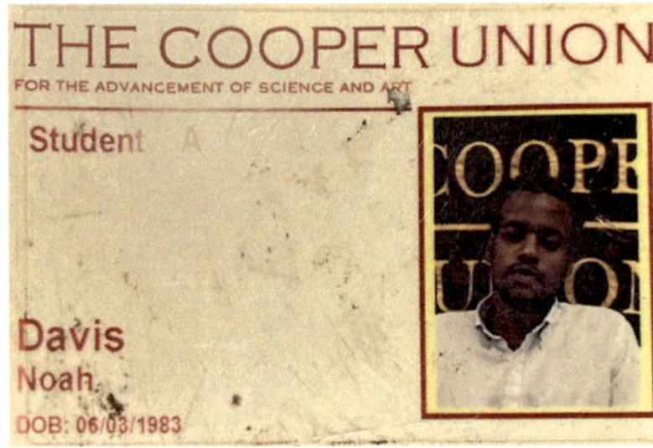

Davis drops out of Cooper Union, struggling to reconcile the school's emphasis on conceptual training with his desire to paint. He later reflects: 'I think it's very important that art remains to be about ideas, but it shouldn't be an either-or battle between concepts versus painting. They can exist together. I guess when my school force-fed us a conceptual education I reacted against it. I left school because it wasn't teaching me anything.'[4]

Davis moves to Los Angeles and takes a job working for the City of Los Angeles Public Art Division.

2005

Davis leaves his job at the Public Art Division and begins working at Art Catalogues, an independent bookstore specialising in exhibition catalogues, run by Dagny Corcoran. The store had recently relocated to the Pacific Design Center, the Museum of Contemporary Art's (MOCA) satellite space in West Hollywood. Corcoran later recalled how Davis would scour the Art Catalogues bookshelves, building his own imagined library for a speculative museum.[5]

Davis meets Tyler Gibney, who opens the HVW8 Art + Design Gallery in West Hollywood in 2006 with Addison Liu. The gallery becomes a local hangout, bringing together art, music and design. This interdisciplinary ethos extends to the artworks Davis and Gibney later collaborate on, including experimental painting performances and large murals.

2006

Davis studies at the newly opened Mountain School of Arts, a radical, artist-run school founded by Piero Golia and Eric Wesley. The school aims to teach its students how to sustain themselves creatively and professionally, encouraging them 'to engage with the widest possible audience'.[6] With free, part-time tuition, the school has a rotating guest faculty of visiting artists and curators who teach an interdisciplinary programme. It is based at the Mountain Bar in downtown Los Angeles, established in 2003 by artist Jorge Pardo and

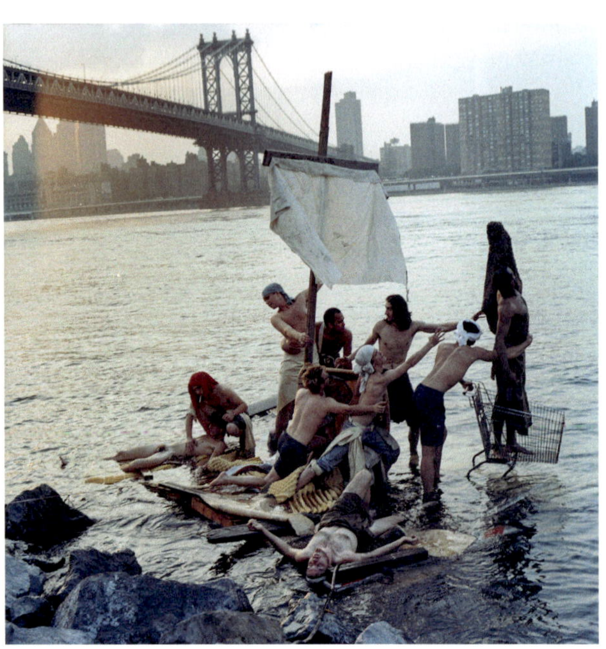

Left Davis's Cooper Union student card, 2004
Right Bruce High Quality Foundation, *The Raft of the Medusa*, 2004

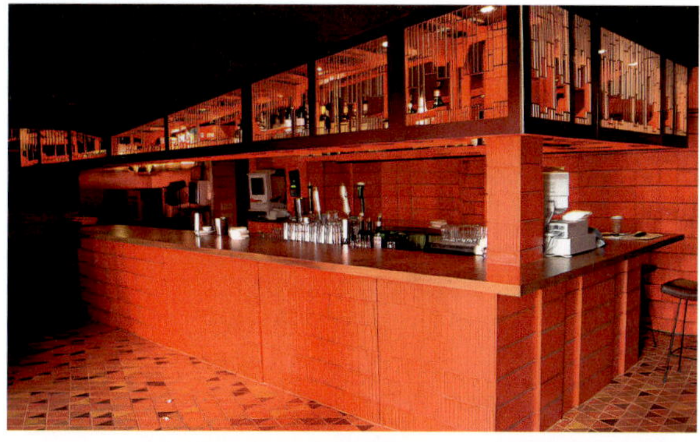
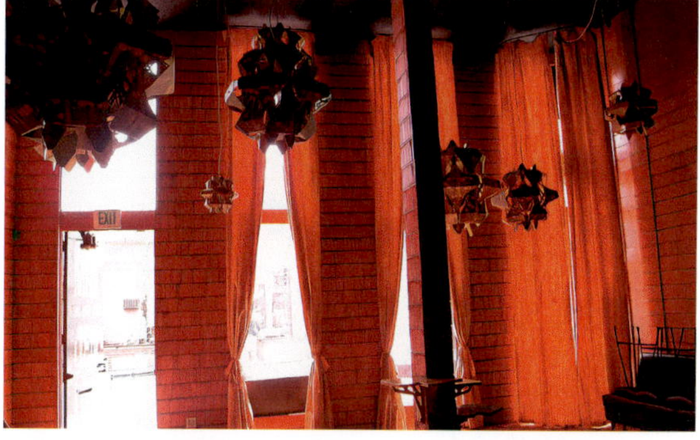

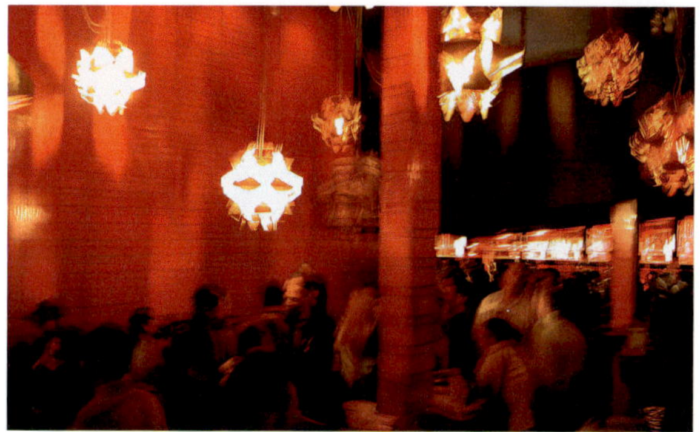
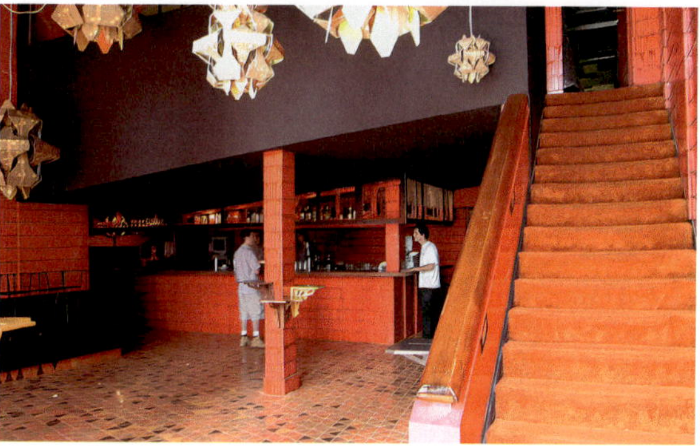

co-founder of China Art Objects gallery Steve Hanson as a place for artists to gather. Davis attends the school with other young artists, including Jordan Wolfson. He later reflects: 'The Mountain School…helped me out massively when I came to LA. Eric Wesley and Piero ran it from a little room in the back of a bar. Students were taken on tours of artists' studios during the two classes a week and I found it to be a really inspiring place.'[7]

In 2009, Jorge Pardo makes a bespoke bar for the school using plexiglass, MDF and fluorescent lights, which operates both as a functioning bar and an art object.

Many years later, Davis will install a bar inspired by Donald Judd's furniture in the Underground Museum, following a similar sentiment of situating art and life in the same space.

2007

Davis and his brother Kahlil Joseph start *FEB MAG* (the title of which is a play on the art journal *October* and Black History Month, which is celebrated in February in the United States). The blog is the brothers' answer to the early website *Tiny Vices*, an online gallery and image archive started by photographer Tim Barber in 2005. *FEB MAG* specifically focuses on images of Black life, featuring old Polaroids found at the Fairfax Flea Market and other swap meets, home video footage by friends, and Joseph's photographs from his trip to the Congo. Some of these latter photos become the reference images for Davis's *Congo* series (2014–15, pp. 211–17).

Lindsay Charlwood (now a director at the Los Angeles gallery Roberts & Tilton) runs into Davis at Art Catalogues.[8] Charlwood is mounting an exhibition exploring the idea of the domestic entitled *Bliss* and invites Davis to exhibit. Davis at first proposes to show a woven blanket depicting a man sleeping on the street but instead submits two paintings: *Bad Boy for Life* (2007) (p. 33) and *Delusions of Grandeur* (2007), which debut at the opening on 13 October. Curator Franklin Sirmans later writes that the palette of *Delusions of Grandeur*, which was installed in the gallery bathroom, recalls Clyfford Still's use of colour and abstract forms.[9]

 Countertop at the Mountain Bar, Los Angeles

2008

In the spring of 2008, Davis meets Karon Vereen, and they fall in love. By the summer, they have moved into a house in West Adams. The neighbourhood is home to many historic turn-of-the-century homes, such as the Fitzgerald House designed by Joseph Cather Newsom in 1903, which Davis would later feature laid over a Rothko-inspired colour field in his painting *The 'Fitz'* (2015). West Adams was also the neighbourhood of Paul Revere Williams, the first Black architect to gain entry to the American Institute of Architects in 1923 and the subject of Davis's painting *The Architect* (2009) (p. 69).

When driving with Lindsay Charlwood to see the Marlene Dumas exhibition *Measuring Your Own Grave* at MOCA, Davis asks Charlwood to stop by an open house at the Fitzgerald House, which Davis and Vereen dream of turning into a public art space.

Dumas is an important influence on Davis, inspiring works like *American Sterile* (2008). He continues experimenting with texture and composition in ways suggestive of Dumas, such as in *Indigo Kid* (2010). He also, like Dumas, increasingly uses found photography as his source material.

On 11 October, Davis opens his first solo exhibition: *Nobody* at Roberts & Tilton. The show is titled after the popular 1905 Bert Williams song of the same name, which was performed by Vereen's father, the acclaimed entertainer Ben Vereen, at Ronald Reagan's All-Star Inaugural Gala – the televised event held on the eve of his inauguration. Vereen's performance, which was an homage to Williams, incorporated elements of Vaudeville and mime to comment on the history of minstrelsy. And, as Williams had in his stage routines, Vereen executed the performance in blackface. Although Vereen had been promised his whole performance would be aired, the broadcast omitted its final section, which implicated the mostly white, Republican viewers.

For the exhibition, Davis is expected to present new figurative paintings (for which he is becoming known) but instead shows three restrained works reminiscent of formalism, with each painting comprised of a single flat geometric plane of purple. Each refers to the shape of a swing state in the 2004 United States presidential election: Colorado, New Mexico and Nevada. These paintings are early precursors to one of Davis's defining fixations: how do the social and political inform the formal development of abstraction? None of Davis's works in the exhibition sell, but Charlwood acquires one at the last minute before they are returned to the artist. Davis destroys the remaining two.

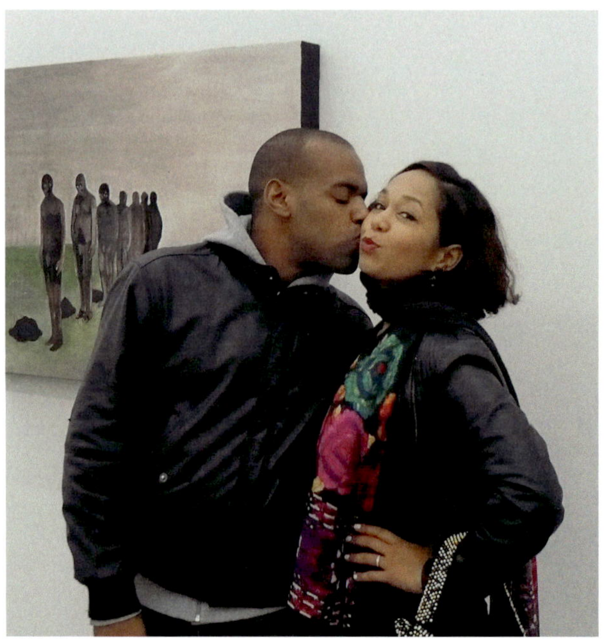

Left Invitation for the group exhibition *Bliss*, Roberts & Tilton, Culver City, 2007
Right Noah and Karon in front of *The Seven Prisoners of the Abyss* (2008) in *30 Americans*, Rubell Family Collection, Miami, 2008

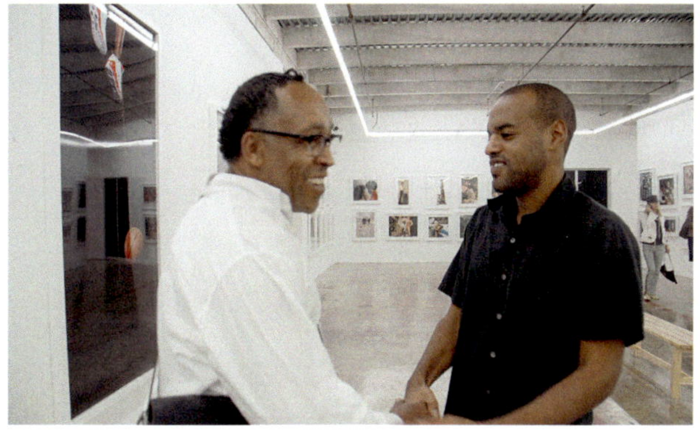

Davis and Karon Vereen influence each other as they live and work together. Vereen's books, including Geraldine Harris's *Gods and Pharaohs from Egyptian Mythology* and Gary Null's *Black Hollywood: The Black Performer in Motion Pictures*, steer Davis's research interests, and Vereen's film *Goat* (2008) directly inspires Davis's painting *The Goat from Grayson* (2008).

On 3 December, the Rubell Family Collection's landmark exhibition *30 Americans* opens in Miami, featuring an influential pantheon of Black artists, including Jean-Michel Basquiat, David Hammons, Barkley L. Hendricks, Glenn Ligon, William Pope. L, Lorna Simpson and Kara Walker. Davis is the youngest artist to be included. Commenting on being shown alongside this group of artists, Davis says: 'For a while, I thought I was being put in a box. But it's probably the most glamorous box I've ever been in, so whatever. I was fucking honoured.'[10] At the opening, Davis meets Henry Taylor for the first time. Taylor would become a close friend of Davis's, painting a portrait of them entitled *Right hand, wing man, best friend, and all the above!* in 2023.

On 4 December, Davis and Vereen get married at the Miami Beach Courthouse.

2009

On 7 April, Davis's first solo exhibition in New York opens at Tilton Gallery. The show includes a series of works on paper that depict the body of Osiris in 14 parts (in reference to the myth of the deity's dismemberment) alongside paintings loosely inspired by Egyptian mythology. The exhibition's opening party is held at the home of collectors A.C. and Thelma Hudgins, where they also celebrate John Outterbridge, who has an exhibition of recent sculptures a floor below Davis's show. Outterbridge's longstanding friend David Hammons, a hero of Davis's, also attends. The Studio Museum in Harlem acquires *The Gardener* (2009) (p. 73) from the show. Leading up to and during the exhibition, Davis and Vereen spend six weeks living in the gallery's basement apartment, where they make a performance painting, pouring chocolate syrup on a canvas covered in gold leaf.

Former Cooper Union student Marlon Rabenreither becomes Davis's studio assistant after the couple returns to Los Angeles. Davis (an avid collector of photos who was increasingly engaged with the burgeoning internet culture) had first connected with Rabenreither through his photo blog. Rabenreither will continue to work with Davis for the rest of the artist's life.

The Nasher Museum of Art at Duke University, Durham, acquires Davis's *Black Widow with Brothers Fighting* (2008).

2010

On 16 January, *Noah Davis: The Forgotten Works* opens at Roberts & Tilton. The show takes its name from Richard Brautigan's *In Watermelon Sugar* (1968), a science fiction novel set on a commune built outside of the 'Forgotten Works', an expanse of refuse that is the ruins of a past society. Many of Davis's paintings for the exhibition take inspiration from the novel's series of vignettes, featuring several characters who all variously repress, venerate or scavenge from the past. Davis makes a video of himself

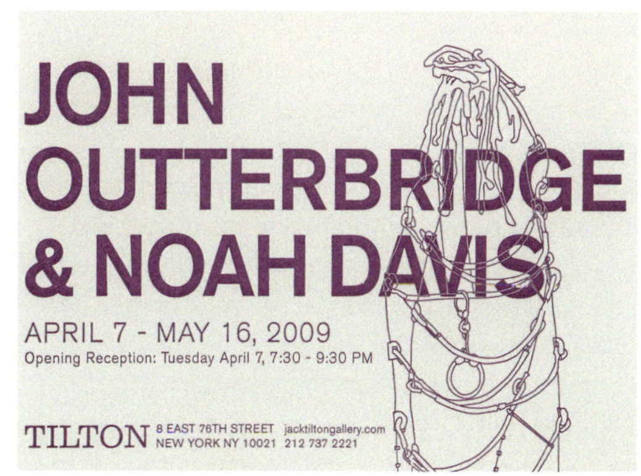

Left Davis meeting Henry Taylor at *30 Americans*, Rubell Family Collection, Miami, 2008
Right Invitation for Tilton Gallery's exhibition featuring work by Noah Davis and John Outterbridge, 2009

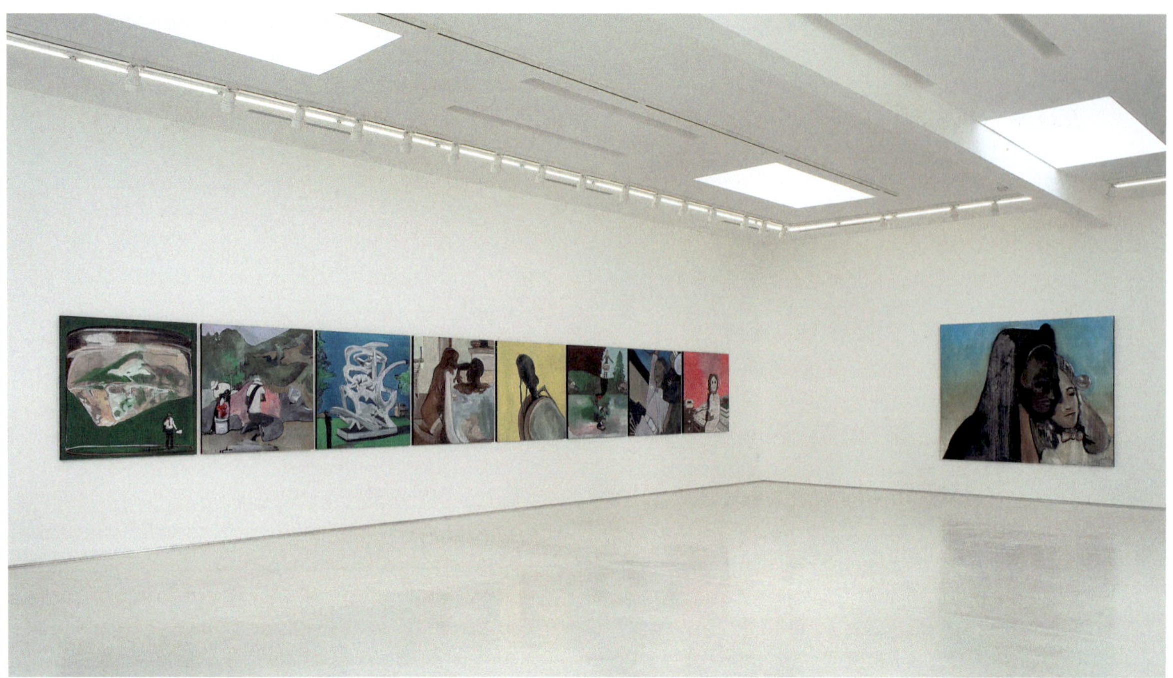

idling around Los Angeles to circulate as a press release. The show sells out and is reviewed by Sharon Mizota for the *Los Angeles Times*, who commends its depiction of 'isolation and mortality'.[11]

On 16 February, Noah and Karon's child Moses is born.

On 20 May, Davis's first exhibition in Europe, *Noah Davis: More Paintings*, opens at Annarumma 404 in Naples. Noah stays in Los Angeles with Karon and Moses instead of travelling to Italy for the show. Paintings exhibited include *Untitled (Kids in the Front Yard)* (2010) and *Untitled (Sketch for Larger More Realistic Painting)* (2010). On the gallery's invitation is a photo of Davis with his face daubed in purple paint, recalling his intrigue with the history of minstrelsy and the colour purple in his past exhibition *Nobody*. In the summer, Davis moves into studios in a formerly disused building on Pico Boulevard between Boyle Heights and Vernon in Los Angeles. Known as Pico Studio, the space is owned by developer Lonnie Blanchard, who leases out studios to artists, often accepting art for rent. Davis rents a large studio previously occupied by Thomas Houseago and moves Daniel DeSure, Kahlil Joseph and Malik Sayeed into the space. Amy Bessone and Aaron Curry are also renting spaces in the building at the time.

Noah and Karon rent a house in Calabasas, around 40 miles from Pico Studio. Davis will come to paint a series of works inspired by the many rockfaces he passes on his long drive into the studio. Tired of the commute, the couple eventually start sleeping on an air mattress at the studio with Moses.

On 14 October, Davis opens *Noah Davis: New Paintings*, his first solo show at James Harris Gallery in his hometown of Seattle.

Top *Noah Davis: The Forgotten Works* at Roberts & Tilton, Los Angeles, 2010
Bottom Invitation for *Noah Davis: More Paintings* at Annarumma 404 in Naples, 2010

Works in the exhibition include *The Future's Future* (2010) (p. 91) and *Spoonfed* (2010).

Davis curates his first exhibition, *Gray Day*, which opens at Roberts & Tilton on 30 October. Concerned with 'the apathy of the present moment', the show is 'an ode to group shows such as Tony Shafrazi [Gallery's] *Who's Afraid of Jasper Johns?* [conceived with Urs Fischer and Gavin Brown] and the Metropolitan Museum of Art's exhibition *Jasper Johns: 'Gray'*.'[12] The exhibition brings together 30 artists to respond to the colour grey, including Larry Bell, the Bruce High Quality Foundation, Daniel DeSure, Inner City Avant-Garde (an 'anarchic collective' Davis formed earlier in the year with his friends Ulysses Pizarro and Darnell Prince) and Davis's studio assistant Rabenreither. Davis also includes Sydney Littenberg, the owner of Fine Art Stretcher Bars, who makes most of Davis's canvases.

On 11 November, Inner City Avant-Garde's exhibition *LOOK MOM, NO TALENT* opens at HVW8 Art + Design Gallery. The show features ten works, including spray-painted works on canvas, sculptures and assemblages made using found objects. The collective's invitation uses the emblem that will later become the logo for the Underground Museum.

On 31 December, Noah and Karon leave Pico Studio and their house in Calabasas and settle into an apartment across the street from MOCA.

2011

Davis temporarily moves to New York to spend time with his father, who has been diagnosed

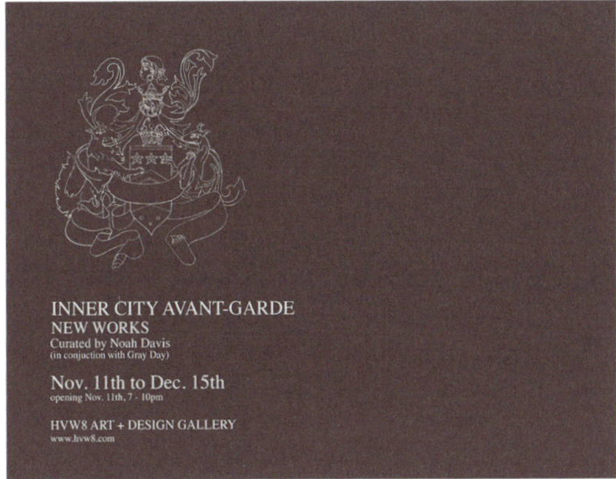

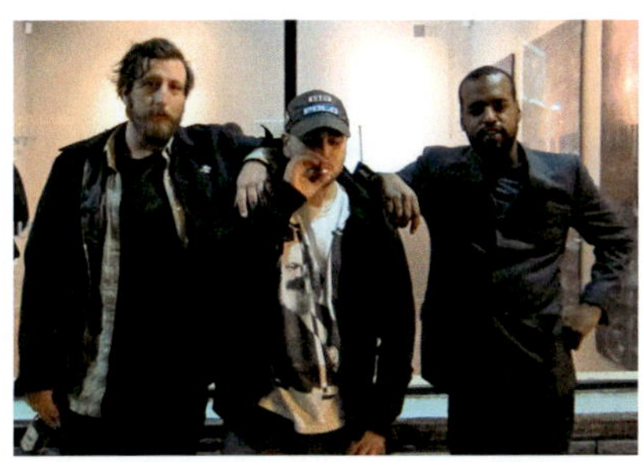

with cancer. He paints at a small studio in Harlem. Along with Henry Taylor, Davis is invited to paint at A.C. and Thelma Hudgins's home in Long Island over the summer.

On 10 November, Davis's second solo show at Tilton Gallery opens in New York. The exhibition pivots on his three *Canyon* (2011) paintings – inspired by the rocks Davis passed on his commute from Calabasas to Pico Studio – and *Painting for My Dad* (2011) (p. 99), a meditation on mortality depicting a lone figure looking into an abyss. The Rubell Family Collection acquire this last painting from the show.

On 23 December, Keven Davis dies.

2012

On 22 January, Noah and Karon perform in *Tirs: Reloaded*, an event organised by curator Yael Lipschutz for the Getty's Pacific Standard Time Performance and Public Art Festival. The event consists of contemporary artists responding to Niki de Saint Phalle's *Tirs* series (c. 1961–64), in which the artist shot a .22 rifle at white plaster-covered assemblages of various objects interspersed with sacks of coloured paint, which would explode upon impact. For the festival, Karon conceives of a work entitled *Boys in the Hoods* (2011), for which she and Davis shoot at Ku Klux Klan effigies with cans of red paint concealed under their white robes.

Davis is included in a group show, *In the Making*, which opens at Roberts & Tilton on 25 February. Instead of submitting paintings, Davis shows a sculpture made from synthetic hair and twigs entitled *Tumbleweave* (2012), inspired in part by David Hammons's hair sculptures. He installs the work in the parking lot outside the gallery.

In June, Davis rents four abutting buildings on West Washington Boulevard

Left Invitation for Inner City Avant-Garde's exhibition *LOOK MOM, NO TALENT* at HVW8 Art + Design Gallery, Los Angeles, 2010

Right Darnell Prince, Ulysses Pizarro and Davis at the opening of *LOOK MOM, NO TALENT*, 2010

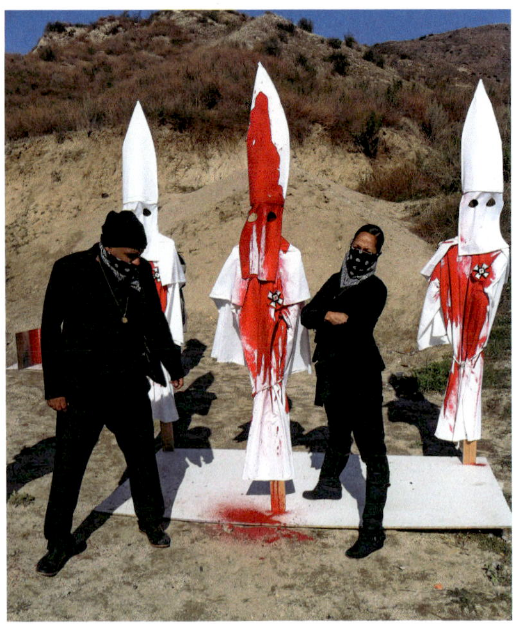

(numbers 3506–12) in Arlington Heights with the money inherited from his father. Davis demolishes the internal walls between the properties to create a gallery space and installs a library, and a bar inspired by Donald Judd's furniture. At first, the library is filled with Noah and Karon's own books. Later, Dagny Corcoran lends books from Art Catalogues before helping to set up the library with vendor accounts. Noah and Karon install a screen in the parking lot at the back of the buildings to function as a community cinema and start planning the Purple Garden, a glade of purple flora dreamt up by Davis in notebook collages. The space is initially known as the Inner City Avant-Garde (after Davis's collective) but is officially named the Underground Museum (UM) by 2014. In one of Davis's notebooks, he writes that the museum's mission is 'to provide inner-city neighbourhoods with free access to world-class art'.

On 12 July, *Noah Davis: Savage Wilds* opens at James Harris Gallery in Seattle. The exhibition takes its name from Ishmael Reed's 1988 satirical play in which two gameshow hosts hire a Black comedian to be hunted on reality television, with an ensuing farce that comments on the paranoia and spectacle of American racism. The works in the show are based on stills from daytime chat shows, subverting formal visual elements such as perspectival framing devices and the superimposition of graphics to conceal, reveal and encase figures. Certain paintings, like *Maury Mondrian* (2012) (p.109), bring these formal elements into conversation with representational tactics of modern European abstraction.

In August, Davis is invited to participate in *The Bearden Project*, an exhibition organised by curator Lauren Haynes at the Studio Museum in Harlem, featuring 100 contemporary artists influenced by artist and writer Romare Bearden. Davis submits a collage on paper entitled *The Frogs* (2011).

On 11 November, the Studio Museum opens *Fore*, a group show of emerging artists organised by Lauren Haynes, Naima J. Keith and Thomas J. Lax. In *Artforum*, Ara H. Merjian describes Davis's work in the show, *Found Photo* (2012), as 'a characteristically arresting portrait of a foregrounded young man in three-quarter profile, set against a window frame and an abstract section recalling a vagrant Clyfford Still painting.'[13] The San Francisco Museum of Modern Art takes Davis's *The Messenger* (2008) into its collection.

2013

On 23 February, *Noah Davis: The Missing Link* opens at Roberts & Tilton. The exhibited series marks a turning point in Davis's practice.

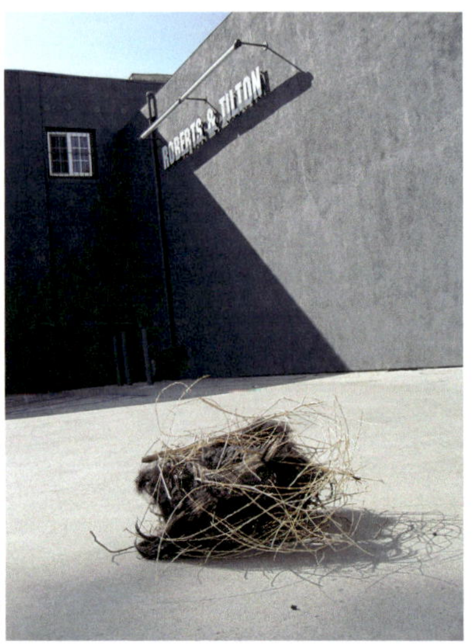

Left *Tirs: Reloaded*, 2012
Right *Tumbleweave* in the group show *In the Making* at Roberts & Tilton Gallery, Culver City, 2012

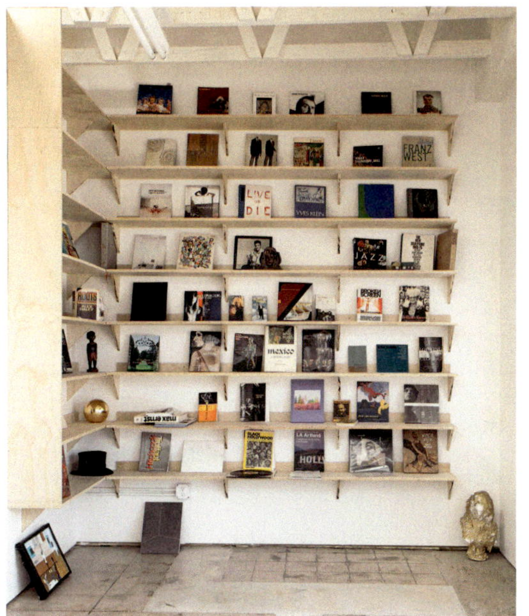

The Missing Link 3 (2013) (p. 121) centres a working man in an urban environment, which is translated into an array of abstract colour fields, while *The Missing Link 4* (2013) (p. 125) takes the gridded façade of one of the modernist housing blocks in Mies van der Rohe's Lafayette Park in Detroit as a backdrop. In *The Missing Link 6* (2013) (p. 129), a figure in repose among a dense thicket of colour alludes to a scene from Alfred Hitchcock's *The Trouble With Harry* (1955), and Manet's subjects painted in states of leisurely recline.[14] The show demonstrates Davis's ability to bring the concerns of modern European painting to contend with Black figuration. On the eve of the opening, Lipschutz interviews Davis for *Art in America*, and Davis speaks about *The Missing Link 4*, saying, 'I am fascinated with instances where Black aesthetics and modernist aesthetics collide.'[15]

Davis holds the afterparty at the Underground Museum, serving a rather dandyish spread of champagne and frog legs. On show are the museum's first exhibitions: *Karon Davis: new sculptures and photographs* and *Imitation of Wealth*.

The latter's title references Douglas Sirk's 1959 film *Imitation of Life*, in which two single mothers, one Black and one white, move between various identity categories defined by race and class. Museums do not agree to loan work to the UM and so Davis decides to present facsimiles of easily replicable works by Constantin Brancusi, Christo and Jeanne-Claude, Marcel Duchamp, Dan Flavin, Donald Judd, On Kawara, Jeff Koons, Barnett Newman, Fred Sandback and Robert Smithson, thereby bringing 'world-class' art to Arlington Heights while playing with the history of institutional critique and the readymade. The works also have personal resonance for Davis: the date depicted in *Imitation of On Kawara* (2013) is his father's birthday (7 October 1957), and

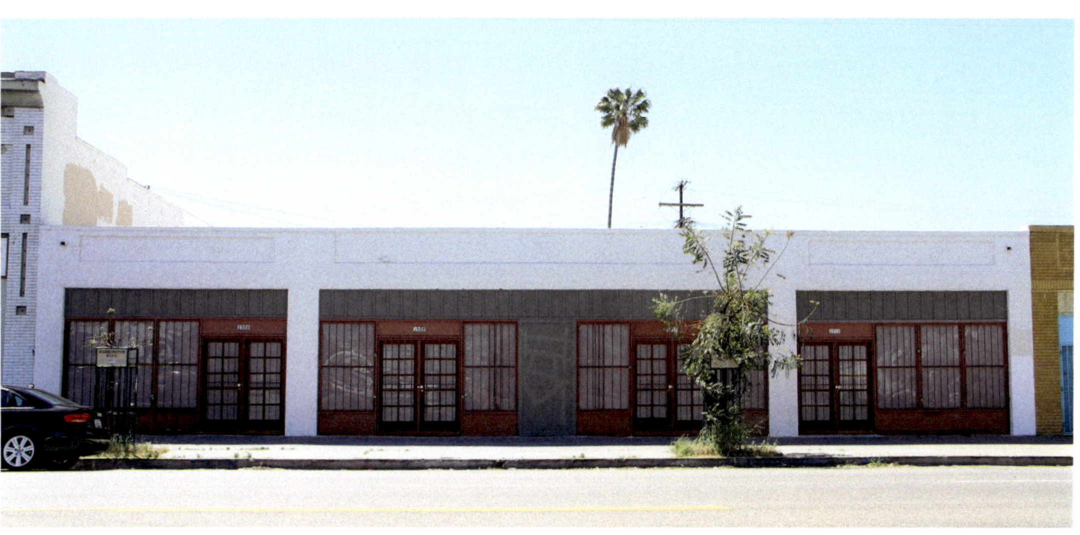

Top The Underground Museum's lending library, 2012
Bottom Exterior facade of the Underground Museum, 2012

Imitation of Marcel Duchamp (2013) was given to Davis by James Harris after the artist noticed an unassuming bottle rack at his home while visiting Seattle for the *Savage Wilds* exhibition the year before.

Around this time, a number of curators at the Los Angeles County Museum of Art (LACMA) take interest in Davis's work. On 7 March, Franklin Sirmans (curator and department head of contemporary art at LACMA) chairs a panel discussion at the Studio Museum in Harlem with Davis and artists Sadie Barnette and Brenna Youngblood, whose work is also included in *Fore* (the Studio Museum exhibition that opened the year before).

As part of LACMA's Art Here and Now programme (which supports acquisitions from emerging artists based in and around Los Angeles), a curatorial committee, including Sirmans and led by Rita Gonzalez and Christine Y. Kim, decide to acquire Davis's *The Missing Link 4*. Kim also organises a roundtable to discuss the future of the space led by Noah and Karon. Participants include Edgar Arceneaux, Mark Bradford, Dagny Corcoran, Karin Higa, Bob Johnson and Rochelle Steiner.

Davis refines the Underground Museum's mission. As he and Karon build the institution, they host six-week residencies in the space and invite artists to display their work.

On 26 June, Brooklyn-based artist Aaron King opens an exhibition at the space following a residency. In the invitation email, Davis explains: 'The Inner City Avant-Garde Residency Program is committed to providing space and resources to artists of merit. The ICAG encourages the artist in residence to collaborate with at least one local business on a piece that can be integrated into the artist's practice.'[16]

On 23 December, Davis is diagnosed with liposarcoma, a rare form of cancer, after a tumour is found next to his heart. He starts a six-month treatment plan of chemoradiotherapy at Cedars-Sinai.

2014

While in and out of hospital, Davis creates his *Seventy Works* series (pp. 168–81), which consists

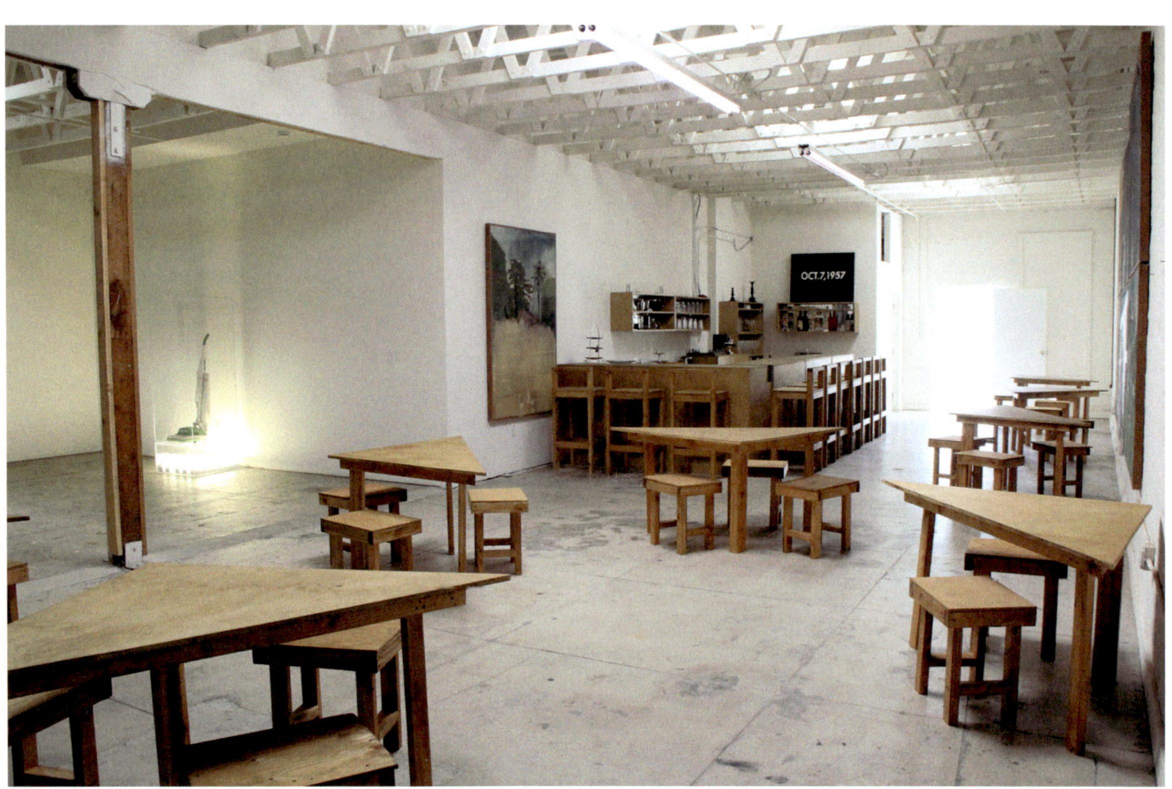

The Underground Museum's bar, inspired by Donald Judd, 2013

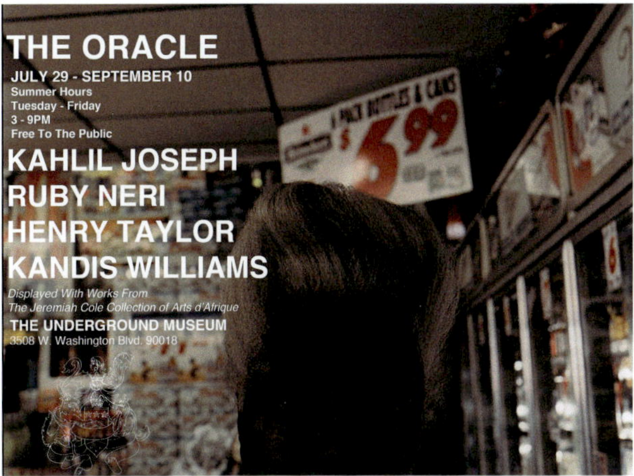

Invitation for *The Oracle* at the Underground Museum, 2014

of 70 small-scale drawings, collages and paintings on archival paper. These works provide Davis with a source of income to support his family and become gifts for loved ones while allowing him to continue to make work from his hospital bed.

Davis's tumour is successfully removed, and he begins to recover.

On 17 May, *Noah Davis: Garden City* opens at PAPILLION, Los Angeles. Davis takes as his subject the Pueblo del Rio public housing project in South Los Angeles, designed in part by Paul Revere Williams and completed in 1942. Against bruised skies and the austere geometry of the architecture's modernist functionalism, Davis paints Black figures immersed in acts of creativity and leisure, reflecting his hopes for the UM. The Hammer Museum acquires one of the works from the show: *Pueblo del Rio: Public Art Sculpture* (2014) (p. 199).

On 29 July, *The Oracle*, a group show curated by Davis, opens at the UM, featuring work by contemporary practitioners alongside loaned objects from the private collection of Jeremiah Cole, an African antiquities dealer from Sierra Leone. The loan is enabled by Davis's mother, Faith Childs-Davis, who encourages Cole to meet her son after buying an African drum from his Collection of Arts d'Afrique. Cole agrees to lend the UM five objects, persuaded by the idea of Arlington Heights locals seeing the works without having to pay museum admission. Davis originally wanted to show the artefacts alongside sculptures by Thomas Houseago (as Houseago often used forms derived from modernist artists such as Picasso and Matisse, who appropriated traditional African art), but instead presents Cole's objects in dialogue with works by Kahlil Joseph, Ruby Neri, Henry Taylor and Kandis Williams.

In the summer, a comprehensive book of Davis's *Seventy Works* is co-published by the UM and Omid Fatemi. The book includes an epilogue by Dagny Corcoran, who writes that for Davis, 'it is the life that is the work of art.'[17]

Davis meets artist Deana Lawson when Joseph invites Lawson and Henry Taylor to a barbeque in the UM's Purple Garden. Davis is already aware of Lawson's work from a previous job organising slides for the William H. Johnson Prize, being particularly struck by her photograph *Daughter* (2007). Davis asks Lawson to exhibit at the UM, suggesting they show her work opposite Diane Arbus.

Davis is told that his cancer has returned, and he begins further treatment.

On 17 September, Helen Molesworth, the new chief curator at MOCA, conducts her first Los Angeles studio visit with Joseph, who has recently moved his studio into the UM. There, she meets Davis, and they talk for hours about Black Mountain College, Walter De Maria's *The New York Earth Room* (1977), Marcel Duchamp, David Hammons and Henry Taylor. They also talk about their shared love for the work of Kerry James Marshall, whom Molesworth is working with on his first major retrospective in the United States (which will open at the Museum of Contemporary Art Chicago in 2016). Molesworth would later write that the UM felt like an artwork in itself, following the tradition of historic projects such as Katherine S. Dreier, Duchamp and Man Ray's Société Anonyme, Inc., Marcel Broodthaers's Musée d'Art Moderne, Département des Aigles and David Wilson's Museum of Jurassic Technology.

Davis's *Black Wall Street* (2008) (p. 49) is acquired by the Studio Museum in Harlem.

2015

Through Molesworth's advocacy, MOCA formalises a partnership with the UM. MOCA's

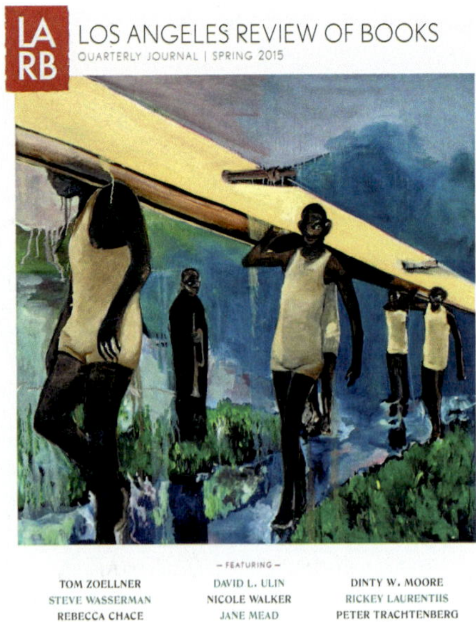

recently appointed director, Philippe Vergne, approves the lending agreement. Molesworth would later write that for Vergne, 'it was a way to rethink museum expansion: No big-name architect needed! Let's move horizontally, not vertically.'[18]

Molesworth brings a large three-ring binder containing MOCA's complete collection (known as 'the bible') to Davis's bedside at Cedars-Sinai, from where he plans 18 exhibitions of works from MOCA's collection. One exhibition Davis conceives, entitled *Non-fiction*, includes a 1995 Kara Walker work, *The Means to an End… A Shadow Drama in Five Acts*, which recalls the works he had seen as a 14-year-old at the Henry Art Gallery at the University of Washington, Seattle.

The Bruce High Quality Foundation University (an alternative, unaccredited art school established in the autumn of 2009 by BHQF, with whom Davis had collaborated at Cooper Union) open a gallery on 431 East 6th Street in New York and invite Davis to be in their first exhibition. On 4 April, the gallery presents *Noah Davis and the Underground Museum*, featuring works by Davis, Henry Taylor, Lyle Ashton Harris, Kahlil Joseph and Deana Lawson.

Hernan Bas, a painter greatly admired by Davis, selects a portfolio of Davis's works to be featured in the *Los Angeles Review of Books* Spring 2015 issue. The portfolio includes Davis's *The Year of the Coxswain* (2009) (p. 79), which appears on the magazine's cover.

On 3 June, Henry Taylor surprises Davis on his 32nd birthday by bringing David Hammons to the UM.

On 25 June, the first exhibition made possible by the MOCA loan agreement opens at the UM: *William Kentridge: Journey to the Moon*. Alongside *7 Fragments for Georges Méliès* (2003) and *Day for Night* (2003), the show features Kentridge's titular 2003 video work in which drawings and everyday objects from the artist's studio become animated, blurring and smudging the boundaries between the real and the represented. The piece's whimsical dissolution of the distinctions between art, the studio and life chimes with the UM's ethos, while the exhibition allows the two institutions to test-run their agreement (with works that do not require specific environmental conditions and are not at risk of theft). The exhibition also features a Kentridge print, *LARGE TYPEWRITERS* (2003), lent to the UM by Dagny Corcoran.

Molesworth spearheads MOCA's acquisition of Davis's *The 'Fitz'* (2015), which consists of a Rothkoesque colour field with two photograph-like images of Fitzgerald House painted in the centre of the canvas. Molesworth later hangs the painting outside the gallery where MOCA's Rothko works are installed.

In July, Davis moves with his family to a house in Ojai, about 80 miles north of Los Angeles, and uses the garage as a studio to create what will become his last works.

On 29 August, a restaging of *Imitation of Wealth* opens at MOCA. On the same day, Davis passes away.

Cover of the *Los Angeles Review of Books: Quarterly Journal*, No. 6, Spring 2015

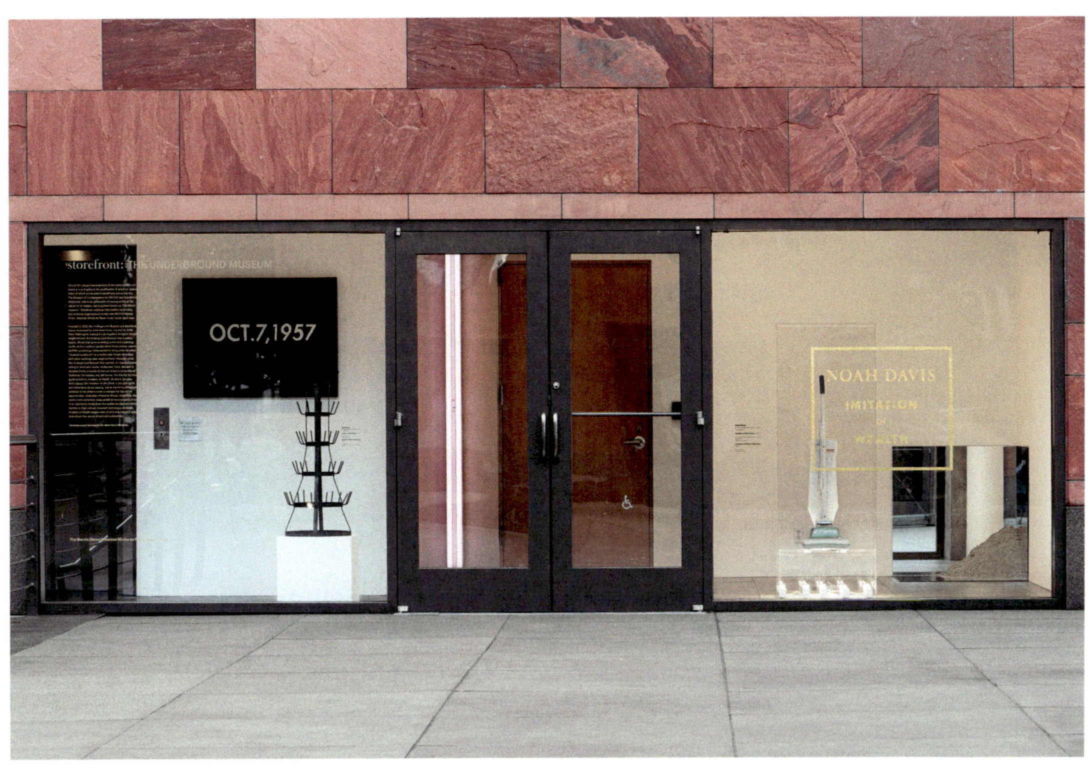

 Installation view, *storefront: Noah Davis: Imitation of Wealth*, MOCA Grand Avenue, 2015–16

1 *Noah Davis: In Detail* (New York: David Zwirner Books, 2023), p. 178.
2 Hamza Walker, 'Presenting Negro Scenes Drawn Upon My Passage Through The South And Reconfigured For The Benefit Of Enlightened Audiences Wherever Such May Be Found, By Myself, Missus K.E.B. Walker, Colored', The Renaissance Society, https://renaissancesociety.org/publishing/84/presenting-negro-scenes-drawn-upon-my-passage-through-the-south-and-reconfigured-for-the-benefit-of-enlightened-audiences-wherever-such-may-be-found-by-myself-missus-keb-walker-colored.
3 Roberta Smith, 'Museum and Gallery Listings', *New York Times*, 16 May 2008, www.nytimes.com/2008/05/16/arts/design/16wart.html?pagewanted=all.
4 Ben Ferguson, 'Noah Davis', *Dazed Digital*, 9 February 2010, dazeddigital.com/artsandculture/article/6483/1/noah-davis.
5 Dagny Corcoran, 'Epilogue', *Noah Davis: Seventy Works* (Los Angeles: The Underground Museum/Omid Fatemi, 2014), n.p.
6 Piero Golia in Steven Henry Madoff (ed.), *Art School (Propositions for the 21st Century)* (Cambridge, MA: MIT Press, 2009), p. 321.
7 Ferguson, 'Noah Davis', *Dazed Digital*.
8 Now Roberts Projects.
9 *Noah Davis: In Detail*, p. 53.
10 Jen Graves, 'Mystery and Strangeness: A Seattle Painter Makes It', *The Stranger*, 21 October 2010, https://www.thestranger.com/visual-art/2010/10/21/5244421/mystery-and-strangeness.
11 Sharon Mizota, 'There Are Truths Underneath', *Los Angeles Times*, 29 January 2010.
12 Davis's annotated press release for *Gray Day*, Roberts & Tilton, Los Angeles, 2010.
13 Ara H. Merjian, 'Critics' Picks: "Fore": The Studio Museum in Harlem', *Artforum*, 2012, https://www.artforum.com/events/the-studio-museum-in-harlem-194790.
14 Yael Lipschutz, 'Links: Q+A with Noah Davis', *Art in America*, 7 March 2013, https://www.artnews.com/art-in-america/interviews/noah-davis-roberts-tilton-56309.
15 Ibid.
16 E-invitation, *Hold Still*, Aaron King, 26 June 2013. Shared by The Estate of Noah Davis.
17 Dagny Corcoran, 'Epilogue', *Noah Davis: Seventy Works*.
18 Helen Molesworth, 'Some Years Count as Double', Helen Molesworth (ed.), *Noah Davis*, exh. cat. (New York: David Zwirner Books/The Underground Museum, 2020), p. 165.

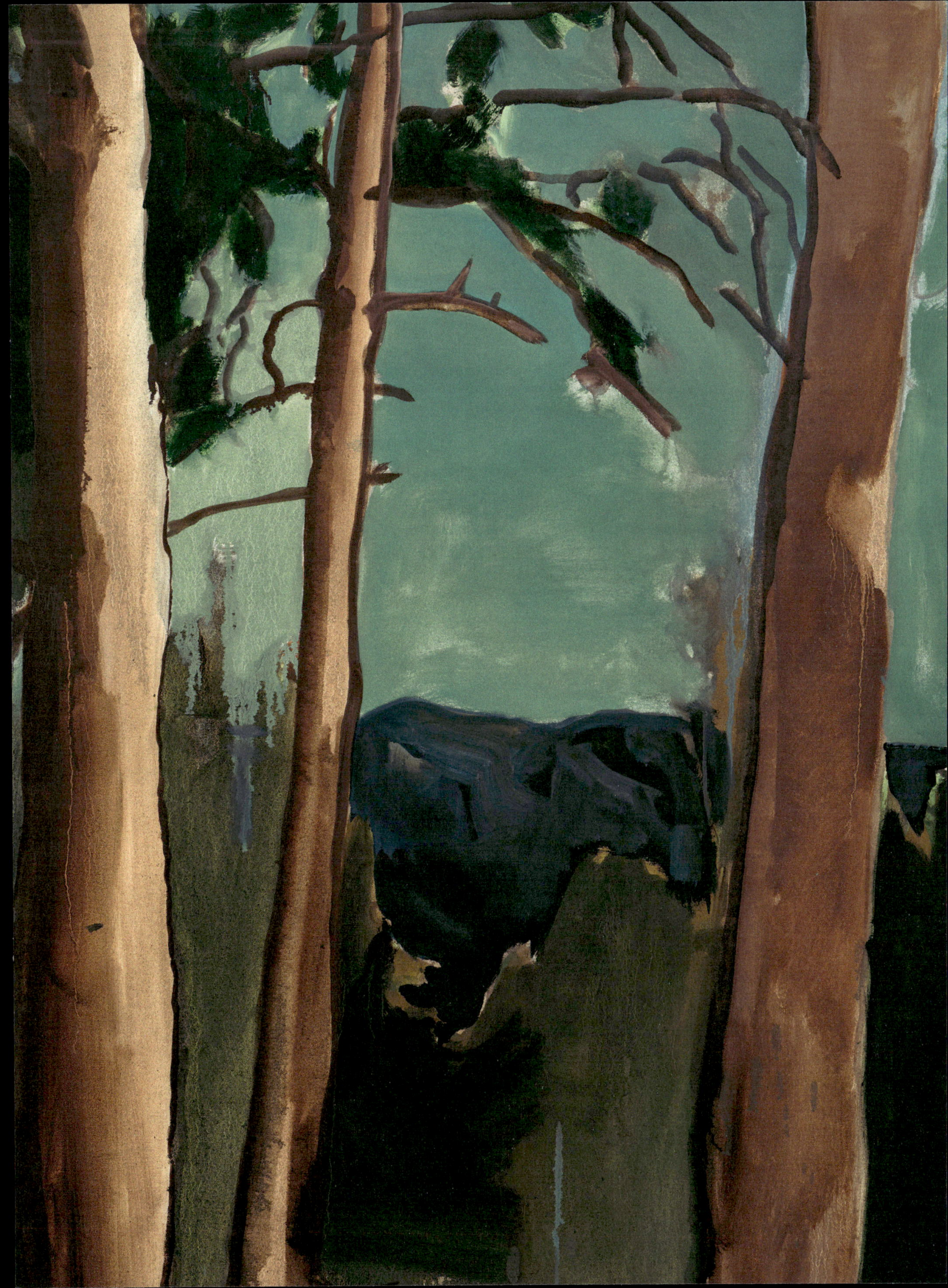

LIST OF WORKS

40 Acres and a Unicorn, 2007
Acrylic and gouache on canvas
76.2 × 66 cm (30 × 26 in)
Private collection; courtesy of David Zwirner
(p. 29)

Bad Boy for Life, 2007
Acrylic, gouache and Conté crayon on canvas
76.2 × 76.2 cm (30 × 30 in)
The Estate of Noah Davis
(p. 33)

Candyman, 2007*
Acrylic and gouache on canvas
61 × 92.1 cm (24 × 36¼ in)
Collection of Ryan Murphy and David Miller
(p. 35)
* Only exhibited at DAS MINSK Kunsthaus in Potsdam

Single Mother with Father out of the Picture, 2007–8
Oil, acrylic and graphite on canvas
101.6 × 76.8 cm (40 × 30¼ in)
Private collection
(p. 37)

Mary Jane, 2008
Oil and acrylic on canvas
152.4 × 132.7 cm (60 × 52¼ in)
Private collection; courtesy of David Zwirner
(p. 41)

LA Nights, 2008*
Oil on wood panel
64.8 × 49.5 cm (25½ × 19½ in)
Private collection
(p. 45)
* Not exhibited

NO-OD for Me, 2008*
Oil and acrylic on canvas
152.4 × 133.3 cm (60 × 52½ in)
Private collection
(p. 47)
* Only exhibited at the Hammer Museum, Los Angeles

Black Wall Street, 2008*
Oil and acrylic on canvas
152.4 × 157.5 cm (60 × 62 in)
Studio Museum in Harlem; gift of David Hoberman
(p. 49)
* Not exhibited

The Last Barbeque, 2008*
Oil on canvas
152.4 × 132.1 cm (60 × 52 in)
Collection of Sam and Shanit Schwartz
(p. 51)
* Not exhibited

Nobody, 2008
Dutch Boy house paint on linen
153 × 153 cm (60¼ × 60¼ in)
Collection of Lindsay Charlwood and Ryan McKenna
(p. 53)

The Seven Prisoners of the Abyss, 2008*
Oil on canvas
76.2 × 102.2 cm (30 × 40¼ in)
Rubell Museum
(p. 65)
* Not exhibited

Museum Guard Fishing, 2009*
Oil and acrylic on linen with rabbit skin glue
121.9 × 121.9 cm (48 × 48 in)
Private collection
(p. 67)
* Not exhibited

The Architect, 2009
Oil and wax on canvas
73.7 × 61 cm (30 × 24½ in)
Studio Museum in Harlem; gift of Martin and Rebecca Eisenberg
(p. 69)

The Gardener, 2009*
Oil on canvas
123.2 × 123.2 × 3.8 cm (48½ × 48½ × 1½ in)
Studio Museum in Harlem; Museum purchase with funds provided by the Acquisition Committee
(p. 73)
* Not exhibited

Isis, 2009
Oil and acrylic on linen
121.9 × 121.9 cm (48 × 48 in)
Mellon Foundation Art Collection
(p. 75)

The Year of the Coxswain, 2009
Oil on canvas
123.2 × 123.2 cm (48½ × 48½ in)
Studio Museum in Harlem; gift of Martin and Rebecca Eisenberg
(p. 79)

1984, 2009
Oil on canvas
122.5 × 122 cm (48½ × 48 in)
Private collection, London
(p. 83)

Another Balcony, 2009*
Oil and acrylic on linen
121.9 × 121.9 cm (48 × 48 in)
Kravis Collection
(p. 87)
* Not exhibited

Imaginary Enemy, 2009*
Oil on wood panel
213.4 × 243.8 cm (84 × 96 in)
Private collection
(p. 89)
* Not exhibited

The Future's Future, 2010*
Oil on canvas
152.4 × 188 cm (60 × 74 in)
Arora Collection, UK
(p. 91)
* Only exhibited at DAS MINSK Kunsthaus in Potsdam

A Snail's Pace, 2010*
Oil, acrylic and gold leaf on canvas
122 × 139.5 cm (48 × 54 7/8 in)
Private collection
(p. 93)
* Not exhibited

Untitled (Birch Trees), 2010*
Oil on canvas
138.4 × 92.7 cm (54 1/2 × 36 1/2 in)
Private collection
(p. 95)
* Not exhibited

Leni Riefenstahl, 2010*
Oil on canvas
187.3 × 152.4 cm (73 3/4 × 60 in)
Private collection
(p. 97)
* Only exhibited at DAS MINSK Kunsthaus in Potsdam

Painting for My Dad, 2011
Oil on canvas
193 × 231.1 cm (76 × 91 in)
Rubell Museum
(p. 99)

Sugartown, 2011*
Oil on canvas
236.2 × 157.5 cm (93 × 62 in)
Fredriksen Family Art Collection
(p. 105)
* Not exhibited

The Maury, 2012
Oil on canvas
61.6 × 76.2 cm (24 1/4 × 30 in)
James Harris and Carlos Garcia, Dallas, Texas
(p. 107)

Maury Mondrian, 2012
Acrylic and inkjet on vinyl
121.9 × 139.1 cm (48 × 54 3/4 in)
The Scantland Collection
(p. 109)

You Are..., 2012
Oil on canvas over panel
121.9 × 183.8 cm (48 × 72 1/3 in)
Private collection
(p. 111)

The Missing Link 1, 2013
Inkjet print and oil on canvas
137.2 × 115.3 cm (54 × 45 1/3 in)
Private collection
(p. 115)

The Missing Link 2, 2013*
Oil on canvas
152.7 × 188 cm (60 1/8 × 74 in)
Private collection
(p. 119)
* Not exhibited

The Missing Link 3, 2013
Oil on canvas
198.4 × 304.8 cm (78 1/8 × 120 in)
Collection of Heidi Hertel and Greg Hodes
(p. 121)

The Missing Link 4, 2013
Oil on canvas
198.1 × 219.1 cm (78 × 86 1/4 in)
Los Angeles County Museum of Art, purchased with funds provided by AHAN: Studio Forum, 2013 Art Here and Now purchase
(p. 125)

The Missing Link 6, 2013
Oil on canvas
198.4 × 304.8 cm (78 1/8 × 120 in)
The Estate of Noah Davis
(p. 129)

Imitation of Dan Flavin, 2013
Two fluorescent lights, purple gels and standard light fixture
243.84 × 10.16 × 5.08 cm (96 × 4 × 2 in)
The Estate of Noah Davis
(p. 139)

Imitation of Marcel Duchamp, 2013
Iron bottle rack
99.06 × 43.18 × 43.18 cm
(39 × 17 × 17 in)
James Harris and Carlos Garcia, Dallas, Texas
(p. 140)

Imitation of Jeff Koons, 2013
Hoover vacuum, fluorescent lights and acrylic
175.26 × 63.5 × 63.5 cm
(69 × 25 × 25 in)
Private Collection of Aileen Getty
(p. 140)

Imitation of Robert Smithson, 2013
Mirrors and sand
91.44 × 91.44 × 91.44 cm
(36 × 36 × 36 in)
The Estate of Noah Davis
(p. 141)

1975 (1), 2013
Oil on canvas in artist's frame
125.7 × 184.2 cm (49 1/2 × 72 1/2 in)
Private collection
(p. 148)

1975 (2), 2013
Oil on canvas in artist's frame
125.7 × 184.2 cm (49 1/2 × 72 1/2 in)
Private collection
(p. 149)

1975 (3), 2013
Oil on canvas in artist's frame
125.7 × 184.2 cm (49 1/2 × 72 1/2 in)
Private collection
(p. 150)

1975 (4), 2013
Oil on canvas in artist's frame
125.7 × 184.2 cm (49 1/2 × 72 1/2 in)
Private collection
(p. 151)

1975 (5), 2013
Oil on canvas in artist's frame
125.7 × 184.2 cm (49 1/2 × 72 1/2 in)
Private collection
(p. 155)

1975 (7), 2013
Oil on canvas in artist's frame
125.7 × 184.2 cm (49 1/2 × 72 1/2 in)
The Ankner Family
(p. 157)

1975 (8), 2013
Oil on canvas in artist's frame
125.7 × 184.2 cm (49 1/2 × 72 1/2 in)
Private collection
(p. 158)

1975 (9), 2013
Oil on canvas in artist's frame
125.7 × 184.2 cm (49 1/2 × 72 1/2 in)
The Ankner Family
(p. 159)

Untitled, 2014
Mixed media and collage on paper
19.7 × 13 cm (7 3/4 × 5 1/8 in), unframed
30.8 × 23.2 cm (12 1/8 × 9 1/8 in), framed
The Estate of Noah Davis
(p. 168, left)

Seventy Works (9), 2014
Mixed media on paper
19.1 × 13.3 cm (7½ × 5¼ in), unframed
30.8 × 23.2 cm (12⅛ × 9⅛ in), framed
The Estate of Noah Davis
(p. 168, right)

Untitled, 2014
Mixed media and collage on paper
19.7 × 13.3 cm (7¾ × 5¼ in), unframed
30.8 × 23.2 cm (12⅛ × 9⅛ in), framed
The Estate of Noah Davis
(p. 169)

Untitled, 2014
Mixed media on paper
20.3 × 13.2 cm (8 × 5⅕ in), unframed
30.8 × 23.2 cm (12⅛ × 9⅛ in), framed
The Estate of Noah Davis
(p. 170, top)

Untitled, 2014
Mixed media on paper
20.3 × 13.2 cm (8 × 5⅕ in), unframed
30.8 × 23.2 cm (12⅛ × 9⅛ in), framed
The Estate of Noah Davis
(p. 170, bottom)

Untitled, 2014
Mixed media on paper
22.9 × 15.2 cm (9 × 6 in), unframed
30.8 × 23.2 cm (12⅛ × 9⅛ in), framed
The Estate of Noah Davis
(p. 171, left)

Untitled, 2014
Mixed media on paper
20.3 × 13.2 cm (8 × 5⅕ in), unframed
30.8 × 23.2 cm (12⅛ × 9⅛ in), framed
The Estate of Noah Davis
(p. 171, right)

Seventy Works (17), 2014
Mixed media on paper
19.1 × 13.3 cm (7½ × 5¼ in), unframed
30.8 × 23.2 cm (12⅛ × 9⅛ in), framed
The Estate of Noah Davis
(p. 173)

Seventy Works (30), 2014
Mixed media on paper
19.1 × 13.3 cm (7½ × 5¼ in), unframed
30.8 × 23.2 cm (12⅛ × 9⅛ in), framed
The Estate of Noah Davis
(p. 174, left)

Seventy Works (15), 2014
Mixed media on paper
19.1 × 13.3 cm (7½ × 5¼ in), unframed
30.8 × 23.2 cm (12⅛ × 9⅛ in), framed
The Estate of Noah Davis
(p. 174, right)

Seventy Works (28), 2014
Mixed media on paper
19.1 × 13.3 cm (7½ × 5¼ in), unframed
30.8 × 23.2 cm (12⅛ × 9⅛ in), framed
The Estate of Noah Davis
(p. 175, top)

Seventy Works (45), 2014
Mixed media on paper
19.1 × 13.3 cm (7½ × 5¼ in), unframed
30.8 × 23.2 cm (12⅛ × 9⅛ in), framed
The Estate of Noah Davis
(p. 175, bottom)

Seventy Works (61), 2014
Mixed media on paper
19.1 × 13.3 cm (7½ × 5¼ in), unframed
30.8 × 23.2 cm (12⅛ × 9⅛ in), framed
The Estate of Noah Davis
(p. 176, top)

Seventy Works (36), 2014
Mixed media on paper
19.1 × 13.3 cm (7½ × 5¼ in), unframed
30.8 × 23.2 cm (12⅛ × 9⅛ in), framed
The Estate of Noah Davis
(p. 177, top)

Seventy Works (50), 2014
Mixed media on paper
19.1 × 13.3 cm (7½ × 5¼ in), unframed
30.8 × 23.2 cm (12⅛ × 9⅛ in), framed
The Estate of Noah Davis
(p. 177, left)

Seventy Works (43), 2014
Mixed media on paper
19.1 × 13.3 cm (7½ × 5¼ in), unframed
30.8 × 23.2 cm (12⅛ × 9⅛ in), framed
The Estate of Noah Davis
(p. 177, right)

Seventy Works (64), 2014
Mixed media on paper
19.1 × 13.3 cm (7½ × 5¼ in), unframed
30.8 × 23.2 cm (12⅛ × 9⅛ in), framed
The Estate of Noah Davis
(p. 178)

Seventy Works (68), 2014
Mixed media on paper
19.1 × 13.3 cm (7½ × 5¼ in), unframed
30.8 × 23.2 cm (12⅛ × 9⅛ in), framed
The Estate of Noah Davis
(p. 180, top)

Seventy Works (67), 2014
Mixed media on paper
19.1 × 13.3 cm (7½ × 5¼ in), unframed
30.8 × 23.2 cm (12⅛ × 9⅛ in), framed
The Estate of Noah Davis
(p. 180, bottom)

Seventy Works (70), 2014
Mixed media on paper
19.1 × 13.3 cm (7½ × 5¼ in), unframed
30.8 × 23.2 cm (12⅛ × 9⅛ in), framed
The Estate of Noah Davis
(p. 181, left)

Untitled, 2014
Mixed media on paper
19.1 × 14 cm (7½ × 5½ in), unframed
30.8 × 23.2 cm (12⅛ × 9⅛ in), framed
The Estate of Noah Davis
(p. 181, right)

Pueblo del Rio: Concerto, 2014*
Oil on canvas
121.9 × 182.9 cm (48 × 72 in)
Kravis Collection
(p. 183)
* Not exhibited

Pueblo del Rio: Arabesque, 2014
Oil on canvas
121.9 × 182.9 cm (48 × 72 in)
Miguel
(p. 187)

Pueblo del Rio: Prelude, 2014
Oil on canvas
121.9 × 182.9 cm (48 × 72 in)
The Estate of Noah Davis
(p. 189)

The Conductor, 2014
Oil on canvas
175.3 × 193 cm (69 × 76 in)
Glenstone Museum,
Potomac, Maryland
(p. 193)

Pueblo del Rio: Vernon, 2014
Oil on canvas
175.3 × 193 cm (69 × 76 in)
ASOM Collection
(p. 195)

Pueblo del Rio: Public Art Sculpture, 2014
Oil on canvas
182.9 × 121.9 cm (72 × 48 in)
Hammer Museum,
Los Angeles. Purchase
(p. 199)

Pueblo del Rio: Stain Glass Pants, 2014
Oil on canvas
182.9 × 121.9 cm (72 × 48 in)
Private collection
(p. 201)

Congo #7, 2014*
Oil on canvas
125.7 × 184.2 cm (49½ × 72½ in)
Private collection, New York
(p. 211)
* Only exhibited at Barbican Art Gallery, London, and Hammer Museum, Los Angeles

Congo, 2015
Oil on canvas in artist's frame
125.7 × 186.7 cm (49½ × 73½ in)
Private Collection of Aileen Getty
(p. 213)

Congo #2, 2015
Oil on canvas in artist's frame
125.7 × 186.7 cm (49½ × 73½ in)
Private Collection of Aileen Getty
(p. 217)

Untitled, 2015
Oil on canvas
121.9 × 182.9 cm (48 × 72 in)
The Estate of Noah Davis
(p. 221)

Untitled, 2015
Oil on canvas
81.3 × 127 cm (32 × 50 in)
The Museum of Modern Art, New York. Gift of Marie-Josée and Henry R. Kravis in honor of Jerry Speyer's 80th birthday, 2020
(p. 225)

Untitled, 2015
Oil on canvas
203.2 × 137.2 cm (80 × 54 in)
The Estate of Noah Davis
(p. 233)

Untitled, 2015*
Oil on canvas
120.7 × 175.9 cm (47½ × 69¼ in)
The Estate of Noah Davis
(p. 235)
* Not exhibited

William Kentridge
Journey to the Moon, 2003*
35 mm and 16 mm film transferred to video (black and white, sound)
7 min 10 secs
William Kentridge and Goodman Gallery
(p. 136)
* Only exhibited at Barbican Art Gallery, London

CONTRIBUTORS

Dawoud Bey

For almost five decades, MacArthur Fellow Dawoud Bey has been making evocative work about subjects and communities that are often marginalised and mining the histories of Black communities and their people. He began his career as a photographer in 1975, and his work has since been shown in numerous exhibitions at museums and galleries worldwide, including a 2021 retrospective organised by the San Francisco Museum of Modern Art and the Whitney Museum of American Art. His work has been the subject of several monographs, and he has been recognised with a John Simon Guggenheim Memorial Foundation Fellowship (2002) and a Lifetime Achievement Award from Howard University (2017), among others.

Tina M. Campt

Tina M. Campt is Roger S. Berlind '52 Professor of Humanities at Princeton University, where she holds a joint appointment between the Department of Art and Archaeology and the Lewis Center for the Arts. She is the author of five books: *A Black Gaze: Artists Changing How We See* (2021); *Listening to Images* (2017); *Image Matters: Archive, Photography and the African Diaspora in Europe* (2012); *Other Germans: Black Germans and the Politics of Race, Gender and Memory in the Third Reich* (2004); and *Imagining Everyday Life: Engagements with Vernacular Photography*, co-edited with Marianne Hirsch, Gil Hochberg and Brian Wallis (2020).

T.J. Clark

T.J. Clark is Professor Emeritus at UC Berkeley, where he taught art history for twenty years. His books have dealt mainly with the aesthetic character and social fate of modern art. Among them are *The Painting of Modern Life: Paris in the Art of Manet and His Followers* (1984), *Farewell to an Idea: Episodes from a History of Modernism* (1999), *Picasso and Truth: From Cubism to Guernica* (2013), and *If These Apples Should Fall: Cézanne and the Present* (2022). He has been associated with Retort, the Bay Area group of artists and activists, and since 2000, he has written regularly for the *London Review of Books*. His next book is *Those Passions: On Art and Politics*.

Francesco Clemente

Francesco Clemente embodies the figure of the nomadic artist, travelling through geography, culture and mediums. He works in oil, fresco, encaustic, pastel, watercolour and sculpture. In the 1970s, he fostered the return to painting as a relevant medium. Before establishing his studio in New York in 1980, Clemente lived in India, where he studied Sanskrit as well as Hindu and Buddhist literature in the library of the Theosophical Society in Chennai. In New York, Clemente collaborated with poets such as Allen Ginsberg and Robert Creeley, published the Hanuman Books with Raymond Foye and was elected a member of the American Academy of Arts and Letters. His work is featured in many prominent museum collections worldwide, including the Art Institute of Chicago; the Tate Gallery, London; Kunstmuseum Basel; Solomon R. Guggenheim Museum, Bilbao and New York; the Metropolitan Museum of Art, New York; and the Museum of Modern Art, New York. Clemente lives and works in New York and India.

Karon Davis

Karon Davis is a sculptor, performer, mother and Executive Director of the Estate of Noah Davis. Davis creates sculptures, multimedia installations and performances that explore issues of history, race, performance and violence in the United States. Davis, alongside her husband, founded the Underground Museum in South Los Angeles. Together, they created a unique arts and culture centre that sought to bring free art experiences traditionally reserved for major institutions to the surrounding Black and brown neighbourhoods while also hosting events focused on education, wellness and community. She currently resides in New York City with her and Noah's son, Moses.

Marlene Dumas

Marlene Dumas came to the Netherlands in 1976 after completing a BA in Fine Art at the University of Cape Town. Her paintings and drawings, mostly devoted to depictions of the human form, are culled from the artist's vast archive of images, including art historical materials, mass media sources and personal snapshots of friends and family. Gestural, fluid and frequently spectral, Dumas's works re-contextualise her subjects, with the relationship between images, titles and text as a central concern. She lives and works in Amsterdam.

Wells Fray-Smith

Wells Fray-Smith is a Curator at the Barbican Art Gallery, London, where she co-curated *Unravel: The Power and Politics of Textiles in Art* (2024). She was formerly Curator: Special Projects at the Whitechapel Gallery, London, where she ran the Max Mara Art Prize for Women. Previous exhibitions include *Emma Talbot: The Age* (2022), *The London Open* (2022) and *Helen Cammock: Che si può fare* (2019). She has held similar positions at Pace Gallery and The Metropolitan Museum of Art, New York. She lives in London.

Colm Guo-Lin Peare

Colm Guo-Lin Peare is an Assistant Curator at the Royal Academy, London. He previously worked at the Barbican Art Gallery, London, where he assisted in the curation of exhibitions, including *Noah Davis*.

Paola Malavassi

Paola Malavassi, founding Director of DAS MINSK Kunsthaus in Potsdam, is a Berlin-based curator and author. She works in an interdisciplinary manner, frequently involving the areas of jazz music and contemporary dance. Malavassi has curated exhibitions of Stan Douglas, Dan Perjovschi and Ruth Wolf-Rehfeldt, among others. Most recently, she co-curated the group exhibition *I've Seen the Wall: Louis Armstrong on Tour in the GDR 1965* with Jason Moran. She formerly was Head of the Julia Stoschek Collection Berlin, and Curatorial Assistant to the director Kasper König at Museum Ludwig, Cologne.

Helen Molesworth

Helen Molesworth is a writer, podcaster and curator based in Los Angeles and Provincetown. In 2023, Phaidon published *Open Questions, Thirty Years of Writing About Art*, an anthology of her essays. Her podcasts include *Death of an Artist*, about the intertwined fates of Carl Andre and Ana Mendieta, and the inaugural season of *Recording Artists* with the Getty. She is also the host of *DIALOGUES*, featuring interviews with artists, writers, fashion designers and filmmakers hosted by the David Zwirner Gallery. She has curated major exhibitions at institutions including the Hammer Museum, the Museum of Contemporary Art, Los Angeles, and the Wexner Center for the Arts, among others. She has organised one-person exhibitions of Ruth Asawa, Moyra Davey, Noah Davis, Louise Lawler, Steve Locke, Anna Maria Maiolino, Josiah McElheny, Kerry James Marshall, Catherine Opie, Amy Sillman and Luc Tuymans. Her writing has appeared in *Artforum*, *Art Journal*, *Documents* and *October*. The recipient of the 2011 Bard Center for Curatorial Studies Award for Curatorial Excellence, in 2021, she received a Guggenheim Fellowship, and in 2022, she was awarded The Clark Art Writing Prize.

Jason Moran

Jason Moran is a jazz pianist, composer and visual artist. He earned a degree from the Manhattan School of Music, where he studied with Jaki Byard. He was named a MacArthur Fellow in 2010 and was recently inducted into the Academy of Arts and Sciences. He is currently Artistic Director for Jazz at the Kennedy Center and teaches at the New England Conservatory. Moran has recorded 19 critically acclaimed solo recordings and has collaborated with major artists, including Stan Douglas, Joan Jonas, Glenn Ligon, Julie Mehretu, Adam Pendleton, Adrian Piper and Kara Walker. He recently curated the permanent exhibition *Here to Stay* for the newly opened Louis Armstrong Center in Queens and co-curated the exhibition *I've Seen the Wall: Louis Armstrong on Tour in the GDR 1965* at DAS MINSK Kunsthaus in Potsdam.

Eleanor Nairne

Eleanor Nairne is the Keith L. and Katherine Sachs Curator and Head of Modern and Contemporary Art at the Philadelphia Museum of Art. She was formerly Senior Curator at the Barbican Art Gallery, London, where her exhibitions included *Alice Neel: Hot Off The Griddle* (2023), *Jean Dubuffet: Brutal Beauty* (2021), *Lee Krasner: Living Colour* (2019) and *Basquiat: Boom for Real* (2017). She is a regular contributor to the *London Review of Books* and has written for publications including *frieze* and *The Art Newspaper*.

Claudia Rankine

Claudia Rankine is the author of five books of poetry, including *Citizen: An American Lyric* (2014) and *Don't Let Me Be Lonely: An American Lyric* (2004); three plays, including *HELP*, which premiered in March 2020 (the Shed, New York), and *The White Card*, which premiered in February 2018 (ArtsEmerson/American Repertory Theater, Harvard University) and was published by Graywolf Press (2019); as well as numerous video collaborations. Her recent collection of essays, *Just Us: An American Conversation*, was published by Graywolf Press in 2020. She is also the co-editor of several anthologies, including *The Racial Imaginary: Writers on Race in the Life of the Mind* (2015). In 2016, Rankine co-founded The Racial Imaginary Institute (TRII). Among her numerous awards and honours, Rankine is the recipient of the Bobbitt National Prize for Poetry, the Poets & Writers' Jackson Poetry Prize, and fellowships from the Guggenheim Foundation, the Lannan Foundation, the MacArthur Foundation, United States Artists and the National Endowment for the Arts. A former Chancellor of the Academy of American Poets, Claudia Rankine joined the NYU Creative Writing Program in 2021. She lives in New York.

ACKNOWLEDGEMENTS

The Barbican Art Gallery, DAS MINSK Kunsthaus in Potsdam and the Hammer Museum would like to thank the lenders:

The Estate of Noah Davis
The Andrew W. Mellon Foundation
The Ankner Family
Arora Collection, UK
ASOM Collection
Collection of Lindsay Charlwood and Ryan McKenna
Private Collection of Aileen Getty
Glenstone Museum, Potomac, Maryland
Hammer Museum, Los Angeles
James Harris and Carlos Garcia, Dallas, Texas
Collection of Heidi Hertel and Greg Hodes
William Kentridge and Goodman Gallery
Los Angeles County Museum of Art
Collection of Ryan Murphy and David Miller
The Museum of Modern Art, New York
Miguel
Rubell Museum
Studio Museum in Harlem
The Scantland Collection

and all those who wish to remain anonymous.

Our gratitude to the below individuals for their invaluable help in the development and realisation of this exhibition: Mark Ankner, Laci Blackford, Lindsay Charlwood, Daniel DeSure, Aileen Getty, Tyler Gibney, Eric Gleason, James Harris, Aleen Jaghalian, Justen LeRoy, Helen Molesworth, Meg Onli, Marlon Rabenreither, Josh Rabineau, Julie and Bennet Roberts, Connie Rogers Tilton and Megan Steinman.

Special thanks to The Estate of Noah Davis for their collaboration and trust.

IMAGE CREDITS

All images © The Estate of Noah Davis. Courtesy The Estate of Noah Davis and David Zwirner unless otherwise stipulated.

All artworks by Noah Davis © The Estate of Noah Davis

Front cover, pp. 33, 37, 38–39 (detail), 41, 43 (detail), 45, 47, 51, 56, 60, 75, 76 (detail), 89, 95, 97, 99, 102–3 (detail), 158, 160–61 (detail), 164 (right), 180 (bottom), 183, 184 (detail), 187, 193, 201, 225, 226 (detail): Photos: Kerry McFate

Inside front cover and pp. 18/3, 18/4, 20/11, 20/15, 22/19, 23/23, 24/29, 24/30, 26/39, 132/1, 133/5, 134/9, 136/19, 137/26, 239/12, 240/17, 240/19, 241/22, back cover: Photos: Chase Barnes

pp. 2 (detail), 135/16*, 136/20, 148, 149, 151, 162 (detail), 166, 167, 189, 190–91 (detail), 207 (top), 221, 223 (detail), 233, 245 (left)**: Photos: Joshua White/JWPictures.com
* Original photo: Karon Davis
** Courtesy Lindsay Charlwood

p. 13: © Christian-Schad-Stiftung Aschaffenburg (CSSA)/VG Bild-Kunst 2024, Bonn

pp. 14 (top) (detail), 87, 105: Photos: Dan Bradica

pp. 14 (bottom), 147 (detail), 150, 153 (detail), 157, 199, 217, 218–19 (detail), 235, 245 (right), 259 (detail): Photos: Elon Schoenholz

p. 15: Photo: bpk / Smithsonian American Art Museum / Art Resource, NY

pp. 18/2, 20/14, 22/18, 23/24, 23/26, 25/33, 26/36, 26/37, 133/4, 133/8, 134/11, 134/12, 134/13, 135/14, 135/16, 137/23, 137/25, 138/27, 139/30, 139/31, 140/34, 141/36, 142/39, 236/3, 238/8, 240/20, 249 (left), 253 (bottom), 254: Photos: Karon Davis

pp. 19/8, 21/16, 24/27, 243: Courtesy Patrick O'Brien-Smith. Photos: Patrick O'Brien-Smith

p. 20/12: Photo: Jack Tilton

p. 21/17: Courtesy Melodie McDaniel. Photo: Melodie McDaniel

p. 22/20: Courtesy Ed Templeton. Photo: Ed Templeton

pp. 25/34, 26/40, 248 (left): Courtesy Roberts Projects, Los Angeles, California. Photos: Joshua White/ JWPictures.com

pp. 26/35, 53, 58 (top), 67, 115, 117 (detail), 119, 121, 123 (detail), 129, 130–31 (detail), 204 (detail), 250 (top), 252 (right): Courtesy Roberts Projects, Los Angeles, California. Photos: Robert Wedemeyer

pp. 29, 30 (detail), 79, 80–81 (detail), 83, 85 (detail), 93, 144 (detail), 155, 159, 164 (left), 195, 197 (detail), 211, 213, 215 (detail): Photos: Anna Arca

p. 49: Photo: Courtesy Studio Museum in Harlem. Photo: John Berens—Brooklyn, NY

p. 57: © VG Bild-Kunst, Bonn 2024. Photo: © Rheinisches Bildarchiv Köln, rba_d048643_01

p. 58 (bottom): © VG Bild-Kunst, Bonn 2024. Photo: József Rosta/ Ludwig Museum – Museum of Contemporary Art

p. 59: Courtesy National Gallery of Art, Washington

p. 61: © Nicole Eisenman. Courtesy the artist and Hauser & Wirth. Photo: Robert Wedemeyer

p. 65: Courtesy Rubell Museum. Photo: Chi Lam

pp. 69, 70 (detail): Courtesy Studio Museum in Harlem; gift of Martin and Rebecca Eisenberg. Photo: John Berens – Brooklyn, NY

p. 73: Courtesy Studio Museum in Harlem. Photo: Marc Bernier

p. 91: Photo: Jack Hems

pp. 107, 140/35: Courtesy James Harris and Carlos Garcia, Dallas, Texas. Photos: Kevin Todora Photography

p. 109: Courtesy The Scantland Collection

pp. 111, 112–13 (detail): Photos: Jonathan Tan

pp. 125, 127 (detail), 205 (detail): Courtesy Los Angeles County Museum of Art, purchased with funds provided by AHAN: Studio Forum, 2013, Art Here and Now purchase. Photos: Robert Wedemeyer

p. 132/2: Photo: Rhys Gaetano

pp. 135/15, 239/13, 241/23: Courtesy Nicole Otero. Photos: Nicole Otero

p. 136/18: © William Kentridge. Courtesy of The Museum of Contemporary Art (MOCA). Photo: Brian Forrest

p. 137/21: Photo: Andrea Bowers

pp. 138/28, 236/1, 237/6, 253 (top): Courtesy Semra Sevin. Photos: Semra Sevin

pp. 139/29, 139/32, 140/33, 141/37, 142/38: Courtesy of The Museum of Contemporary Art, Los Angeles (MOCA). Photos: Cameron Crone and Carter Seddon

pp. 168, 169, 173, 174, 175, 176, 177, 178, 179 (detail), 180 (top), 181 (left): Photos: Stephen Arnold

pp. 170, 171, 172 (detail), 181 (right): Photos: Marlon Rabenreither

p. 203: Courtesy J. Paul Getty Trust. Getty Research Institute, Los Angeles (2004.R.10). Photo: Julius Shulman Photographic Archive

p. 206: Courtesy Housing Authority Collection/Los Angeles Public Library. Photo: Louis Clyde Stoumen

p. 207 (bottom): Courtesy Housing Authority Collection/Los Angeles Public Library

p. 238/9: Courtesy of The Museum of Contemporary Art, Los Angeles (MOCA). Photo: Justin Lubliner and Carter Seddon

p. 238/10: © David Hammons. Courtesy of The Museum of Contemporary Art, Los Angeles (MOCA). Photo: Justin Lubliner and Carter Seddon

p. 239/14: Marion Palfi artwork © Center for Creative Photography, Arizona Board of Regents; Robert Gober artwork © Robert Gober. Courtesy of The Museum of Contemporary Art, Los Angeles (MOCA). Photo: Justin Lubliner and Carter Seddon

p. 246 (left): Photo: Rachel Kaadzi Ghansah

p. 246 (right): © The Bruce High Quality Foundation. Courtesy The Estate of Noah Davis and Bruce High Quality Foundation

p. 247: Courtesy Jorge Pardo and Petzel, New York

p. 248 (right): Photo: Lindsay Charlwood

p. 249 (right): Courtesy Tilton Gallery. Photo: Joshua White/JWPictures.com

p. 250 (bottom): Courtesy Galleria Annarumma, Napoli

p. 251 (left): Courtesy HVW8 Art + Design Gallery

p. 251 (right): Courtesy HVW8 Art + Design Gallery. Photo: Tyler Gibney

p. 252 (left): Photo: Yael Lipschutz

p. 256: © Los Angeles Review of Books. Courtesy Los Angeles Review of Books

p. 257: Courtesy of The Museum of Contemporary Art, Los Angeles and Fredrik Nilsen. Photo: Fredrik Nilsen

Plates with details: p. 2: *Untitled*, 2015; p. 30: *40 Acres and a Unicorn*, 2007; pp. 38–39: *Single Mother with Father out of the Picture*, 2007–8; p. 43: *Mary Jane*, 2008; p. 70: *The Architect*, 2009; p. 76: *Isis*, 2009; pp. 80–81: *The Year of the Coxswain*, 2009; p. 85: *1984*, 2009; pp. 102–3: *Painting for My Dad*, 2011; pp. 112–13: *You Are...*, 2012; p. 117: *The Missing Link 1*, 2013; p. 123: *The Missing Link 3*, 2013; p. 127: *The Missing Link 4*, 2013; pp. 130–31: *The Missing Link 6*, 2013; p. 144: *1975 (9)*, 2013; p. 147: *1975 (7)*, 2013; p. 153: *1975 (3)*, 2013; pp. 160–61: *1975 (8)*, 2013; p. 162: *1975 (1)*, 2013, p. 172: *Untitled*, 2014; p. 179: *Seventy Works (70)*, 2014; p. 184: *Pueblo del Rio: Concerto*, 2014; pp. 190–91: *Pueblo del Rio: Prelude*, 2014; p. 197: *Pueblo del Rio: Vernon*, 2014; p. 215: *Congo*, 2015; pp. 218–19: *Congo #2*, 2015; p. 223: *Untitled*, 2015; p. 226: *Untitled*, 2015; p. 259: *1975 (7)*, 2013

Accompanying illustrations in the essays: p. 13: Christian Schad, *Agosta, der Flügelmensch und Rasha, die schwarze Taube*, 1929. Private collection; p. 15: Palmer Hayden, *The Janitor Who Paints*, c. 1937, repainted after 1940. Smithsonian American Art Museum; gift of the Harmon Foundation, 1967.57.28; p. 57: Max Ernst, *La Vierge corrigeant l'enfant Jésus devant trois témoins: André Breton*, Paul Éluard et le peintre, 1926. Museum Ludwig, Köln, Inv. no. ML 10056; p. 58 (bottom): Wolfgang Mattheuer, *Der Nachbar, der will fliegen*, 1984. Ludwig Museum – Museum of Contemporary Art, Budapest; p. 59: Max Beckmann, *Abstürzender*, 1950. Gift of Mrs. Max Beckmann. National Gallery of Art, Washington, 1975.96.3; p. 61: Nicole Eisenman, *Heading Down River on the USS J-Bone of an Ass*, 2017. Ovitz Family Collection, Los Angeles.

Front cover:
The Conductor (detail), 2014
Oil on canvas
175.3 × 193 cm (69 × 76 in)
Glenstone Museum, Potomac, Maryland

EXHIBITION

Barbican Art Gallery

Curators: Wells Fray-Smith, Eleanor Nairne
Curatorial Assistants: Ada Egg Koskiluoma, Colm Guo-Lin Peare
Exhibition Organisers: Isabel Hesketh, Lily Morgan
Assistant Exhibition Organiser: Joe Shaw
Project Team: Lotte Allan, Lily Booth, Louise Carreck, David Corbett, Chinenye Ezeuko, Ian Fowles, Dan Gunning, Jacob Harrison, Adam Holdway, Georgia Holmes, Sharon Kent, Hannah Moth, Natasha Powell, Christopher Spear

In collaboration with
Exhibition Design: Freehaus
Exhibition Graphics: A Practice for Everyday Life

DAS MINSK Kunsthaus in Potsdam

Curator: Paola Malavassi
Assistant Curator and Project Lead: Marie Gerbaulet
Registrar: Monika Grzymislawska
Project Team: Stefan Baum, Yvonne Benesch, Daria Bormann, Verena Daub, Johanna Engemann, Heike Kraeft, Nadine Müller, Julia Nowak, Andreas Papadimitriou, Daniela Schaube, Sebastian Semmler, Simon Spannig, Marco Surma, Ulrike Techert, Josefine Weiß

In collaboration with
Conservation: Catherina Blohm and Anke Klusmeier
Exhibition Design: Kooperative für Darstellungspolitik, Berlin
Exhibition Setup: Abrell & van den Berg, Berlin; Philipp Ricklefs, Berlin
Lighting: Georg & Paul, Hamburg
Exhibition Graphics: Fasson Freddy Fuss, Berlin, Freddy Fuss, Larissa Starke
Press: A R T Communication + Brand Consultancy, Berlin
Shop: mu.se, Tina Kabot and Jörg Klambt, Berlin

The C& Center of Unfinished Business in the exhibition at DAS MINSK is a project by Contemporary And (C&).

Barbican Art Gallery

Director for Arts and Participation: Devyani Saltzman
Head of Visual Arts: Shanay Jhaveri
Deputy Head of Visual Arts: Katrina Crookall
Senior Manager, Exhibitions and Partnerships: Alice Lobb
Gallery Manager: Priya Saujani
Production Manager: Maarten van den Bos
Media Relations Manager: Hannah Carr
Marketing Manager: Isobel Parrish
Director of Development: Natasha Harris
Head of Creative Collaboration and Learning: Karena Johnson

DAS MINSK Kunsthaus in Potsdam

Director and Curator: Paola Malavassi
Managing Director: Janine Meyer
Head of Communications: Natanja von Stosch
Education: Janet Röder
Events: Caroline Stummel
Security Coordination and Head of Guest Management: Nikolaos Dokalis
Head of IT and Digitalization: Stefan Scholze
Head of Building Services: Carsten Loeper

Hammer Museum

Director: Ann Philbin
Deputy Director, Curatorial Affairs: Cynthia Burlingham
Deputy Director, External Affairs: Fred Yeries
Deputy Director, Finance, Operations & Administration: Michael Harrison
Interim Chief Curator: Aram Moshayedi
Director & Chief Curator, Grunwald Center for the Graphic Arts: Naoko Takahatake
Chief Communications Office: Scott Tennent
Chief Development Officer: Aiza Keesey
Chief of Human Resources: Ebony Wyatt

The exhibition at the Barbican has been made possible as a result of the Government Indemnity Scheme. Barbican would like to thank HM Government for providing Government Indemnity and the Department for Digital, Culture, Media and Sport and Arts Council England for arranging indemnity.

The exhibition at the Barbican has also been made possible through support from Clore Wyndham and the Noah Davis Exhibition Circle.

First published in 2024 by Prestel Verlag, Penguin Random House Verlagsgruppe GmbH in association with Barbican Art Gallery and DAS MINSK Kunsthaus in Potsdam on the occasion of the exhibition *Noah Davis*.

DAS MINSK, Potsdam
7 September 2024 – 5 January 2025
Curated by Paola Malavassi

Barbican Art Gallery, London
6 February – 11 May 2025
Curated by Eleanor Nairne
and Wells Fray-Smith

Hammer Museum, Los Angeles
8 June – 31 August 2025
Curated by Eleanor Nairne, former Senior Curator, Barbican and Wells Fray-Smith, Curator, Barbican

The presentation at the Hammer is organised by Aram Moshayedi, Interim Chief Curator, with Ikechúkwú Onyewuenyi, Curatorial Associate

Exhibition initiated by Barbican, London and DAS MINSK, Potsdam

Barbican Art Gallery
Barbican Centre
Silk Street, London EC2Y 8DS
barbican.org.uk

DAS MINSK Kunsthaus in Potsdam
Max-Planck-Strasse 17, Potsdam 14473
dasminsk.de

Hammer Museum
10899 Wilshire Boulevard, Los Angeles 90024
hammer.ucla.edu

PUBLICATION

Editors: Wells Fray-Smith, Paola Malavassi, Eleanor Nairne
Assistant Editor: Marie Gerbaulet
Editorial Support: Ada Egg Koskiluoma
Editorial Coordination: Rochelle Roberts
Copyeditor: Emma Capps
Design: A Practice for Everyday Life
Production: Corinna Pickart
Printing and Binding: LEGO
Origination: Reproline Mediateam, Unterföhring
Typeface: Starling, TWK Lausanne
Paper: Magno Volume

A CIP catalogue record for this book is available from the British Library.

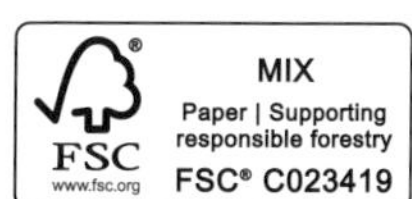

Penguin Random House
Verlagsgruppe FSC® N001967

Printed in Italy

ISBN 978-3-7913-7774-2

prestel.com

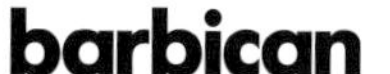

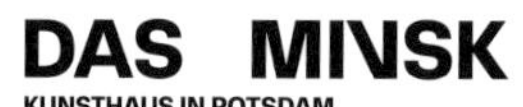

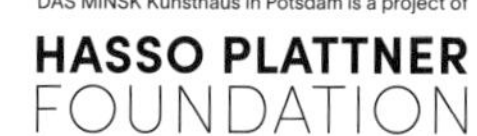

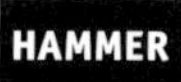